Inheritance in Psychoanalysis

SUNY series, Insinuations: Philosophy, Psychoanalysis, Literature

Charles Shepherdson, editor

INHERITANCE IN PSYCHOANALYSIS

EDITED BY
Joel Goldbach
and James A. Godley

Cover image: Salvador Dalí, "Morphology of Skull of Sigmund Freud" © Salvador Dalí, Fundació Gala-Salvador Dalí, Artists Rights Society (ARS), New York 2016.

Published by State University of New York Press, Albany

For information, contact State University of New York Press, Albany, NY
www.sunypress.edu

Production, Jenn Bennett
Marketing, Michael Campochiaro

Library of Congress Cataloging-in-Publication Data
Names: Goldbach, Joel, editor. | Godley, James A., editor.
Title: Inheritance in psychoanalysis / edited by Joel Goldbach and James A. Godley.
Description: Albany, NY : State University of New York Press, [2018] | Series: SUNY series, insinuations: philosophy, psychoanalysis, literature | Includes bibliographical references and index.
Identifiers: LCCN 2017004237 (print) | LCCN 2017012794 (ebook) | ISBN 9781438467894 (e-book) | ISBN 9781438467870 (hardcover : alk. paper) | ISBN 9781438467887 (pbk. : alk. paper)
Subjects: LCSH: Psychoanalysis.
Classification: LCC BF173 (ebook) | LCC BF173 .I464 2018 (print) | DDC 150.19/5—dc23
LC record available at https://lccn.loc.gov/2017004237

10 9 8 7 6 5 4 3 2 1

Contents

THE INHERITANCE OF PSYCHOANALYSIS

Acknowledgments

This project was a collaborative effort on the part of the Center for the Study of Psychoanalysis and Culture (CSPC) at the University at Buffalo (SUNY). It would not have been possible without the assistance of both its faculty and graduate students. In particular, the editors would like to thank Tim Dean, who, in his tenure as director of the CSPC, encouraged and advised us during the early stages of the project; Steven Miller and Ewa Ziarek, the current director and executive director of the CSPC, respectively, whose support and guidance has been indispensable; Bridget O'Neill, whose input helped orient this project from the beginning; and each of the following graduate students, who assisted us during the production of the manuscript: Chris Bomba, Jen Braun, Woody Brown, Arian Cato, Josh Dawson, Zia Dickson, Adam Drury, Angela Facundo, Martin Goffeney, Elsa Gudrunel, Daae Jung, Min Young Godley, Nicole Lowman, Amanda McLaughlin, Ajit-paul Mangat, Keiko Ogata, Morgan Pulver, Daniel Schweitzer, Kellie Jean Sharp, Doruk Tatar, Eric Vanlieshout, and Kezia Whiting.

We are also immensely grateful to Charles Shepherdson and Andrew Kenyon for their enthusiasm and keen interest in this volume.

Finally, the editors would like to thank the contributors for their inspiring work, kindness, and generosity throughout this process. Above all, we would like to thank Joan Copjec, whose unswerving commitment to this project cannot be overstated. This volume is dedicated to the legacy she bequeaths—a legacy true to the spirit of inheritance in psychoanalysis.

Inheritance in Psychoanalysis

James A. Godley

The etymology of *inheritance* reveals a problematic concerning the fundamental ambiguity of the subject that inherits. To inherit—coming from the Latin *inhereditare*, "appoint as heir," by way of the Middle English *enherite*, "receive as a right," and the Old French *enheriter*—originally meant "to bequeath," as in the phrase "I inherit you." In a complete reversal of what it means today, the word was used in the sense of deliberately ceding an object to another, rather than passively receiving something as an heir. To inherit, in this first sense, is thus not unlike bestowing a gift—or, as becomes especially legible in the sense of the pathological, a *curse*. What to make of this curious etymological slippage of the word inherit, as though either its source or its heir is not quite in place?

While it may seem odd to think that psychoanalysis and inheritance belong together, since inheritance, as such, rarely appears in discussions of psychoanalytic theory and practice, it is nonetheless everywhere implied at the heart of an experience marked by repetitions, returns, and *après-coups*. In psychoanalysis, inheritance takes on a special significance when it is approached from the side of the indeterminacy of the subject that inherits, where the heir of an inheritance is determined retroactively through the pathways of the unconscious "it" that "speaks." In the experience of analysis, what I inherit is often felt to be almost autonomous, like an invention without an inventor. Although the subject of the unconscious is itself substance-less—lacking, as Sigmund Freud claims, any relation to time[1] (and, hence, without a substantive past or future)—it is nonetheless what structures the experience of the "I" in terms of a narrative destiny that can, in principle, be reinvented. Hence, the "it speaks" (*ça parle*) of the unconscious could also be read as "it inherits"—or, better, "it invents," as in Freud's aphorism, "Where it was, there I shall become" (*Wo Es war, soll Ich werden*).[2] That is, understood in the sense of a bequeathing in which the heir returns to the source, inheritance in psychoanalysis doubles as the potential for an act that would transform inheritance.

Here, the past and the future, in a sense, trade places: What has come before is the potentiality of an act that would change one's heredity. At its most radical level, such a reinvention of one's inheritance would signify a change, not only in one's self (as in the limited sense of self-invention) but also to oneself, that is, to the way that one is attached to the social reality in which one takes part. In light of psychoanalysis, then, what is inherited is not exactly given or received, according to a specific biological or cultural order, so much as it is reinvented and openly bestowed, in turn, upon the world of discourse in which the subject is imbricated. The mask of selfhood falls, revealing the depersonalized subject at stake in the discursive movements of symbolic tradition and the seeming paradox that in order to change who "I" am I must change the coordinates of what determines my place in the chain of the "world." By acting in accordance with my unconscious desire, I take responsibility for the singular meaning and effects of an inheritance that I both receive and bequeath.

Herein, an unheard-of task falls to the one who would take responsibility for this act of inheritance: to change both one's self and the world on behalf of something that is not a part of either, the lost object of desire. Inheritance thereby poses an ethical question *in* psychoanalysis, which could equally well be asked *of* psychoanalysis: How can an individual assume responsibility for an act whereby he or she is radically transformed, in which his or her heredity—constituting the given objects of inheritance (symbolically, biologically, structurally)—is reinvented?

It is not hard to find examples today of instances in which the meaning and effects of (trans)individual inheritance are not sufficiently attended to. In February 2016, the United Kingdom passed a law approving the manipulation of CRISPR (clustered regularly interspaced short palindromic repeats) gene sequences in experiments that would alter the genetic composition of the human germ line. CRISPR, a naturally occurring biological defense mechanism found in bacteria and certain viruses, has already demonstrated a wide applicability to the human genome through a technology that enables the "cutting" of undesirable genetic strands and their replacement with altered gene sequences. The CRISPR gene-editing technique has recently proven to have heritable effects and to effectively change the epigenome responsible for gene activation and expression.[3] Hence, this historic legislative act enables the existence of programs that would alter, edit, and even reinvent genetic inheritance. Much of the controversy that surrounds the new biogenetic research has tended to circulate around the excitement generated by the possibility of reinventing the biological makeup of the individual human body—including the possibility of eliminating certain heritable diseases, like HIV and sickle-cell anemia—that could cause people to overlook the potential damage these changes may have beyond the individual. For example, a growing number of scientists warn that while the new research may be promising in terms of its treatment of illness, it can also have potentially harmful effects for subsequent generations. In response to such concerns, the state, insurance companies, hospitals, and medical boards appoint bioethics committees to hold debates about the ethical implications of the new research programs and (sometimes) to make their findings available to the general public. But this "solution" to the ethical problems attending the reinvention of inheritance fails to fully appreciate the problematic of inheritance in the depersonalized sense discussed above. If the subject of inheritance, taken in the abstract, is fundamentally indeterminate, then how could it be made intelligible through some comprehensive report made by a panel of experts, let alone decided upon in any concrete sense? At the very heart of the subject's desire to change his or her body lies an ambiguity that may only be approached immanently, since what it concerns—an unconscious truth—is only answerable to the subject of its experience and is "reported" only in the aberrant form of the symptom that the subject "inherits." Psychoanalysis takes up this aberrant form, not in order to study, debate, or inform the public about it, but in order to help the subject transform the social bond as a consequence of his or her encounter with it. The ethics of psychoanalysis concerns the act of assuming responsibility for inheritance. As such, it offers an ethical alternative to the denaturalization and reinvention of inheritance promoted by other disciplines and practices at a time when such possibilities are increasingly available.

Against the establishment of heredity, either natural or cultural, *inheritance in psychoanalysis* names the ethical process whereby the analyst, in alliance with the subject of the unconscious, maintains the opening for an act that would radically transform not only the individual but also the discourses in which the individual is inhabited. This volume addresses the transformative potential of inheritance in the spirit of this ethical act, which, as a new bequest, also transforms one's given heritage into a new acquisition, as in Johann Wolfgang von Goethe's lines from *Faust*, a play that haunted Freud throughout his career: "What thou hast inherited from thy fathers, acquire it to make it thine."[4] The contributors to this volume intervene into three domains wherein inheritance deserves to be called into question and rendered into the means of reinvention: problems of natural or biological inheritance, such as innateness, heredity, and ontogenesis; problems of cultural transmission, genealogy, and writing; and problems that form the material of psychoanalytic practice, in the concrete space that preserves the revolutionary potential for the subject's transformation. In their responses to the question of inheritance in psychoanalysis, they have each made a bequest that intervenes into the circuit of received meaning within various fields, creating a hole where the problems are that is also an opening necessary for radical change.

In one of his last writings, the unfinished *An Outline of Psychoanalysis*, Freud begins and ends his text by insisting that both the id and the superego are transmitters of natural and cultural heritages, respectively. Despite their wide divergence in aim and expression, they "both represent the influences of the past—the id the influence of heredity, the super-ego the influence, essentially, of what is taken over from other people—whereas the ego is principally determined by the individual's own experience, that is by accidental and contemporary events."[5] On the one hand, the id is the "oldest" psychical agency, which "contains everything that is inherited, that is present at birth, that is laid down in the constitution—above all, therefore, the instincts, which originate from the somatic organization and which find a first psychical expression [. . .] in forms unknown to us."[6] On the other hand, there is the superego, "heir to the Oedipus complex,"[7] which represents not only the influences of one's parents but also "everything that had a determining effect on them themselves, the tastes and standards of the social class in which they lived and the innate dispositions and traditions of the race from which they sprang."[8] Between the two, the natural and cultural heritages, Freud situates the locus proper to what inherits as the mediation of past influences. But the agent of this mediation in fact diverges within the same text, as though Freud cannot decide what the proper heir is. In the first instance, he indicates the ego (as Freud ends the sentence above, "the *ego* is principally determined by the individual's own experience, that is by accidental and contemporary events"). Then, at the end of the text, where he stops writing due to an impending appointment to treat his terminal illness, this formulation of the two sources of inheritance appears again, but this time it is not the ego but "external reality" that mediates between them:

> Those who have a liking for generalizations and sharp distinctions may say that *the external world*, in which the individual finds himself exposed after being detached from his parents, *represents the power*

of the present; that his id, with its inherited trends, represents the organic past; and that the super-ego, which comes to join them later, represents more than anything the cultural past, which a child has, as it were, to repeat as an after-experience during the few years of his early life. It is unlikely that such generalizations can be universally correct. Some portion of the cultural acquisitions have undoubtedly left a precipitate behind them in the id; [. . .] not a few of the child's new experiences will be intensified because they are repetitions of some primaeval phylogenetic experience.

> Was du ererbt von deinen Vätern hast,
> Erwirb es, um es zu besitzen.
> [What thou hast inherited from thy fathers,
> acquire it to make it thine.]

Thus the super-ego takes up a kind of intermediate position between the id and the external world; it unites in itself the influences of the present and the past. In the establishment of the super-ego we have before us, as it were, an example of the way in which the present is changed into the past. . . .[9]

The text ends here. In the editor's note, James Strachey informs us that Freud broke away from his writing in September 1938, due to his having to undergo surgery upon his jaw (he died the following September, and *An Outline of Psychoanalysis* was published posthumously in 1940). But one cannot help but wonder whether there is not something enigmatic about this ending. If the text is considered Freud's last will and testament, a kind of bequest to his followers containing, *in nuce*, his final attempt to run the circuit of his invention, then its final words are instructive. The text concludes just after mentioning the inheritance of the superego as emblematized in Goethe's lines from *Faust*, as if therein lies the key to the riddle of the relationship between psychoanalysis and inheritance: "What thou hast inherited from thy fathers, acquire it to make it thine." In this final moment, when Freud contemplates the invention to which he had devoted almost his whole life, in this final attempt at an outline of psychoanalysis, was there something in the notion of inheritance that made the end return once again to the beginning? Is there, in this ambiguous "power of the present," the potentiality of an inheritance that has not yet been acquired?

Jacques Lacan said he inherited Freud, even in spite of himself.[10] As early as 1954, in a lesson about what it means that the unconscious is the

discourse of the Other, Lacan describes an inheritance in the "discourse of
the circuit in which I am integrated," by which he implicates, also, the transmitted effects of his teaching of psychoanalysis:

> I am one of its links. It is the discourse of my father for instance, in
> so far as my father made mistakes which I am absolutely condemned
> to reproduce—that's what we call the *super-ego*. I am condemned to
> reproduce them because I am obliged to pick up again the discourse
> he bequeathed to me, not simply because I am his son, but because
> one can't stop the chain of discourse, and it is precisely my duty to
> transmit it in its aberrant form to someone else. I have to put to
> someone else the problem of a situation of life or death in which the
> chances are that it is just as likely that he will falter, in such a way that
> this discourse produces a small circuit in which an entire family, an
> entire coterie, an entire camp, an entire nation or half of the world
> will be caught. The circular form of a speech which is just at the limit
> between sense and non-sense, which is problematic.[11]

Given that his point bears upon the father's discourse, how can it be denied
that Lacan's "father" could just as well be Freud and that the "aberrant form"
that he is obliged to transmit includes the "mistakes" of the father of psychoanalysis (for example, Freud's reliance upon the centrality of the Oedipus
myth in his account of the heritage of the superego that Lacan alternatively
describes in this passage as the unstoppable chain of discourse)? Is this to
concede to the naysayers, to admit that the above confirms what has long
been thought about psychoanalysis, that it is a specialized language that
belongs to a "small circuit" or "coterie" of devotees who pass on their occult
knowledge in a self-enclosed circle? But this explanation cannot satisfy us
if we reflect upon the significance of the fact that Lacan describes it as his
duty to transmit a "problematic" discourse, in what amounts to bequeathing
a *curse* to his followers, even a violent betrayal.

The betrayal is not so much reflected in the son's attitude toward the
father, or in the father's betrayal of his progeny, as much as it is in the
betrayal inherent to an inheritance one is obliged to transmit faithfully, if
only because one cannot stop the chain of discourse. In being obliged to
transmit mistakes, aberrations, and failures, what Lacan is seeking to place
before his listeners' awareness is that the inheritance dealt with in psychoanalysis is, above all, the inheritance of the symptoms of society's discontents. In taking up the thread of this "aberrant form," one necessarily
takes up a certain number of problems, the provenance of which cannot

be limited to any single "I" in the unstoppable chain of discourse, even as each individual in the chain is responsible for what is transmitted. What Freud's invention of psychoanalysis bequeaths to the world is an elaboration of problems brought to light through a discourse that is the "circular form of a speech [. . .] at the limit between sense and non-sense." Such a problem is not only negative, in other words, but also what provides the necessary conditions for (re)invention. This is analogous to one of the key points of Lacan's early teaching upon the symptom—a symptom can be read or interpreted because it is "already inscribed in a writing process"[12] and, thereby, already subject to an active, creative agency that is not bound in advance to reproduce or anticipate a given significance. In alliance with the writing of the symptom, the subject becomes capable of rewriting his or her destiny and what is worth living and dying for.

In academia, those who adopt psychoanalytic theory perennially turn or return to it as a more or less useful critical tool for supposedly shedding light upon the way, for example, historical events "return from the repressed," or how unconscious fantasies play a role with, against, and with-and-against the forces of ideological mystification. And yet, this university reception of psychoanalysis is nothing if not a mystifying response itself, in which the scholar or critic avoids the abyssal encounter with the subject of the unconscious and its ethical subversion of self and world in favor of the placid abstraction of "subjective structures," which are routinely mined for ready-made academic "solutions." Why is this, if not that something in Freud's legacy seems to fundamentally disturb one of the most comfortable illusions of intellectual discourse, namely, that there is an inherited and inheritable system of knowledge that can explicate the real? The intention of this volume is to show how far this is from the case. Psychoanalysis is not an object of inheritance, even a problematic one, but a practice that sustains the potential for a certain ethical violence, a new departure of thought and action apart from the given, received, and imposed forms of heredity. The question of its legacy is thus deeply fraught with all of the ambiguities of the subject of the unconscious and calls for a conceptual reinvention of inheritance *in* psychoanalysis.

As an orientating principle, Lacan summarizes Freud's most fundamental recommendation to analysts as follows: "Everything in an analysis is to be gathered up [. . .] as though nothing had ever been established elsewhere."[13] In saying this, he not only gives analysts a word of procedural caution to avoid making each case fit the prevailing theories, he also reminds them that everything—including the inheritance of psychoanalysis itself—has to be gathered up without the fantasy that there is any established knowledge.

In this way, psychoanalysis perpetually reencounters its own beginning, always returning to the place from which "it speaks." Perhaps this is why, as often as it is declared dead or back from the dead, there have been so many reintroductions to psychoanalysis, and why every attempt to "synthesize" psychoanalytic theory in the form of an accessible manual or textbook necessarily fails. Psychoanalysis cannot be inherited; it can only be reinvented.

The overarching argument of this volume is that, in contrast to the way in which notions of inheritance are understood and taken up in various other disciplines, inheritance in psychoanalysis ultimately concerns the reinvention of the social bond, broadly speaking. In order to demonstrate this, the volume enacts a critical traversal of inheritance within select disciplines in addition to psychoanalytic theory and practice. The order of its sections reflects the logic of this traversal: from biological notions of inheritance that are intuitive and seemingly straightforward, like innateness, heredity, and genesis, through cultural notions, like the recasting of cultural traditions and literary filiations, to the ethical reinvention of inheritance in psychoanalytic praxis, in which the idea of inheritance as an ethical problematic concerning the individual's responsibility for the reinvention of the social bond is fully realized and taken to its logical conclusion. Because of this arc, the volume is not as much a collection of variations upon the theme of inheritance as it is a collection dedicated precisely to traversing this theme. That is, inheritance *in* psychoanalysis is not the same as inheritance *and* psychoanalysis, insofar as the former amounts to the conceptual realization of inheritance as an act of reinvention.

As in Lacan's famous aphorism "There is no sexual relationship" (*Il n'y a pas de rapport sexuel*),[14] wherein this impossibility is, in effect, supremely generative and makes possible the invention of new relations and dispositions, we should say "There is no inheritance in psychoanalysis." Rather, *inheritance in psychoanalysis* stands for the transformative potential to reinvent one's inheritance—including the inheritance of psychoanalysis—and the responsibility that this entails.

Natural Inheritance

In the growing field of evolutionary developmental theory (evo-devo), the concept of inheritance is undergoing a veritable revolution. The discovery of the human genome has made possible far greater knowledge of biological inheritance systems and enabled some scientists to see the way that local, human historical events—environmental changes, wars, famine, and disease—affect the heritable biological information of human beings. For example, in the field of transgenerational, epigenetic inheritance, one of the profound discoveries—the implications of which are still only beginning to be felt—is that evolutionarily recent events affect the human genome indirectly through the epigenetic expression of DNA that determine which genes are "switched" on or off. Just as more short-term evolutionary changes, such as specific historical events, can directly affect the human genome, so too do their effects have a demonstrably far greater reach. A traumatic event may affect an individual not only at a biological level but also at the level of his or her succeeding generations, as in the well-documented case of the Dutch famine, in which pregnant women whose estrogen levels were affected by malnutrition during the famine passed on the RNA methylation process to their children and their children's children, who ended up with the biological effects (low birth weight, for example, or compensatory obesity) of the original trauma.[15] The emerging consensus in this field is that DNA can no longer be seen as the *leader* in the evolutionary process; instead, it is becoming more of a *follower* of epigenetic and environmental changes, including those actively made by organisms within the same biological lineage.[16] Hence, natural selection is nowhere near as straightforward as had previously been assumed.

In *Beyond the Pleasure Principle*, Freud takes up the problem of the retrogressive dimension of the drive in order to account for various clinical phenomena, such as the compulsion to repeat troubling experiences, rather than remember them, and the riddle of primary masochism. To account for such phenomena, and the famous tendency of the drive to "restore an earlier state of things,"[17] Freud turns to multiple scientific theories, most especially in biological fields, such as embryology, wherein his theory of the retrogressive tendency of the psyche draws upon Ernst Haeckel's recapitulation theory ("ontogeny recapitulates phylogeny"), the ethological notion of instinct, as in the case of the transgenerational repetition of the migratory patterns of birds and certain fish, and a distinctly Lamarckian brand of evolutionary theory. Although a generation of critics has pointed out the problems attendant upon Freud's turn to biology for a metaphysical biologism that overemphasizes this retrogressive dimension, some theorists have more recently suggested a more nuanced, dialectical reading of Freudian biology, which returns to Freud's biological materialism as well as to some formerly maligned scientific figures, such as Haeckel and Jean-Baptiste Lamarck, who are also starting to make something of a comeback. The essays in this first section situate themselves amid these new developments and address the bio-logics of inheritance from a psychoanalytically inspired orientation, a position that forces them to invent new frameworks for thinking innateness, evolution, transmission, and the bio-logics of sexuality.

In each of their articles, Samo Tomšič and Lorenzo Chiesa argue that one of the most significant problems, not only in psychoanalytic practice but also in the dominant understanding of evolution, is the persistence of the myth of telos—the end of human action. In "Against Heredity: The Question of Causality in Psychoanalysis," Tomšič identifies Freud's three key revisions to the notion of causality—its nonlinearity, nonrelationality, and nonidentity with the signifier—in order to show that psychoanalysis reinvents the very notion of heredity by making it depend upon what Aristotle calls *tyche*, the contingency of the encounter as a specifically subjective causality. In a similar vein, Chiesa's "Lacan with Evo-Devo?" develops Lacan's critique of the theo-teleology of evolutionism in order to show that this critique remains topical today; at the same time, however, he also shows how Lacan misses out on the opportunity for self-critique in the process of criticizing the life sciences. Against over a century of Mendelian-Darwinian hegemony, the argument recently put forward by authorities in the field of evo-devo that genes are not the leaders in the selection process but followers of more decisive changes to the environment has delivered a powerful blow to biological determinism. However, if some of the teleological assumptions and illogical presuppositions of Darwinian evolutionary theory have been successfully critiqued in modern, dialectical theory (as promoted by the likes of Steven Jay Gould), then evolutionary theory still remains problematically close to a tautology. Lacan's criticism of the field back in the 1970s thus still holds as a contemporary challenge—that, even without the supposition of a telos of organized life, the theory of natural selection devolves into the formula that "those who survive are those who have survived."

According to one of the earliest definitions in the *Oxford English Dictionary*, to *inherit* is to derive "by natural descent" or possess "by transmission from parents or ancestry." Already in this definition, at the level of the letter, there is an ambiguous conflation between that which is inherited as an innate or natural constitution and that which is acquired by transmission. Plumbing this ambiguity of the logic of inheritance, Adrian Johnston outlines an ontogeny without descent, one that does not presuppose any priority of lineal ancestry. In "The Late Innate: Jean Laplanche, Jaak Panksepp, and the Distinction between Sexual Drives and Instincts," Johnston points to the anatomical and physiological reality of prolonged prematurational helplessness (*Hilflosigkeit*) in human beings that Freud theorizes as essential to understanding the degree to which humans are thoroughly dependent upon and shaped by others. Not only is this primary or originary helplessness a condition that helps to explain the intercession of the symbolic function within human affairs, but it is also, qua deficit, the motivation and catalyst for the further development of sexuality. Drawing upon Jean Laplanche's late theoretical writing in the largely neglected field of adolescent sexuality, as well as the recent affective neuroscience of Jaak Panksepp and Lucy Biven, Johnston argues that, contrary to what is supposed, the acquired (symbolic inheritance) temporally and logically precedes the innate (biologically constitutive). That is, the innate is only retroactively determined once the acquired is enlisted and actuated by the unconscious subject when sexuality reemerges in puberty. Johnston poses this logic of retroactivity as a critical corrective to key concepts within the emerging field of neuropsychoanalysis.

Frank Ruda also takes up the paradoxical rapport of transmission and ontogenesis in "Hegel's Mother." In a hitherto little-remarked-upon moment in *Philosophy of Mind*, G. W. F. Hegel describes the passage of genius from the mother to the child as the condensation of all of the givens of individuality. Yet, even within this concentration of the given, the acquired precedes the innate: Genius is the genesis of transmission that appears to the human animal, en passant, as an almost autonomous process. Between mother and child stands the genius of genesis, "a possibility that is not—although it is necessarily mistakenly perceived as if it were—a natural disposition." According to Hegel's logic of transmission, the mother, in the very act of becoming a mother—bringing a new being into existence—also thereby passes on the capacity for bringing the new into being. The child inherits this capacity in the genesis or genius of an act whereby the mother becomes a mother by means of the presupposition of a disposition (motherhood) that also passes away in passing on this potentiality. Hence, the mother, according to Hegel, is a vanishing mediator of genius. The act of making new is not the inheritance of an innate substance but the inheritance of that which conditions the innate: "Genius is that which names the quality to posit new presuppositions." It is this quality of positing the unheard-of that makes the latter term resonate with the creative potential, or jouissance, of inheritance.

Such a potentiality exceeds the restrictive limits imposed by the contemporary logic of *bios*, as A. Kiarina Kordela's "Biopower in Lacan's Inheritance; or, From Foucault to Freud, via Deleuze, and Back to Marx" makes clear. Kordela dismantles some of the more persistent metaphysical strands of Michel Foucault's critique of biopower—time, sex, and the real—by showing how the psychoanalytic concept of primary fantasy reorients their coordinates and makes biopolitical administration seem even more excessive than previously supposed. Not content with the managing or care of living bodies, contemporary biopolitics seeks the ultimate jouissance of immortality through the commodification of labor and surplus-value that only the Lacanian theory of sexual difference, and its insight into the overdetermination of sexuality implanted within bios, can critique effectively.

Cultural Inheritance

In "Lituraterre," Lacan proposes a strategic "intrusion" of psychoanalysis into literary criticism, "because if literary criticism could effectively renew itself, this would be as a result of psychoanalysis being there for texts to pit themselves against it, the enigma residing on the side of the latter."[18] Such an approach would allow the enigma to stay within the site of its articulation, rather than, say, to close itself off in abstruse theorizing in the name of what psychoanalysis is or means in an artifactual sense. But how would such an approach signal a means of "effectively renew[ing]" literature and literary criticism, and what would it mean for psychoanalysis to "be there" for literary texts? If inheritance in psychoanalysis names the transformative potential of an encounter with the unconscious, then the point of departure could well be a literary one, concerning the creative combinations of letters that result when the speaking being stumbles upon the nonsense of signifying traditions. Other than in genetic science and linguistics, there is perhaps no other domain in which the discordance of letters, with respect to the message they are supposed to convey, is more clearly felt. Psychoanalysis may be said to interfere productively with a cultural tradition when criticism pits itself against the enigma of the letters of the unconscious.

Justin Clemens and Rebecca Comay oversee the site of collision between literature and psychoanalysis wherein new meaning is created. Clemens's "Drug Is the Love: Literature, Psychopharmacology, Psychoanalysis" attempts to align the literary with the psychoanalytic in his criticism of the biotechnical hegemony of drugs and the ways in which it increasingly marginalizes talking cures. Far from sensing the ontological dimension of affects like anxiety and depression that philosophers have regarded for centuries as intrinsic to the riddle of human experience, the current psychopharmacological authorities tend to regard all unpleasant affects as symptomatic of, and reducible to, the terms and program of a chemical cure. In this tendency Clemens recognizes the force of a desire that "there should be an end to talk." By silencing speech, psychopharmacology also attempts to short-circuit the inheritance of the unruliness of love's hidden rule over the desiring subject.

But, despite this antagonism, drugs have always had a rich history in love's letters. In a brief genealogy, Clemens situates the current psychopharmaco-logical love of drugs within a literary and historical register that has surpris-ing parallels with the literary discourse of "the constitutionally ambivalent vicissitudes of love, in and by love itself." In spite of the dominance of drug therapies that would not dream of identifying love as an element of psychi-atric treatment, Clemens suggests that psychoanalysis goes further "where the transference is expressly identified with the work of love in the practice of psychoanalysis." Unique among contemporary approaches, then, psycho-analysis makes love an object of singular knowledge, so that "*Übertragung* or transference in psychoanalysis [is] at once [what] constitutes a repetition, an analysis, and a *détournement* of the paradoxes of inheritance." From the van-tage of love as a guiding problem, talk therapy, literature, and psychoanalysis seem to share a common bond.

In Comay's "Testament of the Revolution (Walter Benjamin)," new meaning takes flight from the evacuation of inherited meaning. Asking the unasked question of why it is that the history of critical theory, and the Frankfurt School in particular, is traditionally thought in patrilineal, dynas-tic terms as a succession of "generations," Comay examines the founda-tionalist desires attendant upon projects of historical remembering. A line from René Char—"Our heritage was left to us without a testament" (*Notre héritage n'est précédé d'aucun testament*)[19]—well expresses the retrospective sensibilities of such figures as Hannah Ardent and, at least allegedly, Walter Benjamin (each of whose position within any critical lineage is notoriously difficult to fix), who memorably lamented the cultural disarray of our dehis-toricized times. But Comay hazards a reversal of this poetic formula. What if a better expression of our contemporary predicament is one in which "Our testament comes to us without a heritage"? Picking up from the most mate-rial level of the letter, Comay points to the potentiality inherent in the unfin-ished projects of these writers, including Benjamin's *The Arcades Project* and strewn writings, such as reading lists, in order to plumb the potentiality of testamentarity itself as the material for a new invention of a cultural coun-tertradition against the grain of official narratives.

In the language of the unconscious, we find an essential support for the conceptual refoundation of cultural tradition. Seizing upon the pow-erful political potential implicit in this idea, Oxana Timofeeva and Donald E. Pease acquire new inheritances. Timofeeva's "'We' and 'They': Animals behind Our Back" reconceptualizes the "we" and "they" of the so-called human community at the basis of political culture. The language of the unconscious at its purest is an untranslatable, inarticulate noise, "like a beast's cry." She daringly advances a notion of community that is organized according to such difficult-to-articulate truths at the "nonhuman core of the human." "Animals do not *have* an unconscious; they *are* the unconscious," Timofeeva contends. At the level of the dream, there is a nonhuman potentiality that is common to all but that belongs only to the shadowy animal multitude: "The community is not for us but for them." Tracing this unconscious "animal negativity" through biblical and other mythic traditions, Timofeeva dedicates herself to the dream of a future communist community in accordance with the shared terrain of our animal unconscious.

Tracing another pathway in its recasting of tradition is Pease's "F. O. Matthiessen: Heir to (American) Jouissance." Taking up a problematic kernel of American myth, its literary canon, Pease analyzes literary critic F. O. Matthiessen's invention, in 1941, of the tradition he called "American Renaissance" in *American Renaissance: Art and Expression in the Age of Emerson and Whitman*. Although the latter work was created in line with the Popular Front movement to construct a national heritage that would defend against Nazi ideology, this canonical and academic field-defining work of Americanist criticism also notoriously configures this heritage restrictedly according to its nationalist agenda and heteronormative, progress-oriented teleology. In a kind of *détournement* of this heritage, Pease resituates Matthiessen within the register of his suppressed desire—through his work with displaced European persons after the war and his clandestine love affair with painter Russell Cheney—to conceive of an alternative articulation of American Renaissance.

The question of what psychoanalysis has to do with cultural tradition necessarily confronts the legacy of psychoanalysis within culture. Sigi Jöttkandt and Lydia R. Kerr provide surprising cases of this through the writings of two notoriously outspoken critics of psychoanalysis: Vladimir Nabokov and Ishmael Reed. There is a popular anecdote about one of Nabokov's tirades against Freud according to which the celebrated belletrist, upon being interrupted by the loud noise of the heating pipes in his Cornell University classroom, cried out, "The Viennese quack is *railing* at me from his grave!"[20] As Jöttkandt shows, both in his real life and fiction (which Nabokov does not regard as opposed, as in traditional notions of art versus life, but as two "manners of being" that emerge "from the same wellspring of inscription," as Jöttkandt puts it), such Freudian hauntings are not atypical. In "A Mortimer Trap: The Passing of Death in *The Real Life of Sebastian Knight*," paternal figures in Nabokov's novels can be seen to compose a general pattern of deceptive or counterfeit meaning. As opposed to the imaginary mimeticism of most psychobiographical approaches, Jöttkandt is able to show, via the decisive turn to Lacan's understanding of the paternity of letters, that what this retracing also reveals—or, better, invents—is a masque of death. This reading allows us to savor the full piquancy of the closing scene of mistaken identity in *The Real Life of Sebastian Knight*.

As for Ishmael Reed, the question of the cultural inheritance of psychoanalysis is more deeply vexed as a consequence of the racism inherent to the governing logics of tradition. Yet, Reed's novel *Mumbo Jumbo* shows how the argument that inheritance, from a psychoanalytic perspective, is truly the subject's invention has perhaps the most evident and far-reaching effects. The novel concerns a mythic signifier of the inheritance of Black American culture, "Jes Grew," an apparent "plague" attacking the foundations of (Eurocentric, white supremacist) "Civilization As We Know It." Jes Grew's symptoms, like ragtime and jazz, are foreign objects within American history that "only appear as inassimilable excesses." Kerr's "Freud Fainted; or, 'It All Started 1000s of Years Ago in Egypt . . .'" picks up upon the fact that Reed situates Freud as one of the primary conspirators behind the inoculation measures taken by civilization against this plague. Reed's analyst-like protagonist PaPa LaBas, tasked with solving the mystery of Jes Grew, ends up reconstructing a repressed racial history and a myth "that traces the mysteries of inheritance in America to the trauma of an ancient Egyptian fratricide." Yet, despite the fact that Reed figures Freud (in cahoots with Carl Jung) as participating in the Egyptian conspiracy that threatens to eradicate Jes Grew, Kerr points out that Freud's *Moses and Monotheism* provides a similar account of an Egyptian conspiracy to cover up a primal crime in the name of civilization, namely, Freud's myth of the two Moseses. This latter myth, reconstructed by Freud upon the basis of a "historical truth" that he deduces through testamentary distortions, seems almost as though it were reconfigured, in turn, in Reed's novel. That is, if the Jes Grew virus is an inheritance of Black American culture in Reed's sense, it is just as much, Kerr argues, the signifier of "the transmissions of unconscious inheritance that Freud himself detected in the hidden after hours of Civilization As We Know It." Such an enigmatic inheritance is perhaps best understood as what a symbolic heritage tries, and fails, to repress, and the specific way in which the subject attempts to manage this symptom of inheritance to which it is nonetheless deeply, perhaps irrevocably, attached. LaBas's mythic reconstruction thus functions in a parallel way to Freud's myth-construction of the Egyptian Moses as the ur-father of civilization: an attempt to gather up a repressed historical truth in order to reinvent a cultural tradition.

The Inheritance of Psychoanalysis

In its relatively short history, the psychoanalytic movement has been subject to tumultuous upheaval, besieged by the doubts, fears, and wishes of supplicants and detractors alike, arising from both inside and outside the clinic. Therefore, the question of what might constitute its inheritance—not only in the sense of how it has become known to a broad public, or what it has become as a clinical praxis, but also in terms of its survival and the cultural legacy resulting from encounters with it—is an extremely difficult one. Yet, inheritance in psychoanalysis entails an ethical commitment that assumes the most apparent and lively urgency when it is situated within the space of the clinic. Here, inheritance ceases to be a matter of tracing certain effects; instead, it is a prerogative for future generations of analysts, a matter of the inheritance of psychoanalysis in the field—and, by the weight—of its own specific action in the lives of subjects. Coming up against some of the thorniest problems of human agency, as well as the most questionable inheritances of the Freudian unconscious, the contributors to this section explore the problematic dimension of Freud's myths as well as the challenging new symptoms facing psychoanalysis today.

Notoriously, Freud resorts to myth in answer to the riddles enunciated by the speaking being. Such a move is almost incomprehensible from a scientistic standpoint, for, who, in the name of science, would dare ascribe epistemic significance to *myth*? Nonetheless, it is in the interest of scientific truth that Freud puts forward his "Darwinian myth" of the primal horde, the myth of Oedipus, and, indeed, his phylogenetic myths of the id's archaic inheritance, which outline a natural history of the unconscious, dating from primeval times. In "Freud's Lamarckian Clinic," Daniel Wilson retraces the condemned intellectual heritage at issue in these mythic constructions, from Lamarck's conception of the evolution of culturally acquired traits, continuing through Haeckel's theories of the ontogenetic recapitulation of phylogenetic history, followed by the replacement of need by the "power of unconscious ideas" in the psycho-Lamarckist theories of Ewald Hering. Wilson foregrounds the issues accordingly: Freud resorts to myths in the same way he commits himself to daring and controversial new developments in the sciences—in order to follow the torsions of neurotic symptoms and, in so doing, shed a glimmer of light upon universal symptomatic structures. Wilson thereby argues that Freud's myth of phylogenesis bears witness to the orientation of the individual drive towards something that does not correspond to any object in the individual's environment and to which the subject responds with the invention of the symptom.

Philippe Van Haute takes on one of the central mythic motifs of psychoanalysis, the formulations of the Oedipus complex. Against the standard reception, Van Haute draws out a vastly different intellectual history of Freud, pointing out that, despite what is roundly supposed, the Oedipus complex is never mentioned in the original 1905 edition of Freud's *Three Essays on the Theory of Sexuality*, nor is it mentioned in the "Dora" case history, which was published around the same time. He even goes so far as to contend that the supposed references to the complex are susceptible to projection on the part of those eager to read Freud's later theories into these works. "Freud against Oedipus" proposes a decentering of the Oedipal focus of traditional Freudian psychoanalysis in favor of an alternative methodology that would rely upon the pathological disturbances in mental functioning, rather than complexes and myths, to provide the key to understanding mental life more generally, including the pathological basis of so-called normal mental life.

Freud invented the practice of psychoanalysis in recognition of the fact that subjects articulate the most difficult truths in symptomatic form. The turn of the twenty-first century has brought a veritable sea change in terms of the emergence of new subjective problematics. The experiences of trans subjects, for example, bring to the surface the most paradoxical truths about sexual difference and make manifest the difficulties and inventive potential resulting from the impossibility of the sexual relationship for each and every subject. Patricia Gherovici's "Plastic Sex? The Beauty of It!" provides a note of uplift upon this score. Under the reign of neoliberal ideology, the acceleration of technology in capitalism today supports conceptions of sex that reduce it to a commodity in some way serviceable or customizable to the "owner's" will. Yet, the experiences of trans subjects in psychoanalysis challenge this contemporary *doxa*, providing a glimpse into the possibilities for sexual reinvention that do not make sex conform to consumer user-friendliness. Rather than despair of this failure, Gherovici enjoins us to embrace the fruits of what sexual difference means for such subjects. Against the mirages of neoliberal self-invention (often reducible to merely topical alterations in one's life, occupation, or relationship status) and the epistemology of failure that too often serves as its sole critical counterpoint, Gherovici foregrounds the real of sex and sexual difference as the constitutive basis for the (re)invention of the body and its potentiality.

Another significant challenge and opportunity for psychoanalysis today is that of autism. In "The Autistic Body and Its Objects," Éric Laurent extends psychoanalytic themes and approaches to a traditionally nonpsychoanalytic context. He develops a psychoanalytic approach to the treatment of autistic subjects that has echoes with other efforts, like affinity therapy. Through several case studies, he presents some topological aspects of the autistic body that have to be taken into account in order to develop this approach. In this vein, Laurent develops a novel, psychoanalytically inspired account of a number of features of autism that have been neglected by cognitive neuroscience, including the importance of role-playing, voice modulation, and the interplay between two- and three-dimensional objects.

As exciting as these new challenges may be for the future of psychoanalysis, it is becoming increasingly clear that they may only bode well provided that those who have been marked in some way by the inheritance of psychoanalysis culturally, intellectually, and personally are willing to resist the resistances that would stopper up the articulations of unconscious desire. In the interview that closes the volume, "The Insistence of Jouissance: On Inheritance and Psychoanalysis," Joan Copjec remarks upon the urgency of the task of tending to the exigency of the unconscious. Reflecting upon the position that she has found herself in throughout her career as an intellectual who "inherits" psychoanalytic concepts into various fields (feminism, film theory, philosophy), Copjec indicates that the space or gap between meaning and enjoyment in which psychoanalysis is situated is not reducible to either a given or an imposed heritage, but rather unstoppably insists by forging new means of conjugating enjoyment and sense. Within the interval of fatigue lies the potentiality of a psychoanalytic act that would chart a new course—the transformative power of *inheritance in psychoanalysis*.

Notes

1. See Sigmund Freud, "The Unconscious," in *The Standard Edition of the Complete Psychological Works of Sigmund Freud* (hereafter *SE*), ed. and trans. James Strachey et al. (London: Hogarth Press, 1953–1974), 14:187.

2. Freud, *New Introductory Lectures on Psycho-Analysis*, in *SE* 22:80; translation modified. See also, for example, Jacques Lacan, "The Instance of the Letter in the Unconscious, or Reason since Freud," in *Écrits: The First Complete Edition in English*, trans. Bruce Fink (New York: W. W. Norton, 2006), 435; *The Seminar of Jacques Lacan, Book II: The Ego in Freud's Theory and in the Technique of Psychoanalysis, 1954–1955*, ed. Jacques-Alain Miller, trans. Sylvana Tomaselli (New York: W. W. Norton, 1988), 246; and *L'acte psychanalytique* (1967–1968), unpublished seminar, lesson of January 10, 1968, http://gaogoa.free.fr/.

3. See Ari E. Friedland et al., "Heritable Genome Editing in *C. elegans* via a CRISPR-Cas9 System," *Nature Methods* 10 (2013): 741–43.

4. Johann Wolfgang von Goethe, *Faust: Der Tragödie erster und zweiter Teil*, ed. Erich Trunz (München: C. H. Beck, 1986), 29. See also Freud, *Totem and Taboo* in *SE*, 13:158; and *An Outline of Psychoanalysis*, in *SE* 23:207.

5. Freud, *An Outline of Psychoanalysis*, in *SE* 23:147.

6. Ibid., 145.

7. Freud, *The Ego and the Id*, in *SE* 19:48.

8. Freud, *An Outline of Psychoanalysis*, in *SE* 23:206.

9. Ibid., 206–7; emphasis added.

10. See Lacan, *Le Séminaire de Jacques Lacan, Livre XXIII: Le sinthome, 1975–1976*, ed. Jacques-Alain Miller (Paris: Éditions du Seuil, 2005), 12.

11. Lacan, *The Seminar of Jacques Lacan, Book II: The Ego in Freud's Theory and in the Technique of Psychoanalysis*, 1954–55, 89–90; emphasis in original.

12. Lacan, "Psychoanalysis and Its Teaching," in *Écrits: The First Complete Edition in English*, 371.

13. Lacan, "Introduction à l'Édition allemande des Écrits," in *Autres écrits*, ed. Jacques-Alain Miller (Paris: Éditions du Seuil, 2001), 556; my translation.

14. See, for example, Lacan, *The Seminar of Jacques Lacan, Book XVII: The Other Side of Psychoanalysis*, ed. Jacques-Alain Miller, trans. Russell Grigg (New York: W. W. Norton, 2007), 116; and *The Seminar of Jacques Lacan, Book XX: Encore, On Feminine Sexuality, the Limits of Love and Knowledge, 1972–1973*, ed. Jacques-Alain Miller, trans. Bruce Fink (New York: W. W. Norton, 1999), 12, 34.

15. See Richard C. Francis, *Epigenetics: How Environment Shapes Our Genes* (New York: W. W. Norton, 2011), 6–8.

16. See Mary Jane West-Eberhard, "Genes as Followers in Evolution," in *Developmental Plasticity and Evolution* (New York: Oxford University Press, 2003), 157–58.

17. Freud, *Beyond the Pleasure Principle*, in *SE* 18:36.

18. Lacan, "Lituraterre," *Hurly-Burly* 9 (2013): 31.

19. René Char, *Feuillets d'Hypnos*, in *Oeuvres complètes* (Paris: Gallimard, 1983), 190.

20. See Brian Boyd, *Vladimir Nabokov: The American Years* (Princeton: Princeton University Press, 1991), 308. See also Leland de la Durantaye, "Vladimir Nabokov and Sigmund Freud, or a Particular Problem," *American Imago* 62, no. 1 (2005): 59–73.

Natural Inheritance

CHAPTER 1

Against Heredity

The Question of Causality in Psychoanalysis

Samo Tomšič

Restating the Problem

Psychoanalysis begins with etiology as a science that investigates the causes of mental illness. Yet, unlike most of his contemporaries, Sigmund Freud sought these causes in the mental rather than the physiological realm. He thereby flouted normal medical science, which strived to root these illnesses in a neurological hereditary factor. In this same move, from the hereditary to the symbolic, Freud developed a general theory of the mental apparatus, which broke radically from the regimes of knowledge still grounded in a centralized model of consciousness. What is striking in this inaugural move is that Freud mobilized the notion of cause, the scientificity of which had been questioned throughout modernity and had almost become redundant in the sciences by the time psychoanalysis was invented. With the accomplishment of the modern scientific revolution, the sciences no longer aimed at determining the causality underlying natural phenomena, but instead aimed at mathematizing their laws. In Isaac Newton's *Principia Mathematica*, the historical movement that grounded positive science upon the combination of formalization and experimentation was stabilized. Newton's general theory seemed to have solved the majority of problems that preoccupied physics following the downfall of the Aristotelian paradigm. Consequently, the notion of cause, which had been imported into science from Aristotelian metaphysics, appeared redundant, if not pseudoscientific.

The theory of causality was indeed one of the last remainders of Aristotelianism that needed to be removed from positive science. In philosophy, the development from David Hume's skepticism to Immanuel Kant's critique produced a similar result, with the difference being that it restricted causality to the realm of human cognition and transformed it from an ontological to a purely epistemological concept.

The main problem was that causality still presupposed the central position of human observation in the field of knowledge. This centralization contradicted the main achievement of Galileanism, which postulated the autonomy and sufficiency of the mathematical apparatus in the exploration of the physical real. Mathematics is a science without a human observer; it does not rely upon a subject of cognition (consciousness), which implies that its tools and procedures do not describe the world of appearances but rather something that thinking experiences as impossible.[1] In the regime of knowledge, where its centralization around the fixed and immovable point of the human observer had been abolished—in other words, where scientific knowledge had been radically depsychologized—the notion of cause necessarily became a remainder of the old epistemic regime. Recall that, for Hume, the continuity and connectedness postulated by the linear causal relation inevitably mixes human habitus into science and makes knowledge obtained through the technological-mathematical apparatus depend upon the psychological observer.[2] In opposition to the claims of classical metaphysics, natural laws contain no stable and invariable necessity, and the notorious awakening from the dogmatic slumber that Kant described in *Prolegomena to Any Future Metaphysics*[3] concerns precisely the downfall of etiology as an essential ingredient of episteme, an awakening of philosophical thinking from the closed world of the ancients into the infinite universe of the moderns.[4] Kant seems to suggest that precritical thinkers such as Gottfried Wilhelm Leibniz and René Descartes did not entirely integrate the revolutionary consequences of the modern scientific revolution into philosophical knowledge. An important pillar of Aristotelian epistemology was still standing, and this is what the critique was supposed to challenge. We know that the Kantian solution consisted in maintaining that science can drop the concept of causality, but the notion nevertheless persists in the mental apparatus. Causality is the *subjective* conceptual reaction to the *objective* appearance of nature. Kant evidently shared Hume's epistemological skepticism, but he transformed it into a weapon of critique, thereby indicating a possible transformation of the concept. However, if, for Kant, causality remains limited to human cognition, psychoanalysis will take the additional and surprising step of renewing its ontological dimension.

Freud's intervention into the problematics of causality will consist in detaching the causal relation from the context in which it designated a stable and seemingly unproblematic continuity and in linking it to a disturbance or rupture of regularity and automatic repetition. In the context of psychoanalysis, causality will describe dysfunction rather than function. Furthermore, the Freudian theory of trauma will introduce a crucial change in the (topological and temporal) representation of causality by replacing linearity with retroactivity.

By reformulating the problem of causality, psychoanalysis will imply that philosophy and positive science may have been too hasty in their dismissal, insofar as what was rejected along with etiological inquiry was the dimension of production. Freud situated production—notably, the production of jouissance—at the very heart of psychoanalysis, which showed language and sexuality in an entirely different light and, in both cases, repeated the same decentering gesture as the concept of the unconscious in relation to thinking. Indeed, Freud did much more than propose an etiological explanation of neuroses. When reading his early writings on hysteria—as well as some of his mature works, including *The Interpretation of Dreams* and "Papers on Metapsychology"—it is difficult not to see that the interplay of contradictory forces or psychical conflict is central to etiology. Freud did not analyze unproblematic causal *relations*; rather, he reinterpreted causality as an inherently conflictual *nonrelation* between the insatiable unconscious formation (desire or drive) and the mental labor needed for its satisfaction. The nonrelational aspect of causality became evident once neurosis was acknowledged as being more than a simple illness or disorder. Recall that psychoanalysis was established as a *talking cure* (as the first patient, Bertha Pappenheim, whom Freud and Josef Breuer identified by the pseudonym Anna O, describes it),[5] a treatment in which the patient assumes the position of the subject. But is it really the patient who speaks, that is, does the fact that he or she speaks as a conscious subject mean that he or she is a neutral observer? Freud drew a different conclusion, and Jacques Lacan later expressed this conclusion in the famous apothegm *ça parle*, "it speaks."[6] The impersonal "it" stands for the autonomy of discourse, but it also designates the subject of the unconscious, and it is possible to conclude that, as soon as the presence of a decentered subject is determined in the impersonal unconscious process, Freud's etiology becomes a theory of the subject, while neurosis—and, in particular, hysteria, the central topic of Freud's early writings—becomes a form of protest against the unconscious mode of enjoyment.

With Kant causality became a synthetic a priori that conditions human experience and is reserved for the relation between the subject of cognition and the production of knowledge. By contrast, psychoanalysis will return to the ontological dimension of causality, but without simply regressing to pre-critical or premodern thinking. The Freudian reformulation of causality is overtly anti-Aristotelian in at least three ways: The first two, as I have already indicated, correspond to the nonlinearity of causality (retroactivity) and the nonrelation (psychical conflict), while the third corresponds to the signifier, which Aristotle (or, for that matter, Kant) would never have counted among possible causes. Lacan sees this reconceptualization of causality as the most crucial *critical* contribution of psychoanalysis:

> I shall certainly have to indicate that the impact of truth as cause in science must be recognized in its guise as formal cause.
>
> But that will be so as to clarify that psychoanalysis instead emphasizes its guise as material cause, a fact that qualifies psycho-analysis' originality in science.
>
> This material cause is truly the form of impact of the signifier that I define therein.
>
> The signifier is defined by psychoanalysis as acting first of all as separated from its signification.[7]

Lacan returns here to the Aristotelian quadrivium (formal, efficient, mate-rial, and final cause), associating each form of causality with an epistemic practice: *causa efficiens* with magic; *causa finalis* with religion; *causa forma-lis* with science; and *causa materialis* with psychoanalysis.[8] Lacan thereby implicitly refers to Freud, for whom the history of knowledge begins with a belief preoccupied with the omnipotence of thought (the paradigmatic example of which is totemism, which Freud links to obsessional neurosis), progresses to canonical religion (the epitome being revealed religion), and ends with science, where experimentation and the rigorous production of positive knowledge about natural phenomena overcome the various forms of belief.[9] Setting magic and religion aside, it should be noted here that Lacan moved beyond Freud, who attempted to inscribe psychoanalysis into the frame of positive science. The move to the material cause consists in the inclusion of the signifier among the possible causes that produce real con-sequences, including the subject of the unconscious and jouissance, which are of primary interest in psychoanalysis. The subject is intimately related to causality because the causal relation stems from a minimal gap, a compli-cation in the link between the libidinal and the biological. All of the efforts of psychoanalysis follow from the fact that the existence of language intro-duces this rupture into the body. With regard to this rupture, both traditional mind-body dualism and physiological monism fall short, insofar as the former all too precipitously identifies the autonomy of the signifier with immaterial substance, while the latter, a vulgar materialism, denies this autonomy outright. The crucial lesson of Freudianism is that the body is not one, but it is not simply two either. Indeed, Freud's theory of sexuality follows not only from his early etiological preoccupations but also from this insight into the problematic status of the body. The sexual etiology of neuroses was the first major epistemological contribution of psychoanalysis; in Freudian theory, however, sexuality was never meant to designate the anatomical or the biological but rather a specific complication in the relation between the biological and the symbolic, the hereditary and the acquired.

The move from the formal to the material cause complicates the relation between science and psychoanalysis, and this complication proceeds from the detachment of the signifier from its presumed and stable relation to signification. Only once the signifier has been detached from this relationality and envisaged in its absolute autonomy can the notion of the material cause be transformed and psychoanalysis ground its specific materialist orientation, which mobilizes the subversive potential of modern science. In a brief report on Seminar XI that contains an original rearticulation of epistemology and ontology, Lacan describes the core of his project as the move from the essentially Freudian question "Is psychoanalysis a science?" to the more subversive question "What is a science that includes psychoanalysis?"[10] This displacement assumes that psychoanalysis altered the established conception of scientificity, notably the positivist and empiricist vision of science in which an entire set of ontological problematics is rejected as impertinent. In Seminar XI, Lacan proposes a list of the fundamental concepts of psychoanalysis with which Freud challenged the "dogmatic" notion of scientificity: the unconscious, repetition, transference, and the drive. It is indeed paradoxical that modern science could detach the production of knowledge from the central position of human observation *and* lay the foundations for a vulgar empiricism and reductionist positivism that strive to cleanse science of its dialectical and materialist potential. Lacan's engagement in epistemological and philosophical matters consists in reclaiming the right for "speculation" in science, following Freud's example of a subversive scientific practice, an example that leaves hardly any established doctrine of science unchallenged, insofar as the unconscious is a form of knowledge without a subject of cognition; repetition—subdivided into the compulsion to repeat (*automaton*) and traumatism, a form of repetition grounded in disruption (*tyche*)—addresses the relation between the necessary (appearance) and the impossible (the real); transference thematizes the link between knowledge

and desire (the figure of the subject supposed to know); and, finally, the
drive exposes the proximity of knowledge to jouissance. With these four
cornerstones of psychoanalysis in mind, Lacan proposes a condensed redefinition of cause: *Il n'y a de cause que de ce qui cloche*, there is no other cause
than the cause of dysfunction. Kant and Hume were right to criticize the link
between causality and function. In modernity, natural mechanisms follow
laws susceptible to mathematization (unlike in Aristotelian causality); however, causality reenters the picture as soon as the flawless functioning of a
given mechanism is disrupted:

> Cause is to be distinguished from that which is determinate in a
> chain, in other words the *law*. By way of example, think of what is
> pictured in the law of action and reaction. There is here, one might
> say, a single principle. One does not go without the other. [. . .]
>
> Whenever we speak of cause, on the other hand, there is always
> something anti-conceptual, something indefinite. The phases of the
> moon are the cause of tides—we know this from experience, we
> know that the word cause is correctly used here. Or again, miasmas
> are the cause of fever—that doesn't mean anything either, there is a
> hole, and something that oscillates in the interval. In short, there is
> cause only in something that doesn't work.
>
> Well! It is at this point that I am trying to make you see by
> approximation that the Freudian unconscious is situated at that
> point, where, between cause and that which it affects, there is always
> something wrong.[11]

The problem is not simply that causality is rendered inoperative as soon as
positive knowledge fills in the gap between two phenomena; rather, something in the automaton, in the necessity of laws, always persists as contingent, tyche. I am not talking about contingency in the Humean and Kantian
sense, where it designates an ungrounded change or the occurrence of a
radical break with the existing lawful regime, but in the sense of something
closer to gradual becoming.[12] Lacan's reformulation of causality could not
be further from a Kantian synthetic a priori, in which causality is an intellectual construction that provides consistency to the multitude of appearances, its main function in human cognition being precisely to fill in the
gap between appearance and the real, thereby establishing a regular chain
of causes and effects. The idea of causality that emerges from a disruption
of the chain instead presupposes the epistemological model offered by Alexandre Koyré, who never subscribed to the empiricist theory of science and

was always interested in the history of scientific failures and the speculative-philosophical theses contained in scientific theories. Koyré insisted that what is crucial in the history of science is not the linear and continuous movement or progressive accumulation of knowledge but the deadlocks, failed attempts, errors, and discontinuities that draw attention to the fact that science itself is internally split between normal and revolutionary science[13]—or, in Lacan's formulation, between the discourse of the university (normal) and the discourse of the hysteric (revolutionary). The notion of science is a battlefield of concurrent epistemologies, among which Lacan sided with Koyré's. As far as causality is related to dysfunction, a real of a different order than that of phenomenality is in question. As Lacan concludes,

> [i]n this gap, something happens. Once this gap has been filled, is the neurosis cured? After all, the question remains open. But the neurosis becomes something else, sometimes a mere illness, a *scar*, as Freud said—the scar, not of the neurosis, but of the unconscious. [...] Observe the point from which he sets out—*The Aetiology of the Neuroses*—and what does he find in the hole, in the split, in the gap so characteristic of cause? Something of the order of the *non-realized*.[14]

Here we reach the point at which the move from "Is psychoanalysis a science?" to "What is a science that includes psychoanalysis?" is inevitable. Departing from the etiology of neuroses, which establishes a link between sexuality and traumatism, something unprecedented in the history of medical science, psychoanalysis constitutes itself as a science of disruptions, discontinuities, and breakdowns of functioning, examining nothing other than the possible causes that inflict scars upon thinking. But this is also true for modern science in general. Modern science is no longer preoccupied with sustaining appearances but with realizing the "impossible." The scientific real is essentially nonphenomenological.[15] It manifests as the gap that discloses the world of appearances. The evocation of the scar of the unconscious should be understood in its double meaning: A traumatic event leaves a scar in the unconscious, but the very existence of the unconscious, the unconscious as such, is also a scar of thinking that undermines the central status of consciousness.

When, in his later teaching, Lacan speaks of the real as being without law, he refuses to be labeled an anarchist.[16] The idea of a real without law does not suggest that the real is not structured or that no structure is inscribed in the real (the thesis of Lacan's materialism is rather the opposite);[17] it simply means that the law should be altered in light of what science *and* psychoanalysis discover within the realm of appearances, something nonrealized or not fully constituted ontologically—an ontological incompleteness[18]—that seriously challenges the idea of a stable and unchangeable law and that, incidentally, served modernity by replacing the notion of cause. This does not necessarily mean that science should abandon the exploration of natural laws and assume the contradiction between law and cause, automaton and tyche. On the contrary, it has to think their intertwining, raising the question of a law-in-movement, an unstable and contingent law. This is how Lacan formulates the same problematic in 1974 at a press conference in Rome:

> I happened to come across a short article by Henri Poincaré regarding the evolution of laws. [. . .] Émile Boutroux, who was a philosopher, raised the question whether it was unthinkable that laws themselves evolve. Poincaré, who was a mathematician, got all up in arms at the idea of such evolution, since what a scientist is seeking is precisely a law insofar as it does not evolve. It is exceedingly rare for a philosopher to be more intelligent than a mathematician, but here a philosopher just so happened to raise an important question. [. . .] [I]t is not at all clear to me why the real would not allow for a law that changes.[19]

A dynamic law is much closer to the problematic of causality than a static law, and it is possible to conclude that, notwithstanding a rather oversimplified notion of contingency,[20] Hume's critique of causality indicated precisely this persistence of contingency within necessity. The entire problem comes down to the recognition of an irreducible *ontological* gap between reality and the real. Regularity is an appearance that allows the human habitus to discover an automatic repetition in natural laws. Kant admitted this and incorporated Hume's skepticism into his critical epistemology. But with this step Kant already went too far, overlooking the fact that causality is an exceptional phenomenon inscribed into the grey area between the phenomenal and the mathematical. This inscription becomes apparent only once it has been acknowledged that what is at stake in causality is dysfunction rather than function, structure-in-becoming rather than structural transcendence. At the other end of the scientific revolution, Freud's etiology renews the ontological dimension of causality in an encounter with a law-in-movement or a structure that precisely *is* becoming. Freud's break with his predecessors, who saw in hysteria either a pseudoillness or a result of inherited organic predispositions, stems from this problem—traumatism is a form of causality that disrupts the organic. Moreover, trauma is not a singular occurrence but a process that constitutes the tissue of the subject's history and that *occurs* only retroactively. In this retroactive causality, the past determines the present but is not immune to modifications through subsequent events. Freud's case history of the Wolf Man remains exemplary in this respect, because it clearly shows that a trauma is not always (or not above all) a singular event in early childhood but a spatiotemporal relation that unites both modes of repetition, automaton and tyche. Contingent events in the present, like the anxiety dream of wolves for Freud's patient,[21] can be a creative repetition of the trauma that retroactively associates a series of arbitrary past events and de facto generates the traumatic event.

The specific feature of psychoanalytic etiology is that it detects in the subject a privileged effect of dysfunction. Whenever Freud or Lacan speaks of causality he inevitably addresses the production of subjectivity rather than presupposing the conscious and centered subject that both Hume and Kant took for granted. Freud's etiology contains a materialist theory of the subject, an effort to explain the mechanisms that bring the subject into being. But this materialism is rather unusual because Freud's etiology rejects existing medical accounts that strive to trace the genesis of neurotic dysfunction back to the physiological and, hence, to the laws of heredity. In the following section I would like to return to Freud's early writings on hysteria in order to examine his break with the positivist model upon which Jean-Marie Charcot and the French school relied.

Freud against Heredity

Freud began with the etiology of neuroses, which notoriously placed sexuality at the core of neurotic illness. The advancement of this theory involved a long battle with the scientific community's systematic resistance. In a letter to Wilhelm Fliess from 1896, for instance, Freud describes the cold reception his lecture on the etiology of hysteria received at the Vienna Society for Psychiatry and Neurology. The session was presided over by Richard von Krafft-Ebing, the author of *Psychopathia Sexualis*, the famous catalogue of sexual aberrations, who reportedly commented, "It sounds like a scientific fairy tale."[22] However, this was not to be the only resistance Freud's theories would encounter. Subsequent developments were to encounter a more challenging *internal* resistance that manifested through the proliferation of biological metaphors, the primacy of phylogenesis over ontogenesis, collective cultural history over individual sexual development, and so on. Biology would become a model science for Freud, and this would later give rise to misunderstandings that, importantly, determined the development of post-Freudian psychoanalysis.[23] The early lessons concerning the epistemological scandal of hysteria were to be forgotten or declared outdated. However, it is precisely here that Freud linked causality with sexuality and traumatism, while also giving voice to an enigmatic malady that psychiatric positivism and medical science had systematically ignored.

Freud's etiology departed from the epistemological obstacle that the established medical discourse encountered in hysteria. For Charcot, under whom Freud studied in Paris in the late 1880s, hysteria was caused by hereditary predispositions, the sole invariable cause of neuroses, in relation to which other influences behave as agents provocateurs or contingent triggers that merely activate an inborn predisposition. But this etiological model did not in fact explain anything, since hysterical symptoms, despite their physiological manifestations, lacked evident organic causes. For this reason, hysteria was considered at once a simulacrum and a pseudoillness that expressed some mysterious "degeneration." Freud entered the scientific arena by adopting the simulation theory but quickly acknowledged that a symptom, such as paralysis, "can be more dissociated, more systematized, than cerebral paralysis. The symptoms of organic paralysis appear piecemeal, as it were, in hysteria."[24] The body is dismembered by the symptom, testifying to some sort of intrusion of a foreign body into the physiological body. The intruder is nevertheless indistinguishable from anatomy and appears to mimic all too consequentially the symptoms of physiological maladies. If, like Charcot, one assumes that hysteria consists in imitation, one nevertheless has to acknowledge that this mimesis is selective and excessive, that "it tends to produce its symptoms with the greatest possible intensity," thereby combining excess with precision, since a hysterical symptom is always characterized by "*precise limitation* and *excessive intensity.*"[25] Some sort of *amplifier* is at work that detaches the symptom from its organic context and intensifies its manifestation. Hysterical mimesis is both adequate and inadequate, in continuity and discontinuity with the organic. It isolates the organic symptom and increases its intensity, presenting the symptom in its autonomy as an alien body within the physiological body. This displacement through mimesis raises immediate doubts about the organic rootedness of the malady. It is remarkable to observe that Freud associates the unfaithful reproduction of organic symptoms with a *lack* of knowledge rather than with some presupposed real knowledge carved into the body through heredity. As Freud affirms, "the lesion in hysterical paralyses must be completely independent of the anatomy of the nervous system, since *in its paralyses and other manifestations hysteria behaves as though anatomy did not exist or as though it had no knowledge* [connaissance] *of it.*"[26] In the formation of its symptoms, hysteria ignores anatomy (as a physiological fact and as a branch of medical science). To Freud's later claim that "Anatomy is destiny,"[27] one might oppose the hysterical axiom "Anatomy is chance." However, hysteria is not simply ignorant. It possesses popular rather than scientific knowledge of anatomy, remaining at the superficial level of the appearances it imitates. On the causal level something else precedes anatomy, which is why the assumption of heredity contains an empty etiology that does not explain anything. The hereditary factor merely represses the epistemological deadlock that hysteria represents for normal medical science.

The mimetic factor had led Freud away from heredity toward representations and memories. The hysterical body is marked by fragmentation, where an organ is cut off from mental associations to assume an independent life in which it "behaves as though it did not exist for the play of associations."[28] This is where Freud introduces his etiological proposition, according to which the cause of dismemberment should be sought in a repressed and forgotten memory that nevertheless causes material consequences, a representation cut off from other associations that support a consistent image of the body:

> If the conception of the arm is involved in an association with a large affective value, it will be inaccessible to the free play of other associations. *The arm will be paralysed in proportion to the persistence of this affective value or its decrease through the appropriate psychic means.* This is the solution of the problem we have raised, for, in every case of hysterical paralysis, we find *that the paralysed organ or the lost function is involved in a subconscious association, which is endowed with high affective value, and we can show that the arm is freed as soon as this affective value is erased.* The conception of the arm exists in the material substratum but it is not accessible to conscious associations and impulses because its entire associative affinity, so to say, is saturated in a subconscious association with the memory of the event, the trauma, which produced this paralysis.[29]

We might note in passing that, at this early stage, Freud still uses Pierre Janet's expression "subconscious," which he will soon abandon in favor of the unconscious.[30] However, the context here already points in a direction that will lead Freud to the theory of symbolization, in which a body part obtains the "value of jouissance"[31] and is thus invested as the privileged support for

the production of enjoyment. A hysterical symptom codifies two antagonisms: the mental split, which concerns the fact that a memory trace, representation, or association is cut off from the rest of the chain but nevertheless
keeps its causal power, and the tension between, on the one hand, the anatomical body, explicitly reduced here to its imaginary surface, which forms
a consistent and enclosed totality, and, on the other, the dismembered and
associatively linked body of affects.

Freud thus rejects the hereditary model and introduces his etiology of
neuroses, which, in this early phase, he still believes arises from a real sexual seduction in early childhood. Only a few years later will he write the
famous lines in his letter to Fliess claiming that he no longer believes in his
neurotica, that is, he no longer finds it necessary to differentiate between the
causality of real events and the causality of fantasies.[32] The rational kernel
of his early theory of trauma consists in the link between jouissance (the
affective value of associations and memories, that is, symbolic representations), sexuality (seduction), and traumatism, but the full acknowledgement
of what Lacan will call the autonomy and causality of the signifier is yet to
come, precisely insofar as he had not yet given up the qualitative distinction
between real events and fantasies.

In order to mitigate the scandal of his proposition, Freud claimed, in
his early writings, that the association between sexuality and traumatism,
the kernel of his etiology of hysteria, contained nothing new. Charcot and
others had already acknowledged the presence of this association but subordinated it to heredity and ranked the awakening of sexuality in puberty
among the agents provocateurs. Freud merely abandoned the heredity and
accentuated the sexual factor. But even if this should be the case, his etiology nevertheless contains an additional turn of the screw. He proposes
that repetition through memorization, in fact, retroactively constitutes
the trauma. The case history of the Wolf Man, "From the History of an
Infantile Neurosis," will systematize this retroactive causality, but its germ
is already present in Freud's early writings; for instance, he writes, "*[t]he
memory will operate as though it were a contemporary event. What happens
is, as it were, a posthumous action by a sexual trauma.*"[33] Again, trauma is a
process, not an occurrence, and this process is structured by retroactivity.
This *dispositif* already implies an extension of sexuality beyond the frames
of the anatomical and the biological, insofar as Freud confirms Charcot's
claim that all events that come with puberty "are in fact only concurrent
causes—'*agents provocateurs.*'"[34] But then premature sexual activity confirms that there is some form of sexuality prior to biological and anatomical sexual maturation, and this sexuality later stands in irreducible conflict

to biological development. Freud de facto inverts Charcot: It is not the biological rhythm of sexual maturation that triggers the hereditary predisposition of the neuroses but a "precocious sexual excitation [. . .] [with] a special characteristic of the sexual event in earliest childhood."[35] Trauma becomes fully efficient once sexual maturation connects with the memory of a past event; in this connection, psychoanalysis discovers a fundamental discrepancy or nonrelation between the anatomical and the libidinal body, between reproductive sexuality and sexuality produced through the networks of signifiers. Later, after abandoning the distinction between real events and fantasies, as well as the distinction between real memories and screen memories, Freud will enforce the causal dimension of representations and the symbolic in general. His discussion of screen memories, for instance, will relativize the existence of an unchangeable and invariable memory, leading him to conclude that there is no such thing as a univocal mental archive of facts. Memory is a dynamic process subjected to constant change and reinscription. The full acknowledgment of retroactive causality necessitates the abandonment of the qualitative difference between actual memories and (re)constructions. In this way, fantasies, too, are transformed from imaginary fictions or illusions into symbolic formations that are, as such, endowed with causality.

Thus, Freud's etiology of neuroses assumes an interesting epistemological and ontological position. Already in his early theoretical work, Freud, citing the neurologist Adolph Strümpell, writes, "in hysteria the disturbance lies in the psycho-physical sphere—in the region where the somatic and the mental are linked together."[36] He will later stress this grey area repeatedly; for instance, he will claim that the concept of the drive addresses the grey area between the physiological and the psychological. His early etiological accounts address this problematic in terms of a force that does not hide its physicalist background. An event that causes hysteria or obsession needs to possess a "traumatic force."[37] Recall that the concept of force can be isolated only once physical science no longer aims to explain the phenomena but something in the phenomena that does not appear and is, strictly speaking, unimaginable for the human observer. The materiality of force rejects the traditional representation of matter in combination with positive qualities, such as composition, consistency, impenetrability, and so on. The notion of traumatic force, the notion of trauma, and the reinvention of causality that is associated with it repeat this same move in relation to the physiological body. There is a curious dilemma in Freud's writing regarding the importation of force into a science that no longer deals exclusively with physical or biological objects:

> I refer to the concept that in mental functions something is to be dis-
> tinguished—a quota of affect or sum of excitation—which possesses
> all the characteristics of a quantity (though we have no means of mea-
> suring it), which is capable of increase, diminution, displacement and
> discharge, and which is spread over the memory-traces of representa-
> tions as an electric charge is spread over the surface of a body.[38]

The metaphor of electricity is an unusual forerunner to pleasure and libido,
which lead to the Freudian revolution. Does psychoanalysis really have no
technical means to measure and, thereby, quantify affects, psychical energy,
or traumatic force? Lacan's return to Freud displaced this dilemma. The
question is not one of quantification and measurement but of formalization—or, more generally, logification. Lacan will find in the linguistic, the
mathematical-logical, and the topological apparatus the appropriate tools to
enable the minimal formalization of the entities for which Freud could only
presuppose the susceptibility of their treatment to formal tools. Freud's metaphor of an electric charge is nevertheless a step in the right direction. The
entities in question are not positive substances, but their ontological and epistemological status is equivalent to notions such as force, energy, and wave.
Electricity also serves to describe the topology of unconscious processes and
the production that takes place in the peculiar interstice of the libidinal and
the physiological, in this ambiguous zone in which Freud placed the objects
of psychoanalysis (the unconscious, the drive, libido, and so on). The excitation or psychical energy, later theorized as libido, moves along the surface
of the body and not in some anatomical or biological depth. With the abandonment of the hereditary factor the irreducible gap and radical inexistence
of any homeostatic or stable relation between the sexual and the anatomical
is pushed into the foreground. Libido is essentially nonrelational; it can colo-
nize the entire body and transform the anatomical body into a *Fremdkörper*.
Far from being the hard rock of mental life that would finally solidify the fluidity of infantile sexuality, the anatomical and the biological are subjected to
radical transformation precisely by sexuality. This is due to the fact that sexual development in human beings occurs in two steps, wherein the acquired
(sexuality produced by way of the apparatus of the signifier) precedes the
innate and the hereditary (reproductive genital sexuality).[39]

What matters with regard to the excitation in Freud's metaphor is that
the accent upon quantity avoids the dangers of a substantialist position.
Lacan points this out in a crucial passage that cannot be understood entirely
without Koyré in the background: "Because energy is not a substance,
which, for example, improves or goes sour with age; it's a numerical constant

that a physicist has to find in his calculations, so as to be able to work. [. . .] Without this constant, which is merely a combination of calculations . . . you have no more physics."[40] This, of course, does not mean that energy is a scientific fiction. If anything can be denounced as fictional it is the notion of substance. Scientific discourse isolates entities in the phenomenal world by means of mathematical and technical apparatuses that violate the regime of human cognition, phenomenality, and consciousness, but these apparatuses nevertheless enable the functioning of scientific discourse as epistemological deadlocks that either push science into crisis (where it falls into the discourse of the hysteric) or enable its normal functioning (turning it into the discourse of the university). The excitation Freud talks about possesses all of the characteristics of the desubstantialized and quantified materiality of scientific objects (increase, decrease, displacement, and discharge). Additionally, the unconscious processes that Freud was to discover (resistance, repression, condensation, displacement, and so on) can be translated by means of linguistic, logical, and topological relations. In order to express this excitation in formal terms, however, one does not need to wait for theory, which would find a scientific translation—clinical cases already demonstrate that there is a discursive logic underlying the mobility of affects in the bodily and mental apparatus. For instance, Freud identifies in hysteria the following scenario: "[T]he incompatible idea is rendered innocuous by its *sum of excitation* being *transformed into something somatic*. For this I should like to propose the name of *conversion*."[41] What is conversion other than a metaphor, a linguistic operation that can be thoroughly formalized? Obsessional neurosis follows another model:

> If someone with a disposition [to neurosis] lacks the aptitude for conversion, but if, nevertheless, in order to fend off an incompatible idea, he sets about separating it from its affect, then *that affect is obliged to remain in the psychical sphere*. The idea, now weakened, is still left in consciousness, separated from all association. *But its affect, which has become free, attaches itself to other ideas which are not in themselves incompatible; and, thanks to this 'false connection,' those ideas turn into obsessional ideas.*[42]

This is precisely the structure of metonymy, with its accent on "false connection" or horizontal displacement—unlike in hysteria, where the displacement is vertical, from representations to the body, the incorporation and enactment of repressed memories. The main effort of Lacan's return to Freud was to draw attention to the fact that discourse not only captures but also produces these quotas of excitation or affects. The conclusion at hand is that what the apparatus of language produces in the living body (jouissance) is no less real than what the scientific apparatus (mathematics, technology, and so on) isolates in reality.

Psychoanalytic etiology discovers a contradiction between the biological and the libidinal. When it comes to the theory of sexuality one could para-phrase Freud by saying that sexuality knows nothing of anatomy or biology; instead, it is constituted upon a fundamental non-knowledge, trauma, and repression. If sexuality is both an object of repression and structured upon a fundamental lack of knowledge, it is because a radical inexistence persists at its core. Lacan addresses this inexistence in his famous aphorism "There is no sexual relation"[43] and elaborates a logic of sexuation that formalizes the inexistence in question and links it to the moment of "freedom" that stands in opposition to a presumed biological and anatomical "destiny." However, the assumption of sexual position does not always run smoothly because the signifier has always already colonized the anatomical. How is it possible to translate the anatomical into the sexual and sexual difference into sexuality? As Jacques-Alain Miller writes, "[t]here is not determination according to law. You do not have a law saying that because you have a biological sex 'such,' you are necessarily going to have a psychic sex 'so.'"[44] In Freud's early writings there is the sense that he attempts or implicitly tends to provide an integral translation of anatomical sexual difference into neurotic difference, as in, for example, the coupling of hysteria with women and obsessional neurosis with men. This attempt is doomed to fail, and Freud had already acknowledged the "fluidity" and equivocality of sexuality in his etiology of neuroses. There is always a remainder in the translation of the anatomical into the libidinal, and this remainder—the object *a*—is what Lacan associ-ated with the causality of the signifier.

To recapitulate, then, when biological sexuality enters the picture it inev-itably meets a "preexisting" libidinal sexuality that is entirely conditioned by the signifier. Lacan's axiom "There is no sexual relation" can be understood to mean not only that there is no relation at the level of libidinal sexuality but also that there is no relation between libidinal and biological sexuality. For this reason, Lacan translated the Freudian term *Trieb* as *dérive*, devia-tion, drift, or declination,[45] not because it deviates from some positive and preexisting natural law or regularity but because it deviates from an inexis-tent norm. Nonrelation precedes potential relations, and deviation precedes regularity, which could be attributed to the notion of instinct and from which speaking beings are simply not excepted. However, the drive, as that which interrupts biological rhythm, and its object (*a*) are already there as real consequences of the inscription of the signifier in the living body. The libidinal body precedes biological sexual maturity and is sexually "mature," that is, it is capable of reaching satisfaction before the "awakening" of biological sexuality. The drive inevitably encounters a biological tendency, but its equivocality has already been predetermined, even before biological sexuality can become manifest. Accordingly, Lacan speaks of an *other satisfaction*, thereby aiming at the satisfaction of the drive. He describes this other satisfaction as that which is satisfied through "babbling," adding that "[a]ll the needs of speaking beings are contaminated by the fact of being involved in an other satisfaction [. . .] that those needs may not live up to."[46] The means of satisfaction for this other satisfaction is the signifier, which is, for the speaking being, the privileged apparatus of jouissance, insofar as language is the privileged site of its production. Language is not, as Heidegger would have it, a "house of Being"[47] but a factory of enjoyment.

Thus, psychoanalysis also entails a decentering of language. From the earliest stages, Freud's discoveries imply a materialist theory of language that stands in sharp contrast to a pragmatic tradition in philosophy and linguistics that could be summarized with reference to the Aristotelian understanding of language as an *organon* (tool, organ). Poststructuralist linguistics returned to this tradition insofar as it considered language a means of communication acquired through evolution, not a site of the production of a real that puts the ideals of epistemological positivism into question. This scientific revision of linguistic Aristotelianism also rejects the dependency of the unconscious upon language, and, hence, the central structuralist discovery, upon which rests a materialist theory of language, the autonomy of the signifier. Lacan's well-known dictum "The unconscious is structured like a language"[48] brings together the Freudian decentering of thinking and the Saussurean decentering of language, which both pursue the abandonment of Aristotelianism in linguistics and psychology. This dictum also affirms that the privileged tool for the "measurement" of affects, their logical translation back into the signifiers that cause them, most certainly exists, and it is provided by the possibility of a Galilean science of language.

Notes

1. See Alexandre Koyré, *Études galiléennes* (Paris: Hermann, 1966), 206–7. This impossible is nevertheless realized in the physical world through science. See also Koyré, *Études d'histoire de la pensée scientifique* (Paris: Gallimard, 1973), 58–59.

2. In short, the main difference between Aristotelian and Galilean science is that, whereas the former mathematizes the real as it appears to consciousness, the latter mathematizes the real as it appears to scientific discourse in its absolute autonomy. Premodern science is first and foremost a science of appearance, while modern science is a "science of the real" (to use Koyré's expression later adopted by Lacan to describe mathematical logic).

3. See Immanuel Kant, *Prolegomena to Any Future Metaphysics That Will Be Able to Come Forward as Science*, ed. and trans. Gary Hatfield (Cambridge: Cambridge University Press, 2004), 10.

4. See Koyré, *From the Closed World to the Infinite Universe* (Baltimore: Johns Hopkins University Press, 1957).

5. See Sigmund Freud and Josef Breuer, *Studies on Hysteria*, in *The Standard Edition of the Complete Psychological Works of Sigmund Freud* (hereafter *SE*), ed. and trans. James Strachey et al. (London: Hogarth Press, 1953–1974), 2:30.

6. Jacques Lacan, "The Freudian Thing, or the Meaning of the Return to Freud in Psychoanalysis," in *Écrits: The First Complete Edition in English*, trans. Bruce Fink (New York: W. W. Norton, 2006), 344; and *The Seminar of Jacques Lacan, Book VII: The Ethics of Psychoanalysis, 1959–1960*, ed. Jacques-Alain Miller, trans. Dennis Porter (New York: W. W. Norton, 1992), 206.

7. Lacan, "Science and Truth," in *Écrits: The First Complete Edition in English*, 743; translation modified. Fink's translation renders *comme separé de sa significa-tion* as "as if it were separate from its signification," but this misses Lacan's critical point. Lacan's critical point—and, indeed, the epistemological scandal of psycho-analysis—concerns the *actual separation* of the signifier from its signification, the *absolute autonomy* of the signifier, which means that it is independent of human observation. Again, this same autonomy grounds scientific modernity, which explains why, in this passage, Lacan associates psychoanalysis with science, though he displaces its notion of the formal with the material cause.

8. Ibid., 739–45.

9. See Freud, *Totem and Taboo*, in *SE* 13:75–99.

10. Lacan, "The Four Fundamental Concepts of Psychoanalysis: Report on the 1964 Seminar," *Hurly-Burly* 5 (2011): 18. This text appears in French upon the back cover of *Le Séminaire de Jacques Lacan, Livre XI: Les quatre concepts fondamen-taux de la psychanalyse, 1964*, ed. Jacques-Alain Miller (Paris: Éditions du Seuil, 1973), and it also appears, with minor editorial modifications, in *Autres écrits*, ed. Jacques-Alain Miller (Paris: Éditions du Seuil, 2001), 187–89.

11. Lacan, *The Seminar of Jacques Lacan, Book XI: The Four Fundamental Con-cepts of Psychoanalysis*, ed. Jacques-Alain Miller, trans. Alan Sheridan (New York: W. W. Norton, 1998), 22.

12. Recall that, in Seminar XX, Lacan insists that Heraclitus was right and Parmenides was wrong: A philosophy that combines movement with logos, a philosophy of becoming, is superior to a philosophy that departs from the opposition between eternal being and chance movement. See Lacan, *The Seminar of Jacques Lacan, Book XX: Encore, On Feminine Sexuality, the Limits of Love and Knowledge, 1972–1973*, ed. Jacques-Alain Miller, trans. Bruce Fink (New York: W. W. Norton, 1999), 114.

13. See Thomas S. Kuhn, *The Structure of Scientific Revolutions*, 4th ed. (Chicago: University of Chicago Press, 2012). Koyré's position significantly influenced Kuhn's reading of the history of science in terms of paradigm shifts.

14. Lacan, *The Seminar of Jacques Lacan, Book XI: The Four Fundamental Concepts of Psychoanalysis*, 22.

15. This is also Lacan's thesis and the kernel of his radicalized Koyréianism: "Hertzian waves or other waves—no phenomenology of perception has ever given us the slightest idea of them and it would certainly never have led us to them. We certainly won't be calling this place the noosphere, which we ourselves supposedly populate. [. . .] But in using *aletheia* in a way which, I agree, has nothing emotionally philosophical about it you could, unless you find something better, call it the alethosphere." Lacan, *The Seminar of Jacques Lacan, Book XVII: The Other Side of Psychoanalysis*, ed. Jacques-Alain Miller, trans. Russell Grigg (New York: W. W. Norton, 2007), 161. Again, truth is brought into play in strong continuity with the already quoted theses of "Science and Truth."

16. See Lacan, *Le Séminaire de Jacques Lacan, Livre XXIII: Le sinthome, 1975–1976*, ed. Jacques-Alain Miller (Paris: Éditions du Seuil, 2005), 137–38.

17. "Structure is to be taken in a sense, in which it is most real, in which it is the real itself. [. . .] In general this is determined by the convergence toward an impossibility. It is through this that the structure is real." Lacan, *Le Séminaire de Jacques Lacan, Livre XVI: D'un Autre à l'autre, 1968–1969*, ed. Jacques-Alain Miller (Paris: Éditions du Seuil, 2006), 30; my translation. This is another expression of Lacan's radicalized Koyréianism, inasmuch as we know that, for Koyré, modern science explains the (physical) real with the impossible (the ideal geometrical and mathematical forms, which are, as such, not found in nature).

18. See, for example, Slavoj Žižek, *The Ticklish Subject: The Absent Centre of Political Ontology* (New York: Verso, 1999), 60.

19. Lacan, "The Triumph of Religion," in *The Triumph of Religion*, trans. Bruce Fink (Malden: Polity, 2013), 81.

20. Catherine Malabou refers to this notion of contingency as "occurrence-based," to which she opposes the idea of a "gradual," epigenetic contingency. See *Before Tomorrow: Epigenesis and Rationality*, trans. Carolyn Shread (Malden: Polity, 2016), 149.

21. See Freud, "From the History of an Infantile Neurosis," in *SE* 17:29–47.

22. Freud to Wilhelm Fliess, April 26, 1896, in *The Complete Letters of Sigmund Freud to Wilhelm Fliess, 1887–1904*, ed. and trans. Jeffrey Moussaieff Masson (Cambridge: Harvard University Press, 1985), 184.

23. There is, of course, also reason to doubt the standard tale according to which Freud's biologism meant a regression in his theoretical development. Jean Laplanche has most forcefully and consequentially promoted this negative reading of Freud's biological metaphors. Yet, one also notices that Freud's recurrent reference to biological metaphors and models contains an interesting speculative kernel worth exploring.

24. Freud, "Some Points for a Comparative Study of Organic and Hysterical Motor Paralyses," in *SE* 1:163.

25. Ibid. 164.

26. Ibid. 169.

27. Freud, "On the Universal Tendency to Debasement in the Sphere of Love," in *SE* 11:189.

28. Freud, "Some Points for a Comparative Study of Organic and Hysterical Motor Paralyses," in *SE* 1:170.

29. Ibid., 171; translation modified; emphasis in original.

30. The notion of the subconscious preserves the centralized model of the mental apparatus, since it presupposes the division between surface and depth, which can be modeled with reference to the geometry of the sphere. The notion of the unconscious, by contrast, eliminates this division and progressively shifts the focus onto the surface (the surface of the body in the case referred to above), where repressed memories are inscribed and, so to speak, enacted. What matters for Freud is that, within the body, a conflict and a split takes place that brings two independent chains together. Causality emerges from the intersection of these two chains upon the bodily terrain.

31. Lacan, *La logique du fantasme* (1966–1967), unpublished seminar, lesson of April 12, 1967, http://gaogoa.free.fr/> so that the line reads 12, 1967, http://gaogoa.free.fr/.

32. "I no longer believe in my *neurotica* [theory of the neuroses]" (*Ich glaube an meine Neurotica nicht mehr*). Freud, "Extracts from the Fliess Papers," in *SE* 1:259.

33. Freud, "Heredity and the Aetiology of the Neuroses," in *SE* 3:154.

34. Ibid., 155.

35. Ibid., 156.

36. Freud, "The Neuro-Psychoses of Defence," in *SE* 3:51n2.

37. Freud, "The Aetiology of Hysteria," in *SE* 3:194.

38. Freud, "The Neuro-Psychoses of Defence," in *SE* 3:60; translation modified.

39. As Laplanche puts it concisely, "*acquired* drive sexuality *precedes* innate instinctual sexuality within [man], such that when it surges forth, adaptive instinctual sexuality finds its place 'occupied,' as it were, by the infantile drives, already and always present within the unconscious." Jean Laplanche, "Sexuality and Attachment in Metapsychology," in *Freud and the* Sexual: *Essays 2000–2006*, ed. John Fletcher, trans. John Fletcher, Jonathan House, and Nicholas Ray (New York: International Psychoanalytic Books, 2011), 44; emphasis in original.

40. Lacan, *Television*, in *Television: A Challenge to the Psychoanalytic Establishment*, ed. Joan Copjec, trans. Denis Hollier, Rosalind Krauss, and Annette Michelson (New York: W. W. Norton, 1990), 18.

41. Freud, "The Neuro-Psychoses of Defence," in *SE* 3:49.

42. Ibid., 51–52.

43. See, for example, Lacan, *The Seminar of Jacques Lacan, Book XVII: The Other Side of Psychoanalysis*, 116; and *The Seminar of Jacques Lacan, Book XX: Encore, On Feminine Sexuality, the Limits of Love and Knowledge, 1972–1973*, 12, 34.

44. Jacques-Alain Miller, "To Interpret the Cause: From Freud to Lacan," *Newsletter of the Freudian Field* 3, no. 1/2 (1989): 45–46.

45. See, for instance, Lacan, "The Subversion of the Subject and the Dialectic of Desire in the Freudian Unconscious," in *Écrits: The First Complete Edition in English*, 680; *The Seminar of Jacques Lacan, Book VII: The Ethics of Psychoanalysis, 1959–1960*, 90; and *Television*, in *Television: A Challenge to the Psychoanalytic Establishment*, 24.

46. Lacan, *The Seminar of Jacques Lacan, Book XX: Encore, On Feminine Sexuality, the Limits of Love and Knowledge, 1972–1973*, 51.

47. Martin Heidegger, "Letter on Humanism," in *Basic Writings: From "Being and Time" (1927) to "The Task of Thinking" (1964)*, ed. David Farrell-Krell, rev. ed. (New York: Harper and Row, 1977), 217.

48. See, for example, Lacan, "The Function and Field of Speech and Language in Psychoanalysis," in *Écrits: The First Complete Edition in English*, 223; "Science and Truth," 737; and *The Seminar of Jacques Lacan, Book XI: The Four Fundamental Concepts of Psychoanalysis*, 149, 203.

CHAPTER 2

Lacan with Evo-Devo?

Lorenzo Chiesa

Throughout his work, especially in the seminars of the early 1970s, Jacques Lacan attempts to dismantle the fusional bias of biology's take on sex and the underlying presupposition that man "serves an end," that "[h]e is founded on the basis of his final cause [. . .], which [. . .] is to live or, more precisely, to survive, in other words, to postpone death and dominate his rival."[1] On the one hand, I believe that this staunch attack upon the theo-teleology of mainstream Darwinism remains extremely topical. I would even go so far as to suggest that it is precisely through the *bios* of biology that, as Lacan has it, "today, only the *theo* is left, always there, really solid in its idiocy, and logic has [. . .] evaporated."[2] On the other hand, I am equally of the opinion that, for a question of dates, Lacan missed not only the full extent of the ongoing revolution in the life sciences, as Jean-Claude Milner has already noted,[3] but also their *potential* for theoretical self-critique.

For instance, the psychoanalytic questioning of the imaginary and anthropomorphic basis of our reduction of the real duality of sex to the supposed bipolar complementarity between male and female—a preconception that is particularly strong in the way in which we consider animal copulation[4]—resurfaces in current, cutting-edge debates in fields such as psychobiology and behavioral neuroscience. As Mark S. Blumberg puts it in a chapter title in *Freaks of Nature*, a recent book devoted to the coimplication of development and evolution, "Anything Goes: When It Comes to Sex, Expect Ambiguity."[5] Here, he describes, among others, organisms that lack sex chromosomes, although their sexes (male or female) are as identifiable as they are in most mammalian species (like crocodiles);[6] possess an erectile penis-like clitoris, a scrotum, and no vagina (as in the case of the female spotted hyena);[7] switch sex depending upon circumstances (the tobacco fish); or are technically asexual—that is, clones—and the female mates with males of closely related species, transfer of sperm takes place, but there is no genetic exchange (the Amazon molly).

Without entering into a detailed discussion of these fascinating examples, or intending to use them as an objectively "factual" scientific proof of what psychoanalysis would have merely intuited, we can nonetheless make a number of statements. First, they reinforce Sigmund Freud's broad and, in his time, revolutionary idea that (human) sexuality is not predetermined, that it is not bounded to an unequivocal standard of what is masculine and what is feminine (behaviorally for Freud, and behaviorally, morphologically, and genetically for contemporary psychobiology).[8] As the author of *Freaks of Nature* has it, in a presumably deliberate wink at psychoanalysis, "sex [is] a 'syndrome,' a collection of 'symptoms'" that, however, "as a collective, allow for a 'diagnosis' of *male* or *female*."[9] Note here his clear and crucial reference to how sex yet amounts, for us, to *two* natural sexes.

Second, these scientific discoveries support Lacan's contention that the il-logical real of sexual difference, understood also as natural, goes hand in hand, for us, with the impossibility of establishing sex straightforwardly upon the simple basis of observable physical disparities in genitalia—which are instead phallically constructed as sex organs only in a retroactive way. Seeing a female hyena, rather than a lion, at Vienna's zoo, or a horse in the street would no doubt have made Hans even more perplexed as to his sex and that of his mother.[10] Similarly, it is because of the initial indifference of what Lacan calls, in Seminar XIX, the anatomical "little difference"[11] (even smaller in some other species) with respect to symbolic, sexual difference that, as adults, we can continue to confuse the hyena's clitoris with a gigantic penis.[12]

Third, in line with the late Lacan's resistance to singling out man's openness, in contrast to the closed environment of the animal, such empirical investigations also put into doubt the exceptionality of the convolutedness of human sexuality as irreducible to instincts, in favor of a more comprehensive approach to human *and* nonhuman sex as a "meandering, unfolding path."[13] Genes (when they are present) do indeed have an influence upon such a path, but this does not in the least allow us to invoke the existence of "closed genetic program[s]" in either humans or nonhumans, whereby the biology of sex would ultimately come down to the identity of sex chromosomes.[14]

In this context, however, it is also the case that some *technical* aspects of Lacan's denunciation of the life sciences and, in particular, genetics appear to be obsolete. We should not overlook this in the name of psychoanalytic dogmatism. For example, his remark in Seminar XIX that "things are far from being such that we have, on the one hand, the network [*filière*] of the gonad, what Weismann [and Freud after him] called the *germen*, and, on the other hand, the *soma*, the branch of the body,"[15] as well as other observations similar to this, have by now lost most of their polemical undertones and sound rather conservative from the standpoint of contemporary evolutionary developmental theory (with which Blumberg, and his discussion of sex, shares a general orientation). Lacan stresses, contra Weismann, the interdependency of the genotype (the germen) and the phenotype (the soma), yet without renouncing the primacy of the former over the latter: "The genotype of the body conveys something that determines sex, but this is not sufficient," insofar as, "from its production of the body, [...] [the genotype] detaches hormones that can interfere with this determination."[16] But, for their part, leading contemporary biologists, such as Eva Jablonka and Mary Jane West-Eberhard—arguably, the leading authorities in the field—not only acknowledge that the view according to which differences in (sexual) phenotype are the result of both genes and the developmental environment[17] is nowadays shared by most researchers in the life sciences, but also go as far as suggesting, against mainstream biology, that genes are *followers* in evolution.[18] As Jablonka writes, "developmental responses to the environment are *primary*, and can be fine-tuned, stabilized, or ameliorated by *subsequent* genetic changes in populations."[19]

These new and particularly inspiring directions in the life sciences do indeed, for what we have just said, have the potential to shake the very foundations of the Mendelian appropriation of Darwin, if not Darwinism tout court. They should, however, be approached with caution from a psychoanalytically informed, philosophical perspective intending to demystify the theo-teleological kernel still prevalent in evolutionary theory. The datedness of some of Lacan's tirades is not an excuse not to test so-called evo-devo, evolutionary developmental biology, through his own—even now—persuasive anti-bio-logical discourse. While the deconstructive impetus of evolutionary developmental biology stands out as undoubtedly strong, the "new synthesis" it advocates remains at best vague, if not confusing. Theoretically, evo-devo leads, in fact, to quasi-paradoxical conclusions, such as the following: "Selection is still seen as crucial, but the nature, origins, construction, and inheritance of developmental variations are deemed to be just as important."[20] To put it bluntly, what, then, is "selection" in this framework and, above all, what is "evolution" for evo-devo? What is it that is being selected once genes are no longer *leaders* in evolution? Does this refer to the increasingly fitter, that is, increasingly plastic, phenotypic responses to the environment? If so, independently of overthrowing genetic determinism, there is clearly a risk here of propounding a notion of environment, and plastic phenotypic responses to it, that continues to partake of the old Darwinian finalism of adaptation aimed at an incrementalist evolution of Life, and, ultimately, at justifying the fact that "consciousness has to appear, the world, history converge on this marvel, contemporary man, you and me, us men in the street."[21]

At this stage, one should invoke the dialectical Darwinism of Stephen Jay Gould, who lists the alleged increase in "flexibility of behavioral repertoire" and, hence, phenotypic plasticity as one among other possible criteria concocted to defend—more or less explicitly—the tale of "progress," that is, "the fallacy that evolution embodies a fundamental trend or thrust leading to a primary and defining result."[22] Against this stance, he famously proposes that "life has always been, and will probably always remain until the sun explodes, in the Age of Bacteria."[23] More philosophically, he puts forward a "claim about the nature of reality," according to which "*variation* itself [is] irreducible, [. . .] '*real*' in the sense of 'what the world is made of'"[24]—whereby we seem to be left to infer that selection is just the way in which variation, as a first principle of life, varies. He then proceeds to understand the unpredictable, contingent, and unrepeatable (all adjectives he uses) "excellence" of *Homo sapiens* in terms of sheer "*trends* properly viewed as results of expanding or contracting variation, rather than concrete entities moving in a definite direction,"[25] and, more specifically, the fact that, while not showing any general thrust toward improvement, "life [. . .] just adds an occasional exemplar of complexity in the only region of available anatomical space."[26]

Leaving aside Gould—but not without noting that the idea that life as a presupposed agency (albeit occasionally and contingently) adds some complexity remains problematic for its lingering vitalism and anthropocentrism[27]—we can suggest that, in all likelihood, Lacan would not have supported the view that "genes are followers in evolution." This is for the simple reason that he problematizes the very notion of evolution in the first place (to which Gould instead clings—we would have to ask him bluntly: How can there be evolution without progress?).[28] Basically, Lacan sees evolutionary theory as unsubstantiated by the very facts it claims to observe objectively and derive its knowledge from, while nonetheless it resists its self-demise by fashioning a tautological discourse. As he states in Seminar XIX, "it is in the most improper fashion that we put there [in matter] a meaning, an idea of evolution, of perfectioning, while in the animal chain that is presupposed we see absolutely nothing that bears witness to this so-called continual adaptation."[29] This is so misleading that "it was necessary all the same to renounce it and to say that after all those who get through are those who have been able to get through. We call this natural selection. It strictly means nothing."[30]

In other words, natural selection does not mean anything, since eventually evolutionary theory rests upon the tautology according to which those who survive are those who have survived. Developing Lacan's cursory remark, and taking on board more recent speculation in the life sciences, which he seems to anticipate, we could suggest that evolutionary theory leads to the redundant idea that those who have survived would prove, through the very fact of having survived, that they are those who evolve or adapt. Instead, stressing the role of contingency in "evolution," some respected evolutionary biologists, examining fossils, have had to conclude that surviving organisms do not seem better adapted than their now-extinct contemporaneous neighbors.[31]

This specific attack against the tautological character of evolutionary theory (whether based upon an explicit teleology or a professedly nonfinalistic "thrust" of life, whether genetically or environmentally deterministic) should be read together with Lacan's more comprehensive onto-logical debunking of what he deems to be the Aristotelian "animism" of biology, which we should tentatively define as the imaginary presupposition of a correspondence between thought and what is being thought. Molecular biology is not exempt from such a presupposition, given that it operates upon the supposed correspondence between the linguistic notion of information and "the level of the gene's molecular information and of the winding of nucleoproteins around strands of DNA, that are themselves wrapped around each other, all of that being tied together by hormonal links—that is, messages that are sent, recorded, etc."[32] Nobel Prize-winning life scientists unhesitatingly support this supposition: Evolution "entails the generation of information," and man's development of language as a species-specific faculty involves a "plane of information transfer, similar to the primary plane of genetic information."[33]

However, we should also stress that, for Lacan, animism does not apply exclusively to bio-logy but must be referred to what he considers the unfinished character of Galilean science in toto. Modern science is only in principle nonanimistic. According to Lacan, modern science proceeds in a contradictory manner. Thanks to the use of numbers and letters, it has undone—and this is its great achievement—the ancient association between nature and sensible substance, that is, between nature, qua what is being thought, and the perceived unity of the human body and its senses, qua a presupposition for thinking. Yet, modern science nevertheless equally promotes a new kind of animism, that is, a form of naturalist reductionism for which the presumed totalizability of man's body, including his brain, could eventually be mathematized—for example, by means of a synergy of statistics, genetics, and cognitive science—as a numerical segment of the whole of nature.[34] The alleged correspondence between thought and what is being thought is thus not eliminated but only displaced.

Upon the basis of these considerations, we need to conclude that, even if biology were finally to become a full-blown algebraic Galilean science, it would still be amenable to the same kind of criticism Lacan shifts to Galilean science.[35] Jacques-Alain Miller thus moves too quickly when he argues that, even though "Freudian biology is not biology," for it is primarily an energetics, from the moment that biology no longer has life as its object[36] but what François Jacob calls "the algorithms of the living world," Lacan could unreservedly support it.[37] I would be inclined to reverse this claim: There can be a psychoanalytical biology that is not a bio-logy as soon as Freudian energetics is challenged, and this can be achieved only if one does not take it for granted that "the algorithms of the living world" are necessarily done once and for all with animism.

Moreover, contemporary biology, albeit at a much simpler level than that of Galilean sciences such as physics, could be said to remain firmly imaginary, since, fundamentally, it still treats the letters of its algebra in an analogical way. Everything proceeds from the idea that genes are discrete and divisible particles. For instance, in population genetics, basic mathematical models have, until recently, considered only one gene locus at a time. Can we say, despite the advanced statistics of, say, the gene-finding algorithms elaborated by bio-informatics, that, following Lacan's definition of formalization, in genetics, "whatever the number of ones you place under each [. . .] letter"—for example, in the formula of inertia ($mv^2/2$)—"you are subject to a certain number of laws"?[38] To put it bluntly, does this also apply to the G, T, A, C of guanine, thymine, adenine, and cytosine that compose the nucleobases of DNA and their forming pairs? Or, is our scientific approach to genetic material still intimately tied to "the idea of evolution," ending up "at the top of the animal scale, with this consciousness that characterizes us," an idea that thus simply proposes "a new figure of progress" in the guise of programming?[39] If so, is this new theo-teleological mutant not already heavily influencing all science?

Our stance toward recent developments in the life sciences should, in my opinion, consequently be twofold. On the one hand, we need to listen attentively to Milner's exhortation to Lacanian discourse to take seriously the current consolidation of a "Galileanism of the living."[40] This is decisive to the extent that the latter manages to threaten doxastic Darwinism and its long shadow. The work of Adrian Johnston has already demonstrated how fruitful such an opening can be theoretically in terms of a psychoanalytic-philosophical rethinking of the broad notions of realism and materialism, which, more than half a century ago—availing himself of the findings of zoology, ethology, embryology, and *Gestalt* theory—Lacan rescued from the swamps of phenomenology.[41] Rather than hastily giving up all that is Darwin-related—if not the biological tout court—as Lacan sometimes does,[42] taking seriously the "Galileanism of the living" must here go together with the awareness that establishing whether evolutionary theory can be reformulated in a novel manner, in line with the principles of Galilean formalization, is in no way an easy task. An "evolution" without progress, like the one Gould implicitly proposes, stands as a thought-provoking oxymoron, but Lacan-informed philosophy should push it further theoretically.

On the other hand, and this is even more important, we should not lose sight of the complex positioning of psychoanalysis vis-à-vis Galilean science. Lacan condemns the fact that modern science's relentless expansion—or, better, intensification of the real—goes together with an increasing attempt at totalizing knowledge that forecloses this very intensification. More specifically, in confronting contemporary biological perspectives, such as evolutionary developmental theory, it is important to stress that its proponents are, at present, in search of what they themselves label a new synthesis—one that would be able to replace the hegemonic link between Darwinism and Mendelianism with a Darwinian, epigenetical genetics that recovers the credible elements of the Lamarckian legacy.[43] Although this move could strike a definitive blow to the most untenable (nineteenth and early twentieth-century) theo-teleological aspects of evolutionism[44] (that is, in brief, following Lacan, the aprioristic presupposition that life, as an inexhaustible, continuous, and incrementalist force, binds One and One into two-as-One), as has been noted in debates internal to the same scientific circles, such a change of biological paradigm would hardly diminish overall the intolerance of ambiguity.

Sex, for instance, could well be regarded as an agglomeration of "symptoms" more and more recalcitrant to being understood as the bi-univocal fusion of complementary (organic, cellular, or molecular) partners, and this in line with the advancements of physics, which has long ceased to consider matter as reducible to binding particles that are easily identifiable. Yet, such an ever-more apparent, and empirically testable, real "decomposition" of the world, as Lacan calls it,[45] would still most probably aim at the delineation of a unitary worldview (*conception du monde*), which is what psychoanalysis refuses to begin with as fundamentally onto-theo-logical.[46] This future

Weltanschauung could eventually even rest upon the algebraic formula of an acausal, chaotic universe and an evolutionary algorithm accounting for sexual reproduction—if not life tout court—compatible with it, without, for this reason, diminishing in the least science's attempted totalization of knowledge.[47] In this sense, the retarded animism of traditional biology, together with the life and cognitive sciences's current effort to overcome its embarrassing delay, could, by contrast, unexpectedly teach us a lot about the unsurpassable character of the whole of modern science's contradictory stance upon the real. Lacan's claim that the theory of natural selection, strictly speaking, "means nothing" also indicates that, as such, it amounts, at present, to a point of emergence of the real qua symbolic impasse, the structural impasse of formalization that runs parallel to modern science.

Notes

1. Jacques Lacan, *The Seminar of Jacques Lacan, Book XX: Encore, On Feminine Sexuality, the Limits of Love and Knowledge, 1972–1973*, ed. Jacques-Alain Miller, trans. Bruce Fink (New York: W. W. Norton, 1999), 105.

2. Lacan, *Le Séminaire de Jacques Lacan, Livre XIX: . . . ou pire, 1971–1972*, ed. Jacques-Alain Miller (Paris: Éditions du Seuil, 2011), 34. All translations of the text appearing here are my own.

3. See Jean-Claude Milner, *Clartés de tout: De Lacan à Marx, d'Aristote à Mao* (Lagrasse: Éditions Verdier, 2011).

4. "As if [. . .] what constitutes the tropism of one sex for the other were not as variable, for each species, as their bodily constitution." Lacan, *Le Séminaire de Jacques Lacan, Livre XIX: . . . ou pire, 1971–1972*, 43.

5. Mark S. Blumberg, *Freaks of Nature: What Anomalies Tell Us about Development and Evolution* (New York: Oxford University Press, 2009), 191.

6. "[W]hat determines sex in these species is the *temperature* at which the embryos are incubated." Ibid., 226; emphasis in original.

7. Interestingly, this clitoris "can be erected and displayed during nonsexual interactions referred to as *meeting ceremonies*." Ibid., 232; emphasis in original.

8. This is not to say that Freud does not unproblematically posit an a priori distinction between masculinity and femininity (that he never defines in detail)—whereas Lacan starts off from the empirical evidence of the absence of the sexual relationship—but that what, for Freud, falls under these two categories may have been thought, more intuitively, as falling under the opposite category. For instance, the little girl's psychosexual development is masculine, while an adult man never completely loses a certain feminine disposition. It is also worth emphasizing that,

as he pointed out as early as 1905, "a certain degree of anatomical hermaphroditism occurs normally." Sigmund Freud, *Three Essays on the Theory of Sexuality*, in *The Standard Edition of the Complete Psychological Works of Sigmund Freud* (hereafter *SE*), ed. and trans. James Strachey et al. (London: Hogarth Press, 1953–1974), 7:141.

9. Blumberg, *Freaks of Nature: What Anomalies Tell Us about Development and Evolution*, 198; emphasis in original.

10. To stress this, let us remember that Hans takes a cow being milked as "milk coming out of its widdler" and attributes a widdler to a lion as well as to a steam engine: "[H]e saw some water being let out of an engine. 'Oh, look,' he said, 'the engine's widdling. Where's it got its widdler?'" Freud, "Analysis of a Phobia in a Five-Year-Old Boy," in *SE* 10:7, 9. This more complex reference to the widdler points to the fact that the penis, as sex *organ*, is always already a (symbolic-imaginary) phallus, but it can be identified as such even before it is materially located.

11. Lacan, *Le Séminaire de Jacques Lacan, Livre XIX: . . . ou pire, 1971–1972*, 16.

12. Thus, Lacan again notes that, as adults, we are in many respects not exempted from Hans's perplexity: "If you knew the variety of organs of copulation that exist in insects, [. . .] you could certainly be astonished that it is like that in particular that it functions in vertebrates." Lacan, *Le Séminaire de Jacques Lacan, Livre XVIII: D'un discours qui ne serait pas du semblant, 1971*, ed. Jacques-Alain Miller (Paris: Éditions du Seuil, 2006), 67; my translation.

13. Blumberg, *Freaks of Nature: What Anomalies Tell Us about Development and Evolution*, 215.

14. The biologist Ernst Mayr first developed the notion of a "closed genetic program," or "the program for recognizing the appropriateness of the future mate" that is "contained completely in the original fertilized zygote." Mayr, *Evolution and the Diversity of Life: Selected Essays* (Cambridge: Harvard University Press, 1976), 697. Note, however, that, in Seminar I, Lacan seems to defend Konrad Lorenz's closely related ethological notion of an "innate releasing mechanism" in the case of animals. Like Lorenz, Lacan believes that "[t]he mechanical throwing into gear of the sexual instinct is [. . .] essentially crystallised in a relation of images," which "serves as [a] support for the sexual instinct on the psychological plane." Lacan, *The Seminar of Jacques Lacan, Book I: Freud's Papers on Technique, 1953–1954*, ed. Jacques-Alain Miller, trans. John Forrester (New York: W. W. Norton, 1988), 122, 121. See also *The Seminar of Jacques Lacan, Book III: The Psychoses, 1955–1956*, ed. Jacques-Alain Miller, trans. Russell Grigg (New York: W. W. Norton, 1993), 94–95. Lacan further contends that humans depart from this model—or, better, complicate it—by alienating themselves in the image of the other.

15. The "network [*filière*] of the gonad" refers to the sexual organs (ovary and testes) responsible for the production of gametes (spermatozoa and egg cells). The

quotation is from Lacan, *Le Séminaire de Jacques Lacan, Livre XIX: . . . ou pire, 1971–1972*, 43.

16. Ibid. Not to mention what Richard Lewontin—one of the first authoritative proponents of a neat disassociation of Darwin from genetic determinism—refers to as a good amount of sheer contingency, that is, the random variation in growth and division of cells during development or so-called developmental noise. See Richard C. Lewontin, *Biology as Ideology: The Doctrine of DNA* (New York: HarperCollins, 1991), 27.

17. See Mary Jane West-Eberhard, "Genes as Followers in Evolution," in *Developmental Plasticity and Evolution* (New York: Oxford University Press, 2003), 157–58.

18. Eva Jablonka, "Introduction: Lamarckian Problematics in Biology," in *Transformations of Lamarckism: From Subtle Fluids to Molecular Biology*, ed. Snait B. Gissis and Eva Jablonka (Cambridge: MIT Press, 2011), 146; emphasis added. As Jablonka also states, "certainly there is no requirement that developmentally acquired variations in the phenotype should be directly transformed into corresponding changes in the genome. This may sometimes happen [. . .], but soft inheritance does not require such specific phenotype-to-genotype transfer." Ibid., 154.

19. Ibid., 145.

20. Lacan, *The Seminar of Jacques Lacan, Book II: The Ego in Freud's Theory and in the Technique of Psychoanalysis, 1954–55*, ed. Jacques-Alain Miller, trans. Sylvana Tomaselli (New York: W. W. Norton, 1988), 48.

21. Stephen Jay Gould, *Full House: The Spread of Excellence from Plato to Darwin* (Cambridge: Belknap Press, 2011), 20, 19.

22. Ibid., 33.

23. Ibid., 3; emphasis added.

24. Ibid., 16; emphasis added.

25. Ibid., 33.

26. We can speak of lingering anthropocentrism in view of the claim that "humans are uniquely complex," and lingering vitalism to the extent that life is still seen as a "floridly arborescent bush of life." Ibid., 3, 18.

27. Consider the following sentence: "Darwin's revolution will be completed when we smash the pedestal of arrogance and own the plain implications of *evolution* for life's nonpredictable nondirectionality." Ibid., 29; emphasis added. This means either that (a) life is still seen as a (nondirectional, qua non-uni-directional and, hence, multi-directional?) movement that, as such, evolves (but why is this the case if there is no "towards"?) or that (b), if there is no real movement after all, evolution is to be acknowledged as a misleading term. Independently of the idea of progress, life does not evolve and, in turn, its supposed propulsive agency (which Gould takes for granted) needs to be tackled accordingly.

28. Lacan, *Le Séminaire de Jacques Lacan, Livre XIX: . . . ou pire, 1971–1972*, 78.

29. Ibid.

30. Again, this is first and foremost Gould. See especially *Wonderful Life*, where his main argument revolves around "the largely random sources of survival or death, and the high overall probability of extinction." Gould, *Wonderful Life: The Burgess Shale and the Nature of History* (New York: W. W. Norton, 1989), 47n. Unsurprisingly, Gould is also a staunch opponent of continual adaptation or, more technically, phyletic gradualism. See his theory of punctuated equilibrium, which "grant[s] stasis in phylogenetic lineages" "interspersed with relatively brief periods of rapid change." Gould, *An Urchin in the Storm: Essays about Books and Ideas* (New York: W. W. Norton, 1987), 38; and Steven Rose, "Introduction," in *The Richness of Life: The Essential Stephen Jay Gould*, by Stephen Jay Gould, ed. Steven Rose (New York: W. W. Norton, 2007), 6. See also Niles Eldredge and Gould, "Punctuated Equilibria: An Alternative to Phyletic Gradualism," in *Models in Paleobiology*, ed. T. J. M. Schopf (San Francisco: Freeman, Cooper, 1972), 82–115. To the extent that Gould nonetheless preserves the idea of evolution, we could perhaps suggest that his thought elegantly, though unintentionally, constructs what appears to be the veritable antinomy of evolutionary theory—there is evolution but there is no progress.

31. Lacan, *The Seminar of Jacques Lacan, Book XX: Encore, On Feminine Sexuality, the Limits of Love and Knowledge, 1972–1973*, 17.

32. Manfred Eigen, "What Will Endure of 20th Century Biology?" in *What is Life? The Next Fifty Years: Speculations on the Future of Biology*, ed. Michael P. Murphy and Luke A. J. O'Neill (New York: Cambridge University Press, 1995), 10, 22.

33. I think this is the reason why, very late in his teaching, Lacan feels the urgency to curb his earlier claim that "[m]athematical formalization is [the] ideal" of psychoanalysis: "I have not said [we should] mathematize everything but [to] start isolating a mathematizable minimum." Lacan, *The Seminar of Jacques Lacan, Book XX: Encore, On Feminine Sexuality, the Limits of Love and Knowledge, 1972–1973*, 119; and "Conférences et entretiens dans des universités nord-américaines: Yale université 24 novembre 1975," *Scilicet* 6/7 (1976): 27; my translation.

34. This is what, in Milner's words, prompts him to "extend" Galileanism through "hyperstructuralism." See Milner, *L'oeuvre claire: Lacan, la science, la philosophie* (Paris: Éditions du Seuil, 1995) and *Le périple structural: Figures et paradigme* (Lagrasse: Éditions Verdier, 2008). See also Lorenzo Chiesa, "Hyperstructuralism's Necessity of Contingency," in *S: Journal of the Jan van Eyck Circle for Lacanian Ideology Critique* 3 (2010): 159–77.

35. This is highly debatable to say the least.

36. Jacques-Alain Miller, "Lacanian Biology and the Event of the Body," in *lacanian ink* 18 (2001): 7.

37. Lacan, *The Seminar of Jacques Lacan, Book XX: Encore, On Feminine Sexuality, the Limits of Love and Knowledge, 1972–1973*, 130.

38. See Lacan, *Le Séminaire de Jacques Lacan, Livre XVIII: D'un discours qui ne serait pas du semblant, 1971*, 90.

39. Milner, *Clartés de tout: De Lacan à Marx, d'Aristote à Mao*, 18.

40. Among Adrian Johnston's vast production, I would single out "The Weakness of Nature: Hegel, Freud, Lacan, and Negativity Materialized," in *Hegel and the Infinite: Religion, Politics, and Dialectic*, ed. Slavoj Žižek, Clayton Crockett, and Creston Davis (New York: Columbia University Press, 2011), 159–79.

41. Consider also the political undertones of his condemnation: "The very principle of the idea of progress is that one believe in the imperative [. . .] *Forward March!*" Lacan, "Geneva Lecture on the Symptom," in *Analysis* 1 (1989): 25; translation modified. This should be counterbalanced with Lacan's contemporaneous suggestion, fully compatible with Milner's exhortation, according to which "we are only starting to have some idea of what biology is." Lacan, "Conférences et entretiens dans des universités nord-américaines: Yale université 24 novembre 1975," 26; my translation. Only one month separates these two late statements. Lacan at times also tries to distinguish Darwin from the neo-Darwinian paradigm, as best expressed in the following passage from a little-known 1966 interview:

> There are people who speak about Darwin without having ever read him. What is commonly referred to as "Darwinism" is a bundle of imbecilities. One cannot say that the cited sentences have not been extracted from Darwin, but they are nothing more than patched sentences, with which one claims to solve everything, and in which life is described as a great struggle where all works through the dominion of the strongest. It is enough to open up Darwin to realize that things are rather more complicated.
>
> *Conversaciones con Lévi-Strauss, Foucault y Lacan*, ed. Paolo Caruso
> (Barcelona: Editorial Anagrana, 1969), 107; my translation.

The role of Darwin in the future of biology is a contentious issue for biologists themselves. For the contrasting positions concerning whether evo-devo remains included or not within the Darwinian (or, at least, neo-Darwinian) paradigm, see "Does Evolutionary Developmental Biology Offer a Significant Challenge to the Neo-Darwinian Paradigm?" in *Contemporary Debates in Philosophy of Biology*, ed. Francisco J. Ayala and Robert Arp (Chichester: Wiley-Blackwell, 2010), 195–226.

42. "Today, endorsing 'Lamarckian problematics' does not entail commitment to Lamarck's specific (and sometimes inconsistent) views [. . .]. For example, *acquired* variations do not have to be *required* (adaptive) variations [. . .]. Lamarckian and Darwinian problematics are complementary, not conflicting."

Jablonka, "Introduction: Lamarckian Problematics in Biology," in *Transformations of Lamarckism: From Subtle Fluids to Molecular Biology*, 154; emphasis in original.

43. This is far from guaranteed given the above discussion.

44. See Lacan, *The Seminar of Jacques Lacan, Book XX: Encore, On Feminine Sexuality, the Limits of Love and Knowledge, 1972–1973*, 36.

45. "[T]here is nothing easier than to fall back into what I ironically called a world view [*conception du monde*], but which has a more moderate and more precise name: ontology." Ibid., 31.

46. "This world conceived of as the whole, with what this word implies in terms of limitation, *regardless of the openness we grant it*, remains a conception—a fitting term here—a view, gaze, or imaginary hold. And from that results the following, which remains strange, that some-one—a part of this world—is at the outset assumed to be able to take cognizance of it." Ibid., 43; translation modified and emphasis added.

CHAPTER 3

The Late Innate

Jean Laplanche, Jaak Panksepp, and the Distinction between Sexual Drives and Instincts

Adrian Johnston

For both Sigmund Freud and Jacques Lacan, an apparently small quirk of biology bears ultimate responsibility for the vicissitudes of subject formation and psychical subjectivity in the full sweep of their more-than-biological peculiarities. According to the two giants of psychoanalysis alike, the material facticity at the levels of anatomy and physiology of human beings' distinctive early developmental condition of prolonged prematurational helplessness (*Hilflosigkeit*) is of enormous import and fundamentally influential for who and what these beings subsequently become.[1] In Freud's work, it explains why humans, throughout their entire lives, come to be so thoroughly dependent upon and shaped by relations with others, starting with their first caretakers/protectors and family members. Relatedly, in Lacan's work, this same helplessness is a (if not *the*) key catalyst propelling the immature subject-to-be into forming an ego (*Ich, moi*) via the mirror stage, with all the ensuing, lifelong consequences of this fateful identificatory formation.

Jean Laplanche, in a handful of texts composed close to the time of his death in 2012, makes one of his last (and, hopefully, lasting) contributions among many to psychoanalysis. Specifically, Laplanche's writings gathered together in the volume *Sexual: La sexualité élargie au sens freudien, 2000–2006* insightfully draw attention, as Lorenzo Chiesa has also done perspicuously more recently,[2] to an additional facet or variety of human ontogenetic

prematuration partially overshadowed by Freud's and Lacan's special emphases upon the prematurational helplessness of neonates, infants, and young
children. In particular, Laplanche stresses the significance of the fact that a
biological sexuality (that is, one arising with developments of secondary sex
characteristics and the capacity for sexual reproduction) does not surface in
human beings until the onset of puberty, typically after over a decade of life.
But, as the Freudian tradition indicates, this relatively late advent of instinctual sexuality is forced to irrupt within the framework of a psychical subjectivity already occupied and saturated by a prepubescent sexuality formed by
admixtures of infantile "polymorphous perversity" with the inheritances of
influences transmitted by intersubjective others and transsubjective Others.
Whereas Freud (and, throughout much of his career, Laplanche) zooms in
on the premature intrusions of adult sexuality into the life of the sexually
immature child,[3] the later Laplanche brings to the fore the delayed advent
of sexual maturation in a child already psychically colonized by these premature intrusions. In short, and contrary to received wisdom and "common
sense" about the distinction between nature and nurture, the acquired (the
drives of socio-symbolically mediated sexuality, as taking shape prior to
puberty) precedes the innate (the instincts of [post]pubescent, chromosom-
ally dictated, and hormonally triggered sexuality).[4]

     In touching upon this precise point, Laplanche's final papers generate a
plethora of questions: How, if at all, does this acknowledgment of sexual prematuration affect the psychoanalytic distinction between drive (*Trieb, pul-
sion*) and instinct (*Instinkt, instinct*)? Do drives originating prior to puberty
(over)determine instincts activated in and through puberty? Do these
instincts transform the drives they succeed? Do drives and instincts somehow combine or merge with each other once the latter become efficacious?
This intervention sets out to begin resolving, at least at the level of metapsychological theory, some of these enigmas bequeathed by the late Laplanche.

     I intend to work through these issues, raised by Laplanche's later essays,
via an engagement with the research of Jaak Panksepp, whose investigations
in affective neuroscience have proven to be especially crucial to my own
endeavors as well as those of, for instance, Mark Solms, the founder of neuropsychoanalysis in the English-speaking world. Roughly contemporaneous
with the recent underscoring of humans' protracted sexual prematuration
by the late Laplanche, Panksepp, in a major book coauthored with psychoanalyst Lucy Biven (*The Archaeology of Mind: Neuroevolutionary Origins of
Human Emotions*), addresses this prematuration as well as a host of related
topics.[5] Although anchored first and foremost by empirical, experimental
inquiries into the structures and dynamics of the central nervous systems

of humans, as well as various nonhuman mammals, Panksepp and Biven's substantial tome, thanks to its authors' intellectual sensitivities, does so with a view to the clinical and metapsychological upshots of their findings. After a detailed tour through *The Archaeology of Mind*, I will circumnavigate back to Laplanche's *Sexual* so as to propose tentative answers to a few of the just-mentioned queries prompted by the latter.

Before zeroing in on the specific points of overlap between, on the one hand, (psychoanalytically aware) neurobiology à la Panksepp and Biven and, on the other hand, psychoanalysis à la Laplanche, it would be both appropriate and productive for me first to clarify aspects of Panksepp and Biven's approach—specifically with an eye to easily anticipated reservations and resistances to things biological on the parts of those invested in certain interpretations of the Freudian and Lacanian analytic legacies. To begin with, *The Archaeology of Mind* is staunchly opposed in general to any sort of naturalist, scientistic reductivism or eliminativism. Instead, the authors, like some of their fellow scientific travelers (such as Antonio Damasio, Terrence Deacon, Benjamin Libet, and Mark Solms), explicitly endorse a (quasi-)Spinozistic, dual-aspect monism.[6] Although I have problematized this metaphysical framework and its contemporary life-scientific reception elsewhere,[7] the least that can be said here is that it is far from any kind of crude, vulgar physicalism.

Furthermore, as Panksepp and Biven rightly observe, "there are not enough genes to account for the variety and subtlety of our MindBrain functions."[8] Just at a sheerly quantitative level, the mind-boggling, astronomical number of neurons and their interrelationships, constituting a single human neural network, vastly exceeds the comparatively tiny number of genetic coding specifications for the central nervous system. This fact by itself bears damning witness against all who would argue that the brain and the mindedness it helps to enable are nothing more than mere effects entirely dictated by genetic determinants alone; such pseudoscientific genetic determinism is rendered utterly implausible due to the undeniable absence of anywhere close to the quantity of genes equal and corresponding to the quantity of synaptic connections to be found in the brains of humans.

Very much in line with recent biological findings, Panksepp and Biven account for the massive quantitative excess of synaptic connections over genetic (pre)determinants by supplementing genetics with epigenetics.[9] The latter involves the biologically formative impacts upon the organism of multiple extraorganic mediating forces and factors (environmental, experiential, social, cultural, linguistic, and so on)—more precisely, it involves these mediators insofar as they shape the translation processes between genotypes and phenotypes. In the case of the human central nervous system, *The Archaeology of Mind* proposes that genetic underdetermination (what François Ansermet and his collaborators describe as "genetic indeterminism")[10]—the deficit of genes in relation to the comparative surplus of mental structures and dynamics—actually determines the brain to be significantly and substantially configured by a plethora of entities and events other than genes. Relatedly, Panksepp and Biven, early on in their book, insist that the brains and central nervous systems of mammals in general, albeit to varying extents across different species, are inherently socially mediated,[11] with the species *Homo sapiens* displaying the greatest degrees of such mediation. That is to say, mammals' brains are naturally inclined toward the influences of nurture upon nature, genetically preprogrammed for receptivity to epigenetic, especially social, (re)programming (or, as the neuropsychoanalytic duo of Ansermet and Pierre Magistretti put it, "genetically determined not to be genetically determined,"[12] and, as Gérard Pommier similarly phrases it, "innate that it not be innate").[13] Similarly, neuroscientist Jean-Pierre Changeux stresses that, like the rest of the neonate's body, the human brain is born in a premature state, with the combination of its genetic underdetermination and ex utero maturation resulting in epigenetic variables playing significant roles in the forming of the central nervous system.[14]

Along similar lines, Panksepp and Biven's treatment of specifically human neurobiology appropriately zeros in on, among other things, the evolutionarily recent neocortex distinctive of the species *Homo sapiens*. Whereas the evolutionarily older components of humans' central nervous systems largely shared with nonhuman mammals exhibit a relatively greater amount of intraorganic closure, qua evolutionary-genetic (pre)determination, the neocortex, by comparison, is especially open to more-than-organic influences. Panksepp and Biven characterize this youngest product of the natural history of brains as a tabula rasa endowed with an enduring plasticity (in the precise Malabouian sense), allowing it to receive as well as retain an indefinite number of myriad forms and functions endowed to it by extracerebral dimensions and milieus.[15] Solms and Oliver Turnbull similarly speak of "blanks" built into the central nervous system, namely, genetic hardwirings for epigenetic rewirings.[16]

Additionally, *The Archaeology of Mind*, from its initial pages onwards, insists upon the nonepiphenomenal reality of a downward causal efficacy of human beings' "emerging higher functions" (that is, their evolutionarily newer neocortical capacities bound up with epigenetic facilitators) vis-à-vis the "lower," evolutionarily older subcortical architectures and operations of their brains[17] (Panksepp and Biven even identify "free will" as a very real exemplar of the powers of the uniquely human neocortex).[18] With these two-way interactions and struggles between distinct brain regions and sub-regions (older and newer, higher and lower, neocortical and subcortical, and so on) in view, Panksepp and Biven wink at psychoanalysis, with its charac-teristic emphases upon tensions and antagonisms of multiple sorts as cru-cially configuring human mindedness and like-mindedness.[19] For instance, they remark that

> the lower BrainMind functions are embedded and re-represented in higher brain functions, which yield not only traditional bottom-up controls but also top-down regulations of emotionality. This pro-vides two-way avenues of control that can be seen to be forms of "circular causality" that respect the brain as a fully integrated organ that can have dramatic intra-psychic conflicts.[20]

Much later, Panksepp and Biven add that this both neurological and psy-chical predicament of humans, after it arises in and through all three levels of evolution, phylogeny, and ontogeny, cannot be undone voluntarily in favor of any regression back to a more "primitive," nonconflictual condi-tion (that is, a mythical, confabulated prelapsarian state of harmonious, Edenic nature):

> [O]nce primal urges are cognitively rerepresented within matur-ing neocortical areas, both humans and other animals come to rely ever more heavily upon those higher, developmentally programmed "software" functions. Once one has started to rely on those fine new cortico-cognitive tools for higher forms of consciousness, one can-not effectively return to simpler ways of being.[21]

Of course, these two authors, in line with convictions and methods integral to the Panseppian brand of affective neuroscience (with its cross-species approach), indicate that differences between mammalian species are of degree rather than kind (that is, that "humans and other animals" all, to varying degrees, employ "cortico-cognitive tools"). However, Panksepp and Biven's own research strongly suggests that the difference in degree between, on the one hand, humans' "top-down regulations"—via "higher, develop-mentally programmed 'software' functions" (experiential and conceptual-linguistic ideational representations ontogenetically acquired, thanks to prematurational helplessness, neural underdevelopment, and epigenetics generally)—and, on the other hand, "higher forms of consciousness" (not to mention, as I will momentarily, the forms of unconsciousness of concern to Freudian analysis) is so great in comparison, even with the human species' nearest mammalian relatives amongst the primates, that it might as well be, or de facto amounts to, a difference in kind. In short, and consistent with the Hegelian dialectics between continuity and discontinuity, the evolution of the human neocortex could be said (as it is by Panksepp and Biven) to mark a revolution in the contingent course of natural history.

Before proceeding to the triangulating links drawn in *The Archaeology of Mind* between the just-summarized neurobiological proposals, an affective neuroscience of motivation, and psychoanalytic drive theory, I feel compelled to note and respond to a facet of Panksepp and Biven's work apparently at odds with the neuropsychoanalytic picture of affective life I preliminarily and programmatically sketch in my half of *Self and Emotional Life: Philosophy, Psychoanalysis, and Neuroscience*, coauthored with Catherine Malabou.[22] Whereas I maintain that there is a meaningful manner of metapsychologically and clinically interpreting the controversial phrase "unconscious affect," Panksepp and Biven categorically assert that "[a]ffect [. . .] is never unconscious."[23] This assertion receives further elaboration and specification:

> [M]emories are not always explicit. Some are implicit, cognitively unconscious but still affectively capable of influencing behavior.
>
> Many emotional memories in humans surely arise without awareness of their causes, but that does not mean their accompanying affects are not experienced. Indeed, although the cognitive reasons for changing feelings may typically be unconscious (perhaps retrievable with psychoanalysis), the feelings themselves are not. Since affect is a form of phenomenal consciousness, experienced feelings should not be deemed to be unconscious, although their reasons may be cognitively impenetrable.[24]

Subsequently, as the authors comment,

> [m]any others believe emotions, indeed affective *feelings*, can be dynamically unconscious. Perhaps, but that may only occur if feelings are denied or repressed by excessive cognitive activities, a common disposition of the human mind, which can surely inhibit subcortical emotional turmoil to some extent. But those pressures of mind will seep out in unexpected ways and create chaos in people's lives.[25]

They soon go on to state that

> it may be worth remembering that Freud also often claimed that *the affects* are never unconscious. It feels like something to be in a primal emotional state. They are raw affective experiences—special phenomenal states of mind, a unique category of *qualia*, that arises from the very foundation of the conscious mind.[26]

As I argue in *Self and Emotional Life*, Panksepp and Biven's type of take regarding Freud on affect (one also affirmed by almost all self-identifying Lacanians) is highly selective and misleadingly oversimplifying. It maintains a hard and fast distinction between "cognition" (the domain of Freud's ideational representations and mnemic traces, qua *Vorstellungen,* or Lacan's Symbolic chains of signifiers) and "emotion," with Panksepp and Biven seeming to lump together, under the latter heading, both "affect" and "feeling," too. By contrast, the terms affect (*Affekt*), emotion (*Gefühl*), and feeling (*Empfindung*) are treated as conceptually distinct from each other by both Freud himself and other contemporary affective neuroscientists, such as Damasio.

Inspired by this unconventional, usually unacknowledged Freud, as well as some of Damasio's contributions along these same lines, my portion of *Self and Emotional Life* primarily puts forward the concept of *misfelt feelings*. According to this concept, the guises in which intrapsychically defended-against "pressures of mind," qua "emotional turmoil," manage to "seep out in unexpected ways and create chaos in people's lives," as Panksepp and Biven put it, often involve, due to the interferences of such psychical mechanisms as repression, the emotions thus combatted being consciously felt as feelings different from what these emotions would feel like if they were not submitted to intrapsychical defense mechanisms. These mechanisms can result in a splitting of affect into two different qualia: one an unfelt, unconscious (but potentially feelable) emotion (for example, guilt, love, or excitement); and another, a correspondingly misfelt, conscious (and actually felt) feeling (in these examples, guilt "seeping out" into being consciously misfelt as anxiety, love "seeping out" into being consciously misfelt as hate, or excitement "seeping out" into being consciously misfelt as terror). The idea of misfeeling admits that affects always manage to register themselves consciously (that is, to seep out) while, at the same time, enabling the phrase "unconscious affect" to retain a precise, valid meaning. Relatedly, my labor in *Self and Emotional Life* severely problematizes the above-quoted fashions of talking about "primal emotional states" and "raw affective experiences" as pure, qualitative immediacies. Whereas Panksepp and Biven appear to consider such "rawness" the rule for human animals (in addition to nonhuman mammals), I recast them as the exception—with the nonprimal, "cooked" (mis) feelings of affects/emotions as mediated by the cognitive, conceptual, linguistic, and so on being the rule for psychical subjects instead.

However, other moments in *The Archaeology of Mind* look like they might allow for a rapprochement with my proposals in *Self and Emotional Life*, despite the nonnegligible differences. For instance, as Panksepp and Biven state in their first chapter,

> we are most concerned with, first, the instinctual emotional responses that generate raw affective feelings that Mother Nature built into our brains; we call them *primary-process* psychological experiences (they are among the evolutionary "givens" of the BrainMind). Second, upon this "instinctual" foundation we have a variety of learning and memory mechanisms, which we here envision as the *secondary processes* of the brain; [. . .] we believe these intermediate brain processes are deeply unconscious. Third, at the top of the brain, we find a diversity of higher mental processes—the diverse cognitions and thoughts that allow us to reflect on what we have learned from our experiences—and we call them *tertiary processes*. Recognizing such levels of control helps enormously in understanding the fuller complexities of the BrainMind.[27]

Much later, in the context of addressing genetics and epigenetics, they observe the following:

> There are many strengths and weaknesses that we inherit directly from our parents, but much also emerges from the genetic changes, after birth, from how we are reared—namely, the *epigenetic* moldings of brain networks that result in various patterns of sensitization and desensitization in the primary-process emotional and motivational networks of the brain.[28]

One should not be fooled by false cognates here: The Freudian binary distinction between primary and secondary processes, designating the differences in kind between unconscious and conscious thinking, respectively, is far from exactly what Panksepp and Biven have in mind with their tripartite distinction between primary, secondary, and tertiary processes (for instance, insofar as the Freudian unconscious is irreducible to the id, with the latter being very close to what the authors of *The Archaeology of Mind* associate with their primary processes, this unconscious-beyond-the-id would consist of mental structures and dynamics characteristic of Panksepp and Biven's secondary and tertiary processes). That said, Panksepp and Biven grant that aspects of intrapsychical affect regulation are unconscious—in the two block quotations above, taken together, they admit that epigenetically mediated configurations and functions of "BrainMind" (these, presumably, would be at the levels of secondary and tertiary processes) can and do come to exert downward influences upon primary processes as "the evolutionary 'givens'" of the "raw affective feelings that Mother Nature built into our brains." Consequently, these "affective feelings" would not remain quite so thoroughly "raw" in human beings after all. Moreover, and of a piece with my own hybrid philosophical and neuropsychoanalytic reconceptualization of unconscious affects as misfelt feelings, I would suggest, blending Freud with Panksepp and Biven, that the unconscious dimensions of Panksepp and Biven's secondary and tertiary processes sometimes eventuate in entwined cognitive and qualitative distortions of the conscious registrations and self-interpretations of the very feel of feelings.

This defense of the central thesis of my contribution to *Self and Emotional Life*, in the face of a select few of the claims advanced in *The Archaeology of Mind*—despite, perhaps, appearances to the contrary—does not amount to a complete digression from the main thread of my reconstruction of Panksepp and Biven's relevance for a certain neuropsychoanalysis. This is especially so to the extent that this defense involves the topic of the mutually modulating exchanges and comminglings between, on the one hand, the cognitive (Panksepp and Biven's secondary and tertiary processes, processes bound up, for psychoanalysis, with Freud's *Vorstellungen* and Lacan's signifiers) and, on the other hand, the emotional and motivational (as per the immediately prior block quotation, "the primary-process emotional and motivational networks of the brain"—or, in analytic terms, affective and libidinal forces and factors). The matter of "emotional memory"—which concerns mnemic traces (that is, signifier-like ideational representations) acquired through a life history inseparably interwoven with material and socio-symbolic surroundings, charged with affective resonances, and inflecting the vicissitudes of drives (*Triebe*)—is situated right at the crossroads of the neuroscientific triad of cognition, emotion, and motivation. And this matter receives sustained attention from Panksepp and Biven.[29]

The coauthors of *The Archaeology of Mind* observe, at one point, that "[e]motional memories remain forever malleable, subject to influence by future events—through a phenomenon called reconsolidation."[30] They even proceed, correctly, to credit Freud with profound foresight about just this:

[M]emory storage is an ongoing dynamic process. Memories are not only constantly subject to the dynamic process of consolidation but they are also affected by "reconsolidation" [. . .]. This means that when humans and other animals are using their memories, and the memories thereby revert to an active processing mode, they can be remodeled and then reconsolidated in forms that are different from the original memories. Such reconstituted memories typically include information about new emotional contexts that were not present when the original memory was consolidated. Thus, old memories become temporarily labile when retrieved in new contexts, and they are re-processed accordingly. Even though Freud did not know anything about such brain mechanisms, it seems that he was already well aware of the fact that memory processes operate in this way, and he invented the word *Nachträglichkeit* to describe the kind of mental process that is characterized by psychic temporality and construction [. . .]. This basically means that memories can be reconstructed from not only the past to the future, but from an imagined future to the past.[31]

Pansepp and Biven are indeed right to recognize Freudian "deferred action" (*Nachträglichkeit*)—although other, related Freudian concepts, such as *retranscription, day's residues,* and *screen memories,* would be relevant in this context as well—as a presciently discerned set of psychical phenomena anticipating an eventual somatic corroboration/substantiation in the form of neurobiological reconsolidation.[32] (Incidentally, Ansermet and Magistretti, drawing upon the work of neuroscientist Cristina Alberini, provide Lacanian neuropsychoanalytic elaborations of reconsolidation and its various implications.)[33] After this highlighting of an instance of psychoanalysis foreshadowing neurobiology, the latter having to catch up to the former, I want to remind readers that Pansepp and Biven discuss reconsolidation specifically as a mnemic process integrally involving both cognitive and emotional dimensions of "MindBrain" functioning. But, for neuroscience, whether cognitive or affective, there is, as I mentioned above, a third dimension too, namely, the motivational (in addition to the cognitive and the emotional). Examining the entwining of motivations (specifically as drives or instincts) with the cognitions and emotions entangled in potentially or actually reconsolidated, affectively charged memories will lead into a neuroscientifically informed return to the Laplanche-inspired psychoanalytic questions I posed at the outset of this intervention.

Panksepp's version of affective neuroscience is centered upon a taxonomy of seven basic emotional systems deeply etched by evolution into mammalian central nervous systems (a taxonomy adopted by, for instance, Solms and Turnbull).[34] Foregoing here a summary of this taxonomy in its entirety, I will instead focus especially upon the emotional and motivational system Panksepp labels SEEKING, which is associated with stimulus-bound appetitive behavior and self-stimulation. At the very start of *The Archaeology of Mind*, Panksepp and Biven declare, "[w]e are happy to note that the SEEKING system provides an interesting parallel to Freud's libidinal drive (insofar as he saw libido as a generic appetitive force, rather than in narrowly sexual terms)."[35] A Freudian (or Lacanian) would take issue with Panksepp and Biven's contrast between "a generic appetitive force" and a "narrowly sexual" one as a false opposition missing and masking the proper analytic conception of sexuality as between the polar extremes of genericness and narrowness. Nonetheless, the subsequent elaborations apropos of the SEEKING system in *The Archaeology of Mind* contain valuable insights for psychoanalysis well worth appreciating. Moreover, this system, as highly distributed in humans across a wide range of different regions and subregions of their brains,[36] brings into play all three dimensions of BrainMind operations: cognition, emotion, and motivation.

One of the features of SEEKING, as per Panksepp and company, is that its distinctive motivating emotional tonalities are not equivalent to pleasurable gratification or satisfaction. As he and Biven put this, "it [. . .] feels good in a special way."[37] They proceed to specify that

[t]his positive feeling (euphoria?) of anticipatory eagerness, this SEEKING urge, is entirely different from the pleasurable release of consummation. And this feeling exists as an emotion within certain subcortical networks of the mammalian brain long before the brain develops exuberant object-relations with the world [. . .]. Initially, it is just a goad without a goal.[38]

They then encapsulate this by stating, "the SEEKING system [. . .] promotes [. . .] anticipatory euphoria [. . . ,] as opposed to any 'pleasure' of consummation."[39] If, as seems entirely reasonable to surmise, pleasurable consummations generally are brought about as consequences, effects, outcomes, or results of behaviors motivated by the SEEKING system, then the latter could be depicted fairly as paving the way for pleasure, qua gratification/satisfaction. Seen in this light, SEEKING centrally involves something equivalent to Freudian "repetition compulsion" (*Wiederholungszwang*), specifically as a preparatory precondition for the pleasure principle (as per *Beyond the Pleasure Principle*).[40] Additionally, as originally "just a goad without a goal," SEEKING, thus characterized, resembles Freud's drives as primordially "objectless" (that is, without naturally preordained, innate teloi).[41]

Another parallel between the SEEKING system and the later Freud of *Beyond the Pleasure Principle*, as well as related aspects of Lacan's thinking inspired by the latter, is rather striking. Speaking of the anticipatory eagerness generated by SEEKING, Panksepp and Biven point out that

> [p]eople and animals clearly like this feeling, although it too can become excessive. They will work relentlessly until they are utterly exhausted (sometimes to the point of death, in the case of laboratory rats that are allowed to eat only one meal a day just at the same time when they are also allowed to self-activate the brain "euphoria" system). Animals will expend much effort in order to achieve electrical or chemical stimulation of this circuitry.[42]

Not only are the implications of this for an understanding of the neurobiological substrates of the myriad "addictions" of human animals glaringly obvious, but also echoes of the (self-)destructive Freudian death drive (*Todestrieb*) and the overwhelming surpluses of Lacanian (lethal) jouissance are audible here too. Panksepp and Biven's observations can be interpreted as implying that, at least with mammalian species, the individual organism's organic body generally, and brain specifically, is far from organic, qua organized holistically. To be more exact, the animating affects of the SEEKING system can and do conflict with and override other motivational and emotional systems, such as those tending to push in the direction of the organism's self-preservation. This appears to be an instance of the central nervous system as, to reuse terminology I use elsewhere, a kludgy, anorganic system of systems—with the lack of thoroughgoing organic systematization, qua coordination, harmonization, integration, synthesis, and so on, of these multiple brain systems and subsystems opening up the potential, inevitably actualized, however frequently or infrequently, for clashes and imbalances between them (that is, intraorganic discord and lopsidedness).[43]

However, as the invocations of epigenetics and neuroplasticity above already hint, such intraorganic conflicts as those featuring the death-drive-like excesses of the SEEKING system are not, in human beings, purely and entirely intraorganic, especially insofar as the (an)organic systems of the human central nervous system are, to varying degrees, always already shot through with the mediating influences of the non- or extraorganic, the more-than-biological. Indeed, Panksepp and Biven drive home this contention specifically as regards SEEKING:

> In animals that are not as intellectually bright as we are, the SEEK-ING system operates without the admixture of forethought and strategic planning that is so characteristic of humans. In humans, strategic thinking plays a major role in SEEKING arousal because this system, like all our emotional systems, has abundant connections to the frontal neocortex, the most highly developed part of the cognitive MindBrain. When the SEEKING system arouses the human neocortex, it energizes thinking processes—a kind of virtual world—yielding complex learned behaviors that are not instinctual and may even be counterinstinctual.[44]

Several pages later, they add,

> [i]n certain "lower" mammals like rats, the ascending dopamine pathways that energize this system do not project beyond the frontal cortical regions. In humans, however, this system reaches much further, into the sensory-perceptual cortices concentrated in the back of the brain. This is consistent with the fact that SEEKING in humans arouses cognitive functions that do not have clear homologues in other animals.[45]

First of all, Panksepp and Biven assert here that, in human beings, each and every major emotional (and motivational) system, rather than remaining, as it were, naturally immediate (a purely evolutionary-genetic given of mammalian animality), is instead mediated by neocortical neural networks, themselves highly plastic conduits between, on the one hand, the brain and, on the other hand, the body's surrounding extraneural, extrabodily contexts, both natural and nonnatural. As regards what is said about the SEEKING system in the preceding two quotations, the "virtual world" of "thinking processes" that are "energized" (a Freudian might say "cathected," qua libidinally invested) by this system's emotional and motivational powers presumably would not be the neocortex in itself, as an anatomical and physiological region of living brain tissue, but, instead, this region as an intrabiological site of more-than-biological influences (in Lacanian terms, the neocortex as "extimate," qua "in the brain more than the brain itself").[46] Insofar as the SEEKING system in humans is inextricably intertwined with such a site, with neocortically facilitated inter- and transsubjective mediations both phenomenal/experiential and structural/socio-symbolic (that is, Panksepp and Biven's "virtual world" or Lacan's "reality" as both Imaginary and Symbolic), this system is portrayed in *The Archaeology of Mind* as caught up in processes of denaturalizing deinstinctualization that can and do go so far as antinatural counterinstinctuality.

With Panksepp and Biven's talk of the "instinctual" and the "counterinstinctual" apropos of a SEEKING system that they themselves equate with the drives, as per Freud, the moment has arrived to return to Laplanche's final texts and the questions they raise, questions that I underscored at the outset of this text. In staging this critical encounter between affective neuroscience and Freudian psychoanalysis, I can begin, at this juncture, by noting that Laplanche, when reflecting, in his later thinking, upon the conditions of possibility underpinning his career-long emphasis upon the topic of the formation of psychical subjectivity around introjected "enigmatic signifiers" transmitted to the subject(-to-be) by its significant Others,[47] acknowledges that "[f]or the other's message to be *implanted* we must acknowledge the existence of a primary somatic receptivity."[48] Both here and elsewhere, I have made the case that the contemporary biology of the human, via such concepts as epigenetics and neuroplasticity, significantly substantiates and specifies the precise nature of this "primary somatic receptivity" in ways dovetailing with the psychoanalytic stress upon prolonged, prematurational helplessness shared by Freud, Lacan, and Laplanche.[49] As seen above, Panksepp, Biven, and other like-minded neurobiologists and neuropsychoanalysts reinforce this picture of a biological, natural soma always already exposed and sensitive to more-than-biological, nonnatural (other) psyche(s).

Moreover, *The Archaeology of Mind* contains an observation that ought to grab the attention of those familiar with Lacan and Laplanche especially. Therein, as Panksepp and Biven note, "[f]etuses begin to integrate extrauterine sounds, even recognize their mothers' voices, before birth [. . .] and perhaps to imprint on those melodic intonations—the *motherese*—that will eventually open up the full potential for language acquisition."[50] They subsequently add that "little babies first become engaged with the prosodic intonations and melodies of their languages before they begin to assimilate the propositional contents. Our 'musical' emotional intonations may be the gateway to language acquisition."[51] Laplanche's "primary somatic receptivity" is quite primary indeed, starting in utero (as well as even earlier than Panksepp and Biven suggest, to the extent that, prior to biological conception, the symbolic orders and unconsciouses of future parents already begin preparing places for the yet-to-be-conceived child). For both Lacanians and

Laplanchians, then, several facets of Panksepp and Biven's observations are worth highlighting. To start with, the discourses and messages of the maternal Other (the *motherese*) are received and invested in by the fetal child as early as is physically possible. These "mother tongues" are "enigmatic" (Laplanche) qua material, rather than meaningful, making music rather than sense (as per Lacan's doctrine of the materiality of the signifier in general and his concept of *lalangue* in particular, with motherese as [leading to] lalangue—at one point, Lacan even speaks precisely of the poetic proclivities of prepubescent children).[52] Nonetheless, such meaninglessness and nonsense make possible meaning and sense insofar as they are crucial for later language acquisition itself (and, of course, Panksepp and Biven show how humans already are acquired by language before they properly acquire it). This "imprinting" of motherese has more to do with the emotional/affective and the motivational/libidinal than with the cognitive/representational ("propositional contents"). And, finally, these emotional/affective and motivational/libidinal dimensions are, for both mother and child (albeit differently for each of them), intimately bound up with inter- and transsubjective relationships.[53]

Taking into account all of the preceding (that is, the epigenetic and neuroplastic human brain; this brain and its body being affected already in utero by extrauterine inter- and transsubjective influences; the consequent neural receptivity to and shaping by more-than-neural forces and factors of this brain's SEEKING system; the equivalence of this system to the psychoanalytic libidinal economy of drives *als Triebe*; this system's hybrid emotional-motivational-cognitive status; and, lastly, its denaturalized character), it should be noticed that Panksepp and Biven still seem to imply, by describing human beings as having to "learn" to be "counterinstinctual," that such beings are, if only initially, instinctual, remaining, however briefly, creatures of nature before nurture. But Panksepp and Biven's own evidence and observations, especially when viewed side by side with Laplanche's insights regarding sexual prematurity, suggest that they fail to do justice to the groundbreaking radicalness of their own findings by complacently adhering to the entrenched, traditional model, a long-standing bias of thinking, in which nature always precedes nurture—an adherence that these findings indicate is a 180-degree inversion of reality, at least in certain instances. As Laplanche underscores, when it comes to the sexuality of the human libidinal economy, acquired drives precede innate instincts:[54] "What psychoanalysis teaches us—which seems utterly foreign—is that in man the sexuality of intersubjective origin, that is, drive sexuality [*pulsionnel*], *the sexuality that is acquired, comes before the sexuality that is innate. Drive comes before instinct*, fantasy comes before function; and when the sexual instinct arrives, the seat is already occupied."[55] In other words, for (neuro)psychoanalysis, "second nature" comes first and "first nature" comes second.

The depiction in *The Archaeology of Mind* of the upsurge of genital-centric sexuality with the onset of puberty further reinforces the impression that its two authors cling to a philosophical/theoretical naturalism that remains too standardly naturalistic in relation to their actual empirical, experimental data. As Panksepp and Biven maintain,

> [d]uring puberty, the early imprint of maleness and femaleness comes to life under the sway of massive secretions of sex hormones from the testes and ovaries. This *activational period* of sexual maturation carries forward the preconscious brain imprints of fetal development. Although the cultural impact of an intensely lived childhood also plays its role in sexual development, puberty activates the fetal legacy. And like an ancient "impish orchestra," it begins to play insistent biological tunes down in the deep LUSTful recesses of the brain.[56]

Here, the authors write as though the irruption of adolescent sexuality amounted to nothing more than a straightforward activation of dormant codes and programs (the "brain imprints" of "the fetal legacy" as "insistent biological tunes"). This sexuality is allegedly colored by the socio-symbolically molded ("culturally impacted") life history of the individual between conception and puberty only in the extreme, exceptional case of "an intensely lived childhood" (implicitly in contrast with a not-so-intensely lived one that could be qualified as "normal" and nontraumatic). But, in addition to Panksepp and Biven pledging loyalties to a Freudian psychoanalytic orientation frontally challenging from its inception all such reductively naturalizing descriptions of human sexuality, their own insistences upon the thoroughgoing neocortical cognitive/representational mediation of all emotional/affective systems (including the intertwined SEEKING and LUST systems) undermine the above (pre-Freudian, depth-psychological) image of "an ancient 'impish orchestra'" making its evolutionary-genetic music perfectly audible without any epigenetic, phylogenetic, and ontogenetic filters modifying or muffling its purportedly archaic, authentic sound.

Laplanche, in contrast to Panksepp and Biven, furnishes a more nuanced conceptualization of the advent of (post)pubescent sexuality. Furthermore, I would maintain that Laplanche's conceptualization does more justice to Panksepp and Biven's empirical findings than do their own theoretical interpretations of these findings. At the level of psychoanalytic metapsychology, Laplanche argues against the two opposed extremes of either naturalistically reducing drives to instincts (a reduction crystallized in James Strachey's consistent [mis]translation of *Trieb* as "instinct" in the *Standard Edition* of Freud's writings) or antinaturalistically reducing instincts to drives (a gesture characteristic, in Laplanche's eyes, of Lacan and his followers).[57] Subsequently, he specifies that human sexuality is distinctively marked by a conflict between infantile (prepubescent) and adolescent/adult ([post]pubescent) sexuality. The former (in)consists of the polymorphous perversity of acquired pregenital drives, while the latter, which arrives upon a scene already occupied and dominated by these drives, is centered upon a genital instinct arising from evolutionary-genetic imperatives with respect to reproduction. For this Laplanche, one of the many conflicts brought to light by analysis is the conflict between drives and instinct(s).[58]

I wish to suggest that Laplanche too, like Panksepp and Biven, might not be sufficiently consistent with his own discipline's radical consequences. In this instance, his third way, between the opposed poles of naturalistically reducing drive to instinct and antinaturalistically reducing instinct to drive, is simply to preserve both concepts unaltered and immediately posit an antagonism between them. Now, I think Laplanche's basic intuition that a rejection of naturalism-versus-antinaturalism apropos of psychoanalysis generally, and the metapsychology of the libidinal economy specifically, is fundamentally correct and compelling. Nonetheless, I suspect that he still concedes too much internal integrity and self-cohesion to the adolescent sexuality arising in puberty when promptly and inevitably faced with the previously established and operative network of prepubescent drives. To be more precise, Laplanche seems to imply that an innate reproductive sexual instinct, as an evolutionarily genetically dictated and stabilized circuit of— to borrow Freud's categories from "Drives and Their Vicissitudes"[59]—source (the genitals and sex hormones), pressure (felt genital-centric sexual urges), aim (genital-centric sexual satisfaction), and object (suitable conspecific partner), thrusts itself forward upon the field of the libidinal economy as a rival to (and as remaining henceforth essentially unchanged in its natural core by) the already-there partial drives acquired during the protracted prepubescent prematurity of the young human being. This implication risks undoing the ability of psychoanalysis to accomplish one of the tasks originally set for it by Freud at its very founding, namely, to account for the incredible richness and teeming diversity of human sexuality well beyond the narrow confines of "normal heterosexuality," a task that is the main agenda of the trailblazing *Three Essays on the Theory of Sexuality*. Much evidence from the analytic clinic and beyond bears witness against what Laplanche, given his particular fashion of retaining a qualified, attenuated naturalism in the guise of a genital/reproductive sexual instinct, must assert as universal, to the extent that anything instinctual, qua innate to the species, would have to exhibit itself in all the species' members. That is to say, the evidence that each and every human being, even when not a "normal heterosexual," is still perturbed, however slightly and subtly, by specifically genital/reproductive tendencies, is not overwhelmingly strong, to say the least. What about those analysands and various persons who would insistently testify that their sexual desires are in no way shaped or buffeted by an urge to reproduce via copulation with a member of the opposite sex? Are they merely deceiving themselves?

At the same time, there is indeed no denying that, with the onset of puberty, some sort of new, ontogenetically unprecedented adolescent sexuality insistently intrudes into the life of the human animal. I would be the first to agree enthusiastically with Laplanche (as well as Panksepp, Biven, and those of similar mind) that an antinaturalistic denial of there being underlying biological (that is, evolutionary, genetic, neural, and hormonal) elements and processes affecting humans' sexualities is untenable and absurd. Nonetheless, Laplanche's manner of attempting to accommodate this quasi-naturalist admission strikes me as putting in danger too many of the explanatory gains unique to the Freudian psychoanalytic theorization of psychical sexuality.

My alternate hypothesis, relying upon Freud's metapsychology of drive (as per the aforementioned paper "Drives and Their Vicissitudes"), is that, in the epigenetically and socio-symbolically mediated psyche, qua Brain-Mind (as per a synthesis of neurobiology and psychoanalysis), what would have been an instinct is instead amputated, although not stifled or eliminated altogether, in the process of being forced into the mold of a drive, one competing with other drives. Put differently, the sexual instinct of puberty is a "vanishing mediator," an instinct that loses its instinctual nature as soon as it arises between pre- and postpubescent sexual-libidinal economies. To be more exact, this instinct's source (the genitals and sex hormones) and pressure (felt genital-centric sexual urges) are activated at puberty within a psyche in which all aims and objects, including those involving others as potential or actual providers of genital-level gratifications, are constituted in and through more-than-natural phenomenological and structural representational mediations of aims and objects thoroughly immersed within temporal dynamics stretching across the full arc of the subject's life history.[60] Hence, there is no way that the aims and objects of purportedly instinctual adolescent/adult sexuality would not always be at least colored (if not dominated) by ontogenetic/historical dimensions long preceding the onset of puberty. Therefore, the instinctual component of adolescent, (post)pubescent sexuality stays confined to the levels of source and pressure, with its aims and objects bringing into play numerous other variables over and above strictly natural instinctuality. Or, one could say that the late innateness of the adolescent/adult sexual instinct, preceded by the early acquisition of the infantile/childhood drives, makes this instinct, as soon as it surfaces, always already a Frankenstein-like, hybrid drive-instinct, namely, an innate source and pressure automatically and inevitably routed through previously acquired aims and objects (perhaps the bastard compound phrase "instinctual drives" of certain Anglo-American analytic circles is not entirely without redeemable merit). Not only do I believe this metapsychological hypothesis to be more in line with Freud's own views, as well as with the accumulated evidence of clinical experience, but I am also confident that it is robustly defensible upon neurobiological grounds too.

On one occasion, during his very first annual Seminar, Lacan briefly comments upon the sexual prematuration that was to be of concern decades later in Laplanche's final essays:

> This prematurity of birth hasn't been invented by the psychoanalysts. Histologically, the apparatus which in the organism plays the role of nervous system [*appareil nerveux*] [. . .] is not complete at birth [*inachevé à la naissance*]. Man's libido attains its finished state before encountering its object [*L'homme a atteint l'achèvement de sa libido avant que d'en rejoindre l'objet*]. That is how this special fault [*faille spéciale*] is introduced, perpetuated in man in the relation to the other who is infinitely more fatal [*infiniment plus mortel*] for him than for any other animal.[61]

Lacan is referring specifically to the prematurity-at-birth and consequent ex utero environmentally mediated maturation of human brain tissue (that is, the histology of the human organism's central nervous system). With the implied ontogenetic formation of brain and subject, via the complex ensemble of structures and dynamics illuminated by psychoanalysis (among other disciplines) transpiring between birth and puberty (including during Freud's "latency period"),[54] a libidinal economy of drives (that is, a SEEKING system) congeals into "its finished state," prior to "encountering its object," precisely as the potential and/or actual sexual partners of a pubescent and post-pubescent genital sexuality. These "objects" of adolescent and adult libido, as soon as they come on the scene of the subject's libidinal life, already are overshadowed, however visibly or invisibly, partially or completely, by the spectral revenants of prepubescent libidinal objects (or, in the language of affective neuroscience, by emotional-motivational-cognitive configurations of the SEEKING system already under construction starting in the womb). Although this line of thought is extremely familiar Freudian fare (going back to such a source as, again, Freud's foundational and path-breaking *Three Essays on the Theory of Sexuality*),[63] Lacan, at this moment in 1954, points to something Freud awaited: biological corroboration of analytic discoveries regarding human sexual life.[64]

Interestingly, Lacan's just-quoted assertions concerning the interlinked neural and sexual immaturities in humans are immediately preceded by some intriguing remarks apropos of conceptions of animality and nature. As Lacan declares,

> [i]n animals, the securing of the guide-rails [*La sûreté du guidage*] is so much more in evidence that it is precisely what has given rise to the great fantasy [*le grand fantasme*] of *natura mater*, the very idea of nature, in relation to which man portrays his original inadequacy to himself [*son inadéquation originelle*], which he expresses in a thousand different ways. You can spot it, in a perfectly objectifiable manner, in his quite special impotence at the beginning of life.[65]

These "guide-rails" are (human imaginings of) animal instincts as predetermined, fixed, and invariant teleological templates for survival-conducive behavior. These templates are envisioned as being a kind of sure-fire savoir faire hardwired by evolution and genetics, an instinctual know-how with which the living being comes inherently preequipped, thanks to a benevolent "Mother Nature" interested in ensuring the existence and flourishing of her offspring. This vision, this "very idea of nature" (qua idea rather than whatever *Natur an sich* extra-ideationally might be) as "natura mater," is diagnosed by Lacan as nothing other than a "great fantasy" (I have scrutinized problematizations of pictures of merger and integration with Nature as a kindly parental big Other by Lacan and others at some length on separate occasions).[66] Furthermore, this quotation from Seminar I identifies the distinctively human, anatomical, and physiological real(ity) of extremely drawn out *Hilflosigkeit* (that is, "his original inadequacy to himself" [*son inadéquation originelle*], "his quite special impotence at the beginning of life") as the key ur-catalyst spurring the formation of both organicist fantasies of omniscient, omnipotent Nature defensively repressing this ur-catalyst, as well as representative sublimations (such as the paintings of Hieronymus Bosch to which Lacan refers in the 1949 *écrit* on the mirror stage)[67] of it (that is, the "thousand different ways" of a spectrum spanning everything from repression to sublimation). Arguably, Panksepp and Biven, to a greater extent, as well as Laplanche, to a lesser extent, still do not utterly abandon a fantasized *natura mater* generously bequeathing to her progeny an id-level instinctual knowledge in the real, however minimal or modified.

Of course, the general Lacanian lesson along the preceding lines is that, as regards nature too (in addition to God and the like), "*le grand Autre n'existe pas*" (the big Other does not exist—here, "the great fantasy [*le grand fantasme*] of *natura mater*"). Stated very broadly, evolutionary biology can be seen, through the combined lenses of Freudian psychoanalysis and affective neuroscience, to be so delicate, so fragile that, through just a few of its own self-wrought quirks (such as the accidental, contingent geneses of opposable thumbs, neocortices, ex utero maturation, delayed reproductive capability, and the like), it blindly brings about its own partial subversions. This immanent, self-undermining of nature—its autogenerated disruption of its own causal/determinative authority, embodied specifically by human (non)natures—consists in both the natural-historical revolutions of humanity's phylogeny as well as the ontogenetic rebellions of sexualities nudged by instinct into leaving the instinctual behind. Hence, upon the multiple time scales in which humans are embedded and entangled, it is always already, for these particular, peculiar beings, too late for the innate.

Notes

1. See Sigmund Freud, *Project for a Scientific Psychology*, in *The Standard Edition of the Complete Psychological Works of Sigmund Freud* (hereafter *SE*), ed. and trans. James Strachey et al. (London: Hogarth Press, 1953–1974), 1:318; *Inhibitions, Symptoms and Anxiety*, in *SE* 20:154–55, 167; *The Future of an Illusion*, in *SE* 21:17–19, 30; Jacques Lacan, "Les complexes familiaux dans la formation de l'individu: Essai d'analyse d'une fonction en psychologie," in *Autres écrits*, ed. Jacques-Alain Miller (Paris: Éditions du Seuil, 2001), 33–35; "The Mirror State as Formative of the *I* Function as Revealed in Psychoanalytic Experience," in *Écrits: The First Complete Edition in English*, trans. Bruce Fink (New York: W. W. Norton, 2006), 76, 78; "Aggressiveness in Psychoanalysis," in *Écrits: The First Complete Edition in English*, 92; *Le Séminaire de Jacques Lacan, Livre VI: Le désir et son interpretation, 1958–1959*, ed. Jacques-Alain Miller (Paris: Éditions de La Martinière,

2013), 27–30; and *Le Séminaire de Jacques Lacan, Livre VIII: Le transfert, 1960–1961*, ed. Jacques-Alain Miller (Paris: Éditions du Seuil, 1991), 427.

2. See Lorenzo Chiesa, *The Not-Two: Logic and God in Lacan* (Cambridge: MIT Press, 2016).

3. See Freud, "Extracts from the Fliess Papers," in *SE* 1:221–31, 236, 238–40, 247, 250–51, 269, 276; *Project for a Scientific Psychology*, in *SE* 1:333; and Jean Laplanche, *Life and Death in Psychoanalysis*, trans. Jeffrey Mehlman (Baltimore: Johns Hopkins University Press, 1976), 35–36, 46.

4. See Laplanche, "Drive and Instinct: Distinctions, Oppositions, Supports and Intertwinings," in *Freud and the* Sexual: *Essays 2000–2006*, ed. John Fletcher, trans. John Fletcher, Jonathan House, and Nicholas Ray (New York: International Psychoanalytic Books, 2011), 14; "Sexuality and Attachment in Metapsychology," in *Freud and the Sexual: Essays 2000–2006*, 44; "Gender, Sex and the *Sexual*," in *Freud and the* Sexual: *Essays 2000–2006*, 180; and "Three Meanings of the Term 'Unconscious' in the Framework of the General Theory of Seduction," in *Freud and the* Sexual: *Essays 2000–2006*, 205–7.

5. See Jaak Panksepp and Lucy Biven, *The Archaeology of Mind: Neuroevolutionary Origins of Human Emotions* (New York: W. W. Norton, 2012), 275.

6. See Panksepp and Biven, *The Archaeology of Mind: Neuroevolutionary Origins of Human Emotions*, 185, 417, 422–23; Mark Solms and Oliver Turnbull, *The Brain and the Inner World: An Introduction to the Neuroscience of Subjective Experience* (New York: Other Press, 2002), 56–57, 72; Antonio Damasio, *Looking for Spinoza: Joy, Sorrow, and the Feeling Brain* (London: William Heinemann, 2003), 12, 214–15; Benjamin Libet, *Mind Time: The Temporal Factor in Consciousness* (Cambridge: Harvard University Press, 2004), 6, 17, 86–87, 163, 184; and Terrence W. Deacon, *Incomplete Nature: How Mind Emerged from Matter* (New York: W. W. Norton, 2012), 138, 155, 237, 480, 484.

7. See Adrian Johnston, *Adventures in Transcendental Materialism: Dialogues with Contemporary Thinkers* (Edinburgh: Edinburgh University Press, 2014), 13–64.

8. Panksepp and Biven, *The Archaeology of Mind: Neuroevolutionary Origins of Human Emotions*, 239.

9. See ibid., 239–41, 342.

10. See François Ansermet, "Des neurosciences aux logosciences," in *Qui sont vos psychanalystes?* ed. Nathalie Georges, Nathalie Marchaison, and Jacques-Alain Miller (Paris: Éditions du Seuil, 2002), 383; Pierre Magistretti and Ansermet, "Introduction," in *Neurosciences et psychanalyse: Une recontre autour de la singularité*, ed. Pierre Magistretti and François Ansermet (Paris: Odile Jacob, 2010), 11; and Ansermet and Ariane Giacobino, *Autisme: À chacun son génome* (Paris: Navarin, 2012), 9–10, 13–14, 16–17, 20–21, 58–60, 71, 82.

11. See Panksepp and Biven, *The Archaeology of Mind: Neuroevolutionary Origins of Human Emotions*, xviii.

12. Ansermet and Magistretti, *Biology of Freedom: Neural Plasticity, Experience, and the Unconscious*, trans. Susan Fairfield (New York: Other Press, 2007), 8.

13. Gérard Pommier, *Comment les neurosciences démontrent la psychanalyse* (Paris: Éditions Flammarion, 2004), 27; my translation.

14. See Jean-Pierre Changeux, *The Physiology of Truth: Neuroscience and Human Knowledge*, trans. M. B. DeBevoise (Cambridge: Harvard University Press, 2004), 189, 208–9.

15. See Panksepp and Biven, *The Archaeology of Mind: Neuroevolutionary Origins of Human Emotions*, 10–11, 197–98, 427–28.

16. See Solms and Turnbull, *The Brain and the Inner World: An Introduction to the Neuroscience of Subjective Experience*, 122–23, 133–34, 277–78.

17. See Panksepp and Biven, *The Archaeology of Mind: Neuroevolutionary Origins of Human Emotions*, xii, 12, 17.

18. See ibid., 448.

19. See ibid., 77, 199, 396, 451.

20. Ibid., 77.

21. Ibid., 451.

22. See Johnston, "Preface: From Nonfeeling to Misfeeling—Affects Between Trauma and the Unconscious," in *Self and Emotional Life: Philosophy, Psychoanalysis, and Neuroscience* (New York: Columbia University Press, 2013), ix–xviii; and "Misfelt Feelings: Unconscious Affect between Psychoanalysis, Neuroscience, and Philosophy," in *Self and Emotional Life: Philosophy, Psychoanalysis, and Neuroscience*, 73–210.

23. Panksepp and Biven, *The Archaeology of Mind: Neuroevolutionary Origins of Human Emotions*, 136.

24. Ibid., 204.

25. Ibid., 426–27; emphasis in original.

26. Ibid., 427; emphasis in original.

27. Ibid., 9; emphasis in original.

28. Ibid., 239; emphasis in original.

29. See ibid., 208, 214, 220, 456, 467, 473.

30. Ibid., 208.

31. Ibid., 220.

32. See Freud, "Extracts from the Fliess Papers," in *SE* 1:233; Freud and Josef Breuer, *Studies on Hysteria*, in *SE* 2:133; "Screen Memories," in *SE* 3:322; *The Interpretation of Dreams*, in *SE* 5:573; "Notes upon a Case of Obsessional Neurosis," in *SE* 10:206; "Remembering, Repeating and Working-Through," in *SE* 12:149; *Introductory Lectures on Psycho-Analysis*, in *SE* 16:369; and Johnston, *Time Driven:*

Metapsychology and the Splitting of the Drive (Evanston: Northwestern University Press, 2005), 5–22, 218–27.

33. See Christina M. Alberini, "La dynamique des représentations mentales: Consolidation de la mémoire, reconsolidation et intégration de nouvelles informations," in *Neurosciences et psychanalyse: Une recontre autour de la singularité*, 31–32, 37–38; Magistretti and Ansermet, "Introduction," 10–12; Magistretti and Ansermet, "Plasticité et homéostasie à l'interface entre neurosciences et psychanalyse," in *Neurosciences et psychanalyse: Une recontre autour de la singularité*, 18–19; and Johnston, "Drive between Brain and Subject: An Immanent Critique of Lacanian Neuropsychoanalysis," *The Southern Journal of Philosophy* 51 (2013): 64–65.

34. See Panksepp, *Affective Neuroscience: The Foundations of Human and Animal Emotions* (Oxford: Oxford University Press, 1998), 47, 52–54; Solms and Turnbull, *The Brain and the Inner World: An Introduction to the Neuroscience of Subjective Experience*, 112–33, 277–78; Johnston, "Misfelt Feelings: Unconscious Affect between Psychoanalysis, Neuroscience, and Philosophy," 186–87; and "Drive between Brain and Subject: An Immanent Critique of Lacanian Neuropsychoanalysis," 71.

35. See Panksepp and Biven, *The Archaeology of Mind: Neuroevolutionary Origins of Human Emotions*, xv. Solms and Turnbull, relying upon Panksepp's earlier work, emphatically endorse this asserted parallel between affective neuroscience and psychoanalytic metapsychology. See Solms and Turnbull, *The Brain and the Inner World: An Introduction to the Neuroscience of Subjective Experience*, 117–19.

36. See Panksepp and Biven, *The Archaeology of Mind: Neuroevolutionary Origins of Human Emotions*, 96.

37. Ibid., 95.

38. Ibid., 96.

39. Ibid., 97.

40. See Freud, *Beyond the Pleasure Principle*, in *SE* 18:14–17, 23, 32–36, 62.

41. See Johnston, *Time Driven: Metapsychology and the Splitting of the Drive*, 168.

42. Panksepp and Biven, *The Archaeology of Mind: Neuroevolutionary Origins of Human Emotions*, 98.

43. See Johnston, "The Weakness of Nature: Hegel, Freud, Lacan, and Negativity Materialized," in *Hegel and the Infinite: Religion, Politics, and Dialectic*, ed. Slavoj Žižek, Clayton Crockett, and Creston Davis (New York: Columbia University Press, 2011), 159–79; "Misfelt Feelings: Unconscious Affect between Psychoanalysis, Neuroscience, and Philosophy," 175–78; "Reflections of a Rotten Nature: Hegel, Lacan, and Material Negativity," *Filozofski vestnik* 33, no. 2 (2012): 23–52; "Drive between Brain and Subject: An Immanent Critique of Lacanian

Neuropsychoanalysis," 48–84; "Points of Forced Freedom: Eleven (More) Theses on Materialism," *Speculations: A Journal of Speculative Realism* 4 (2013): 95–96; François Jacob, "Evolution and Tinkering," *Science* 196 (1977): 1161–6; Francisco J. Varela, Evan Thompson, and Eleanor Rosch, *The Embodied Mind: Cognitive Science and Human Experience* (Cambridge: MIT Press, 1991), 106–7; Damasio, *Descartes' Error: Emotion, Reason, and the Human Brain* (New York: Penguin, 1994), 185; *The Feeling of What Happens: Body and Emotion in the Making of Consciousness* (New York: Harcourt, 1999), 331; *Self Comes to Mind: Constructing the Conscious Brain* (New York: Pantheon, 2010), 250–51, 314; Joseph LeDoux, *The Emotional Brain: The Mysterious Underpinnings of Emotional Life* (New York: Simon and Schuster, 1996), 16, 105–6, 127; *Synaptic Self: How Our Brains Become Who We Are* (New York: Penguin, 2002), 31; Keith E. Stanovich, *The Robot's Rebellion: Finding Meaning in the Age of Darwin* (Chicago: University of Chicago Press, 2004), xii, 12–13, 15–16, 20–22, 25, 28, 53, 60, 66–67, 82–84, 122, 142, 186–7, 247; David J. Linden, *The Accidental Mind: How Brain Evolution Has Given Us Love, Memory, Dreams, and God* (Cambridge: Harvard University Press, 2007), 2–3, 5–7, 21–24, 26, 235–46; Gary Marcus, *Kludge: The Haphazard Evolution of the Human Mind* (New York: Houghton Mifflin Harcourt, 2008), 6–16, 161–3; and Changeux, *Du vrai, du beau, du bien: Une nouvelle approche neuronale* (Paris: Odile Jacob, 2008), 78.

44. Panksepp and Biven, *The Archaeology of Mind: Neuroevolutionary Origins of Human Emotions*, 102.

45. Ibid., 105.

46. See Lacan, *The Seminar of Jacques Lacan, Book VII: The Ethics of Psychoanalysis, 1959–1960*, ed. Jacques-Alain Miller, trans. Dennis Porter (New York: W. W. Norton, 1992), 139; *The Seminar of Jacques Lacan, Book XI: The Four Fundamental Concepts of Psychoanalysis*, ed. Jacques-Alain Miller, trans. Alan Sheridan (New York: W. W. Norton, 1998), 268; and *Le Séminaire de Jacques Lacan, Livre XVI: D'un Autre à l'autre, 1968–1969*, ed. Jacques-Alain Miller (Paris: Éditions du Seuil, 2006), 224–25, 249.

47. Laplanche, *Life and Death in Psychoanalysis*, 46; "Temporalité et traduction: Pour une remise au travail de la philosophie du temps," in *La Révolution copernicienne inachevée: Travaux, 1967–1992* (Paris: Aubier, 1992), 331; "The Kent Seminar," in *Jean Laplanche: Seduction, Translation and the Drives*, ed. John Fletcher and Martin Stanton, trans. Martin Stanton (London: Institute of Contemporary Arts, 1992), 22; *La sexualité humaine: Biologisme et biologie* (Le Plessis-Robinson: Institut Synthélabo, 1999), 52; "The Unfinished Copernican Revolution," in *Essays on Otherness*, ed. John Fletcher, trans. Luke Thurston (New York: Routledge, 1999), 78; "The Drive and Its Source-Object: Its Fate in the Transference," in *Essays on Otherness*, trans. Leslie Hill, 129; "Interpretation between Determinism

and Hermeneutics: A Restatement of the Problem," in *Essays on Otherness*, trans. Philip Slotkin, 146–7, 160, 164; and Johnston, *Time Driven: Metapsychology and the Splitting of the Drive*, 129–43.

48. Laplanche, "Sexuality and Attachment in Metapsychology," 49; emphasis in original.

49. See Johnston, "Reflections of a Rotten Nature: Hegel, Lacan, and Material Negativity," 23–52; "Drive between Brain and Subject: An Immanent Critique of Lacanian Neuropsychoanalysis," 48–84; "The Object in the Mirror of Genetic Transcendentalism: Lacan's *Objet petit a* between Visibility and Invisibility," *Continental Philosophy Review* 46, no. 2 (2013): 251–69; "Lacking Causes: Privative Causality from Locke and Kant to Lacan and Deacon," *Speculations: A Journal of Speculative Realism* 6 (2015): 19–60; "Humanity, That Sickness: Louis Althusser and the Helplessness of Psychoanalysis," *Crisis and Critique* 2, no. 2 (2015): 216–61; and *Prolegomena to Any Future Materialism: A Weak Nature Alone*, vol. 2 (Evanston: Northwestern University Press, forthcoming).

50. Panksepp and Biven, *The Archaeology of Mind: Neuroevolutionary Origins of Human Emotions*, 306; emphasis in original.

51. Ibid., 475–76.

52. See Lacan, *The Seminar of Jacques Lacan, Book VII: The Ethics of Psychoanalysis, 1959–1960*, 157.

53. See Lacan, *La savoir du psychanalyste* (1971–1972), unpublished seminar, lesson of November 4, 1971, and December 2, 1971, http://gaogoa.free.fr/; *The Seminar of Jacques Lacan, Book XX: Encore, On Feminine Sexuality, the Limits of Love and Knowledge, 1972–1973*, ed. Jacques-Alain Miller, trans. Bruce Fink (New York: W. W. Norton, 1999), 138–39; *Les non-dupes errent* (1973–1974), unpublished seminar, lesson of January 8, 1974, and June 11, 1974, http://gaogoa .free.fr/; *Le Séminaire de Jacques Lacan, Livre XXIII: Le sinthome, 1975–1976*, ed. Jacques-Alain Miller (Paris: Éditions du Seuil, 2005), 117; *L'insu que sait de l'une-bévue, s'aile à mourre* (1976–1977), unpublished seminar, lesson of April 19, 1977, http://gaogoa.free.fr/; *Le moment de conclure* (1977–1978), unpublished seminar, lesson of November 15, 1977, and April 11, 1978, http://gaogoa .free.fr/; *Television*, in *Television: A Challenge to the Psychoanalytic Establishment*, ed. Joan Copjec, trans. Denis Hollier, Rosalind Krauss, and Annette Michelson (New York: W. W. Norton, 1990), 9–10; "Alla 'Scuola Freudiana,'" in *Lacan in Italia/En Italie Lacan, 1953–1978*, ed. and trans. Giacomo B. Contri (Milan: La Salamandra, 1978), 104–47; "Columbia University: Lecture on the Symptom," in *Culture/Clinic 1: Applied Lacanian Psychoanalysis*, ed. Jacques-Alain Miller and Maire Jaanus, trans. Adrian Price with Russell Grigg (Minneapolis: University of Minnesota Press, 2013), 12–13; Colette Soler, *Lacan: The Unconscious Reinvented*, trans. Esther Faye and Susan Schwartz (London: Karnac, 2014), 25–38; *Les affects*

lacaniens (Paris: Presses Universitaires de France, 2011), 84, 103, 106–7; Ansermet and Magistretti, *Biology of Freedom: Neural Plasticity, Experience, and the Unconscious*, 8; Pommier, *Comment les neurosciences démontrent la psychanalyse*, 23–28, 45–47; Panksepp, *Affective Neuroscience: The Foundations of Human and Animal Emotions*, 47, 52, 149, 302, 318–19; Changeux, *Neuronal Man: The Biology of Mind*, trans. Laurence Garey (Princeton: Princeton University Press, 1997), 246–9; *The Physiology of Truth: Neuroscience and Human Knowledge*, 37, 39, 58, 60–62, 113–4, 118, 129, 132, 140–1, 184–5, 201–2; *Du vrai, du beau, du bien: Une nouvelle approche neuronale*, 293–94, 296–97; LeDoux, *Synaptic Self: How Our Brains Become Who We Are*, 72–74; Lesley Rogers, *Sexing the Brain* (New York: Columbia University Press, 2001), 21–22; Stanovich, *The Robot's Rebellion: Finding Meaning in the Age of Darwin*, 82, 201–2; and Johnston, "Misfelt Feelings: Unconscious Affect between Psychoanalysis, Neuroscience, and Philosophy," 141–46, 195–200.

54. See Laplanche, "Sexuality and Attachment in Metapsychology," 44.

55. Laplanche, "Drive and Instinct: Distinctions, Oppositions, Supports and Intertwinings," 22; emphasis in original.

56. Panksepp and Biven, *The Archaeology of Mind: Neuroevolutionary Origins of Human Emotions*, 275.

57. See Laplanche, "Drive and Instinct: Distinctions, Oppositions, Supports and Intertwinings," 8–9.

58. See Laplanche, "Three Meanings of the Term 'Unconscious' in the Framework of the General Theory of Seduction," 206–7.

59. See Freud, "Instincts and Their Vicissitudes," in *SE* 14:122–23; translation modified.

60. I have in mind here, in the background, my reworking of Freudian-Lacanian drive theory. See Johnston, *Time Driven: Metapsychology and the Splitting of the Drive*.

61. Lacan, *The Seminar of Jacques Lacan, Book I: Freud's Papers on Technique, 1953–1954*, ed. Jacques-Alain Miller, trans. John Forrester (New York: W. W. Norton, 1988), 149.

62. See Freud, *Three Essays on the Theory of Sexuality*, in *SE* 7:173–79.

63. Ibid., 222–29; and Lacan, *Le Séminaire de Jacques Lacan, Livre IV: La relation d'objet, 1956–1957*, ed. Jacques-Alain Miller (Paris: Éditions du Seuil, 1994), 52–53.

64. See Freud, "The Claims of Psycho-Analysis to Scientific Interest," in *SE* 13:179–82; "On Narcissism: An Introduction," in *SE* 14:78; *Introductory Lectures on Psycho-Analysis*, in *SE* 16:320; and "Female Sexuality," in *SE* 21:240.

65. Lacan, *The Seminar of Jacques Lacan, Book I: Freud's Papers on Technique, 1953–1954*, 171.

66. See Johnston, "The Weakness of Nature: Hegel, Freud, Lacan, and Negativity Materialized," 159–79; "Second Natures in Dappled Worlds: John McDowell, Nancy Cartwright, and Hegelian-Lacanian Materialism," *Umbr(a): The Worst*, no. 1 (2011): 71–91; "The Voiding of Weak Nature: The Transcendental Materialist Kernels of Hegel's *Naturphilosophie*," *Graduate Faculty Philosophy Journal* 33, no. 1 (2012): 103–57; "Reflections of a Rotten Nature: Hegel, Lacan, and Material Negativity," 23–52; "Misfelt Feelings: Unconscious Affect between Psychoanalysis, Neuroscience, and Philosophy," 175–78; "Points of Forced Freedom: Eleven (More) Theses on Materialism," 95–96; "Drive between Brain and Subject: An Immanent Critique of Lacanian Neuropsychoanalysis," 48–84; *Prolegomena to Any Future Materialism: The Outcome of Contemporary French Philosophy*, vol. 1 (Evanston: Northwestern University Press, 2013), 37, 206–9; *Adventures in Transcendental Materialism: Dialogues with Contemporary Thinkers*, 148, 150, 153–55, 158–59; "Humanity, That Sickness: Louis Althusser and the Helplessness of Psychoanalysis," 216–61; and *Prolegomena to Any Future Materialism: A Weak Nature Alone*, vol. 2.

67. See Lacan, "The Mirror State as Formative of the *I* Function as Revealed in Psychoanalytic Experience," 78.

CHAPTER 4

Hegel's Mother

Frank Ruda

Once Upon a Time . . .

Once upon a time philosophical anthropology was a wasteland. Within its terrain, nearly all endeavors were subjected to harsh and fundamental criticism, to far-reaching de(con)structions of many different kinds—or, even worse, blunt repudiations. How did this peculiar situation come about? In presenting the internal logic and structure of the natural constitution of human beings as such, philosophical anthropology seemed not only to rely constitutively upon an objective and objectifying comprehension and conception of the human but also, at the same time, to produce and postulate concepts of human being and human life with highly problematic implications. This was partly because it provided the ground for what was, at first, a widely ignored and then, after a transitory and affirmative period, widely rejected and allegedly idealist Weltanschauung of humanism. Such humanism was supposedly enabled politically to criticize really existing social conditions by emphasizing that they are opposed to, or in contradiction with, the true end(s) of human nature. Humanism, thereby, was always a closet Aristotelianism. In other words, a humanist perspective or stance encouraged a criticism of existing social and political circumstances, but only by paying the high price of returning to a metaphysical conception of human nature. Hence, as a consequence of humanism (that is, Aristotelianism), philosophical anthropology was led into a Scylla and Charybdis situation. If human nature is the basis for changing, or at least critically evaluating existing worldly conditions, then a stable basis for performing this very act of criticism is required. Yet, even if this very basis enables us to change or criticize the world, we thereby also implicitly agree that we will never be able to change what allows us to change the world, namely, our own nature. In this way, philosophical anthropology, tending toward humanism, Aristotelianized itself and immediately became a substantialist, human-nature-and-life metaphysics.

A slightly different phrasing of this same conceptual concatenation, which is often associated with the work of the early Karl Marx,[1] emphasizes not only that human beings are the only beings that constantly transform their own nature but also that any society that is fixated has to rely upon a fiction/*fixion* of what human beings are.[2] Such a fiction/fixion may allow for the constitution of a certain form of society (a capitalist one, for example), but as human life constitutively and constantly redetermines itself, any kind of fixion of human nature ultimately turns out to be nothing but an inhuman fiction alienating society from its own subjective life impulse and, therefore, its natural basis. Human nature, in this depiction, is different from the nature of all other beings because it can only properly realize itself within a self-transforming and self-transformative practice. Yet, with this conceptual move, in defining human nature as essentially unfixable, history or historical transformation is turned into the proper nature of mankind. This conception, in other words, basically implies that *history is human nature.*[3] In consequence, we are led to the conclusion that as long as society is alienated from its substantial, subjective ground, we are still living within "the prehistory of human society."[4] Even if one claims that humans do not have a pregiven nature but are only what they are through historical processes of self-transformation (that is, through their very own practices), one cannot but once again naturalize history. History is the nature of human being, and human being, therefore, has no other nature than a self-transforming nature. One thereby establishes not only a normative but also a fundamentally substantialist groundwork. Hence, the essential instability of human nature turns out to be a surprisingly stable assumption. Critical or (self-proclaimed) emancipatory anthropology inferred from this, among other things, that the present state of (capitalist) affairs must be criticized because it fixates, and thereby oppresses, the true, human realization of human nature and hinders real human life and practice.

Anthropology's conception of human nature is either never or always changing, but in both of these "left-wing" versions, so to speak, the characterization of human being cannot but produce a problem when linked to the concept of history or historicity. Both of these versions end up with an ahistorical and invariable nature of human beings: either one that grounds any kind of social or political change and, thus, history (that is, nature is turned into the very basis of history and history is thereby essentially naturalized), or one that ends up with a supposedly historical and transformative nature of the very agent of history (human being) claimed to be so fundamentally historical that it implies the very abolition of any substantial human nature.[5] Yet—and this is the apparent paradox—this very abolition proves itself to be a renewed reinscription of a substantialist nature. Why? Because the only thing that cannot or is not supposed to change—this is the very normative implication of its principal concept—is the constantly changing nature of human beings.

Anthropology, in these first versions, ends up eliminating history conceptually, which means that it ends up in nature. From this, one can see why it may not be overly surprising that both of these anthropological versions were easily converted and then incorporated into the very opposite political orientation, namely, a conservative orientation. The first version, depicting an invariantly unchanging human nature, became quite prominent, with its (still) often-repeated claims about how human nature is essentially self-seeking and egotist (one may think here of Thomas Hobbes and many others) and about how it is thereby only fitted for a competitive surrounding that is best provided by a capitalist mode of social organization.[6] If, in consequence, human nature has substantial character traits, then one could argue that these very traits, which essentially determine any form of human conduct and interaction, contradict any demand to transform society in a fundamental way. In this first, conservative, and anthropological articulation, human nature serves not as an unchangeable foundation, allowing for transformation, but as an unchanging natural ground that prevents change from happening.[7] The given state of society is what it is because of human nature, and those who dream of another state of the world either dream unnatural (and often violent) dreams or have the wrong idea of human nature and, therefore, have to be reminded of it.

The second version—that of the constantly changing nature of human being—reappeared in two different, literally conservative, stances. The first contends that any kind of social construction that is not as dynamic as human nature necessarily hinders productive, creative, and transformative potential deriving from human nature and human life activity. So, in order to function properly, social and political organization has human nature and its internal transformative dynamic as its normative standard. This very normative standard, derived from the substantial constitution of human nature, is then rendered as necessary for a society and its members to be constantly dynamic, moving, and flexible. Societies can only survive if they allow for, and are themselves constantly in the process of, self-transformation. Yet, the laws of these self-transformations are not decided upon deliberately by those subjected to them but are rather presented as natural (one "natural environment" is, for example, the market and its specific laws).[8] The second possible option of how to integrate the self-transforming nature of human beings into an often rather (although not necessarily) conservative framework within anthropology is to emphasize that human beings are deficient by nature, that their nature is weak and given to malfunctioning, and that, therefore, they have to rely upon the compensatory operations of strong institutions in order for them to function.[9] Human nature is thus so weak that it allows only for a social and cultural process of prosthetization that constantly transforms it, precisely because there is no surviving human nature before its cultural and institutional transformation, education, and formation. Human nature is thus unable to determine the society one lives in, because it requires the society it was formed by. Society thus presents itself and culture as the natural destiny of a weak human nature that enables it to overcome its own weakness. In these conservative articulations, one either opted for a human nature that naturally determined a given form of society, or one ended up with a kind of human nature that was unable to decide upon its own laws of transformation, whereupon these very laws were naturalized.

Philosophical anthropology became a conceptual wasteland, as one can infer from this, because all of these versions, conservative as well as emancipatory, remained in one way or another imprisoned within a metaphysical (that is, substantializing) account of (human) nature. The discourse upon human beings and their nature became an uninhabitable terrain because of the naturalizing tendency of this very discourse, ultimately eliding any kind of historicity proper. Anthropology became a wasteland because, in its kingdom, nature ruled and history withered away. Hence, all of the struggles between the conservatives and the emancipators fought upon this now-deserted battleground have mostly turned out to be struggles about (the) ahistorical nature (of human beings). The aftermath of these battles produced a lot of collateral damage for any kind of discourse that came with even the slightest anthropological timbre, which is one of the reasons why, for example, psychoanalysis in general, and Sigmund Freud's theory of the drives in particular, was criticized for turning "historical contingencies into biological necessities"[10] (and some of Freud's critics then further contended that one can infer from his theory the general mechanisms of naturalization and, hence, ideology).[11] Once upon a time philosophical anthropology was a wasteland because it stank of substantialism, metaphysics, and, more precisely, a metaphysics of (human) nature. It naturalized human nature and history became its anathema, an anathema to which it nonetheless constantly referred. Yet, the naturalizing tendency brought with it problems that even exceeded the conflict between emancipatory and conservative positions. The reason for this is conceptual: Substantialism cannot but turn into exclusivism—this is the inheritance of the underlying Aristotelianism[12]—and to exclude some from not only the social and political sphere but also the sphere of humanity as such proves politically (and historically) more than disastrous. Thereby, any discourse that sought to define the human (being) substantially became a highly forbidden and justifiably avoided territory. The dangers of such an attempt included substantializing nature or naturalizing substance (either both at the same time or both at the same time while trying to avoid both at the same time); political and ontological exclusivism; and so on.

Then Habit . . .

Then, not so long ago, there was a resurgence of interest in philosophical anthropology. Neobiologisms or non-neobiologisms are now in vogue, and many forms of philosophical vitalism encourage the return to anthropological speculations. Nature philosophy has also returned, as well as new materialisms that not only redefine matter but also, with the same stroke, revivify (even if explicitly seeking to downplay) the definitions of human nature. And theories of second nature have become predominant in many philosophical camps. How did this happen, if, prior to this moment, things had stood so badly for anthropology? This question is less difficult to answer than it may initially appear, since the resurgence of interest in anthropology was, in a certain sense, already inscribed in what brought about its very decline. What was needed was a nonsubstantialist discourse upon human nature, and taking seriously the different versions of substantialist, anthropological claims brought this about.[13] If one is left with the option of an unchangeable human nature that grounds or prohibits social and political change, or a constantly changing nature that allows for or prohibits it, then one can infer that the very conflict between the two different versions of the two different sides is responsible for defining not only human nature but also anthropology. Human nature in anthropology is split between dynamic and static, unchanging and unchangeably changing, determinations, and this very split also splits the very discourse that seeks to determine human nature. In this sense, anthropology lost substance because of its substantialism, and this made returning to anthropology and human nature possible.

To make this more comprehensible, consider the following (highly reductive) schema.

Human Nature and Change in Anthropology

Unchangeable Human Nature	Constantly Changing (Determinate or Indeterminate) Human Nature	Unchangeable Human Nature	Constantly Changing (Determinate or Indeterminate) Human Nature
Pro-change	Pro-change	Against Change	Against Change

Where does the real struggle reside? Where does the lack of substance occur? Obviously, between the first two and second two columns, where an antagonism runs through the very definition of human nature and, thus, anthropology, its defining discourse. There is a contradiction in the conception of human nature, and the unity of this difference is the very structure of anthropology. Yet, by understanding its structure—reading it as a wasteland or battlefield—it loses its substantialist character. That is, by taking the overdetermined (overdetermined because it is finally determined by some unchangeable determining factor) contradiction at its heart seriously (positing the two columns against each other), anthropology is led to the insight that there is no stable definition of human being and life, either as simply transformative or as simply resisting transformation. It is constitutively both, as well as both changing and unchanging. Human nature is a battlefield (and its definition results from the anthropological struggles fought thereon). Taking this seriously means that anthropology has lost its inherent substantialist character and has to address its immanent contradiction. And, because, as a famous saying goes, this must be undertaken "not only as *Substance*, but equally as *Subject*,"[14] this may be one of the reasons why most, if not all, of the currently resurgent renewals or revivifications of anthropology start from or, at one point, turn to G. W. F. Hegel—and this goes for so-called continental as well as analytic and pragmatic approaches.

After all, is Hegel not the thinker of contradictions between contradicting positions that are, at the same time, peculiarly bound together in a unity of opposition? This is why it is not a great surprise that the resurgence of interest in anthropology coemerged with a resurgence of interest in a part of the Hegelian system that was, for quite a long time, not only neglected but also considered an uninhabitable wasteland of its own, namely, his philosophy of nature (as well as his philosophy of human nature included within his philosophy of subjective spirit). Of course, Hegel's anthropology is seemingly not a part of his philosophy of nature, but in some sense it still is, since it is the transition out of nature that is both part of nature and also no longer nature. So, anthropology is both in nature and not in nature, or, in other words, it deals with the specificity of human nature.[15] But what can one learn from Hegel's anthropology that exceeds anthropology's previous substantialism? It was the achievement of Catherine Malabou[16] and Slavoj Žižek,[17] among others, to have brought attention to the centrality of the concept of habit in Hegel's philosophy, a concept that provides the answer to the question above. Habit is a concept that is supposed to circumvent, conceptually, all unchanging, substantialist traits of human nature, as well as being crucial to any kind of human practice. It thus stands at the heart of properly human life. It is relevant not only to Hegel's account of the formation of subjectivity or subjective spirit but also to his account of socio-political phenomena, or what he calls "objective spirit," and one may go so far as to assume that it plays a crucial role even for the constitution of absolute spirit, that is, the spheres of art, religion, and philosophy. The concept of habit appears in the transition from his philosophy of nature to his philosophy of mind, in the first part of the third and final volume of *Encyclopedia of the Philosophical Sciences*, entitled "Subjective Spirit," where he deals with the (natural and spiritual) formation of the subject. This part begins with anthropology (before moving on to phenomenology, psychology, and then objective and absolute spirit).[18]

Habit is an element of what Hegel calls the "feeling soul."[19] As has been argued many times before, it is a formational category, since, by means of habit, one is able to transform one's nature into another kind of nature; hence, *habit* is synonymous with *second nature*. Habit is formational and transformative because it is only through habit that one is able to get used to things and activities (from breathing to walking, talking, and so on) by making these activities part of one's own self-feeling (that is, one cannot imagine oneself without having these capacities), which is why habit is part of the "feeling soul." Habitualized things seem as if they were inscribed into our very nature because they are habitualized, second *nature*, and yet acquired and, hence, cultural—precisely because this nature is *second* nature. Everything we are is, in an abstract sense, habitualized and, hence, not naturally inherited. By means of habit, one is able to do several complex things at once (speaking while walking, smoking while thinking, and so on). I do not intend to present a detailed study of habit here; however, the present return to anthropology—and, more specifically, Hegel's anthropology—raises the issue when one asks a simple question: If there is only a transformed, always only second nature, a nature determined by the very practice that habitualizes the subject, what is the nature of the transformed nature? This question becomes even more pertinent if one takes into account that Hegel's anthropology does not start with habit but with something else, to which I will return shortly. So, what is the nature that is transformed through the practice of spirit? Or, to put the question differently, does spirit inherit anything from nature? Is there anything that naturally determines spirit? Or, again, we can ask, is there a first nature? Is there, and can there be, any theory of inheritance in Hegel, or does his theory of habit systematically exclude it?[20]

The first answer would seem to be a straightforward "No"—there is no inheritance whatsoever that would not fundamentally be an inheritance of spirit to spirit. Of course, by means of habit, culture is formed and one inherits cultural practices that have already been created; yet, there seems to be no natural element of inheritance involved (although some claim that second nature is simply another kind of nature and, hence, spirit never leaves behind what it tries to liberate itself from).[21] If, in "Subjective Spirit," spirit begins to form itself only by forming a second nature, then one can see why Hegel can explicitly state that "spirit does not naturally emerge from nature."[22] If spirit does not naturally emerge from nature, this is simply because it always is "its own result," and thus nature cannot be "the absolutely immediate, first, originary positing," but rather one of the preconditions that spirit "makes for itself,"[23] and from which it emerges. Spirit does not emerge from nature naturally, but because, in the beginning, spirit cannot but (also) naturalize itself, the emergence of spirit is fundamentally spiritual. This is the seemingly paradoxical movement: Spirit naturalizes itself—taking nature as its precondition—yet naturalization is an act of spirit.

Might one not therefore assume that the only thing spirit inherits is the product of spirit, which spirit dedicates to inherit itself? Yes, but what precisely does this mean? If Hegel claims that, "as it is by nature or immediately, humanity is what it ought not to be, and that, as spirit, humanity has instead the vocation to become explicitly [for itself] what in its natural state it still is only implicitly [in itself],"[24] then it seems that the only thing that transforms humanity into humanity, spirit into spirit, is the very act of transforming what seems to have the status of an immediate, natural givenness, and that one of the means to do this—maybe the most crucial one—is habit, that is, the formation of a second nature. Furthermore, everything that appears to be an immediate, natural given is already posited by spirit in an act of naturalization. Does it not therefore seem useless to inquire into a Hegelian conception of inheritance? One can complicate this picture by asking the following question: What does spirit inherit, as that which it needs to transform, such that it is what spirit posited, as that which it needs to trans-form? If there is nothing given in Hegel, not even nothing, how does one conceive of that which is less than nothing, which we somehow inherit?

Before Hegel introduces the concept of habit in the "Anthropology" sec-tion of *Encyclopedia of the Philosophical Sciences*, he unfolds a concept that, at least at first sight, seems to provide the ground for unfolding a Hegelian conception of inheritance. This concept is what he calls *Naturell*,[25] which can be translated as "disposition." Yet, in German, the reference to nature is obvious if there is a Naturell of spirit, and one aspect of this concept provides an answer to the question above, that is, the concept of "genius," which I will expound below. To approach this concept, one should first note that, while introducing it, Hegel first explains why he begins his exposition the way he does. This is because "[o]ne [. . .] cannot begin with spirit as such, but must begin with its inadequate reality. Spirit *is* already spirit in the beginning, but it does not know that it is spirit."[26] Spirit begins inadequately. Spirit's beginning is a failed beginning. The inadequate reality of spirit is what Hegel refers to as *nature*.[27] So, nature is spirit in an inadequate form, but this is also to say that, in the very beginning, spirit is natural simply because it is not (yet) spirit. It is *a* spirit, which is not spirit, because it is spirit that does not know what it is; therefore, it is not what it is. Its inadequacy is measured and articulated in terms of knowledge. Spirit is there in the beginning, but it does not know that it is there in the beginning;[28] therefore, it *is*, positively, *not-there*, *not-spirit* in the beginning. It does not know that it is there and, hence, it is a spirit that does not know where, what, or even that it is. In its beginning, spirit is disoriented and will only slowly start to sense that it is and what it is (once it is the "feeling soul"). Spirit springs from its own inad-equacy, which is why it will ultimately be its own result. It springs from its own inadequacy because spirit cannot simply begin with itself as such, but it emerges from its own failure to grasp itself. In this sense, one may say that spirit begins even before spirit begins and that it is there before it is properly there. Yet, if "[s]pirit is essentially only what it knows about itself,"[29] and spirit does not yet know it is spirit, then spirit is not spirit in the beginning of spirit. Spirit begins before spirit begins, yet this beginning is a beginning because the spirit that begins before spirit begins is not (yet) spirit, simply because spirit has not yet begun. Spirit is there before spirit is there, but only as the absence of spirit (as spirit that does not know what it is and, therefore, that is not what it is). Spirit is there and not there before its own beginning. It is there only as the absence of spirit and is thus its own failed anticipation. The name for this presence of spirit in the mode of its absence is *nature*. Why nature? Because the positive (in both the trivial as well as Hegel's sense of the term) concept of the absence of spirit—the other of spirit—is nature. But, given the foregoing, how does spirit emerge from its own absence?

Spirit's Nature

As Hegel states, "[s]pirit, *for us*, has its *presupposition in nature*."[30] Does spirit thus inherit anything from and by nature if nature is the other of spirit, that is, if nature is spirit's absence, or, more precisely, if spirit is not (yet) being spirit? Is there anything that the presence of the absence of spirit hands over to spirit? What is the status of this peculiar presupposition? In order to elaborate this, recall that Hegel classifies three forms of spirit: first, a spirit immanently relating to itself; second, a spirit relating to something outside of itself; and, third, a spirit relating to something outside of itself as being (posited by) itself. These are subjective, objective, and absolute spirit, respectively. It is important to note that spirit, from the very beginning, is part of (absolute) spirit, which is why it is only "for us" (from the perspective of absolute spirit, that is, philosophy) that it has its presupposition in nature (that is, in the absence of spirit). But it is also important to note that, "as such," spirit does not presuppose nature, since there is simply no given, nor is there an objective nature there before spirit that could serve as its prespiritual precondition. Spirit presupposes nature, that is, its own absence, and the name of this presupposition is *nature*. Yet, it does not simply presuppose itself negatively as absent; instead, it presupposes its own absence by determining this very absence and assigning (natural) qualities to it. If spirit is absent, then there is an other (of spirit ultimately in spirit) that fills (and physically embodies) this very absence, namely, nature, and thus nature can be determined.

The way in which spirit presupposes itself as a natural determination is by assigning to its own absence qualities marked by the absence of spirit, and it does this in such a way that these qualities bear the traits of its absence. In other words, if spirit is what is able to determine itself, then the absence of spirit (as spirit's precondition) is marked by unchangeable laws, natural cycles, heteronomous determinations, and so on. Spirit thereby determines its own absence (we are thus dealing with the positive feature of a determinate negation). Yet, to repeat, spirit, at its own beginning—that is, at the beginning of subjective spirit—does not know that it is spirit and, therefore, appears to itself in the form of (given) natural determinations that are what determine its own absence.[31] Spirit thereby appears to itself in the form of something other than what it is.[32] Yet, spirit is "not the mere result of nature, but rather truly its own result; it yields itself from the presuppositions that it lays itself."[33] This is why nature is thus not simply a given presupposition; it is posited by spirit as the absence of spirit, but this very absence of spirit—of which spirit does not know it has posited—starts to determine spirit. One can therefore say that nature emerges as soon as spirit believes there are given presuppositions (and that it does not know them as self-posited).

However, as soon as one starts believing in the givenness of the objective presuppositions one has posited, but forgets or ignores the act of positing, then these very presuppositions start to determine oneself externally. It is precisely this form of determination that is at stake at the beginning of spirit. Nature is then the name for the idea that there is something, anything at all, before it is posited. It is the assumption that there is a *there is* before positing, yet it is this very assumption that is posited and then forgotten. This means that one is determined by something posited as if it was not posited. Nature, here, thus appears as a posited myth of the given whose act of positing is forgotten. One can, in an abstract way, contend that if there is any kind of natural inheritance at work here, it is natural precisely in the sense delineated above. What one inherits from nature one inherits because one does not know that one posited what determines oneself, taking it as a given. In other words, it seems there is only inheritance at the beginning of spirit because spirit fails to grasp that there is nothing to inherit (since everything is posited by spirit). Yet, spirit, in the beginning, cannot but fail to know that there is nothing to inherit, and this is why there is natural inheritance. Spirit thus inherits a peculiar "nothing" that it brought about and onto itself.

Spirit springs from the process of spirit itself positing a precondition and ignoring the positedness of this very precondition. This leads spirit to believe that there is a (natural and objective) ground for its own being. Spirit should know that any presupposition is posited (since spirit is the positing agent), but it somehow does not know what it knows. Yet, this is how spirit emerges from nature, that is, from spirit not knowing that it knows something it does not know. Because it does not know what it knows, spirit inherits something from and by nature. To simplify matters, this means that, conceptually, there is, for Hegel, no natural path that leads from nature to spirit (since there is no nature without spirit misconceiving itself).[34] The only way to get from nature to spirit is by means of spirit, simply because nature is failed spirit. Yet, this very failure makes the move from nature to spirit appear as if there is also a natural determination involved.

But how can we account more precisely for the transition from a spirit that does not know what it is, and thus appears as the natural determination of spirit, to the awakening of spirit to itself? Hegel situates this beginning in "Subjective Spirit," which further divides into three distinct domains: "Anthropology," "Phenomenology," and "Psychology." "Anthropology" deals with spirit in itself, which Hegel calls "soul," "natural spirit," or (literally) "spirit in nature" (*Naturgeist*). Spirit, in the very beginning, is in nature (it is there only by being *not-there*). "Phenomenology" deals with consciousness, and "Psychology" deals with spirit as such, that is, spirit that can be differentiated into three forms, namely, abstract universality (soul), particularity (consciousness), and singularity (spirit for itself). But it is "Anthropology" that deals with the overall "groundwork of man."[35] As Catherine Malabou formulates succinctly,

> [t]he course of the *Anthropology* as a whole explicates the process whereby originary substance, leaving behind the natural world, progressively differentiates itself until it becomes an individual subject. This movement unfolds in three moments which structure the exposition: self-identity, rupture, return to unity. The meaning of this division organizes itself in the process of the soul's *singularization* which, from its beginning in the "universal" (understood as "the immaterialism of nature" or "simple ideal life"), moves progressively towards self-individuation until it becomes "singular self." From the "sleep of spirit" to the "soul as work of art" the genesis of the individual is accomplished, that individual which, configured as the "Man," finally stands forth in the guise of a statue.
>
> If the anthropological development appears to be a progressive illumination, it does produce some abrupt returns to obscurity, some moments of trial and error, some aberrations. The spirit that awakens knows also crises of somnambulism, delirious manias; at times it consults the stars or magnetizers, at times it weeps endlessly over those it has lost whom it never managed properly to mourn. It haunts its own depths, its own night, failing to commit to the individuation which will be its definitive splendour.
>
> The unfurling of the process of individuation is the constitution of the "Self" (*Selbst*), the founding instance of subjectivity.[36]

The course of Hegel's "Anthropology" begins with "spirit that is still based in nature, and still related to its embodiment."[37] This is why the primary object of "Anthropology" is "the soul bound to natural determinations,"[38] that is, natural determinations that determine that which appears to be determined by the absence of spirit (which is nonetheless posited by spirit, albeit unknowingly). These natural determinations of spirit appear to spirit, for example, in the form of racial differences (in the form of an assumption that, say, the French think differently than the Japanese, simply because of the natural, geographical determining factors of France and Japan). As Malabou again states,

> [t]he soul's determinations are in the first instance the "natural qualities" which make up its initial "being-there" (*Dasein*). [. . .] But what, for the *Anthropology*, are these "qualities"?
>
> They are divided into three types following a hierarchy based on their degree of differentiation. The first type includes such qualities as "differences of climate, changes of the seasons, times of the day, etc.," connected to "the general planetary life." Spirit lives this life "in agreement with it" [. . .]. These first natural qualities can be classified under the generic term of "influences," in the original sense of that physical and fluid force believed by ancient physics to proceed from the heavens and the stars and act upon men, animals and things. These "physical qualities" determine the soul's correspondence to "cosmic, sidereal, and telluric life." [. . .]
>
> The second group of "natural qualities" contains those of the specialized "nature-governed spirits" (*Naturgeister*) which constitute the "diversity of races."
>
> The third set of "qualities" consists of those which can be called "local spirits" (*Lokalgeister*). These are "shown in the outward modes of life (*Lebensart*) and occupation (*Beschäftigung*), bodily structure and *disposition* (*körperlicher Bildung und Disposition*), but still more in the inner tendency and capacity (*Befähigung*) of the intellectual and moral character of the peoples."[39]

So, the first and, therefore, most inadequate natural form with which spirit presupposes itself (as being absent or, more precisely, not-yet spirit) is the form of the soul. Spirit knows itself as soul and not yet as spirit. The soul thus appears to be something that is given, besides the givenness of the absence of spirit. This is an important point, since the soul is natural in the sense that it appears to spirit as a given and not as posited, yet it appears to spirit as given to the presence of spirit itself, whereby the complete (but nonetheless posited) absence of spirit is overcome. Yet, as the very givenness of the soul still implies the absence of spirit conceptually (since it is not conceived of as being posited), it ends up being determined conceptually by physical, natural, and local determinations. The soul is thus spirit not knowing what it is and taking an always already naturally determined form of itself as given. Spirit assumes that it is naturally given to itself in the form of the soul. But it is important to observe that, with the soul, an important differentiation appears. For the soul is not simply nature but immaterial; it is the beginning of spirit (Hegel calls this the "immateriality of nature,"[40] since the soul still appears to spirit as naturally determined, and it is natural in view of the fact that it comes with seemingly nonposited given qualities). Hegel calls it a "*simple* universality."[41] Spirit posits a determinate presupposition of itself that is separate from nature as such (the pure absence of spirit), and its determination is as general and simple as it can be—it is just that there is a givenness of spirit. Spirit assumes itself to be given; yet, it does not recognize that there is always already an act of positing involved, that it posits itself as a presupposition of itself. If the unacknowledged positing of a given presupposition leads spirit into nature, the unacknowledged positing of itself as a given presupposition—that is, as a presupposition of its own givenness—leads spirit to assume a (naturally given) soul that differs from nature because of its immaterial (yet still natural) qualities. This is why Hegel can contend that the soul names "the universal immateriality of nature [. . .], the sleep of spirit [. . .], that is *potentially* everything."[42] The soul is spirit sleeping, but with sleep also comes dreams (of oneself).

Spirit posits itself as its own presupposition and, thereby, posits itself as being different from nature. Yet, this difference from nature still appears to be a difference that is given and is, therefore, still natural (and not posited). Spirit posits itself as a soul that is different from nature yet still in nature (spirit as given and not as its own result). One can see here how the seemingly unavoidable failure of spirit to take its own act of positing into account leads to the assumption that spirit is not simply given but, because of this very givenness, determined by factors that exceed the grasp of spirit. Spirit sleeps and dreams of itself, but what and how it dreams does not appear to spirit to be its own fabrication (although it is, as Freud will also expound). Spirit's dreams seem to come from a source outside of spirit and, thereby, spirit seems to inherit its very being (or existence) through nature. Spirit inherits its dreams as well as itself. But wherefrom? This question is what awakens spirit.

The soul thus grounds the process of the awakening of spirit (to itself) because it does not appear merely as a simple universality but as a "singularity,"[43] that is, in the steps that follow, Hegel will start to differentiate and individualize the assumption of the givenness of determinations by differentiating these very determinations of givenness. Spirit assumes that it has a given, determined nature (a nature of spirit whose nature is different from nature as such), and it slowly starts to grasp and conceive of it. This makes a difference because spirit thereby unknowingly acknowledges that there are different forms of how to posit a presupposition, and positing the soul as the form of how spirit is given determinately specifies the act of positing a presupposition. Spirit slowly begins to make a real difference.

Soul Mates

For Hegel, the soul is generally divided into three different forms: the natural soul, the feeling soul, and the actual soul. Thus far, I have discussed the natural soul, the assumption of the natural givenness of spirit. The natural soul is not yet individualized in any specific manner. Its concept is the embodiment of the assumption that there are general qualitative determinations, "the physical as well as psychical *racial differences* in humanity,"[44] that is, differences that allow for individualization and differentiation of the one, simple, universal, and natural soul (one differentiates and individualizes the presupposition that there is a presupposition).[45] Yet, this process of differentiation not only produces external, natural differences (of races) but also allows for an inner differentiation and individualization of human beings as such. For example, it generates the assumption that there are unchangeable natural ages not only of individuals but also of races and states (childhood, youth, adult life, and so on). This is because a natural form of change determines the soul and also because spirit assumes that it cannot but be subject to these same natural determinations. Hegel demonstrates this movement by showing that the (universal) natural soul lives a "universal planetary life"; in other words, it is determined by "the differences of climates, the changes of the seasons, and the periods of the day."[46] The life of spirit, in the form of the natural soul, is a natural life determined by natural changes (climatic changes, for instance). Spirit presupposes itself as given, in the form of the soul—as something that is different from nature (the absence of spirit)—only thereby to reintroduce nature as the determining instance of its own givenness. Yet, this determining instance is thereby particularized and individualized, which is why this process of internal differentiation continues such that one moves from races to "local spirits,"[47] that is, local cultures, local ethical communities, and so on. One may say that one moves here from racial to national differences and that this move is the reassertion of spirit, since spirit is determined by nature, yet this very determination leads spirit to redetermine that which determines it—and, in this process, it is again and again led back into naturalizing that which it assumes to be a determining instance.

It should be obvious that this continuous differentiation of different determinations leads to an increasing degree of particularization of what spirit assumes to be a given precondition for itself (for example, spirit assumes that being born in Italy and, thereby, into certain Italian customs, which are given, makes a different spirit than being born, say, in Turkey). One moves from effects of climatic conditions to races, national communities and their customs, intra-family relations (that is, the naturally determining impact of mothers upon their children), and so on. Hegel claims that this particularization appears in the form of "special temperament, talent, character, physiognomy, or other dispositions and idiosyncrasies of families or singular individuals."[48] We thus move from planetary to geographically and climatically determined life, from national, communal life to the individual family, and the individual within a family to life as an individual. It is precisely here that one can draw nearer to the concept of inheritance. Hegel states that the effect of natural determinations within a family operate such that "the peculiarity of an individual has different sides to it. One distinguishes it by means of the determination of the disposition [Naturell], temperament, and character."[49] But what is a Naturell?

Approaching Genius

Hegel defines Naturell in §395 of Encyclopedia of the Philosophical Sciences as "natural dispositions in contrast to that which a human being has acquired by means of its own activity."[50] A natural disposition is thus not a habit (although it is unknowingly posited in the sense elaborated above). This is why this disposition can be characterized as "innate"[51]—an astonishing claim for (any Hegelian) spirit! Spirit unknowingly presupposes itself as given, that is, as soul, and yet, some part of the determinate character of this very givenness (the natural disposition) is, or at least appears to be, innate. This implies at least two things. First, spirit unknowingly presupposes itself such that it is given as different to nature; at the same time, however, it presupposes itself such that it still has the fundamental quality of nature, namely, the unchangeability of its constitution (although, here, the natural disposition is highly individualized). Spirit presupposes itself as given and takes this to be an unalterable fact. At the beginning of spirit, and for spirit, spirit has no beginning, which is why its beginning is a necessarily and conceptually failed beginning. Second, this clarifies why spirit cannot but presuppose a natural disposition of itself (which is why it is innate). Spirit—that is, at least, subjective spirit, spirit in the beginning, ignoring its beginning—is stuck with the assumption that it has a given ground that it cannot alter. Spirit cannot alter the assumption that there is something it cannot alter. That which spirit cannot alter is the assumption of the givenness of itself; thus, it presupposes an innate ground, namely, itself in the form of a natural disposition.

Part of this unalterable, natural disposition of spirit, Hegel asserts, is what one calls *talent* and *genius*: "Both words express a determined direction which the individual spirit has received by nature."[52] Yet, whereas talent produces something new within a given, particular field (someone is talented in painting pictures, for example), genius is able to "create a new species."[53] Talent is a given, but a given that remains within the domain of the given. Genius is a given that alters the given and creates something new. Within the unalterable given, natural condition of spirit, there is one that is repetitive and one that is transformative. Spirit thus differentiates here its own presupposition into two different, innate parts. Yet—and here things get even more complex—both talent and genius "have to be cultivated in a universally valid way."[54] It gets more complex when this very cultivation follows a natural logic (since one assumes that one simply cultivates and does not posit a given), and cultivation thus follows the logic of the life ages of childhood, adult life, geriatric life, and so on. Here, education and institutions (kindergarten, school, and so on) play a crucial role. Spirit thereby constantly senses (this is the feeling soul) that it is not simply given but that it takes itself to be given and, thereby, ends up in natural determinations (which is why Hegel claims that this very oscillation of spirit is the natural change between waking life and sleeping spirit). Hegel thus shows that, because we are still within natural determinations, the very rhythm and law of the waking and sleeping life of spirit is not determined by spirit but nature. It appears to be natural to spirit that it is spirit and that it is also given without positing itself. Yet, only one of the two states (*Zustände*) generates a form of feeling (*Empfindung*), namely, waking life. Only in waking life does spirit sense that it is spirit and, hence, not simply naturally given. This feeling, which is what makes the natural soul into the feeling soul, is not natural but a form of the self-relation of spirit. It is a "judgment,"[55] namely, the judgment that spirit is there and given. Although this judgment ignores the self-positing act of spirit, it posits a relation to that which does not appear to have been posited. But it is an erroneous judgment, a judgment that "is the form of the dull weaving of spirit"[56] in which a particular content appears. Spirit feels itself, and it feels itself as being something particular (it does not feel the whole nature, nor its innate disposition, but something specific). Yet, feeling is the "worst form of spirit,"[57] because it feels something by relying upon the assumption that the very groundwork for that feeling is something simply given, such as the soul.

Hegel then distinguishes between two types of feeling: those that are produced by exterior impulses and those that are expressions of internal impulses. Yet, one can see here that this distinction collapses immediately, since the soul is something internally external because it is assumed to be given to spirit. It is here that Hegel clarifies that the concept of feeling implies at least three things. First, it implies that the determinations appearing within it are transient and singular, although, as such, they also imply a sense of self.[58] Although they do not last, they are always feelings of the soul. Second, feeling implies a passivity of the soul. Hegel here toys around with the etymology of Empfindung, referring it back to *finden*, that is, "to find something" (that is given). The soul finds a feeling whereby it is related to something that did not originate in itself. The soul thereby does what spirit does when there is a soul. The soul takes something to be simply given and not posited. This leads the soul to feel something, and what it feels always actualizes the feeling of its own givenness, which is why feeling is a determining, individualizing factor of the givenness of the soul. Third, feeling can originate, although from what it originates is not immediately and physically present at hand (say, to the senses). One can feel bad as a consequence of something that is not simply physical, so the origin of a feeling can lie in something that is not physical. Feeling thus differentiates the concept of givenness from itself, insofar as a feeling can emerge from something that is given in a form different from objective, apparent givenness (which is why feeling always implies self-feeling, since the self—or, in other words, the soul—is also given, but in a nonobjective way).

Hegel derives from feeling the concept of the individual soul. And it is precisely here, in §405 of *Encyclopedia of the Philosophical Sciences*, that he further specifies the notion of genius. The soul that feels has a sense of individuality, since it also always feels itself. Yet, it does not properly have a sense of self, since what it feels comes to it from something that is as much given as the soul itself. This is why he can state that "[t]he feeling soul in its immediacy" is not itself.[59] The soul feels itself but it does not feel itself as itself, which also means that spirit does not recognize itself in the soul and the soul does not recognize itself as the determining agent of feeling. But as what does the soul feel itself when it feels itself, such that it only passively feels itself? Hegel's answer is *an other subject*.

Inheriting Genius; or, Hegel's Mother

Hegel's paradigm for this other subject is the mother. The mother "is the genius of the child,"[60] and what Hegel here defines as genius is the "intensive form of individuality."[61] First of all, this means that the mother-child relation is somehow like a version of the spirit-soul relation. The child cannot but take the mother as a given, simply because it takes itself as a given (it is given to itself by the mother, which must have been given in order to give a child). But what does the mother give to the child? Hegel's answer is fourfold. First, the mother gives to the child the child itself. Second, the mother gives to the child its (the child's as well as the mother's) individuality, and, thereby, the mother gives itself to the child. It is the paradigm of givenness for the child (the source of all its feelings—before it has been born at least). Third, the mother gives to the child its individuality in the form of genius, as "concentrated individuality."[62] Genius is "concentrated" in that it condenses the individuality of the child with that of the mother. The child within the mother feels what the mother feels and, thereby, the mother becomes the paradigm of the other subject to which spirit constitutively relates. Fourth, the mother gives to the child the concept of givenness (the givenness of the mother, genius, and, most importantly, the child itself).

Here, it is important to recall that genius, for Hegel, also defines that which allows for the creation of a new species. The mother thus gives to the child that which she is herself, namely, what makes her into a mother: the act of creating something new.[63] What the child thus inherits from its mother is nothing but the possibility—not a capacity—to generate something that exceeds the given coordinates, a possibility that exceeds all capacities and that is not a given, that is, a possibility beyond the possible, an im-possibility. Yet, Hegel clearly states that the mother is the genius of the child. Does the mother thus possess genius, in the sense of a kind of capacity that is transmitted to the child? One can unfold here a simple argument, namely, that the mother has been a child and, thus, genius is also something that has been passed on to her. Genius names a possibility that is not—although it is necessarily mistakenly perceived as if it were—a natural disposition. Genius is that which names the quality to posit new presuppositions. And if the mother gives this possibility to the child, can one not conclude that there is no mother of this possibility (not simply because every mother has been a child but, in addition, because one can never assume this possibility is a given)? For every mother there is a mother; at the same time, there is no Mother of all mothers. Hegel's theory of inheritance thus leads to the surprising conclusion that *there is no Mother*; not only is there ultimately no mother of that which is inherited—there is no *sujet supposé de l'avoir* (supposed subject of having)—but also the only thing spirit, reason, and all of us *can* inherit is genius, the im-possibility (*die Un-Möglichkeit*) of positing new presuppositions.

Notes

1. Erich Fromm was one of the most prominent proponents of a humanist Marx. See Fromm, *Marx's Concept of Man* (New York: Continuum, 2004). For a cognitive map of the different reactions to humanism, see Frank Ruda, "Humanism Reconsidered, or: Life Living Life," *Filozofski vestnik* 30, no. 2 (2009): 175–93.

2. Jacques Lacan introduces the term *fixion*, with an *x*, in "L'étourdit," in *Autres écrits*, ed. Jacques-Alain Miller (Paris: Éditions du Seuil, 2001), 483.

3. See Robert B. Brandom, *A Spirit of Trust: A Semantic Reading of Hegel's "Phenomenology of Spirit"* (unpublished typescript, 2014 draft), http://www.pitt.edu/.

4. Karl Marx, "Marx on the History of His Opinions," in *The Marx-Engels Reader*, 2nd ed., ed. Robert C. Tucker (New York: W. W. Norton, 1978), 5.

5. According to one version of this kind of anthropological claim, there is no pregiven nature of mankind, since human nature is essentially indeterminate. Yet, positing the indeterminateness of human nature ultimately means that either human nature is what humans make of it or it is always essentially indeterminate. The former version leads to the consequences described above, whereas the latter substantializes indeterminacy (one may think here of Jean-Paul Sartre).

6. For more on this theory, see two chapters in the (by now) classic study by C. B. Macpherson, "Hobbes: The Political Obligation of the Market" and "The Levellers: Franchise and Freedom," in *The Political Theory of Possessive Individualism: Hobbes to Locke* (New York: Oxford University Press, 2011), 9–106, 107–59.

7. This is why, for example, Max Horkheimer once remarked, opposing such claims, that "[t]he argument that has been advanced against any concept of historically necessary transformations, namely that such a concept is contrary to human nature, must be put to rest once and for all." Horkheimer, "Remarks on Philosophical Anthropology," in *Between Philosophy and Social Science: Selected Early Writings*, trans. G. Frederick Hunter, Matthew S. Kramer, and John Torpey (Cambridge: MIT Press, 1993), 174. One should also mention that Joseph Stalin's idea of creating a new man is somehow a determinately negating conceptual consequence of this definition of human nature.

8. For an analysis of flexibility, in opposition to "plasticity," see Catherine Malabou, "Introduction: Plasticity and Flexibility—For a Consciousness of the Brain," in *What Should We Do with Our Brain?* trans. Sebastian Rand (New York: Fordham University Press, 2008), 1–14.

9. One may think here, for example, of Arnold Gehlen. See, for instance, *Man, His Nature and Place in the World*, trans. Clare McMillan and Karl Pillemer (New York: Columbia University Press, 1988).

10. Herbert Marcuse, *Eros and Civilization: A Philosophical Inquiry into Freud* (Boston: Beacon Press, 1955), 34.

11. See ibid., 34–35: "The 'unhistorical' character of the Freudian concepts thus contains the elements of its opposite."

12. For some implications of this, see Jacques Rancière, *Disagreement: Politics and Philosophy*, trans. Julie Rose (Minnesota: University of Minnesota Press, 1999), and for a complication of this reading, see Giorgio Agamben, *Homo Sacer: Sovereign Power and Bare Life*, trans. Daniel Heller-Roazen (Stanford: Stanford University Press, 1998).

13. It is worth noting that, already in 1970, Theodor W. Adorno (a critic of substantialist anthropology) praised Ulrich Sonnemann's *Negative Anthropologie*. See Adorno, "Zu Ulrich Sonnemanns 'Negative Anthropologie,'" in *Gesammelte Schriften*, ed. Rolf Tiedemann, Gretel Adorno, Susan Buck-Morss, and Klaus Schultz, vol. 20, pt. 1 (Frankfurt am Main: Suhrkamp, 1986), 262–63. The return to anthropological questions is thus neither particularly new nor a proper return, simply because the very historical moment of anthropology's overcoming coincided with a return to it (a very Adornian motive), or, in other words, the moment the substantialist discourse lost all substance (and became a wasteland) is the same moment this discourse can be taken up again.

14. G. W. F. Hegel, *Phenomenology of Spirit*, trans. A. V. Miller (Oxford: Oxford University Press, 1977), 10; emphasis in original.

15. One of the first volumes to deal with Hegel's philosophy of nature is *Hegel and the Philosophy of Nature*, ed. Stephen Houlgate (Albany: State University of New York Press, 1998). Subjective spirit does not play a significant role in it at all.

16. See Malabou, *The Future of Hegel: Plasticity, Temporality, and Dialectic*, trans. Lisabeth During (New York: Routledge 2005).

17. See Slavoj Žižek, "Discipline between Two Freedoms: Madness and Habit in German Idealism," in *Mythology, Madness, and Laughter: Subjectivity in German Idealism*, by Markus Gabriel and Slavoj Žižek (New York: Continuum, 2009), 95–121.

18. I have also contributed to the long list of Hegelian habit studies, investigating the role habit plays in objective spirit. See Ruda, "The Lost Habit: Elements of a Hegelian Theory of Laziness/Foulness," in *Hegel's Rabble: An Investigation into Hegel's Philosophy of Right* (New York: Continuum, 2011), 75–99.

19. The concept of habit appears in §409, after Hegel gives an account of "self-feeling" and the "feeling soul in its immediacy." See Hegel, *Philosophy of Mind*, trans. William Wallace (Oxford: Clarendon Press, 1894), 39.

20. Obviously, Hegel has a legal theory of inheritance that concerns family relations, which he develops in *The Philosophy of Right*. Here, I am focusing solely upon the "biological" or "natural" meaning of inheritance. For more on the former, see Hegel, *Outlines of the Philosophy of Right*, ed. Stephen Houlgate, trans. T. M. Knox (New York: Oxford University Press, 2008), 175–76.

21. One may think here of the work of Hubert L. Dreyfus. One may also recall that, for Hegel, even breathing is something a human child first has to learn when it is born, to which it then becomes immediately habitualized. Yet, the fact that there are human bodies that need to breathe, as well as air and an atmosphere, cannot really be said to be just an effect of culture (although "atmosphere" is clearly a cultural concept).

22. Here, and in the following, I cite the German, critical edition, since it includes the additions (*Zusätze*) provided by Hegel's pupils, which were written in a Hegelian spirit and are often highly instructive. Hegel, *Enzyklopädie der philosophischen Wissenschaften im Grundrisse, Dritter Teil*, in *Werke*, vol. 10 (Frankfurt am Main: Suhrkamp, 1970), 25. All translations of the text appearing here are my own.

23. Ibid., 24.

24. Hegel, *Lectures on the History of Philosophy 1825–6: Medieval and Modern Philosophy*, rev. ed., ed. Robert F. Brown, trans. R. F. Brown and J. M. Stewart, vol. 3 (New York: Clarendon Press, 1990), 21.

25. Hegel, *Enzyklopädie der philosophischen Wissenschaften im Grundrisse, Dritter Teil*, 71; emphasis in original.

26. Ibid., 33; emphasis in original.

27. Obviously, this is a very reductive way of elaborating the concept of nature in Hegel, which is far more complex. Yet, it is only important here to note that nature is what is there if there is an inadequacy of spirit.

28. In the beginning of spirit, there is a spirit that fails to be spirit. Yet, this does not mean it is simply not spirit; rather, it is *not-spirit*. The logic here is similar to that of the famous Freudian anecdote about the patient who claims not to know who the person in his dream is: "You may ask who this person in the dream can be. It's *not* my mother." Sigmund Freud, "Negation," in *The Standard Edition of the Complete Psychological Works of Sigmund Freud*, ed. and trans. James Strachey et al. (London: Hogarth Press, 1953–1974), 19:235; emphasis in original. For Freud, as Alenka Zupančič has shown, this negation does not mean that the patient simply negates his mother; rather, through the very act of negating he brings to the fore a peculiar entity that is the *not-mother*. One can say that, for Hegel, this is the move in the beginning of spirit (and it also may not be an accident that Hegel characterizes the peculiar life of spirit, in its beginning, in terms of dreams). It is as if spirit starts by stating, *whatever there is, it is* not-spirit—and this is the very beginning of spirit. See Zupančič, "Between Aufhebung and Verneinung," in *Backdoor Broadcasting Company: Academic Podcasts*, podcast audio, May 14, 2013, http://backdoorbroadcasting.net/.

29. Hegel, *Enzyklopädie der philosophischen Wissenschaften im Grundrisse, Dritter Teil*, 33.

30. Ibid., 17; emphasis in original.

31. Hegel also calls this move "the shift [*Umschlagen*] of the idea into the immediacy of external and individualized being-there. This shift is the becoming of nature." Ibid., 30.

32. But—and this is important to note—this is only the appearance, for "the emergence of spirit from nature should not be taken as if nature is the absolutely immediate, primary, and originally positing [agency], and as if spirit is, by contrast, only something posited; rather, nature is posited by spirit and the latter is absolutely primary." Ibid., 24. Spirit is here determined by its own appearance (although it posited itself unknowingly), and that it does not know it is ultimately determined by itself forces it to take a natural form.

33. Ibid.

34. Hegel's point here is important and highly relevant (say, for today's ecological discussion): Not even nature should be naturalized. Of course, the same holds for spirit, although spirit, in the beginning, cannot but find itself in nature (whereby spirit constitutively misses itself).

35. Hegel, *Enzyklopädie der philosophischen Wissenschaften im Grundrisse, Dritter Teil*, 40.

36. Malabou, *The Future of Hegel: Plasticity, Temporality, and Dialectic*, 28; emphasis in original.

37. Hegel, *Enzyklopädie der philosophischen Wissenschaften im Grundrisse, Dritter Teil*, 41.

38. Ibid., 40.

39. Malabou, *The Future of Hegel: Plasticity, Temporality, and Dialectic*, 30; emphasis in original.

40. Hegel, *Enzyklopädie der philosophischen Wissenschaften im Grundrisse, Dritter Teil*, 43.

41. Ibid., 43; emphasis in original. At the risk of trivializing this passage, it may be useful to read it in light of the fact that we do not usually think of ourselves as just natural beings (like plants, for example) but as beings endowed with something else, a *something* not as material as the rest of our natural constitution. This something—a surplus that exceeds mere bodily constitution—is what is here called *soul*.

42. Ibid.; emphasis in original.

43. Ibid., 51; emphasis in original.

44. Ibid., 50; emphasis in original.

45. One can see here that Hegel's philosophy of subjective spirit is fundamentally a critique of ideology, since ideology always relies upon naturalization.

46. Hegel, *Enzyklopädie der philosophischen Wissenschaften im Grundrisse, Dritter Teil*, 52.

47. Ibid., 63.

48. Ibid., 70.

49. Ibid., 71. I will set aside, in the following, what Hegel says about temperament, because it is rather "the most general form in which an individual is active," and also what he states about character as that which is determined by "formal energy" and "a universal content of the will," because both are already situated there where "natural determination loses the guise of being fixed." Ibid., 72–74. I am interested here only in investigating the theory of natural disposition and, with it, the question of whether or not there is a theory of natural inheritance in Hegel.

50. Ibid., 71.

51. Ibid., 74.

52. Ibid., 71; emphasis in original.

53. Ibid.

54. Ibid.

55. Ibid., 97.

56. Ibid.

57. Ibid., 100.

58. The feelings I have now, according to Hegel, are always my feelings: "What I feel [. . .], that *is* me, and what I am I feel." Ibid., 119; emphasis in original.

59. Ibid., 124.

60. Ibid., 125.

61. Ibid., 126.

62. Ibid.

63. Here one can see how Marx's infamous saying about a society being pregnant with something new implies, in a specific way, a Hegelian theory of inheritance. See Marx, *Capital: A Critique of Political Economy,* trans. Ben Fowkes, vol. 1 (New York: Penguin, 1990), 916.

CHAPTER 5

Biopower in Lacan's Inheritance

or, From Foucault to Freud, via Deleuze, and Back to Marx

A. Kiarina Kordela

Preamble

Is biopower a conception of power compatible with the psychoanalytic worldview? My short response is *yes*, biopower is the only form of power that can be conceived of within the psychoanalytic worldview—but only on condition that Michel Foucault's concept of *bios* first be fundamentally reconceptualized according to the psychoanalytic worldview.

Foucault's concept of bios—and, hence, biopower—is incompatible with psychoanalysis because it does not take into account the real. A psychoanalytic theory of biopower would conceive of actual beings, bodies, and lives as actualizations of the real Being, Body, or Life—Bios—that is, it would conceive of bios as a *logically necessary hypothesis* that is presupposed in order to explain actual beings, bodies, and lives. This presupposition, at once purely hypothetical and logically necessary, is what Sigmund Freud calls the primary fantasy (*Urphantasien*), which defines psychoanalytic methodology. The foundation of the psychoanalytic method and worldview is the primary fantasy qua real.

Yet, Freud is not the first to include in a systematic worldview such a logically necessary hypothesis. Baruch de Spinoza's concept of substance, qua Nature or God, is another instance of a logically necessary hypothesis, such that every existing concrete being, body, and life is an actualized mode of this substance. However, Freud is the first to consciously express its epistemological and ontological status as *primary fantasy*, that is, to repeat, as at once logically necessary and purely hypothesized (in other words, not actually existing). Jacques Lacan's act in this line of inheritance consists in showing how, in secular or atheist thought, this primary fantasy (or real or God) is both unconscious—that is, structured like a language—and libido (or jouissance or sex) at the level of the real: being qua indestructible life. It is precisely in this sense—a sense that I will attempt to make clear in what follows—that, as the common saying goes, in psychoanalysis everything is about sex. It also remains to be seen in what sense Foucault rightly argues that, in biopower, too, everything is about sex.

Writing within the inheritance of both Spinoza and Lacan, Gilles Deleuze introduces the virtual, ontological, and spatiotemporal dimension of the real as that which is opposed to the actual. While, on the one hand, the actual (Spinoza's modes of substance) exists in duration (that is, in diachrony or the linear time punctuated as the past, present, and future), the virtual or real, on the other hand (Spinoza's substance and its attributes), is, as each of the above thinkers concur, marked by the atemporal temporality that Spinoza calls eternity, Freud calls *Nachträglichkeit* (retroactivity or belatedness), Lacan calls logical time, and Deleuze calls the third synthesis of time.

It follows from the above that, in order to develop a psychoanalytically informed theory of biopower, we will need to reconceptualize three key concepts about which Foucault and psychoanalysis diverge fundamentally: the real, time, and sexuality.

But before we embark upon this task, let us note one of the most explicit points of concurrence between Foucault's conception of biopower and the psychoanalytic conception of power within capitalist modernity. Lacan elucidates the latter through what he calls the discourse of the university (*le discours de l'université*), which he presents as historically coextensive with secular, capitalist modernity, that is, with Foucault's biopolitical epoch. In this discourse, power presents itself qua pure knowledge, that is, as "nothing other than knowledge," not directly mastery or power but *pure* knowledge, which, as such, is said to be "objective knowledge," "science," or what "in ordinary language is called the bureaucracy."[1] Recall that Max Weber defined bureaucracy as a strictly hierarchical form of power freed from the yoke of inherited titles and privileges, as well as all individual favoritism, relying instead upon impersonal and objective systematicity and scientific expertise.[2] In spite of the ostensible division between private and professional life, then, the constitution of individuals in this bureaucratic machinery is thoroughly determined by their profession, with all their upbringing and education aiming at nothing other than developing the skills required for obtaining a professional position. In other words, Lacan and Foucault concur that modern political power is a continuous and scientific form of power that is "individualizing," opposed to "legal power," and "linked with the production of truth," including "the truth of the individual himself."[3] It is due to this ongoing overlap of power and science, or "objective knowledge," that the old, oppressive, and much more vulnerable sovereign power—which Lacan represents in the discourse of the master (*le discours du maître*)—has gradually been replaced by the more elusive and resilient form of a modern power that "is exercised only over free subjects, and only insofar as they are free," with the result that "there is no face-to-face confrontation of power and freedom."[4] Yet, although this is, unanimously indeed, the form of modern power, a psychoanalytic conceptualization of bios will reveal, as we shall see below, that biopower is a term that applies to all historical forms of power.

Biopower of Evolutionist History

According to Foucault, a decisive shift in the form of political power occurred sometime in the seventeenth century, obtaining its full-fledged form by the end of the nineteenth century. During this shift, the old political form of sovereignty—the power of "the sword" as "the right of seizure of things, time, bodies, and ultimately life itself"—gradually yielded to modern biopower, whose base is no longer "the right to *take* life or *let* live" but "the power to *make live*."[5] "This power over life," Foucault continues,

> evolved in [. . .] two poles of development linked together [. . .]. One of these poles [. . .] centered on the body as a machine: its disciplining, the optimization of its capabilities, the extortion of its forces, the parallel increase of its usefulness and its docility, its integration into systems of efficient and economic controls, all this was [. . .] an *anatomo-politics of the human body*. The second [. . .] focused on the species body, the body imbued with the mechanics of life and serving as the basis of the biological processes: propagation, births and mortality, the level of health, life expectancy and longevity, [. . .] *a biopolitics of the population*.[6]

Thus, throughout the era of secular, capitalist modernity, a vast network of biopolitical apparatuses and mechanisms emerge, aiming at "the administration of bodies and the calculated management of life," so as to "exert [. . .]

a positive influence on life," to "optimize [. . .] and multiply it."[7] In short, as Foucault maintains, while political power had always been a threat to human life, with the advent of secular, capitalist modernity, the specific historical phenomenon of modern biopower emerged as the "technology of power over [. . .] men insofar as they are living beings,"[8] that is, insofar as they can be regulated, normalized, and administered upon "the basis of biological processes"[9] in ways that are supposed to protect, foster, and maximize their physiological and productive potential.

Foucault's model of the historical development of political power is predicated upon a one-dimensional notion of time. Biopower, the power whose object and objective is life, always aims at the maximum prolongation and improvement of the biological life of individuals and populations within finite chronological time. By reducing bios to discursively inscribed biological bodies, Foucault conceives of biopolitics as mechanisms charged to propel linear time further, both in terms of its progression or evolution (always improving life) and extension (prolonging the duration of life), even as both remain limited due to biological constraints. In short, in Foucault's biopower, time is reduced to a progressivist, teleological finite duration.

Foucault's linear biopolitical temporality follows directly from his broader thesis, advanced a decade earlier in *Les mots et les choses*, regarding the criterion differentiating secular from presecular epistemes. The presecular, theocratic paradigm, which lasted until the end of the Renaissance, was marked by the divinely sanctioned organic links between words and things—links because of which words and things bore a remarkable resemblance with each other. Hence, the meaning of the word was ultimately always supported by the divine Word and the whole world was a Text, a Text to be incessantly reread and reinterpreted so as to bring its Truth closer to us, albeit only asymptotically. These same divine links also imbued each of the two realms—words and things—with infinite internal resemblances, among the words themselves and among the things themselves, so that everything, from the celestial universe to the tiniest grain of sand, from the macrocosm to the microcosm, was a mirror image, a reiteration of each other, so that the whole world itself consisted of an infinite repetition of the Same, just as knowledge exhausted itself in an infinite rediscovery of the Same. By contrast, the establishment of the secular episteme involved, among other things, the introduction of linear and teleological historical time, a kind of a line of flight (out of the text) whose vector finally broke out of the self-enclosed circular time of the recurrence of the Same. For the first time in history, Foucault maintains, humanity escaped textuality and discovered the real, with its historical, linear, and finite temporality, by introducing the three "quasi-transcendentals" that transcend "the space of representation."[10] The effects resulting from this change concern three levels: (1) in economy, *labor*, which is situated within "the temporal sequence" of "a great linear, homogenous series [. . .] of production,"[11] as opposed to the aspect of the commodity as an exchange value, which is a "system of equivalences";[12] (2) in biology, *life*—both the mortal life of the individual and the life of the species, conceived of in functionalistic and evolutionist (that is, teleological) terms; and (3) in language, *philology*, the study of the historical development of words, from their roots to their resignifications or obsoleteness.[13]

In other words, Foucault's conception of biopower is based upon a concomitant secular ontology that *equates the real with a being that exists within finite, historical (linear and teleological) time.* Here, the first two levels, economy and biology, provide the labor and life out of which Foucault will eventually formulate his notion of bios as the vulnerable and ultimately mortal individual, the biological as well as evolutionist body of the population, both of which live and labor within the teleological chronology of history. In Foucault's words, "[h]istory exists (that is, labour, production, accumulation, and growth of real costs) only in so far as man as a natural being is finite"[14]—"*Finitude*, with its truth, is posited in *time*; and *time* is therefore *finite*."[15] This is why the "great dream of an end to History is the utopia" that characterized that episteme until "Nietzsche, at the end of the nineteenth century [. . .] took the end of time and transformed it into the death of God and the odyssey of the last man," so that he transformed "the great continuous chain of History [. . .] into the infinity of the eternal return."[16] Thus, after Nietzsche's death of God and Man, Foucault maintains, history ceased to be eschatological; yet, Foucault's own theory of biopower remains predicated upon an evolutionist eschatology.

But we cannot complete this account of Foucault's concept of biopower without adding that, ten years later, when Foucault actually introduces the term, he brings to the stage another dimension of bios as the true protagonist, namely, sexuality. As he says in *"Society Must Be Defended"* in 1976—the same year as the publication of *La volonté de savoir*, the first volume of *The History of Sexuality*—the reason he places sexuality at the center of biopolitics, as the privileged "field of vital strategic importance," lies in the fact that "[s]exuality exists at the point where body and population meet."[17] For, on the one hand, sexuality, "being an eminently corporeal mode of behavior, is a matter for individualizing disciplinary controls," while, on the other hand, "it also has procreative effects" and is "inscribed [. . .] in broad biological processes that concern [. . .] the multiple unity of the population," which is why it occupies "the privileged position [. . .] between organism and population."[18]

The Time of the Real

Given the above, two points of comparison between Foucault's account and a possible psychoanalytic approach to bios become immediately evident and can function as our starting point. First, psychoanalysts would fully agree with Foucault upon the centrality of sexuality in biopower, since, in psychoanalysis, sexuality enjoys such a privilege in human life. Second, however, we cannot miss the striking discrepancy between the Foucauldian and psychoanalytic conceptualizations of the real. Both actually concur insofar as they each conceive of the real as that which escapes the realm of representation. However, Foucault's equation of the real with the chronological and teleological time in which both individual consciousness and collective bodies of knowledge narrativize the lives of biological bodies, the development of species, languages, or what is generally perceived as history—all of this bears no affinity with the psychoanalytic conception of the real. In psychoanalysis, duration or chronological time is the time of consciousness, that is, an imaginary temporality—all the more so the more teleological it is—whereas the temporality of the real pertains to the unconscious fantasy, that is, the Other insofar as it does not exist.

In fact, it is not an exaggeration to say that the development of Freud's thought toward a theory divested of all mythical elements depended entirely upon growing out of chronological, historical, or biographical conceptions of temporality, operating instead in terms of what, in 1945, having demonstrated "the function of haste in logic," Lacan calls "logical time."[19] The three chronological moments of past, present, and future reveal themselves in logical time as the three instances of seeing, understanding, and concluding, not as three distinct chronometric units but as different intensities between hesitation and urgency. That such a logical temporality is the unique contribution of psychoanalysis—following from its radical gesture of including, within knowledge, fantasy as an epistemologically legitimate category—is foregrounded in Jean Laplanche and J. B. Pontalis's 1964 article on the origin of fantasy (and the fantasy of origins), which discerned the logic and temporality of structure as the condition of the scientificity of psychoanalysis.[20] In this article, Laplanche and Pontalis trace Freud's long itinerary, from his "seduction theory" in the early 1890s to his work on the "primal fantasy" and "autoeroticism" in the late 1910s, as a series of attempts toward eventually defining and establishing fantasy as the object of psychoanalysis. And what is at stake in this itinerary is precisely the conceptualization of logical or structural time.

Laplanche and Pontalis's article had a major impact upon Deleuze, who, in his 1966 work *Difference and Repetition*, elaborated extensively upon this temporality under the name the "third synthesis of time," which was itself fashioned after Spinoza's "third kind of knowledge," a type of knowledge that perceives everything under the species of *eternity*. Let us note that eternity in Spinoza is not the eternity of traditional logic—the logic that was the very target of critique in Lacan's notion of logical time—since only substance is eternal, and substance "is the immanent, not the transitive, cause of all things," that is, a cause that is itself the effect of its own effects,[21] not unlike the past in Freud's *Nachträglichkeit*, which is itself the effect of its own future. Both Deleuze's and Laplanche and Pontalis's accounts of logical or structural time foreground the fact that real time—the time of the real—is the temporality of a (logical) structure insofar as it is *not* actualized, *not* filled in with actual contents, but consists of *purely virtual* empty spaces and their relations.

Chronological or, to put it in Deleuze's terms, actual time—the time of the succession of past, present, and future—corresponds on the real or virtual level to the "third synthesis" of time, that is, a form "empty and out of joint, with its rigorous formal and static order."[22] Logical time "is necessarily static, since time is no longer subordinated to movement"—which takes place in chronological, transitive space and time—for logical time "is the most radical form of change, but the form of change [itself] does not change."[23] Time is change, that is, it consists of causes that bring about effects, but the form of change itself, the form of this (immanent) causation—the fact that the causes are the effects of their own effects—does not change. Moreover, this static order of logical time pertains to the order of the "death instinct"[24] (or, rather, the death drive, which, as we know from Freud, is the compulsion to repeat).[25] The function of repetition consists in collapsing all empirical oppositions (for example, reality versus imaginary and object versus subject) and eliminating "all content," including any "temporal content,"[26] as is evident in "love's repetition," in which "we realize that our sufferings do not depend on their object":[27] "Each suffering is particular [. . .] insofar as it is produced by a specific being, at the heart of a specific love. But because these sufferings reproduce each other and implicate each other, the intelligence disengages from them something general, which is also a source of joy."[28] That is, "the intelligence's interpretation [. . .] consists in discovering essence as the law of the series of loves," so that, although "the phenomena are always unhappy and particular, [. . .] the idea extracted from them is general and joyous."[29] The essence of the repetition of the particular loves in the series consists not in any of these transitory particulars but in their general, formal, and eternal law, which is itself a source of joy—comparable to Spinoza's Joy of "the third kind of knowledge," which "knows itself and the Body under a species of eternity [. . .] as a formal cause" and "eternal":[30]

"From this kind of knowledge there arises the greatest satisfaction of Mind there can be," namely, the "Joy" that is "accompanied by the idea of God as its cause[, . . .] not insofar as we imagine him as present [. . .] but insofar as we understand God to be eternal."[31] The Spinozian link between repetition and Joy reemerges in Lacan as the interlacing of the death drive with enjoyment, as the "beyond" of pleasure and its principle, which governs only the realm of actuality and its chronological time.

In 1897, however, Freud was still thinking exclusively in terms of the pleasure principle, and, as Laplanche and Pontalis write, after "discard[ing . . .] the seduction theory," he replaced it with the "Oedipus complex"; nonetheless, he "conceive[s]" of it as a "biological" or "endogenous reality," while "sexuality [. . .] is itself supposed to be in conflict with a normative, prohibitory external reality."[32] In this move, fantasy was once again reduced to "no more than the secondary expression of this reality," while chronology united forces with biology to arrive at the conclusion that "the intrusion of the fantasy [. . .] into the subject [. . .] cannot but occur to the organism, the little human being, at a point in time, by virtue of certain characteristics of his biological evolution."[33] Freud fails to grasp that what appear as "temporal characteristics of human sexuality"—as "too early (birth) and too late (puberty)"—are an effect of the projection onto linear time of the *logical* relation between "too much and too little excitation."[34] The past and the future reveal themselves on the logical, virtual, or real level not as instances spread out in diachrony but as two intensities—"too much" and "too little"—that form the "totality of time."[35] The totality of time cannot be conceived of but "in the image of a unique and tremendous event, an act which is adequate to time as a whole,"[36] that is, an act that would amount to the end of the world or, at least, the end of the individual involved. Deleuze's examples include the following: "to throw time out of joint, to make the sun explode, to throw oneself into the volcano, [and] to kill God or the father."[37] The image of such an act "must be called a symbol by virtue of the unequal parts which it subsumes and draws together," that is, "the before and the after" or the absence and presence of the act.[38] It is the "inequality" between the two intensities—too much and too little—that "creates the possibility of a temporal series," that is, it generates actual, chronological, time. For "there is always a time at which the imagined act is supposed 'too big for me,'" and this "defines *a priori* the past or the before"; the "second time [. . .] is [. . .] the present of metamorphosis, a becoming equal to the act" or "a doubling of the self, and the projection of an ideal self in the image of the act," as "is marked by Hamlet's sea voyage and by the outcome of Oedipus's enquiry: the hero becomes 'capable' of the act,"[39] that is, Hamlet finally decides to commit his act, just as Oedipus recognizes that it was he who had committed the act. But, on the level of the real,

> [i]t matters little whether or not the event itself occurs, or whether the act has been performed or not: past, present, and future are not distributed according to this empirical criterion. Oedipus has already carried out the act, Hamlet has not yet done so, but in either case the first part of the symbol is lived in the past, they are in the past [. . .] so long as they experience the image of the act as too big for them.[40]

And "the third time in which the future appears [. . .] signifies that the event and the act possess a secret coherence which excludes that of the self," that is, the event and the act "turn back against the self which has become their equal and smash it to pieces."[41] What matters at the level of the real is not the particular individual called Hamlet but the structure of neurosis—not the man who bears the name Oedipus but the Oedipus complex.

This completes the bridge from the actual to the virtual. Seen from the opposite perspective, from the virtual to the actual, chronological time is generated out of the logical time of the virtual structure: "Time goes from the virtual to the actual, that is, from structure to its actualizations, and not from one actual form to another."[42] Real time "is always a time of actualization," and in this actualization "the elements of virtual coexistence are carried out at diverse rhythms."[43]

It was eventually by addressing the ultimate fantasy of narcissism or autoeroticism that Freud was able to condense actual, linear time into its logical, virtual form. Narcissism, as Laplanche and Pontalis remark, does not operate "in the object-directed sense, as a first stage, enclosed within itself, from which the subject has to rejoin the world of objects."[44] On the contrary, as Freud writes in *Three Essays on the Theory of Sexuality*, "[i]t is only [after] the drive loses [the] object [that] the drive [. . .] becomes autoerotic"[45]—something that presupposes "the existence of a *primary object* relationship," that is, an object that was *never given in actuality*.[46] As Freud continues, as long as "sexual satisfaction" is "linked with the taking of nourishment, the sexual instinct has a sexual object outside the infant's own body in the shape of his mother's breast. It is only later that the instinct loses that object, just at the time, perhaps, when the child is able to *form a total idea* of the person to whom the organ that is giving him satisfaction belongs."[47] This passage, as Laplanche and Pontalis continue, means that "the very constitution of the auto-erotic fantasy implies not only the partial object (breast, thumb or substitute), but the mother *as a total person*, withdrawing as she *becomes total*."[48] In other words, according to Laplanche and Pontalis, "the natural method of apprehending an object is split in two": on the one hand, the "non-sexual functions" of need, such as "the taking of food," and, on the other hand, the "sexual drive," for which the "external object is abandoned," and whose "aim and [. . .] source assume an autonomous existence with regard to feeding," so that its "prototype is not the act of sucking, but the enjoyment of going through the motions of sucking"—the "ideal [. . .] of auto-erotism is 'lips that kiss themselves.'"[49] The origin of autoeroticism is "the moment when sexuality, disengaged from any natural object, moves into the field of fantasy," where *the object is redoubled as totality*, "and by that very fact becomes sexuality" in the human sense.[50]

Now, Freud's as well as Laplanche and Pontalis's references to totality call for a comparison with Lacan's account of the introduction of sexuality in human life offered in 1964—the same year as Laplanche and Pontalis's article. In Seminar XI, Lacan says that what the human being "loses in sexuality," what "is subtracted from the living being by virtue of the fact that it is subject to the cycle of sexed reproduction," is not the breast but *totality*, in its most comprehensive sense, that is, on the one hand, "the libido, *qua* pure life instinct, [. . .] immortal [. . .] or irrepressible [. . .], simplified, indestructible life," and "whose characteristic is *not to exist*, but which is nevertheless an organ" (exemplified in the "lamella," Lacan's zoologically inspired fable for the libido or enjoyment), and, on the other hand, totality as "the locus of the Other, in so far as it is there that the first signifier emerges."[51] The entrance of the subject into language is also the subject's entrance into sexed reproduction, and both entail the loss of a primary, not existing—hence, virtual—object. This lost primary, virtual object is an undifferentiated totality—at once nonexistent, virtual, indestructible life, libido, or jouissance, *and* virtual signifying structure, in the midst of which the first actual signifier will emerge in actual time.

In each of the two texts, Laplanche and Pontalis and Lacan describe the existence—or, strictly speaking, nonexistence, that is, virtual existence—of two things that, far from being mutually exclusive, entail each other. They speak of the two virtual totalities at the basis of the entire psychoanalytic edifice: first, the totality of libido (or enjoyment) or full and indestructible life—*indestructible being*—which is, nevertheless, absolutely identical with the "locus of the Other," the totality of the signifier, that is, complete language, language as not lacking; and, second, totality insofar as, to repeat Laplanche and Pontalis's words, an actual "natural object" withdraws from the field of the living being's experience and "moves into the field of fantasy" to be redoubled as totality. In this second aspect, totality provides the imaginary stuff for all possible "forms of the *objet a* [. . . ,] all the other objects," from a breast to what have you, as long as these imaginary objects can function as stand-ins, as "representatives" or "figures," for the initially presupposed unified totality of being and sign.[52] In short, totality designates, on the one hand, the primary fantasy of virtual—real—plenitude presupposed for the experience of any lack within actuality, and, on the other hand, the imaginary stuff that vainly attempts to make up for the loss of the primal virtual object (the first totality).

To differentiate more clearly between the two totalities, let us recall Bruce Fink's distinction between $Real_1$ and $Real_2$. As Fink writes, Lacan's theory involves

> two different levels of the real: (1) a real before the letter, that is, a pre-symbolic real, which, in the final analysis, is but our own hypothesis (R_1), and (2) a real after the letter which is characterized by impasses and impossibilities due to relations among the elements of the symbolic order itself (R_2), that is, which is generated by the symbolic.[53]

And, I would add, $Real_2$ is generated by the symbolic but not actualized within it, which is why it remains *real*; and it can also be imaginary, like the stuff that fills in the object *a*, but only insofar as it has real effects. By contrast, the primary fantasy of the virtual totality of being and sign is $Real_1$.

Having established the difference between, on the one hand, the real or virtual realm of the absolute, nondifferentiated, totality, with its logical time, and, on the other hand, the realm of the actual, with its linear chronology but also its imaginary, secondary, fantasies of totality, we can now return to our initial subject matter—biopower.

Psychoanalytic Biopolitics

What would a psychoanalytically informed conceptualization and theory of biopower look like, that is, a biopolitical theory based upon the recognition of the two realms discussed above and their respective temporalities?

I shall begin by fully espousing Foucault's thesis that sexuality is a "field of vital strategic importance" for biopower, and so I turn to the treatment of sexuality in psychoanalysis. Sexuality in psychoanalysis is libido, which, as we have seen, on the level of $Real_1$ is the virtual totality of the undifferentiated union of jouissance, qua pure indestructible life, *and* the locus of the Other (the signifier) in its fullness.

Throughout his work, Lacan gradually distinguishes between *sexual jouissance* and real or *asexual jouissance*. As Jacques-Alain Miller stresses, "Seminar XI is about [. . .] the passage from jouissance of the imaginary to [jouissance] of the real," through which real jouissance reveals itself as noth-ing less than the following: (1) that which is "present in sexual reality," by which is meant the sexual real; (2) the *objet a*, as it appears in the formula of the barred subject, which (as the lozenge in the formula of fantasy reads) stands in all possible relations "with jouissance present in sexual reality"; (3) libido, insofar as we refer to the libido "of the real register"; and, conse-quently, due to the "link between libido and [. . .] the death drive," (4) drive, which is why "*jouissance* [is always] beyond the pleasure principle," at once death drive and "pure life instinct" (Eros), insofar as "[t]he activity of the drive is concentrated in this *making oneself* [*se faire*]";[54] and, finally, (5) being, because of which there is an "antinomy between subject and jou-issance," since what the "barred subject" lacks is precisely being, ceaselessly "call[ing] for a complement of being."[55]

From Lacan's statement, in Seminar XX, that "being is the *jouissance* of the body as such, that is, as asexual [*asexué*]," we understand that the sexual real is *asexual*.[56] And as we have seen, jouissance, qua libido of "the real level," is "pure life instinct, [. . .] immortal [. . .], irrepressible [. . .], inde-structible life [. . .], whose characteristic is not to exist."[57] In other words, jouissance lies outside of chronological time and is not "actual" but *pure, indestructible potential*. It is the sheer, irrepressible power of being to actu-alize itself ("making oneself") and, hence, it is the sole cause of itself, not unlike Spinoza's "substance [that] cannot be produced by anything else [. . . ,] therefore it [is] the cause of itself."[58] This jouissance-substance, which "is the power of making itself actual,"[59] or the indestructible potential of self-actualization, is governed by logical time, that is, to put it in Spinoza's terms, it is of an "eternal nature" and exists "under a species of eternity" (*sub specie aeternitatis*).[60] To say, as Lacan and Spinoza do, that jouissance, being, or substance, is to "cause" or "make oneself" entails that jouissance or being is always more and less than itself, which is why jouissance is always surplus-enjoyment (*plus-de-jouir*)—with the French version alone being capable of indicating that surplus (*plus*) entails disequilibrium, regardless of whether this manifests itself as "more" or "less" enjoyment. For in order to make oneself one must be the cause of oneself, which means that one must be both oneself and something beyond or other than oneself—the very thing that causes oneself—not unlike the paradoxical set of all sets, which both is and is not a member of itself. Like the set of all sets, being or jouissance is an *all-not-all*. This relation of self-causation in its pure form pertains only to the level of the real (Real$_1$), that is, only to sheer potentiality, and its temporality is that of logical time.

Importantly, Lacan's logical time, or Spinoza's eternity, is entirely outside chronological time. This is to say that it should not be conflated with infinity, if by this is meant an infinite duration. As Spinoza writes, eternity "cannot be explained by duration or time, even if the duration is conceived to be without beginning or end."[61] Deleuze stresses this point by juxtaposing any "finite existing mode" in duration to eternity as that which cannot involve duration, since it pertains to the "full, unvarying *power* of acting," and not to the actualized action, let alone its actual product, both of which exist in actuality and are, therefore, in linear time.[62]

As follows clearly from the above, and as Lacan emphatically states, jouissance or the sexual real differs radically from sexual reproduction, whose product (offspring) presupposes (1) a cause other than itself, (2) sexual difference, and (3) duration in time. In Lacan's words from Seminar XI, "what the *sexed* being loses in sexuality [. . .] is the libido, qua pure life instinct, that is to say, immortal life, or irrepressible life[; this] indestructible life [. . .] is precisely what is subtracted from the living being by virtue of the fact that it is subject to the cycle of sexed reproduction."[63]

Thus, although both the "asexual real" and sexual difference are real, we can differentiate their status upon the basis of the aforementioned distinction between Real$_1$ and Real$_2$. Since the asexual real is presymbolic and pertains to eternity, it belongs to Real$_1$, whereas sexual difference pertains to Real$_2$. In other words, sexual difference is an effect of the subject's introduction into the symbolic order (and time and, hence, mortality), an effect owing to the symbolic order's failure to grasp Real$_1$ as such—that is, as the asexual real, qua indestructible, eternal power of self-actualization.

That real, asexual jouissance is all-not-all means that it is *self-referential*, insofar as jouissance is the sole substance (an absolute One) and, yet, by dint of the fact that it is self-caused, is internally split (Two). It is One, and yet this One involves an internal relation with itself; hence, jouissance is self-referential—or, more strongly, jouissance or being *is* self-referentiality. The potentiality of self-actualization and self-referentiality are inseparable. It follows that, if the moment of the subject's introduction into language, sexual difference, time, and, hence, mortality—in short, the moment of castration—is the mechanism that prohibits real jouissance, then what castration prohibits is *self-referentiality*.[64] If self-referentiality allows for the undifferentiated coexistence of the One and the Two at the level of Real$_1$, the entrance of the subject into the signifier and its separation from real jouissance bring about the nonnegotiable discord between the One and the

Two. Henceforth, the union of the One and the Two will be relegated to the unconscious, while consciousness will experience them as incompatible. This is why the function of the myth sustaining castration—the myth of Oedipus and the Oedipus complex—consists in displacing the terms One and Two, which to consciousness appear as opposites, onto more negotiable terms. In Claude Lévi-Strauss's words, "the Oedipus myth provides a kind of logical tool which relates the original problem—born from one or born from two?—to the derivative problem: born from different or born from same?"[65] This way the One-Two relation is displaced from the level of pure being to blood. Born from people of different blood or the same, as in incest? If castration is the name for the subject's entrance into the signifier, as an individual experience, the incest prohibition is its corollary name at the level of the population and all society, given that the prohibition of incest, as again Lévi-Strauss has shown, is the precondition for the establishment of the structure of kinship and, therefore, human society. The incest prohibition is the prohibition of self-referentiality—at the *level of blood*.

In other words, the incest prohibition and castration designate one and the same mechanism operative upon collective and individual levels, respectively. The mechanism of castration, qua the incest prohibition, intervenes directly into the body (blood) and the sexual real and is, therefore, a *biopolitical* mechanism.

What can we infer from this regarding a psychoanalytic theory of biopower? The first conclusion is that, in this theory, power is, since its inception, biopower and that, therefore, biopower and biopolitics are not specifically modern but *transhistorical* phenomena. Nevertheless, there are different concrete actualizations of biopower and biopolitics throughout history. Biopower remains, throughout history, the function of power to regulate life, regardless of whether this regulation exercises itself by posing threats to life (as in the paradigm of sovereignty) or by supporting it (as in modern biopower).

The second conclusion is that *the primary object of biopower and biopolitics is jouissance*—including all of its cognates, such as being qua potentiality of self-actualization and self-referentiality. The third conclusion is that biopolitical mechanisms and laws may be concerned with interdicting what is impossible, as is the case with castration, which prohibits real jouissance, something that is inaccessible to the speaking subject. As Lacan puts it, "I have castration anxiety at the same time as I regard it as impossible."[66] The fourth conclusion is that, by introducing into the realm of biopower a psychoanalytic conceptualization of bios, sexuality, the real, and its temporality, we have arrived at a radical reconceptualization of biopower itself. For now body, blood, and the sexual real concern not just those biological processes examined by physical sciences and administered and regulated by medicine, statistics, and all the other disciplines and institutions invoked by Foucault. Bios and sexuality are to be considered simultaneously in two ways: on the one hand, as substance, being, enjoyment, self-referentiality, and everything that pertains to the level of Real_1 and its logical time; and, on the other hand, as the actualized modes of this virtual real within chronological time, including the excess residue caused by the necessary failure of this actualization to be complete (Real_2). And it is at the intersection of the two levels that biopolitics operates. Like castration and the incest prohibition, *biopower intervenes precisely at the moment of the generation of the actual out of the virtual real, the moment of the transfiguration of eternity into chronology.* And, again, like castration and the incest prohibition, *the target of biopower is the prohibition of this asexual jouissance that is common to both sexes.* Sexual difference or Real_2, by contrast, emerges out of *the two ways in which this prohibition fails to enforce itself completely.*

For, as we know from Lacan, castration fails to be complete, and this is the case thanks to the resistance of what we call the body. In Lacan's words, "what Freud discovered under the name [. . .] castration" is best formulated with reference to the Cartesian cogito: "the 'therefore,' the causal stroke, divides inaugurally the 'I am' of existence from the 'I am' of meaning," thereby introducing the fundamental "rift or split" that is "reproduced at all levels of subjective structure."[67] It is this rift in the subject between being and language that prevents access to the totality of real jouissance. However, the rift is not complete; it is marred by a failure, insofar as, as Lacan continues, the body is that "which in many ways resists actualizing the division of the subject."[68] An integral part of castration is the body's resistance to the execution of the subject's rift. It is due to the body's resistance to completely actualize the division of castration that the subject is sexed.

Sexual Jouissance and Sexual Difference

Let us then shift our focus from the one side of the core of biopolitics, asexual jouissance (Real_1), to its other side, sexual difference and sexual jouissance (Real_2), as well as the bridge between the two, the very moment of sexuation, namely, castration.

As we know from Lacan's formulas of sexuation, sexual difference expresses the two possible ways of coping with the failure of reason to constitute a totality. This, as Joan Copjec has foregrounded, is a problematic that is intrinsically correlated with the Kantian antinomies of pure reason. In brief, the female sex fails to form a totality (of representation) by remaining undecided as to whether being ("I am") is reducible to or transcends representation, while the male failure consists in forming a totality (of representation), but only by positing an exception (being, "I am") outside of itself.[69] What the present psychoanalytic theory of biopolitics adds to this is that sexual difference (Real$_2$) constitutes the two possible ways of evading the *complete* enforcement of the biopolitical prohibition of jouissance or self-referentiality. Self-referentiality would be completely inaccessible if the subject were to undergo an absolute split, a split as a consequence of which the subject would literally consist of two distinct parts, the subject as cause (being) and the subject as effect (representation)—we might call this *complete castration*. It is in order to avoid this split that the subject makes recourse to what is conventionally known as castration, that is, the process of the subject's introduction into the signifier and sexuality—what we might refer to as *sexed* or *sexuating* castration. Each sex evades complete castration through its own sexed mode of castration, so that sexuation or sexual difference is the subject's resistance to the biopolitical prohibition of real jouissance. Each sex replaces what for consciousness is the noncompromisable conflict of self-referentiality—One or Two, cause or effect—with its own myth (the myths of the Lacanian formulas of sexuation or the two Kantian antinomies), which replaces this absolute contradiction with more negotiable terms (such as finite and indefinite series or law and freedom).

Each sex can resist the biopolitical law of complete castration by replacing it with its own—male or female—law and mode of sexed castration (law and castration are at the level of Real$_2$).[70] Both sides of Lacan's formulas of sexuation, like both Kantian antinomies, while addressing the question of whether or how totality can form itself, are essentially in revolt against the biopolitical prohibition of self-referentiality, that is, against the fact that totality (Real$_1$) is self-referentially all-not-all. If this thesis is correct, then one must be able to hear the murmur of the paradox of self-referentiality in both formulas of sexuation or antinomies.

In the case of the female sex, the mathematical antinomy—which is concerned with the spatiotemporal limits of the world, asking whether the world in itself is limited or unlimited in time and space—the echo of the precastrated and direct experience of jouissance appears deceitfully conspicuous. In Immanuel Kant's words, the world, qua thing in itself (that is, not as appearance but as Being), "exists neither as *a whole that is infinite in itself* nor as *a whole that is finite in itself*,"[71] in short not as a whole at all but as not-all—hence, in Lacan's words, "woman is *not whole* [*pas toute*]."[72] But the reason woman is "not whole" is that there can always be another condition in the indefinite regress of the series of the conditioned *in time*, or, in Copjec's linguistically inflected paraphrase, "there will always be another signifier" in the signifying chain "to determine retroactively the meaning of all [signifiers] that have come before"[73]—in time. This is the law that establishes the real of the female sex in time (Real$_2$) by maintaining that Being (jouissance) does not form a closed One, yet only because of the indefinite regress of the conditioned appearances in time, not because of the problematic of self-referentiality. In this way, the female sex evades the biopolitical prohibition of the self-referentiality of Being, that is, Being, like the set of all sets, is not a closed One, not only because we may encounter yet another set in time but also because it cannot be determined logically whether or not it (the set of all sets) is itself included in itself (which is the equivalent of the logical undecidability as to whether or not the cause is part of its effect). Yet, the indefinite regress of the conditioned appearances in time enables, as a side effect, the female sex to be alerted to the limitlessness of appearances, which is what raises the question as to whether or not being is reducible to it and, further, even if it were reducible to representation, whether or not the female sex would have to consider being a nontotalizable cognitive object, since appearances are unlimited. It is in this (mathematical, not set-theoretical) sense that woman raises the question as to whether or not being is reducible to appearances, thereby gaining some intuition of the self-referential character of Being.

Before we proceed to the male sex, let us note a major consequence of this intuition for the female sex. Since woman allows for the possibility that being is not reducible to conditioned appearances or the signifier, she may somehow have access to something beyond the indefinite, regressive series of conditioned appearances or signifiers. For Kant, this "beyond" would be the thing in itself, including its two faces, freedom and God. For Lacan, who can "interpret one face of the Other, the God face, as based on feminine jouissance,"[74] woman, not unlike "mystics," has the "idea or sense that there must be a jouissance that is beyond," that is, outside the series of the conditioned appearances or the symbolic order and the signifier, which is why "the essential testimony of the mystics consists in saying that they experience it, but know nothing about it."[75] In other words, the position of woman is essentially transgressive, as her jouissance requires accessing something beyond the given order of both representation and the symbolic. This is evidenced in Lacan's choice of Saint Teresa as the exemplary case of the mystic qua woman.[76] While operating under the constraints of the church, an equally exemplary manifestation of the symbolic order, Saint Teresa's mysticism constitutes a double transgression: On the one hand, she posed a challenge to the established order, engendering the reform of the Carmelite Order; on the other hand, experiencing her ecstasy as a perfect union with God, she had direct access to that which no one else within the church had access. The transgressive disposition of the female sex, both against the established order and towards the absolute, has considerable significance for politics, ethics, and the experience of love. Suffice it to point out the stark discrepancy between the logic of the female sex, on the one hand, and another structure (Paradoxically? Surprisingly? Wrongly?) referred to as "feminization," on the other. The latter designation is frequently used to describe a given phenomenon marked by a tendency away from the absolute and toward pluralization, serialization, dispersion, and the like, which, moreover, is not likely to pose any kind of challenge whatsoever to the established order.

The logic of the male sex, the dynamic antinomy, concerns causality and asks whether the world is governed only by natural necessity or whether there is also freedom. Here, the not-all character, or the self-referentiality of Being, is kept unconscious by means of dividing Being into two distinct realms: law (effect) and its exception (cause). If we accept that, in the realm of appearance, everything is conditioned by natural necessity (law) in time, whereas freedom can only be asserted as an unconditioned cause, then freedom "would not have to be subject to temporal determinations," and, hence, "would have to be taken for a thing in itself," outside the realm of appearances and time, and as their cause.[77] Thus, "if natural necessity is referred only to appearances and freedom only to things in themselves, then no contradiction arises if both kinds of causality are assumed or conceded equally, however difficult or impossible it may be to make causality of the latter conceivable."[78] By positing an exception (freedom), the male sex forms a closed whole (appearance governed by the laws of natural necessity), yet everything under these laws can, in another relation, be free. The male sex evades the biopolitical law of self-referentiality (the fact that Being is the cause of itself) by separating cause from effect, but in ways that enable a compartmentalization of life, rather than a split within each experience (not unlike Kant's, and the overall Enlightenment's, compartmentalization of modern life between the obedient civic servant and the freely thinking world scholar—the basis of the free speech ideal).

Biopower in Capitalist Modernity

I would like to conclude by returning to Real$_1$ in order to remark that the psychoanalytic thesis I am advancing here—asexual jouissance (self-referentiality) is the (transhistorical) real underlying our concrete (historical) actualizations and the modes in which we experience our individual lives in time—is constitutive of what we took as our starting point, namely, the psychoanalytic worldview. In psychoanalysis, self-referentiality is always the impossible and missed/yearned-for real, which is why it always lies at the center of the constitution of both subjectivity and any form of power, from religious-based societies to enlightened democracies, and from explicit totalitarianism to tacitly totalitarian biopolitics. And because self-referentiality is always the same, insofar as it is not an identity but pure difference (a One that is Two), its actualization involves the multiplicity of the variants through which individuals, collectives, and whole historical periods relate to this self-referentiality—history itself being guided, swerved, and, ultimately, constituted by minute decisions about whether or not to call the missed/yearned-for real "totality," "identity," or "difference," whether or not to call our relation to it one of "plenitude" or "lack," and, what is at once more important and subtler, whether or not this relation is (invoking Kant's distinction) one of constitutive or regulatory dreams.

Every historical era has its own object *a* that functions as a stand-in for the presupposed (as always already lost) jouissance, and often more than one object fulfills this function. In capitalist modernity, the central object that occupies the position of the object *a* is *labor-power*.[79] This statement may sound strange, as humans have always had the power to labor, and, indeed, as the sheer potential of the living body and mind to act, there is nothing new about labor-power in modernity. In the capitalist mode of production, however, labor-power is commodified, that is, it enters the market and becomes a major economic object. Karl Marx already conceived of labor-power in terms of the psychoanalytic conception of bios, or being qua real. In his words, labor-power—as the *"capacity* of the living individual"[80] to produce—"is [the laborer's] vitality itself."[81] That is, it "is not materialized in a product, does not exist apart from him, thus exists not really, but only in *potentiality*, as his *capacity*."[82] And because the laborer is no longer considered a slave or serf but a wage laborer—that is, the free owner of labor-power that he or she sells on the market—what we have is the unprecedented social actualization of, in Paolo Virno's words, the "commerce of potential as potential."[83] *With labor-power potentiality itself—jouissance—is commodified.* A psychoanalytic theory of biopower should be concerned, above all, with the *commodification of the real.*

Spinoza already alludes to one of the side effects of the commodification of substance by adding, right after he emphatically distinguishes eternity from infinite duration, that "[i]f we attend to the common opinion of men, we shall see that they are indeed conscious of the eternity of their Mind, but [. . .] they confuse it with duration, and attribute it to the imagination, or memory, which they believe remains after death."[84] Here, Spinoza, who notoriously does not shy away from intellectual snobbery and considering the multitude ignorant and prey to superstition, grants the common opinion of men regarding the idea of eternity; *yet*, this idea can only lead them to confusion, so that they mistake eternity for the continuation of duration after their death, that is, they imagine that there is an afterlife. If the common opinion mistakes eternity for infinite duration and, hence, immortality, then biopower's true function concerns not just the well-being of living individual and collective biological bodies and populations but also, above all, the fact that these same actual bodies and minds, which exist in time, (mis)take themselves for immortal.

Note that Spinoza attributes the people's illusion of immortality not to religiosity but to "confusion" in the mind, as a consequence of which a slippage occurs from eternity to infinite duration. In fact, it is to the specific mind of secular, capitalist modernity that Spinoza's explanation of the illusion of immortality applies. It is only capitalism that introduces—into social reality—a further temporality that is prone to instigate this slippage from eternity to infinite duration. The unprecedented and specifically modern commodification of labor-power entails as its corollary the equally unprecedented accumulation of *surplus-value*, which results in nothing less than the *introduction of a temporality—into actual, empirical, worldly life—of theoretically infinite duration*. For, being by definition the unlimited reproduction of ever-more value—since, in Marx's words, capital is "value which is greater than itself"[85]—surplus-value functions as a kind of temporal valve, as it were, that, as Éric Alliez puts it, "open[s] up the duration of the durable" to infinity, and this takes place *within social reality*.[86] From this point forward, the primordial nature of the durable to remain, however long-lasting and resilient it may be, always confined within its limited durance, is undermined, gradually allowing for the fantasy of the imaginary limitless duration of actual bodies and minds. In its biopolitical twist, capital procures a temporality that functions as a surrogate for the species of eternity, and thereby entices subjects to the pernicious slippage from the presupposed jouissance under a species of eternity to the (fantasy of the) immortality of our actual bodies and minds![87]

One of the things that immediately transpires from this discussion is, of course, the need to examine the relation between the specifically secular fantasy of immortality—as one of the most central, modern, biopolitical mechanisms of control—and sexual difference, as a mode of resistance to the biopolitical prohibition of jouissance.

Notes

1. Jacques Lacan, *The Seminar of Jacques Lacan, Book XVII: The Other Side of Psychoanalysis*, ed. Jacques-Alain Miller, trans. Russell Grigg (New York: W. W. Norton, 2007), 31.

2. See Max Weber, *Economy and Society: An Outline of Interpretive Sociology*, ed. Guenther Roth and Klaus Wittich, trans. Ephraim Fischoff et al. (Berkeley: University of California Press, 1978), 956–1005.

3. Michel Foucault, *"Society Must Be Defended": Lectures at the Collège de France, 1975–76*, ed. Mauro Bertani and Alessandro Fontana, trans. David Macey (New York: Picador, 2003), 247; and "The Subject and Power," *Critical Inquiry* 8, no. 4 (1982): 783.

4. Foucault, "The Subject and Power," 790.

5. Foucault, *"Society Must Be Defended": Lectures at the Collège de France, 1975–76*, 241, 247; emphasis added.

6. Foucault, *The History of Sexuality: An Introduction*, trans. Robert Hurley, vol. 1 (New York: Pantheon, 1978), 139; emphasis in original.

7. Ibid., 140, 137.

8. Foucault, *"Society Must Be Defended": Lectures at the Collège de France, 1975–76*, 247.

9. Foucault, *The History of Sexuality: An Introduction*, vol. 1, 139.

10. Foucault, *The Order of Things: An Archaeology of the Human Sciences* (New York: Vintage, 1994), 250.

11. Ibid., 255.

12. Ibid., 254.

13. Ibid., 280–94.

14. Ibid., 259.

15. Ibid., 263.

16. Ibid.

17. Foucault, *"Society Must Be Defended": Lectures at the Collège de France, 1975–76*, 251–52.

18. Ibid., 251, 252.

19. See Lacan, "Logical Time and the Assertion of Anticipated Certainty: A New Sophism," in *Écrits: The First Complete Edition in English*, trans. Bruce Fink (New York: W. W. Norton, 2006), 161–75.

20. See Jean Laplanche and J.-B. Pontalis, "Fantasy and the Origins of Sexuality," *International Journal of Psycho-Analysis* 49 (1968): 1–18.

21. See Baruch de Spinoza, *Ethics*, in *The Collected Works of Spinoza*, ed. and trans. Edwin Curley, vol. 1 (Princeton: Princeton University Press, 1985), 428.

22. Gilles Deleuze, *Difference and Repetition*, trans. Paul Patton (New York: Columbia University Press, 1994), 111.

23. Ibid., 89.

24. Ibid., 111.

25. See Sigmund Freud, *Beyond the Pleasure Principle*, in *The Standard Edition of the Complete Psychological Works of Sigmund Freud* (hereafter *SE*), ed. and trans. James Strachey et al. (London: Hogarth Press, 1953–1974), 18:33.

26. Deleuze, *Difference and Repetition*, 110.

27. Deleuze, *Proust and Signs*, trans. Richard Howard (Minneapolis: University of Minnesota Press, 2000), 74.

28. Ibid., 73.

29. Ibid., 73–74.

30. Spinoza, *Ethics*, 610.

31. Ibid., 611.

32. Laplanche and Pontalis, "Fantasy and the Origins of Sexuality," 7.

33. Ibid., 7, 5.

34. Ibid., 5.

35. Deleuze, *Difference and Repetition*, 89.

36. Ibid.

37. Ibid.

38. Ibid.

39. Ibid.

40. Ibid.

41. Ibid.

42. Deleuze, "How Do We Recognize Structuralism?" in *Desert Islands and Other Texts, 1953–1974*, ed. David Lapoujade, trans. Michael Taormina (New York: Semiotext[e], 2004), 180.

43. Ibid.

44. Laplanche and Pontalis, "Fantasy and the Origins of Sexuality," 15–16.

45. Freud, *Three Essays on the Theory of Sexuality*, in *SE* 7:222; translation modified.

46. Laplanche and Pontalis, "Fantasy and the Origins of Sexuality," 16; emphasis added.

47. Freud, *Three Essays on the Theory of Sexuality*, in *SE* 7:222; emphasis added.

48. Laplanche and Pontalis, "Fantasy and the Origins of Sexuality," 16n38; emphasis added.

49. Ibid., 16.

50. Ibid.

51. Lacan, *The Seminar of Jacques Lacan, Book XI: The Four Fundamental Concepts of Psychoanalysis*, ed. Jacques-Alain Miller, trans. Alan Sheridan (New York: W. W. Norton, 1998), 197, 198; emphasis added.

52. Ibid., 198.

53. Bruce Fink, *The Lacanian Subject: Between Language and Jouissance* (Princeton: Princeton University Press, 1995), 27.

54. Lacan, *The Seminar of Jacques Lacan, Book XI: The Four Fundamental Concepts of Psychoanalysis*, 184, 195.

55. Jacques-Alain Miller, "Transference, Repetition and the Sexual Real," *Psychoanalytical Notebooks* 22 (2011): 13, 14, 16, 15.

56. Lacan, *The Seminar of Jacques Lacan, Book XX: Encore, On Feminine Sexuality, the Limits of Love and Knowledge, 1972–1973*, ed. Jacques-Alain Miller, trans. Bruce Fink (New York: W. W. Norton, 1999), 6.

57. Lacan, *The Seminar of Jacques Lacan, Book XI: The Four Fundamental Concepts of Psychoanalysis*, 197–98.

58. Spinoza, *Ethics*, 412.

59. Beth Lord, *Spinoza's "Ethics": An Edinburgh Philosophical Guide* (Edinburgh: Edinburgh University Press, 2010), 21.

60. Spinoza, *Ethics*, 481.

61. Ibid., 409.

62. Deleuze, *Spinoza: Practical Philosophy*, trans. Robert Hurley (San Francisco: City Lights, 1988), 67, 63; emphasis added.

63. Lacan, *The Seminar of Jacques Lacan, Book XI: The Four Fundamental Concepts of Psychoanalysis*, 197, 198; emphasis added.

64. Kojin Karatani and Gregory Bateson have pointed this out. See Karatani, *Architecture as Metaphor: Language, Number, Money*, ed. Michael Speaks, trans. Sabu Kohso (Cambridge: MIT Press, 1995), 78; and Bateson, *Steps to an Ecology of Mind* (New York: Ballantine, 1972), 202–3.

65. Claude Lévi-Strauss, *Structural Anthropology*, trans. Claire Jacobson and Brooke Grundfest Schoepf (New York: Basic, 1963), 216.

66. Lacan, "Responses to Students of Philosophy Concerning the Object of Psychoanalysis," in *Television: A Challenge to the Psychoanalytic Establishment*, ed. Joan Copjec, trans. Jeffrey Mehlman (New York: W. W. Norton, 1990), 108.

67. Ibid., 110, 108.

68. Ibid.

69. See, in particular, Lacan, "A Love Letter," in *The Seminar of Jacques Lacan, Book XX: Encore, On Feminine Sexuality, the Limits of Love and Knowledge, 1972–1973*, 78–89; and Joan Copjec, "Sex and the Euthanasia of Reason,"

in *Read My Desire: Lacan against the Historicists* (Cambridge: MIT Press, 1994), 201–36.

70. Here, we can gain further insight into the mechanism of psychosis, which, instead of sexed castration (that is, the repression of the primary signifier that allows the subject to function as if being were not self-referential), involves the foreclosure of the primary signifier. While sexed castration occurs at the level of $Real_2$, we could say that foreclosure occurs when the refusal to be castrated—for the psychotic also does not want to be castrated—occurs directly at the level of $Real_1$. As a result, the psychotic remains trapped within self-referentiality, or, as Karatani puts it, "[p]sychotics live, as it were, within the self-referential paradox." Karatani, *Architecture as Metaphor: Language, Number, Money*, 78.

71. Immanuel Kant, *Critique of Pure Reason*, trans. Werner S. Pluhar (Indianapolis: Hackett Publishing Company, 1996), 515; emphasis in original.

72. Lacan, *The Seminar of Jacques Lacan, Book XX: Encore, On Feminine Sexuality, the Limits of Love and Knowledge, 1972–1973*, 7; emphasis in original.

73. Copjec, *Read My Desire: Lacan against the Historicists*, 205.

74. Lacan, *The Seminar of Jacques Lacan, Book XX: Encore, On Feminine Sexuality, the Limits of Love and Knowledge, 1972–1973*, 77.

75. Ibid., 76.

76. See ibid.

77. Kant, *Prolegomena to Any Future Metaphysics That Will Be Able to Come Forward as Science*, ed. and trans. Gary Hatfield (Cambridge: Cambridge University Press, 2004), 95–96.

78. Ibid., 95.

79. As I argue elsewhere, another central such object is the gaze. See A. Kiarina Kordela, "(Marxian-Psychoanalytic) Biopolitics and Bioracism," in *Penumbr(a)*, ed. Sigi Jöttkandt and Joan Copjec (Melbourne: re.press, 2013), 279–91.

80. Karl Marx, *Capital: A Critique of Political Economy*, trans. Ben Fowkes, vol. 1 (New York: Penguin, 1990), 274; emphasis added.

81. Marx, *Grundrisse: Foundations of the Critique of Political Economy (Rough Draft)*, trans. Martin Nicolaus (New York: Penguin, 1993), 267.

82. Ibid.; emphasis added.

83. Paolo Virno, *A Grammar of the Multitude: For an Analysis of Contemporary Forms of Life*, trans. Isabella Bertoletti, James Cascaito, and Andrea Casson (New York: Semiotext[e], 2004), 84.

84. Spinoza, *Ethics*, 611–12.

85. Marx, *Capital: A Critique of Political Economy*, vol. 1, 257.

86. Éric Alliez, *Capital Times: Tales from the Conquest of Time*, trans. Georges Van Den Abbeele (Minneapolis: University of Minnesota Press, 1996), 6. This homology between economic structures, on the one hand, and the functions of

subjectivity (that is, enjoyment), on the other, is also central to the psychoanalytic methodology, as is already evidenced in Freud's employment of abundant economic terminology. Lacan further foregrounds this point by arguing that surplus-value is not to be understood as a purely economic category, its equivalent at the level of thought and human subjectivity being surplus-enjoyment. See, in particular, Lacan, "Oedipus and Moses and the Father of the Horde," in *The Seminar of Jacques Lacan, Book XVII: The Other Side of Psychoanalysis, 1969–1970*, 102–17. We first find the logic of (though not the term) surplus-enjoyment in Aristotle's analysis of *chrematistics*, a kind of miniature version of capitalism manifest in antiquity in the marginalized practice of exchanging money, not for the acquisition of goods but for the purpose of profit-making. Because the quest is always for ever-more profit, no acquired profit can satisfy one's craving for enjoyment. Hence, it is by being constantly frustrated that enjoyment perpetually renews its urge in an (imaginarily) infinite duration. See Aristotle, *The Politics*, in *"The Politics" and "The Constitution of Athens,"* ed. Stephen Everson, trans. Jonathan Barnes (New York: Cambridge University Press, 1996), 1256a1–1258b8. For Aristotle, however, surplus-enjoyment is a condemnable and "unnatural" aberration, as is *chrematistics* itself, the natural mode of exchanging and enjoying being that of *oikonomia*, that is, the exchange of goods for the satisfaction of needs (enjoyment) here and now. Capitalism is presupposed for the organization of enjoyment as something that constantly defers itself *within* duration—prior to capitalism, the sole enjoyment that could function as surplus to the satisfaction of earthly needs and desires was the absolute and eternal enjoyment of divine transcendence. The homology between economic structures and subjectivity is a principle that psychoanalysis shares with Marx, whose theory of commodity fetishism also implies that no category is ever purely economical or purely a category of thought and subjectivity. For, according to the theory of commodity fetishism, objective relations are the relations of their producers, so that, as Étienne Balibar puts it, "there is no theory of objectivity without a theory of subjectivity." Balibar, *The Philosophy of Marx*, trans. Chris Turner (New York: Verso, 2007), 64–65. See also Marx, "The Fetishism of the Commodity and Its Secret," in *Capital: A Critique of Political Economy*, vol. 1, 163–77. I also address this topic extensively in much of my work.

87. Beyond such directly market-related biopolitical administrations of surplus-enjoyment, science, at least in its popularized forms, significantly contributes to the fostering of illusions about earthly immortality, whether it be immortality of the body (for example, through the increasing development of antiaging technologies, the promise of the cure for all diseases) or immortality of the mind (for example, digital immortality, which has been popularized through films, video games, and other forms of popular culture). See, for example, Tanya Lewis, "'Mind Uploading' and Digital Immortality May Be Reality by 2045, Futurists

Say," Science, *Huffington Post*, June 18, 2013, http://www.huffingtonpost.com/. An at least equally important biopolitical mechanism is the administration of the (real and imaginary) temporalities involved in secular capitalist modernity (finitude, eternity, and infinite duration) for the purpose of constructing the bioracial divisions that are required for the justification of biopower's employment of violence—a subject I explore throughout much of my work. See, for example, Kordela, *Being, Time, Bios: Capitalism and Ontology* (Albany: State University of New York Press, 2013); and "(Marxian-Psychoanalytic) Biopolitics and Bioracism," 279–91.

Cultural Inheritance

CHAPTER 6

Drug Is the Love

Literature, Psychopharmacology, Psychoanalysis

Justin Clemens

> How does opium induce sleep? "By means of a faculty," [...]
> replies the doctor in Molière [...]. But answers like that
> belong in comedy.
>
> — Friedrich Nietzsche[1]

The Current Dominance of Psychopharmacology in Mental Health

Everybody knows that the prognosis for psychoanalysis today is dire. Perhaps not everybody is as forthright as the English psychoanalyst Darian Leader, who has famously announced that psychoanalysts today are "mutants scavenging after a nuclear holocaust."[2] But the consensus is patent. Moreover, the diagnoses of the historical preconditions for this situation seem always to finger the same malevolent culprits. Take Kate Schechter's recent anthropology of Chicago analysts, *Illusions of a Future*.[3] As Schechter details, we live in a time in which the dream of technological solutions to mental disorders dominates the governmental-corporate-medical provision of services, hence the ubiquity of psychopharmacological treatments for an enormous range of disorders, dispensed by a range of state-ratified medical officials (from general practitioners to high-end psychiatrists) and supported by a wide and powerful range of institutions (from private research bodies and universities to governments, the mass media, and Big Pharma itself).

Drug treatments are pragmatic, not exploratory, and biotechnical, not personal or sociological; above all, they are directed at neutralizing sets of psychophysical symptoms, not towards illuminating and transforming analytic structures. So-called evidence-based medicine has trumped the qualitative narratives of psychotherapy; automated management tools have increasingly taken over the burden of diagnosis and prescription for the ever-shorter face-to-face sessions available to practitioners; and commandments issuing from the insurance industry more and more determine the micropractices of psychiatrists and psychologists. Given their clear and present supremacy in the treatment of all sorts of alleged disorders, the new-generation management strategies for mental illness have utterly overrun psychoanalytic methods of diagnosis, treatment, and theory. The latter now appear protracted, expensive, unstable, and untestable—if not downright noxious.

It is certainly not the case that the domination of Big Pharma has gone unnoticed. On the one hand, there is a slew of popular books that itemize the effects of such domination upon economies, mental health provision, and individuals globally; on the other hand, there is a barrage of technical, institutional studies mapping the consequences.[4] As Emmanuel Stamatakis and his collaborators have announced,

> [t]o serve its interests, the industry masterfully influences evidence base production, evidence synthesis, understanding of harm issues, cost-effectiveness evaluations, clinical practice guidelines and healthcare professional education and also exerts direct influences on professional decisions and health consumers. There is an urgent need for regulation and other action towards redefining the mission of medicine towards a more objective and patient-, population- and society-benefit direction that is free from conflict of interests.[5]

One can immediately see how this global domination of the pharmacological industry entails a new kind of total corruption, in which there is no significant countervailing agency able to produce counter effects. In sum, one can see how, since the 1950s, mental health has been reconceptualized as part of general health. As a consequence, mental health has been linked to economic productivity and, thus, to industrial and labor relations within a global frame. As part of general health, mental health can be subjected to the same sort of governmental attentiveness already familiar in, say, epidemiological affairs. Diagnoses are "manualized" according to dominant institutional taxonomies (for example, the *Diagnostic and Statistical Manual of Mental Disorders*, fifth edition [*DSM-5*]), and technological innovations (functional Magnetic Resonance Imaging [fMRIs]). Treatment is now pre-dominantly pharmacological. Prognosis is linked to the ongoing manage-ment of symptoms, including the management of the so-called side effects of treatment itself.

Søren Kierkegaard once wrote that "[t]he more profound the anxiety, the more profound the culture," and "[a]nxiety is neither a category of necessity nor a category of freedom; it is entangled freedom, where freedom is not free in itself but entangled, not in necessity, but in itself."[6] This is not at all a popular opinion in either the official or unofficial worlds of mental health, in which vast investments require happy results. On the contrary—and this is itself a significant development—"anxiety and depressive disorders" (the two now often produced and confounded together) have become the con-temporary targets of political, medical, and chemical interventions, that is, deleterious *symptoms* to be mitigated and monitored. That such a program of eradication may well help to spread the symptoms of anxiety and depres-sion further and further afield is clearly no argument against it.

As Mikkel Borch-Jacobsen noted over a decade ago,

> [a]dmittedly, SSRIs [selective serotonin reuptake inhibitors] some-times lead to diminished libido and even, among men, to impo-tence, but that is surely a small price to pay for a restored capacity for happiness. Twenty million people worldwide are thought to be taking Prozac, and we are hearing reports of a new era of "cosmetic psychopharmacology," in which drugs will be used to treat not only depression, but daily mood swings and existential angst. So farewell Kierkegaard and Heidegger.[7]

This is not even to mention the serious politico-scientific issues around prescription, testing, and governmental ratification. As Peter Kramer notes (surprise, surprise!), "drug companies manage the information about anti-depressants, promulgating positive studies and suppressing evidence of harm or failure. [. . .] It turns out that drug companies are shockingly inept at testing their own products."[8] Yet, for Kramer, the paradox is that drugs may turn out to be even better than their manufacturers claim; moreover, such a situation puts paid to the old-style talk for good. We will return to Kramer shortly, as his own writings proved to be prominent propaganda for the emergent, personalized drug therapies of the 1990s and 2000s, and precisely as an assault against talking cures.

I believe these transformations express the force of a desire. For my pur-poses here, I will reduce this desire to a formula: *There should be an end to talk*. All of the features of contemporary psychological politics I have already elaborated bear integrally upon this desire. There is general agreement that "depressive" and, to a lesser extent, "anxiety" disorders are the greatest threats to personal and social well-being in the current dispensation of mental health; concomitantly, enormous resources are poured into the study and fabrication of "positive emotions"—happiness, for instance. There is general agreement that the most promising research into the causes and solutions for these disorders come from psychopharmacology and the neurosciences. There is general agreement that psychoanalysis and its offspring—including versions of family therapy—have little or nothing to contribute to either research or solutions.

These features have a variety of consequences. In the new world of descriptive psychiatry, affects such as anxiety are at best *symptoms* of biochemical imbalances (genetic or physiological); they are neither irreducible affects nor guides toward truth and freedom but symptoms of the aforementioned imbalances or disorders, themselves now most likely biophysical, if not "genetic."[9] If psychoanalysis was invented in an encounter with hysteria, and if problems of psychosis and perversion came to occupy psychoanalysis in the wake of its Freudian origins, psychoanalysts seem mainly at a loss to know how to situate themselves with respect to these new disorders.

For reasons that will hopefully become clear, I want to reexamine this situation from a slightly unfamiliar angle, by way of a modern genealogy of drugs. This will involve examining the relation between psychoanalysis and drugs, a relation that is not merely contingent but rather goes directly to an issue that persists at the heart of psychoanalysis and its institutions. I will suggest that the present dispensation of drug therapies was established not by research chemists and pioneering doctors but in a literary register by William Shakespeare. Thereafter, the modality of drug therapies was forwarded in an aesthetic register by the great Romantic writers and in a governmental register by plumbers.[10] The subsequent development of drug treatments undergoes four further major shifts. From its origins with Shakespeare, there is its subsequent extension by the Romantic litterateurs; drugs are then subjected to medico-moral scrutiny; thereafter, they are subjected to repressive state apparatuses and a logic of expulsion; and, finally, in our own times, drugs are subjected to administrative control and market restriction.[11]

Having briefly sketched this genealogy, I will focus upon an influential popular text by Kramer about the relations between mental health, psychoanalysis, and drugs in order to show how the new regime of personal psychopharmacology was accompanied by specialist publicity expressly aimed against psychoanalytic theories and practices. In so doing, I will suggest how commonplace understandings of the relation between psychoanalysis and drugs fail to recognize certain crucial antagonistic complicities between psychoanalysis and drug therapies. These solidarities also provide, as we shall see, an unfamiliar angle from which to rebroach the ancient squabble within psychoanalysis in regards to its relation to science. I will offer several propositions about this relation, suggesting that a particular concept of the place, temporality, and powers of language is at stake. Finally, I want to suggest that the "real enemy" of psychoanalysis—if this phrase has any sense—is not the neurosciences or psychopharmacology per se, but rather the expropriation of language itself as an independent force that underpins all of the preceding conditions. Indeed, if psychoanalysis is to survive, it should perhaps forge a compact with other treatments that share the following fundamental axiom: *Language is not simply a technology.* As I will try to show, something troubling remains about psychoanalysis that cannot be dispensed with, even for and by persons who are deeply against it.[12]

Love's Drugs in Shakespeare and Freud

A Midsummer Night's Dream opens with a tormenting imbroglio of love and marriage. As the besotted Lysander declares to his paramour Hermia, whose father Egeus has promised her to Demetrius,

> Ay me, for aught that ever I could read,
> Could ever hear by tale or history,
> The course of true love never did run smooth.[13]

Never did run smooth—*A Midsummer Night's Dream* henceforth shuttles and stutters between the town and the woods, between the high- and low-born, the natural and supernatural, the waking and the dreamed, the real and the pantomimed, and the king and the ass. Moreover, as Lysander's own impassioned discourse suggests, the unquiet course of love is so deeply bound to language's own courses and curses—for which stories of love not only provide the matter but also the form of story itself—that, at the limit, love and language threaten to become coextensive with one another.

Shakespeare was writing the comedy of *A Midsummer Night's Dream* at the same time as the tragedy of *Romeo and Juliet*, where we also find—despite the severe generic differences marked by the ancient names of "comedy" and "tragedy"—much ado about love. On the one hand, misfortune, multiple deaths, and other disasters befall all of the noble families in the

play, through the escalations familiar to us from revenge drama: the Montagues lose Romeo and Montague's wife; the Capulets lose Juliet and Tybalt;
and the Prince loses Mercutio and County Paris. What *A Midsummer Night's
Dream* had comically figured in its Ovidian transmogrifications and in its
play-within-a-play—as Theseus advises Bottom, "Never excuse; for when
the players are all dead, there need none to be blamed"[14]—*Romeo and Juliet*
presents as a real triple death in the family crypt. On the other hand, the play
hinges upon what is essentially a comedy of misrecognition and ends with
reconciliation. The Montagues and Capulets offer each other their hands,
while golden statues of the "star-crossed" lovers are erected as a memorial
and compact. The civil rift in the city is healed.

For Sigmund Freud, precisely along the lines established by Shakespeare,
psychoanalysis is a theory and treatment of the constitutionally ambivalent
vicissitudes of love, in and by love itself. Above all, psychoanalysis considers love as the primal operator of inheritance and inheritability, a course
that can never run smoothly. Just as for Shakespeare, love in psychoanalysis must pass through wild contingencies, prohibitions, misrecognitions,
repetitions, and dissimulations as a matter of course. Love binds the most
intimate affects to affairs of state. Love is a vital disorder that, reciprocally,
inscribes and inspires personal and political disorder. Love's work is at once
the passage and the impasse.

This situation is especially clear in Freud's writings on technique, where
the transference is expressly identified with the work of love in the *practice* of
psychoanalysis. Moreover, as Freud underlines, transference-love acquires a
notably puzzling character. "Firstly," Freud notes,

> we do not understand why transference is so much more intense
> with neurotic subjects in analysis than it is with other such people
> who are not being analysed; and secondly, it remains a puzzle why
> in analysis transference emerges as *the most powerful resistance* to
> the treatment, whereas outside analysis it must be regarded as the
> vehicle of cure and the condition of success.[15]

I would like to underline not only the remarkable intensity and resistance
that Freud assigns to love in the *clinical* moment of psychoanalysis but also
the fact that, in being condemned to such struggle, the course of psychoanalysis *must* never run smoothly.

Why not? Because *Übertragung* or transference in psychoanalysis at
once constitutes a repetition, an analysis, and a *détournement* of the paradoxes of inheritance. The famous Oedipus complex is only a synecdoche of

these paradoxes. Each person is formed by infantile experiences, of which they are thereafter the inheritors. The infantile experiences are themselves destined by a kind of eternal struggle upon two fronts, between the claims of biology, on the one hand, and the social, on the other, each of which is further split. Regarding the biological, we find a kind of developmental singularity divided between the use of an organ and the survival of the organism, in which the infant's experience of its own organs is inherently split between pleasure and necessity. The pleasure of sucking a nipple, for example, which provides the neonate with its vital nutrition, is also inherently linked with the pleasure of sucking per se. Regarding the social, we find a kind of ethical *dressage* bound to the specificity of the infant's familial site, whereby the conflicting pressures of the carers' own sexual, familial, and social positions come to be directed towards the child, where they are taken up according to a range of symptomatic modalities. The vital rift between organ and organism, pleasure and survival, is doubled and compounded by a rift between the organism and its contingent situation, between the individual and its education. As Freud consistently notes, the structural frustrations of this situation are supplemented by hallucinated wish fulfillments that become the fundamental elements of fantasy. Finally, the individual "adult" finds itself caught up in, and as the aftereffects of, this double distress, according to the logic of deferred action.

It is this triple deadlock of inheritance—subsistence through a pleasure that constantly tropes away from survival, the enforced inculcation of actions through mimetic antithesis, and the achronia of the aftershock—that transference at once exemplifies and repeats. Freud can be exceptionally clear upon the matter, particularly when discussing technique. Transference revivifies a sequence of earlier identifications and cathexes in the analysand (and in the analyst, too, under some descriptions!), which, though necessarily unknown to the analysand and, despite being patently preposterous contextually, are nonetheless desperately pumped out by the publishing house of the unconscious as facsimiles of varyingly reliable quality.[16] The metaphor of the facsimile or reedition is Freud's own and implies, among other things, that the unconscious does everything not to stop not reading what it sees fit to print.[17] There is no news but old news for the unconscious—which does not read its own work. One inherits as and through the failures of inheritance.

The emphasis upon transference as an instrument and the exposition of the constitutional failures of multiplying inheritances should alert us to the fact that psychoanalysis is first and foremost an *ethics*, in a very ancient sense of the word. It is not just a theory of human behavior and motivations

but an ethical modality in and for which theory and practice are indissociable. And one of the many crucial features that separate psychoanalysis
from its ancient philosophical and cultic forebears is that, in concert with
its postscientific status, it integrally acknowledges its own rebarbative and
unwelcome nature. This is true to the extent that Freud will end by having
to admit that psychoanalysis is, strictly speaking, impossible.[18] In so doing,
psychoanalysis emerges as a new kind of institution, that is, as a form of
organization that binds economy, practice, theory, training, and transmission under the rubric of *impossibility*.

It is necessary to note here that it is no coincidence that Shakespeare—
whose plays Freud of course cites and analyzes often and enthusiastically—is
also strictly contemporary with the emergence of the epoch of modern science. Even if one fails to believe that Francis Bacon is the author of Shakespeare's plays, and even if one takes Shakespeare's probable ignorance of the
emergent new sciences seriously, one has to take the contemporaneity of
Shakespearean theatre and Galilean science seriously.

Indeed, one might also note the determining roles that friars, apothe-
caries, and their fabular counterparts, spirits such as Puck and Ariel, play
throughout Shakespeare's work as the often-unwilling agents of the crossed
subroutines of narrative fate. The "distilling liquor"[19] that simulates death and
the magical ointment that induces transspecies desire—whatever their char-
acterological, thematic, and technical differences—share at least three crucial
features in the current context. First, as *redirectors of affect*, they incarnate the
irreducible ambivalence of the *pharmakon*, the poison-cure, at once quotidian and spiritual powers, simulators and real dealers of death.[20] Second, as
generic devices, they are necessary conditions and operators that broach and
break the theatrical narratives themselves. They open and reroute narrative
and, thus, the temporality of narrative as such. Third, drugs and love are intri-
cated yet antithetical powers, opposed upon the grounds of the will. Whereas
drugs in Shakespeare already amount to an attempt at the technical seizure of
affect by individuated will—which might have quite varied comedic or tragic
effects—love is what objects to such a seizure. If drugs immediately and
artificially shut down the claims of inheritance, love opens a space wherein
inheritance and individuation duke it out at the limits of both.

It is for such reasons that the suggestively paradoxical terms of the cross,
crossroads, and crossing—the cross as simultaneously torture device and
emblem of salvation, the crossroads as a place of decision and destiny, and the
crossing as the fateful encounter of the heterogeneous—are regularly bela-
bored by both Shakespeare and Freud alike. Aside from *Romeo and Juliet's*
celebrated "star-crossed lovers,"[21] we find Hermia responding to Lysander:

If then true lovers have been ever crossed,
It stands as an edict in destiny.
Then let us teach our trial patience,
Because it is a customary cross,
As due to love as thoughts, and dreams, and sighs,
Wishes, and tears, poor fancy's followers.[22]

One can see how tempting it might be, following Harold Bloom, to take psychoanalysis as an immense and detailed gloss upon Shakespeare's plays, even if Freud himself would perhaps have preferred to advert to a distinguished philosophical inheritance for his theses.[23] As Freud famously writes in the preface to the fourth edition of *Three Essays on the Theory of Sexuality*, "as for the 'stretching' of the concept of sexuality which has been necessitated by the analysis of children and what are called perverts, anyone who looks down with contempt upon psycho-analysis from a superior vantage-point should remember how closely the enlarged sexuality of psycho-analysis coincides with the Eros of the divine Plato."[24] Psychoanalysis, in other words, authors the *Symposium* of scientific modernity.

But perhaps the "superior vantage-point" of which Freud speaks here should best be considered the rim of a volcano, given that he would later invoke the pre-Socratic Empedocles as another august forefather. In "Analysis Terminable and Interminable," Freud writes that "[t]he two fundamental principles of Empedocles—$\varphi\iota\lambda\iota\alpha$ and $\nu\varepsilon\tilde{\iota}\chi o\varsigma$—are, both in name and function, the same as our two primal instincts, *Eros* and *destructiveness*, the first of which endeavours to combine what exists into ever greater unities, while the second endeavours to dissolve those combinations and to destroy the structures to which they have given rise."[25] Yet, as Freud ambiguously notes, "we should be tempted to maintain that the two are identical, if it were not for the difference that the Greek philosopher's theory is a cosmic phantasy while ours is content to claim biological validity."[26] Of course, the difference loses "much of its importance" insofar as those principles can now be regrounded biologically. Nonetheless, what breaks the continuity with the ancients is the very practice of modern science—Copernican, Galilean, Baconian, to advert to the standard references—to which Freud himself was expressly committed.

I have argued elsewhere that psychoanalysis is an antiphilosophy insofar as it emerges by injecting poetic elements into science.[27] I do not wish to further rehearse my arguments here, except insofar as they bear upon the thematic of transference as an expression-treatment for the deadlocks of inheritance. In this context, this requires revisiting the changing relationship between drugs and love in modernity in order to show how psychoanalysis at once conforms to certain of this episteme's ground-features as it attempts to depart from them—or, at least, to leverage them against itself.

Drug Archaeologies of the Modern Episteme

Let me now suggest that there are five key dispensations of drugs in the modern episteme.[28] I will denominate these as follows: (1) theatrical monstrosity, (2) romantic imperialism, (3) medico-moralizing, (4) legislative-repressive, and (5) administrative decriminalization.

Each of these dispensations is marked by particular internal antagonisms, which condition the production, distribution, and uses of "drugs"; these antagonisms are not simply neutralized or supplanted in the shift to the next dispensation but continue to actively interfere with one another. However, despite its integral (if complex) relations with theatrical monstrosity, certain Romantic tropes, modern science, and modern forms of governmentality, psychoanalysis itself moves transversally to the logics of these dispensations. If I begin by summarizing what I see as the essential characteristics of these dispensations, it is ultimately to show how psychoanalysis fails to conform to the dominant modi operandi.

1. *Theatrical Monstrosity.* I have already noted this phenomenon above with regard to Shakespeare. The key point is that love and drugs are there understood as metastable generic elements bound together in their role of affect redirectors yet opposed according to their relations to volition. If drugs, as technologies of will, essay to short-circuit the powers of inheritance, love takes the latter to their limits.

2. *Romantic Imperialism.* Often themselves explicitly drawing from the genius of Shakespeare, Romantic litterateurs set the stage for all subsequent re-visionings of the relation between drugs and the human sensorium.[29] Writers such as Samuel Taylor Coleridge, Thomas Love Beddoes, and, above all, Thomas de Quincey invent the still-contemporary image of the addict as an ambivalent hero of subjectivity. Associated with one of the first recognizable modern drug subcultures, the "Pneumatic Drug Institute," which included the scientist Sir Humphry Davy among its members, these writers take drugs for a number of interconnected reasons: (1) fun, (2) medical complaints, (3) subjective experimentation, (4) political motivations, and (5) ontological-metaphysical enthusiasm. In their experiments with drugs, these writers generate a number of tropes around drug use that remain active today. Drugs are at once a source of what Walter Benjamin would

later call "profane illumination" *and* addiction, that is, a pure reduction to transartificial biophysical necessity. Drugs set their subject in motion, towards the borders of social space, where the drug-subjects will encounter, in liminal and degraded zones, other unacceptable figures (prostitutes, the destitute, petty criminals, and so on).[30] Onto existing theological discourses of sin, these writers graft the extreme consumption of psychologically and physically deranging commodities.[31]

Drugs are not, it must be remembered, illegal at this historical moment; their circulation is not restricted by the state. Nor are they in any way immoral. On the contrary, they are quotidian, widely available, and entirely acceptable commodities. As Victoria Berridge and Griffith Edwards point out in their classic text *Opium and the People*, using a phrase that is now somewhat commonplace, in the nineteenth century, religion was not, as Karl Marx suggested, "the opium of the people": "Opium itself was the 'opiate of the people.'"[32] This immediately points us towards an apparent paradox in the literature: To what is one confessing when one confesses to taking drugs? If de Quincey is addicted to drugs, it is not simply as a deleterious physical compulsion but as an incitement to discourse. Narratives are produced as a rupture with drugs, without ever absolutely departing their ambit. For the Romantics, drugs are technologies that undermine their own therapeutic bases, while language is a technology that permits the transmission of this failure. At the same time, however, both drugs and language are in excess of technology to the extent that they are associated with noninstrumental— and, thus, metaphysically interesting—activities.

In the terms that the Romantics themselves forged, it seems that inventive uses of language become a *treatment*—and not simply a *cure*—for drug addiction. The Romantic addict unveils an immanent toxicity of the will, the will itself as a rapacious drive to toxicity.[33] Moreover, from the Romantics to the present day, such writers are obsessed with drugs as somehow providing the truth of the social body. That this is done in a literary fashion is paramount. The antihero in narratives of addiction is integrally a figure that short-circuits medical and literary genres.[34] Not only does the Freudian unconscious find itself prefigured by Romantic writers, but so too does the death drive, in both its dominant acceptations as destructive aggression and pure repetition automatism. That this happens upon the terrain of drugs is, as we shall see, particularly significant.

It should also be remembered that opiate products are widely available because of European imperialism. Britain fought two opium wars with China, making Queen Victoria the most powerful drug baron of the nineteenth century.[35] And this imperial expansion returns as a question of nation within narratives of drug abuse—de Quincey's title is, after all, *Confessions of an English Opium Eater*.[36] But there is another point to be made here concerning the problem of contagion. Early nineteenth-century Europe was periodically ravaged by such highly infectious diseases as typhoid, smallpox, and cholera, which "were almost entirely traceable to bad sanitation."[37] Barbara Hodgson, the author of a book on opium, has remarked that, when she was going through newspaper obituaries in the 1820s and 1830s, she found, among all the cholera deaths, a scattering of deaths attributed to opium use.[38] Opium, in other words, was literally holding early nineteenth-century Western Europe's shit together. If political theorists often continue to speak of the "social contract" and the "social bond," one would have to say that the real bonding technology of European societies of the late eighteenth to the mid-nineteenth centuries is opium. The drug *is* the bond—but also the rupture of the bond. As Jacques Derrida puts it, in a perhaps surprising allusion to Jacques Lacan, "you might even say that the act of drug use itself is structured like a language and so could not be purely private."[39] Or, as de Quincey puts it in a deidealizing note, "[i]n the whole system of houses, to which this house is attached, there exists but one *Templum Cloacinae*. Now imagine the fiend driving a man thither thro' 8 and 10 hours successively. Such a man becomes himself a public nuisance, and is in some danger of being removed by assassination."[40] Drugs are liable to create a public social nuisance, even in the most private, biological functions of life. As such, they do not merely open onto transcendence but also parasitize the subject, who is thereby revealed as the voiding effect of primordial, meaningless, and physiological repetitions. This exemplarily Romantic relation to addiction (and shit) provides a useful transition to our second dispensation, which, against the dark revelations of the Romantics, aims at cleanliness, order, and sanity.

3. *Medico-moral.* The isolation of the figure of the addict by the Romantics renders it susceptible to immediate recodification by discursive regimes with very different political agendas. The major interlocking developments include the following: (1) a new dominance of urban planning, especially sewage, for which Baron Haussman's rebuilding of Paris is emblematic; (2) the transformation of dye companies into chemical companies;[41] (3) the rise of so-called social purity movements in modern European democracies;[42] (4) the development of modern scientific specializations, notably organic chemistry;[43] (5) a new bond between medical professionals and the state;[44] and (6) developments in medical technologies, such as the hypodermic method. Rather than Romantic writers, it was plumbers such as Thomas Crapper who opened the possibilities.[45] If the early nineteenth century had seen the first isolation of active substances (in 1806 Friedrich Sertürner

isolated morphium from opium, an event that was followed by the isolation of emetine, strychnine, codeine, caffeine, atropine, quinine, and so on), it was not until after mid-century that synthesizing really began to get underway, including, for example, the synthesis of heroin at St. Mary's hospital in London in 1870.

This is the era in which addiction is crystallized as a viable medical category. One immediately sees the relation to Michel Foucault's "history of sexuality."[46] On the other hand, and unlike sexuality, addiction arises out of nowhere, so to speak. Unlike sexual acts, which had always been policed in one way or another, and have always been the subject of possible social— even sovereign—intervention, drug taking has never been subject to the law in the same way, and the addict "himself" is hardly susceptible to the same sort of scientific etiologies as those of supposed sexual deviants. Rather than a pervert of nature, as it were, the addict is considered to be in direct relation to technology, a synthetic production, and not even, in principle, to a "natural" being. The addict is a pervert of technology. "Addiction," as a medical category, is directly generated out of state restrictions upon commodity availability, industrial synthesis, and control of contagions by urban renewal.

4. *Legislative-Repressive*. It was not until the 1860s in England that opium was restricted, and it was not until much later that drugs were banned anywhere.[47] The Pure Food and Drug Act of 1906 in the United States only restricted the importation of coca leaves and required all medicines containing cocaine or opium to be properly labeled. Indeed, into the twentieth century, one could still buy fancy morphine injecting kits at major department stores worldwide. They would have presumably made great gifts: Galeries Lafayette might have even wrapped them for you. Significantly, the United States led the way, moving to render cocaine illegal, before rapidly progressing on to alcohol, marijuana, and opiates in subsequent decades. Many of the players we have already encountered played a determining role in this shift: moral campaigners, the medical profession (which became the only legal trader in drugs in the modern state), organized crime rings, and, above all, law enforcement agencies. In this dispensation, drugs were criminalized, and unauthorized users were to be dealt with by what Louis Althusser called repressive state apparatuses (RSAs): police, courts, and prisons.[48] The twentieth century was mostly organized by an accord between medical and legal arms of governmentality, in which drugs were illegal, addicts were sick and perverted, and the only people who stood up for drug takers were radical literary types.

5. *Administrative Control*. We are today at the limit of the sequence that I have suggested begins with Shakespeare, having reached a limit in the

aims, methods, and institutions that take mental health as their object. This shift has been underway since the 1950s. David Healy has denominated this period "the psychopharmacological era";[49] it has witnessed unprecedented investment in the development of technologies, exemplarily chemical technologies (but also imaging innovations, such as fMRI), for the diagnosis and treatment of mental disorders. The psychopharmacological era, in short, names the emergence of a new alliance between multinational chemical companies, research scientists, and the state in an attempt to manage the competing exigencies of late capitalist profitability, scientific knowledge, and the governmental control of vast populations.

Listening to Prozac

Accompanying this shift has been a concomitant underplaying of the role of "talking cures"—emblematically, psychoanalysis—as legitimate, useful methods of mental health. The triumph of psychopharmacology seems to have been sealed in the 1990s with the extraordinary international public enthusiasm for Prozac. Prozac and the new, "clean" generation of SSRIs, despite their well-known drawbacks (for example, sexual dysfunction, statistically significant rates of suicide, evidence that they are not, in the final analysis, more effective than psychotherapies, and so on), indicate that "anhedonia," for instance, may be the mere consequence of a serotonin imbalance and nothing to do with dysfunctions in infantile relations with the mother. If one refers to such texts as Kramer's massive bestseller *Listening to Prozac*, one discovers that Prozac reveals there is not a single aspect of experience that can or should be exempted from technological manipulation. It is crucial that the diagnoses of this new dispensation are very different from those of previous eras. On the one hand, we find a taxonomic escalation of those capacious grab bags of "anxiety and depressive disorders" I have invoked above; on the other hand, we find an extraordinary proliferation of a thousand tiny mental disorders (as evidenced by the ever-expanding generations of the *DSM*). Moreover, and according to the best authorities, still no one is certain why these drugs work—or, more accurately, fail to work.

At exactly the same moment officially ratified big business pharmaceuticals are proposed as the magic bullet that will finally put the werewolf of mental disorders to rest, an unforgiving public war is underway to obliterate the purveyors of these drugs outside the realm of daylight markets. The two great metaphors that regulate this tropology are those of epidemic and war, organizing two irreducible but indissociable registers of cultural response.

Such drugs—heroin, cocaine, crack, meth, and so on—are, like terrorism, persistently figured as proliferating virally, integrally threatening the integrity of the social body, against which an unforgiving and endless "war" is allegedly the only possible response. That this rhetoric is at once contradictory and coherent should come as no surprise.

Why listen when you can simply dispense? Daily papers are filled with articles about medical drugs, with headlines such as "Doctors 'Forced' to Overprescribe Antidepressants," "Antidepressants Seen as Effective for Adolescents," and "Large Study on Mental Illness Finds Global Prevalence."[50] It is with this context in mind that I want to reexamine Kramer's massive bestseller *Listening to Prozac*. I take this book at once as part of a concerted propaganda program on the part of Big Pharma and as a symptom of the abiding difficulty of psychoanalysis (in both subjective and objective senses of the genitive).

Note how Kramer's title attempts to reconfigure the distinction between *listening* and *dispensing* in favor of dispensing: Prozac is a wonder drug precisely because it is the drug that overcomes the very distinction—to the point that one now listens to it as if it were the true subject of depression.[51] As Kramer puts it in the conclusion to the book,

> [h]aving seen people not unlike ourselves respond to medicine, we experience angst and melancholy differently—our own and others'. Perhaps what Camus' Stranger suffered—his anhedonia, his sense of anomie—was a disorder of serotonin. Kierkegaard's fear and trembling and sickness unto death are at once spiritually significant and phenomenologically unremarkable, quite ordinary spectrum traits of mammals, affects whose interpretation in metaphysical terms is wholly arbitrary.[52]

This is an extraordinary statement, one that it is almost worth reading closely for its significant rhetorical moves. "Having seen people"—the visual metaphor is not just another metaphor in this context. After all, the book is called *Listening to Prozac*, and so the fact that this grand finale makes an unexpected swerve towards the regime of the visible should strike us as at least a little odd. Next, "not unlike"—a syntagm of indefinite resemblance, which seems difficult to pin down. In what ways are they not unlike, exactly, since, after all, Kramer is a psychiatrist and his patients are not? Are they all middle class? All sick? All basically decent human beings? Actually, it turns out that this not unlikeness is more a question of personality. Kramer states it directly: They are not unlike "ourselves." Again, *who*? He has moved out of the first-person voice of his account to include the innumerable, nameless readers in his warm and capacious embrace. The circularity of this rhetoric cannot be overlooked. For example, if psychoanalysis means anything, it is that we *cannot* recognize ourselves, and that such an affirmation of not unlikeness must therefore be the index of a fantasy, an illusion, rather than a firm evidentiary basis for knowledge.

Leaving psychoanalysis aside, what are our visions of others not unlike ourselves actually meant to be of, according to Kramer? We—who, again?—have seen them "respond" to "medicine." In the beginning was the magic bullet. That is, the very responsiveness of others to drugs shows us that their "being" is a contingency that can and, indeed, should be rectified in the most efficient ways possible. What Prozac teaches us—and Kramer's is indeed an ethico-pedagogical tract, as well as a superbly successful marketing exercise—is that there is not a single aspect of our lives that we should consider exempt from medical expertise and pharmacological intervention. If Immanuel Kant's thumbnail formula for morality was *You can because you must!* the ethical imperative of our era has become *We must because we can!* For Kramer, the other is a mirror of the self and Prozac is its Mr. Sheen.[53]

It is all the more interesting that Kramer then invokes literary and philosophical models as his targets. This is interesting for at least three reasons. First of all, Kramer himself began his training as a wannabe *litteratus*, befriending Lionel Trilling (one of the greatest American literary critics of his generation), as well as writing short stories and criticism. Second, Kramer does not mention psychoanalysis, which, given the context, would have to be the real target of his critiques. Literature and philosophy are thus stand-ins for the real enemy. That they can be so suggests, finally, that contemporary technics and accompanying ideologies of scientism take it as absolutely necessary to proclaim that these older therapeutic practices have neither epistemological traction nor psychological effectivity in the brave new world of chemical treatments (yes, a literary allusion, to the drug-popping Aldous Huxley).

Rather than "experienc[ing] angst and melancholy differently" after meditating upon Albert Camus's literary figures, we now do so after watching others responding to drugs. What humans say is corralled here at the level of mere spiritual significance—having nothing whatsoever to do with the brute, physicochemical fact of a determining biological substrate. Reading itself—or the affects and thoughts generated by listening to others—has somehow become just a reflex of "quite ordinary spectrum traits of mammals," and the most intense affects can therefore supposedly be interpreted only in "wholly arbitrary" terms. At base, contemporary drug therapies present *the very possibility of divergent interpretations* as a nonscientific phenomenon, simultaneously presenting themselves as *absolutes*. That new "generations" of drugs are already being packaged seems not to vitiate each new drug's absolute scientific, materialist basis.

But what if that is precisely the point? That a mammal can and would make a specific affect an index of divinity, and then make that very attribution, in all its arbitrariness, count for other mammals of the same species in an unexpected, unprecedented way, should suggest that the putative responsiveness of such minds to drugs is a direct attack upon what used to be called *imagination*, namely, the ability to synthesize the diversity of experience into an unprecedented form, one that has in no way been given with the given.[54] Rather than people not responding to literature and philosophy, the problem for Kramer is that they *do not respond in the right way*, that is, they (madly) refuse the work-ready functionality (not to mention happiness) that he, as a doctor, has to offer them in the form of an authorized representative of a global, pharmaceutical corporation. How dare they! One might wonder whether Kramer's phrase "wholly arbitrary" betrays a certain anxiety: If he had just written "arbitrary," would we suspect that that meant "just a bit arbitrary," "not really arbitrary," or "arbitrary in a specific way that is not actually arbitrary"? In any case, it is irrelevant: Drugs will solve the problem of all of our interpretative *differends* by quashing the conflict of our inheritances.

For the Love of Technology

The kettle logics at work in the formations I have examined upon the politico-scientific status of psychopharmacology express the force of a desire. This desire is that there be an end to talk. As I have outlined, there are several connected features of contemporary psychological politics that bear integrally upon this desire. First, there is a general agreement that "depressive" and, to a lesser extent, "anxiety" disorders are the greatest threats to personal and social well-being in the current dispensation of mental health. Second, there is a general agreement that the most promising research into the causes and solutions for these disorders come from psychopharmacology and the neurosciences. Third, there is a general agreement that psychoanalysis and its offspring—including versions of family therapy—have little or nothing to contribute to either research or solutions. As Bernard Stiegler frequently argues, part of the problem for the global present is that it is a regime of "psychopower," which "controls the individual and collective behaviour of consumers by channeling their libidinal energy toward commodities."[55] Yet, something troubling remains about psychoanalysis that cannot simply be dispensed with, even for and by scientists who are deeply against it.

One of the noteworthy features of contemporary psychoanalysis is that, to the extent that it survives at all, it has become what Lacan called a "university discourse,"[56] and not just in the particular structural sense Lacan describes, but in the empirical and sociological sense of a predominantly humanities discourse. This makes psychoanalysis a question of a teaching of the inheritance of psychoanalysis that is almost entirely separated from its practice—that is, counter to its origins as a practical psychology—which thereby renders psychoanalysis a bundle of doctrines and authorities that can be compared and contrasted with others, rather than the practice of an urgency of address towards the symptoms of desire. Yet, this separation and diminution also allows something essential to emerge about psychoanalysis that its practical aspect tended to occlude, namely, the properly poetic nature of its intervention into a properly scientific frame. Psychoanalysis is an antiphilosophy insofar as it interrupts science by literature in order to create a *techne-that-is-not-one*. This techne is transference-love; it is arrayed against physiochemical reduction; it requires a trial of inheritances, in which the singular deadlocks of a subject's coming-to-be are revivified in a temporally extended and affectively ambivalent form; and it expressly runs the risk of its own intransigence, impotence, and impossibility.

But it is also because the era opened by Shakespearean-scientific modernity is now in its closure that something of the complicated genealogy of the relation between drugs and love in modernity can reemerge again. As I have tried to show, psychoanalysis takes up what was in Shakespeare already a triple, theatrical monstrosity of drugs in order to connect it directly with the sciences in a way that is at once consonant with, yet irreducible to, all of the major genealogical shifts since. This has meant leveraging the very difficulties of subject-formation into the treatment for their own consequences, a paradoxical and painful process. Now that technology in the form of pharmacology rules the roost, it is the task of psychoanalysis today to reconnect its self-realization as a discourse of failure, hesitancy, and unhappiness to the real lives of people.

Freud—who, lest we forget, was himself euthanized by the new drugs under the direction of his personal physician—knew it too. When Martin Heidegger, confronting what he called "the planetary reign of technology," offers the notorious formula that "[o]nly a god can save us" (*Nur noch ein Gott kann uns retten*), the poetic melancholy of Friedrich Hölderlin remains paramount to his attempts at a postphilosophical "other thinking."[57] For his part, also confronting—if in a very different frame—the problem of technology, Freud finds himself compelled to invoke another great litterateur. "We can only say," he writes, citing Johann Wolfgang von Goethe's *Faust*, "'So muss denn doch die Hexe dran!' [We must call the Witch to our help after all!]—the Witch Meta-psychology."[58] It seems the witchcraft of a love for the literary must today form our last bastion against the totalization of drugs in the marketplace—and, if this will be done, it will require tangling again with the deadlocks of inheritance.

Notes

1. Friedrich Nietzsche, *Beyond Good and Evil: Prelude to a Philosophy of the Future*, trans. R. J. Hollingdale (New York: Penguin, 2003), 42.

2. See Susanna Rustin, "Getting in Touch," *Guardian*, January 26, 2008, http://www.theguardian.com/lifeandstyle/2008/jan/26/familyandrelationships.family1.

3. See Kate Schechter, *Illusions of a Future: Psychoanalysis and the Biopolitics of Desire* (Durham: Duke University Press, 2014).

4. For an interesting instance of a popular critique, see Ethan Watters, *Crazy Like Us: The Globalization of the American Psyche* (New York: Free Press, 2010).

5. Emmanuel Stamatakis, Richard Weiler, and John P. A. Ioannidis, "Undue Industry Influences that Distort Healthcare Research, Strategy, Expenditure and Practice: A Review," *European Journal of Clinical Investigation* 43, no. 5 (2013): 469.

6. Søren Kierkegaard, *The Concept of Anxiety: A Simple Psychologically Orienting Deliberation on the Dogmatic Issue of Hereditary Sin*, ed. and trans. Reidar Thome in collaboration with Albert B. Anderson (Princeton: Princeton University Press, 1980), 42, 49.

7. Mikkel Borch-Jacobsen, "Psychotropicana," *London Review of Books*, July 11, 2002, http://www.lrb.co.uk/v24/n13/mikkel-borch-jacobsen/psychotropicana.

8. Peter D. Kramer, "Should Teenagers Take Drugs? Prozac, Paxil, and Teen Depression," *Slate*, June 4, 2004, http://www.slate.com/. As Kramer continues,

[t]he pharmaceutical companies do shoddy research on the drugs' efficacy. Because the patents on medication have a limited duration, the corporations are always in a rush to bring drugs to market. The companies pressure the subcontractors that perform the studies, demanding that they gather research subjects fast. The recruiters then stretch diagnostic criteria, signing up patients who may not have the disease in question. Studies often include people with a host of shifting complaints, many of which are based less on acute illness than on personality style. The result is a group with poorly defined conditions and

high placebo response rates—enough static to drown out whatever effects the medications have on substantial disease.

Nevertheless, Kramer points to the following:

> Oddly, then, in the "rush to market," drug company studies tend to hide the efficacy of the very medications that the corporations hope to promote. It is the rule, not the exception, for similar medications to fare poorly in drug company trials but to fare well in subsequent (presumably disinterested) government-sponsored research. The NIMH-supervised research on adolescent depression has not been published, which means that it has not undergone its final peer review. But it is known to be well-designed and carefully executed.

Oliver Bennett, citing Arnold Relman, the former editor-in-chief of the *New England Journal of Medicine*, notes that, since the 1970s,

> there had been an erosion of medical ethics as physicians and researchers increasingly entered into financial arrangements with drug manufacturers and investor-owned health-care facilities. Clinical investigators, for example, were holding equity interests in companies whose products they were testing; others were serving as paid consultants or scientific advisors; respected academics were being hired by drug companies to give lectures or write articles about the manufacturers' new products; and physicians were investing in health-care facilities to which they could then refer their patients.
>   Bennett, *Cultural Pessimism: Narratives of Decline in the Postmodern World* (Edinburgh: Edinburgh University Press, 2001), 121.

9. See, for example, Éric Laurent, "Désangoisser?" *Mental* 13 (2003): 21: "Il va de soi, en médecine, que le symptôme est quelque chose qu'il s'agit de faire disparaître. L'angoisse est un symptôme comme un autre à faire disparaître." We can see the shift towards the symptomization of anxiety in the work of cognitive behavioral therapy (CBT). According to Aaron T. Beck, for instance, anxiety and depression are characterized by a "negative cognitive shift." See "Cognitive Therapy: A 30-Year Retrospective," *American Psychologist* 46, no. 4 (1991), 369.

10. Hence, psychoanalysis has always been the close associate of various waste disposal experts: sewage engineers, plumbers, maids, mothers, and so on. Aside from Freud and Lacan's remarks upon the topic of waste, see Dominique Laporte, *History of Shit*, trans. Nadia Benabid and Rodolphe el-Khoury (Cambridge: MIT Press, 2002).

11. Psychoanalysts themselves often seem to demonize drug treatments in a way that elides certain essential complicities. See, for example, Élisabeth Roudinesco, "Anti-Freudian Revisionism Triumphant in the United States," *Virtuosity: The Newsletter of the Australasian Society for Continental Philosophy* 4 (1997): 4; Ellie Ragland, *Essays on the Pleasures of Death: From Freud to Lacan* (New York: Routledge, 1995), 106; and Bruce Fink, *A Clinical Introduction to Lacanian Psychoanalysis: Theory and Technique* (Cambridge: Harvard University Press, 1997), 116, 252n70.

12. "According to his own declarations, Popper constructed his falsificationist epistemology to the sole end of establishing a demarcation between science and political discourse—in the occasion, Marxism, put at the service of a world-view. [. . .] One will note that Popper aligns Freudian psychoanalysis with politicized Marxism. Pure and simple prejudice: it is, on the contrary, completely obvious that Freud is an illustration of falsificationist epistemology. See, among other examples, the introduction of a beyond of the pleasure principle on the basis of falsifying experience: the *Fort-Da*." Jean-Claude Milner, *Les noms indistincts* (Paris: Éditions du Seuil, 1983), 92–93; my translation.

13. William Shakespeare, *A Midsummer Night's Dream*, in *The Norton Shakespeare: Based on the Oxford Edition*, ed. Stephen Greenblatt (New York: W. W. Norton, 1997), 1.1.132–34.

14. Ibid., 5.1.341–42.

15. Sigmund Freud, "The Dynamics of Transference," in *The Standard Edition of the Complete Psychological Works of Sigmund Freud* (hereafter *SE*), ed. and trans. James Strachey et al. (London: Hogarth Press, 1953–1974), 12:101; emphasis in original.

16. I use the word *preposterous* advisedly in the current context. As K. K. Ruthven points out, the term can mean "ridiculous" or "nonsensical" and can refer to a temporal or hierarchical inversion. See Ruthven, "Preposterous Chatterton," *ELH* 71, no. 2 (2004): 345–75.

17. See Freud, *Fragment of an Analysis of a Case of Hysteria*, in *SE* 7:116.

18. See Freud, "Preface to Aichhorn's *Wayward Youth*," in *SE* 19:273; and "Analysis Terminable and Interminable," in *SE* 23:248.

19. Shakespeare, *The Most Excellent and Lamentable Tragedy of Romeo and Juliet*, in *The Norton Shakespeare: Based on the Oxford Edition*, 4.1.94.

20. For a brilliant reading of "Plato's Pharmacy," see Jacques Derrida, *Dissemination*, trans. Barbara Johnson (Chicago: University of Chicago Press, 1981), 61–171.

21. Shakespeare, *The Most Excellent and Lamentable Tragedy of Romeo and Juliet*, 1.1.6.

22. Shakespeare, *A Midsummer Night's Dream*, 1.1.150–55.

23. See Harold Bloom, *Shakespeare: The Invention of the Human* (New York: Riverhead, 1998).

24. Freud, *Three Essays on the Theory of Sexuality*, in *SE* 7:134.

25. Freud, "Analysis Terminable and Interminable," in *SE* 23:246; emphasis in original.

26. Ibid., 245.

27. See Justin Clemens, "Introduction: Psychoanalysis Is an Antiphilosophy," in *Psychoanalysis Is an Antiphilosophy* (Edinburgh: Edinburgh University Press, 2013), 1–16.

28. This claim develops work originally done in collaboration with Christopher Feik. See Clemens and Feik, "The De-moralisation of the Drug Debate?" in *Heroin Crisis: Key Commentators Discuss the Issues and Debate Solutions to Heroin Abuse in Australia*, ed. Kate van den Boogert and Nadine Davidoff (Melbourne: Bookman Press, 1999), 18–23.

29. The literature on this question is now vast. See, among others, Charles J. Rzepka, *Sacramental Commodities: Gift, Text, and the Sublime in De Quincey* (Amherst: University of Massachusetts Press, 1995); Elisabeth Schneider, *Coleridge, Opium and Kubla Khan* (Chicago: University of Chicago Press, 1953); Alethea Hayter, *Opium and the Romantic Imagination* (London: Faber and Faber, 1968); M. H. Abrams, *The Milk of Paradise: The Effect of Opium Visions on the Works of De Quincey, Crabbe, Francis Thompson, and Coleridge* (Cambridge: Harvard University Press, 1934); and Susan M. Levin, *The Romantic Art of Confession: De Quincey, Musset, Sand, Lamb, Hogg, Frémy, Soulié, Janin* (Columbia: Camden House, 1998).

30. See Walter Benjamin, "Surrealism: The Last Snapshot of the European Intelligentsia," in *Selected Writings, 1927–1930*, ed. Michael W. Jennings, Howard Eiland, and Gary Smith, trans. Edmund Jephcott, vol. 2, pt. 1 (Cambridge: Belknap Press, 1999), 207–21.

31. In this regard, Slavoj Žižek is simply restating the Romantics' case when he writes that

> [p]erhaps the best illustration of the way this reflexivity affects our everyday experience of subjectivity is the universalized status of addiction: today, one can be "addicted" to anything—not only to alcohol or drugs, but also to food, smoking, sex, work. . . . This universalization of addiction signifies the radical uncertainty of any subjective position today: there are no firm predetermined patterns, everything has to be (re)negotiated again and again. [. . .]
>
> [This is evident in] the different versions of the attempt to restore the premodern sovereign gesture of pure expenditure—recall the figure of the *junkie*,

the only true "subject of consumption," the only one who consumes himself utterly, to his very death, in his unbound *jouissance*. [. . .]

Today's preoccupation with drug addiction as the ultimate danger to the social edifice can be properly understood only against the background of the predominant subjective economy of consumption as the form of appearance of thrift: in previous epochs, the consumption of drugs was simply one among the half-concealed social practices of real (de Quincey, Baudelaire) and fictional (Sherlock Holmes) characters.

> Žižek, *Did Somebody Say Totalitarianism? Five Interventions*
> *in the (Mis)use of a Notion* (New York: Verso, 2001),
> 27, 44, 260n31; emphasis in original.

32. Virginia Berridge and Griffith Edwards, *Opium and the People: Opiate Use in Nineteenth-Century England* (London: Allen Lane, 1981), 37.

33. See Eve Kosofsky Sedgwick, "Epidemics of the Will," in *Tendencies* (Durham: Duke University Press, 1993), 130–42.

34. This short-circuiting is critical to the present day, such that—from de Quincey, through Charles Baudelaire, Arthur Rimbaud, Sherlock Holmes, Dr. Jekyll, Dorian Gray, Aleister Crowley, Jean Cocteau, and William Burroughs, to the characters of Irvine Welsh's *Trainspotting*—"reality" and "fiction" are thoroughly confounded. As Nigel Leask puts it, "[a]lthough the *Confessions* had first appeared in a literary journal, and was clearly the work of a man of letters [. . .], contemporary readers tended to take it at its word by reading it as a medical account of opium addiction and an intervention in a current debate about the therapeutic value of opium." Leask, *British Romantic Writers and the East: Anxieties of Empire* (Cambridge: Cambridge University Press, 1992), 172. See Thomas de Quincey, *Confessions of an English Opium Eater* (New York: Penguin, 2003); Théophile Gautier and Charles Baudelaire, *Hashish, Wine, Opium*, trans. Maurice Stang (London: Calder and Boyars, 1972); Aleister Crowley, *Diary of a Drug Fiend* (San Francisco: Weiser, 2010); Claude Farrère, *Black Opium*, trans. Samuel Putnam (San Francisco: And/ Or Press, 1974); Jean Cocteau, *Opium: The Illustrated Diary of His Cure*, trans. Margaret Crosland (London: Peter Owen, 1990); William Burroughs, *Junky* (New York: Penguin, 1977); Kevin Mackey, *The Cure: Recollections of an Addict* (Sydney: Angus and Robertson, 1971); and Melvin Burgess, *Junk* (London: Penguin, 1997).

35. The "wars" were fought from 1839 to 1842 and from 1856 to 1860. See Jack Beeching, *The Chinese Opium Wars* (New York: Harcourt Brace Jovanovich, 1975); and Paul C. Winther, *Anglo-European Science and the Rhetoric of Empire: Malaria, Opium, and British Rule in India, 1756–1895* (Lanham: Lexington, 2003).

36. See John Barrell, *The Infection of Thomas de Quincey: A Psychopathology of Imperialism* (New Haven: Yale University Press, 1991); Alina Clej, *A*

Genealogy of the Modern Self: Thomas De Quincey and the Intoxication of Writing (Stanford: Stanford University Press, 1995); Josephine McDonagh, *De Quincey's Disciplines* (Oxford: Clarendon Press, 1994) and "Opium and the Imperial Imagination," in *Reviewing Romanticism*, ed. Philip W. Martin and Robin Jarvis (London: Macmillan, 1992), 116–33; and Leask, *British Romantic Writers and the East: Anxieties of Empire.*

37. Wallace Reyburn, *Flushed with Pride: The Story of Thomas Crapper* (Clifton-upon-Teme: Polperro Heritage Press, 2010), 29. Cholera had spread to Europe from India in the 1820s, and there were further epidemics in Britain in 1848–1849, 1853–1854, and 1866.

38. She mentioned this during a session at the Melbourne Writers' Festival in 1999. See also Barbara Hodgson, *Opium: A Portrait of the Heavenly Demon* (San Francisco: Chronicle, 1999).

39. Derrida, "The Rhetoric of Drugs," in *Points . . . : Interviews, 1974–1994,* ed. Elisabeth Weber, trans. Michael Israel (Stanford: Stanford University Press, 1995), 250.

40. Quoted in Paul Youngquist, "De Quincey's Crazy Body," *PMLA* 114 (1999): 356.

41. In 1859, J. R. Geigy established a dye company and Alexander Clavel founded the company that would become Ciba; in 1862, Jean Gaspar Dolfus set up what would become Sandoz:

> All were dye producers. Ciba only produced its first pharmaceutical preparation in 1889; Sandoz produced a medical remedy for the first time in 1921 and Geigy in 1940 (although the key compounds from which the psychotropic drugs were later to come had all been synthesized by the turn of the century). After World War I, all three of these companies branched out into textiles and in the 1930s into plastics and insecticides. In addition to setting up a home base, all three quickly moved to set up branches outside Switzerland, establishing the basis for later multinational developments. There were a number of reasons for doing this; one was to circumvent patent laws, another to avoid import duties or export tax.
>
> David Healy, *The Antidepressant Era* (Cambridge: Harvard University Press, 1997), 19.

42. The social purity movements in England bespeak radical middle-class women's rage over the Contagious Disease Acts of 1864, 1866, and 1869, which placed both police and medics under control of the War Office, not local government. Elizabeth Blackwell's work is exemplary here, fusing moral and medical concerns in an image of "Christian physiology." See *Christianity in Medicine: An Address*

Delivered before the Christo-Theosophical Society, December 18th, 1890 (St. Leonards: J. F. Nock, 1890); *Counsel to Parents on the Moral Education of Their Children, in Relation to Sex* (London: Brentano's Literary Emporium, 1879); *How to Keep a Household in Health* (London: Sampson Low, Son, and Marston, 1871); *The Human Element in Sex, Being a Medical Inquiry into the Relation of Sexual Physiology to Christian Morality* (London: J. and A. Churchill, 1894); and *The Laws of Life, with Special Reference to the Physical Education of Girls* (New York: G. P. Putnam, 1852).

43. "Organic chemistry is often regarded as having been clearly established as a separate field with the publication of Marcellin Berthelot's *Chimie Organique*, in 1860." Healy, *The Antidepressant Era*, 18.

44. In England, it was the 1858 Medical Act that "established for the first time the statutory definition of a medical practitioner, together with a register and a General Medical Council to watch over conduct and education." Frank Mort, *Dangerous Sexualities: Medico-moral Politics in England since 1830*, 2nd ed. (New York: Routledge, 2000), 52. Or, in Berridge and Edwards' terms, "[d]octors and pharmacists, until mid-century at least, lacked the organizational structures and professional standing even to begin to define opium use as solely a medical matter." Berridge and Edwards, *Opium and the People: Opiate Use in Nineteenth-Century England*, 62. The locus classicus of this development appears in Gustave Flaubert's *Madame Bovary*, exemplarily in the relation between Monsieur Homais and Charles Bovary. See Avital Ronell's reading of *Madame Bovary* in *Crack Wars: Literature, Addiction, Mania* (Lincoln: University of Nebraska Press, 1992).

45. "It was no wonder that Chelsea proved such a magnet to artists and writers, such as Turner, Leigh Hunt and Thomas Carlyle. There is no record of Crapper clearing a clogged drain for Swinburne, repairing a kitchen tap for Whistler or installing a bidet for Christina Rossetti. But he might very well have done so, for they all lived a mere stone's throw from him and when they had the need of a plumber there is no reason why a maidservant should not have been dispatched to fetch Crapper." Reyburn, *Flushed with Pride: The Story of Thomas Crapper*, 12.

46. See Michel Foucault, *The History of Sexuality: An Introduction*, trans. Robert Hurley, vol. 1 (New York: Pantheon, 1978); and "Introduction," in *The History of Sexuality: The Use of Pleasure*, trans. Robert Hurley, vol. 2 (New York: Vintage, 1990), 1–32.

47. See the essays collected in *Heroin Crisis: Key Commentators Discuss the Issues and Debate Solutions to Heroin Abuse in Australia*, ed. Kate van den Boogert and Nadine Davidoff (Melbourne: Bookman Press, 1999).

48. See Louis Althusser, *On the Reproduction of Capitalism: Ideology and Ideological State Apparatuses*, trans. G. M. Goshgarian (New York: Verso, 2014).

49. See Healy, "The Psychopharmacological Era: Notes toward a History," *Journal of Psychopharmacology* 4 (1990): 152–67.

50. I draw these examples from a decade ago partially to suggest how the public circulation of such sentiments has escalated as it vanishes into normality in and by that very escalation. See Sarah Boseley, "Doctors 'Forced' to Overprescribe Antidepressants," *Guardian*, March 30, 2004, http://theguardian.com/; Gardiner Harris, "Antidepressants Seen as Effective for Adolescents," *New York Times*, June 2, 2004, http://nytimes.com; and Donald G. McNeil Jr., "Large Study on Mental Illness Finds Global Prevalence," *The New York Times*, June 2, 2004, http://www.nytimes.com/.

51. Kramer's book (and others like it) has inspired some extreme and bilious responses. See, among others, the dialogue between Zoë Heller and Roy Porter, "The Chemistry of Happiness," in *Mind Readings: Writers' Journeys through Mental States*, ed. Sara Dunn, Blake Morrison, and Michèle Roberts (London: Minerva, 1996), 165–75; and Healy, *Let Them Eat Prozac: The Unhealthy Relationship between the Pharmaceutical Industry and Depression* (New York: New York University Press, 2004).

52. Kramer, *Listening to Prozac* (New York: Penguin, 1993), 296.

53. Mr. Sheen is a popular brand of cleaning materials created in Australia in the 1950s.—Eds.

54. See, for instance, Jean-François Lyotard, *Lessons on the Analytic of the Sublime*, trans. Elizabeth Rottenberg (Stanford: Stanford University Press, 1994).

55. Bernard Stiegler, "Pharmacology of Desire: Drive-Based Capitalism and Libidinal Dis-economy," *New Formations* 72 (2011): 150.

56. See Jacques Lacan, *The Seminar of Jacques Lacan, Book XVII: The Other Side of Psychoanalysis*, ed. Jacques-Alain Miller, trans. Russell Grigg (New York: W. W. Norton, 2007).

57. Martin Heidegger, "'Only a God Can Save Us': The *Spiegel* Interview (1966)," in *Heidegger: The Man and the Thinker*, ed. Thomas Sheehan (Chicago: Precedent Press, 1981), 57. This is Heidegger's final interview, conducted in 1966 but not published in *Der Spiegel* until after his death in 1976.

58. Freud, "Analysis Terminable and Interminable," in *SE* 23:225.

CHAPTER 7

Testament of the Revolution
(Walter Benjamin)

Rebecca Comay

For Carsten

I have often thought it odd that the posterity of the Frankfurt School has always measured itself in terms of generations—first generation, second generation, and so on. (By some counts we are now up to the fourth or even fifth generation, which means that they must breed them very young.) While feminism surges forward in waves (first-wave, second-wave, third-wave), and Hegelians procreate through mitosis, splitting off horizontally into rival wings, or factions (left and right), or vertically (young and old), critical theory, for some reason, seems to want to propagate dynastically along patrilineal lines.

I am not sure where exactly Walter Benjamin fits into this line of filiation or if he is even really part of the family. Is he a father, a son, a sibling, a foster child, a cousin? Is he one of those uncles who you never even knew existed until one day he leaves you a bequest that you do not quite know what to do with? The genealogical lines had always been a little tangled—between Benjamin and Theodor Adorno, for example, or between Benjamin and Gershom Scholem, to name just two of the many claimants swarming around Benjamin's legacy. Both functioned variously—sometimes as Benjamin's mentor, sometimes follower, sometimes executor of the estate, sometimes heir apparent. The setup has some of the complexity of the strange scene of inheritance Jacques Derrida explores in *The Post Card* when he contemplates the picture of an aged Plato standing behind—that is, genealogically *before*—a youthful Socrates, who is shown sitting at his writing desk, taking dictation from his own follower.[1] This genealogical torsion, a kind of time warp within the testamentary circuit, reminds us that the original meaning of *inherit* was the very opposite of what it means today. To inherit—from the Latin *inhereditare* (compare with the Old French *enheriter*)—meant to bequeath, pass on, transmit one's property or title to someone. "I inherit you" once meant *I bequeath to you, I make you my heir, I appoint you as my successor.* What, then, does it mean to bequeath backwards, so that we leave something to our own ancestors?

A last will and testament is a peculiar kind of speech act. To write a will is to assume the impossible, namely, that after I die my wish can function as a command—in other words, that I can defy mortality. In death I can achieve an agency conspicuously lacking in my own lifetime. I can still the passage of time by willing into a future in which my authority will reign supreme. Max Horkheimer smelled a whiff of piety in Benjamin's obsession with redemption. To respond to the call of "enslaved ancestors"[2] is already to endow the dead with posthumous agency—to confess to a secret faith in resurrection.

This essay is driven by a single question: *Can the concept of inheritance be rendered fully profane?* When we respond to the demands of the dead, when we hear the past addressing us, do we succumb to religiosity? Or can *undeadness*—the relentless pressure of the posthumous—be considered a properly disenchanted category?

***

"*Notre héritage n'est précédé d'aucun testament*—'our heritage was left to us without a testament.'" Our heritage was unwilled. This phrase has been rattling around in my head ever since I first stumbled upon it in the epigraph to Hannah Arendt's *Between Past and Future.* Arendt would continue to cite it like a mantra for many years to come.[3] The phrase is borrowed from the French poet and Resistance fighter René Char. It is one of the entries in *Feuillets d'Hypnos*, a collection of aphorisms, diary jottings, and epigrammatic verses penned during the Nazi occupation while Char was operating a parachute drop in Haute-Provence under the nom de guerre Capitaine Alexandre.[4] A Resistance fighter during the daytime, he would spend his nights writing under the somewhat counterintuitive pen name "Hypnos"—Sleep. The wartime notebooks were hidden in a wall during the last year of the war, when Char was dispatched to join the North African campaign, and were published about a year after the war's end.

For all of their exhilaration, Char's wartime writings have a distinctly anxious and melancholic pathos. Even as he anticipates the liberation, he cannot stop brooding about the morning after. Char is not worrying—not quite yet—about the specific vicissitudes of postwar memory politics. He cannot possibly predict in 1943 just how quickly the French Resistance would come to be embellished, mythologized, and redirected; how effortlessly it would be harnessed to de Gaulle's postwar agenda; how quickly its patriotic energies would be commandeered to promote the French wars of colonial aggression in North Africa and elsewhere; and he cannot anticipate how the official narrative of heroic resistance to the Nazis would suffer such corrosive demystification in later decades, as the stories of collaboration began to multiply—the so-called Vichy syndrome that has vexed France since the 1970s. But, even in the flush of the moment, Char already knows, he is already certain, that the revolutionary energy of the Maquis will dissipate as quickly as it had appeared. Without a testament, without any symbolic means of transmitting the event, there will be no way to bequeath the "treasure" to future generations, no way to harvest its energy, prolong its impact, or even bear witness to what had happened. Char is emphatic that a historical experience of this sort resists prolongation: "If I survive, I know that I will have to break with the aroma of these essential years, silently reject or cast away (not repress) my treasure."[5] Not a whiff of the event will remain in the archive of either the voluntary or the involuntary memory—not even a Proustian aroma.

Char will have to "reject or cast away" (*rejeter*), "not repress" (*refouler*), his treasure. His formulation has an uncanny psychoanalytic precision. Not even "repression" is sufficient to describe the forgetfulness he senses ineluctably looming upon the horizon, perhaps because to speak of repression suggests the possibility of eventual retrieval—only a "rejection" or repudiation that has the distinct force of foreclosure. The blockage relates to a gap between experience and its transcription, between action and its symbolization, an impasse that seems to speak to the structural intestacy of every revolutionary—and perhaps not only revolutionary—event. We might call it the problem of the *day after*. How does a radical interruption *of* history assume consequence *within* history? Or is every prolongation a forcible reintegration within the continuum of empty, homogeneous time?

Char seems to be suggesting that the blockage is irremediable; without any protocol of transmission there can be no lineage, result, or legacy. Unplanned, unpredictable, and arriving suddenly, as if from nowhere, an event such as this cannot outlast its own occasion. It is not that the event is marooned in a delirium of ineffable immediacy, miraculously self-generating and self-consuming, leaving no remainder. On the contrary, the blockage arises from the specific antinomies of resistance itself. Parasitic upon what it opposes, resistance threatens to be *structurally* without issue. This barrenness or intestacy—Char writes of a "sterile sadness"[6]—threatens to haunt every form of activism. This poses a special challenge for revolutionary politics and everyone living in its aftermath.

Char registers this impasse as an intractable antinomy between politics and poetry. "In our darkness there is no place for Beauty."[7] He will refuse the mantle of "Resistance poet"; the very notion is oxymoronic. It either aestheticizes politics—it blunts the edge of action—or turns poetry into propaganda: either bad politics or bad art (or both). Char will publish nothing throughout the war years. After the liberation he will return to publishing poetry.

Arendt relates this intestacy to the specific impasse of revolutionary modernity. Revolution (there are basically only two that count for her) demands a sequel—it solicits an aftermath—that is structurally destined to miscarry. The predicament of revolutionary inheritance is epitomized, for Arendt, by the parallel destinies of its two most exemplary incarnations, the monstrous fecundity of the one mirrored perfectly by the utter sterility of the other. Whereas the French Revolution, in its failure, would manage, literally, to *succeed* all too well—it would breed successor after terrifying successor—the American Revolution, for all its manifest success, would conspicuously fail to produce a successor. The former would keep on cloning itself, spawning an endless chain of uncanny replicants. The latter would betray its own glorious beginnings and fizzle out without posterity. Bereft of progeny, the American Revolution would almost immediately disavow its own revolutionary beginnings, the very word "revolution" becoming disreputable and even inaudible within the American lexicon, while the idea of public happiness would shrivel into a vapid notion of self-fulfillment, and freedom dissipate into the vagaries of free enterprise. The French Revolution would become the template for an endless succession of imitations, plagiarisms, and second editions. Even on American soil, Arendt remarks, it was the French Revolution, not the American one, that would provide the script for subsequent revolutionary change: "The point is unpleasantly driven home when even revolutions in the American continent speak and act as though they knew by heart the texts of revolutions in France, in Russia, and in China, but had never heard of such a thing as an American Revolution."[8]

Revolution, in this way, oscillates between a surfeit and a deficit of generativity. It procreates either mechanically and idiotically or not at all. Its reproductive system is either on overdrive or disabled. In either case, the very thing that defines revolution, by Arendt's own reckoning, is rendered dysfunctional—that is, the unquenchable force of "natality" itself. For Arendt, the primal scene of modernity is thus marked by the twin disasters of an inheritance without testamentary pedigree. Without the legitimating channels of witness, testimony, or testament, the heritage of the Revolution remains as inaccessible as a buried treasure—Arendt speaks of "an island of freedom"[9]—left to us without a map, navigation tools, or operating instructions.

***

Here is a thought experiment: What if Char's formula needs to be reversed? Perhaps the predicament is not intestacy but rather a kind of hyper-testacy or hyper-testamentarity—not a *deficit* but an *excess* of testamentary protocol. It is the heritage that has gone missing, while the testamentary injunction remains in force. Switching things around a little, we might rewrite the sentence as follows: *Notre testament n'est précédé d'aucun héritage* (Our testament comes to us without a heritage). It is not that the thread has been broken, the family jewels scattered and inaccessible. The problem is rather that we are overwhelmed by a surfeit of testamentary material. The past confronts us as a thicket of interpellations—imperatives, injunctions, promises, exhortations, incitements, excitations, obscure messages from the dead, unsigned and undated but nonetheless time-stamped and addressed to us uniquely. Every document is overlaid by a palimpsest of additions, revisions, emendations, codicils, each one seemingly intended for us uniquely, demanding our immediate and undivided attention; but, for this very reason, each one is illegible, every attestation subject to contestation, every testation subject to an intolerable delay of testing, proving, probing, probate, probation. What if the testament itself was the heritage? Or, rather, if there was no heritage—no patrimonial estate to settle, no treasure to be distributed, not even a meaning or value to be retrieved and safeguarded—only the pressure of a demand as enigmatic as it is insistent?

In a 1938 letter to Scholem on Franz Kafka, Benjamin writes of an irremediable "sickening of tradition."[10] He is referring to the specific predicaments of Jewish assimilation, but his larger point relates to the impasses and opportunities of secular modernity more broadly. In the face of the radical insolvency of tradition—the exhaustion of cultural capital, the evacuation of religious authority, the depletion of the consistency and intelligibility of truth and meaning—Kafka opted for *transmissibility* as such. He committed to sheer *testamentarity* in the default of any *heritage*. It is hard to get the language quite right here: To speak of the absence, loss, or withdrawal of meaning, along the lines of some kind of negative theology, is already to speak far too monumentally. (This will be the kernel of Benjamin's debate with

Scholem: Whereas Scholem retrieves a shred of negative epiphany in Kafka's writing—the shadow cast by the law's disappearance—Benjamin evacuates the last crumb of normative positivity.) Kafka registers nothing but the relay of passing in the absence of anything to pass on. He staked a claim upon the passage of passability itself. "Kafka's genius lay in the fact that he tried something altogether new: he gave up truth so that he could hold on to its transmissibility."[11]

This testamentary excess is captured by the "inexhaustible intermediate world"[12] of Kafka's fiction, a world clogged with moldering paperwork, swarming with "agents of circulation"[13]—throngs of emissaries and assistants, traveling salesmen and waiters, couriers and imperial messengers running around everywhere conveying messages in an "unending stream of traffic."[14] Kafka's celebrated commitment to "failure"—his failure to marry, to produce offspring, to leave home, to be a father, to be a son, his failure to finish things, his (by his own estimation) Moses-like[15] failure to arrive at his destination, the multiple inhibitions, insufficiencies, and inabilities from which his writing draws its entire energy[16]—registers only a relentless testamentary pressure to *succeed*. Kafka's whole wager is to secure succession itself in the default of any estate to settle. This is one way of understanding Kafka's peculiar relationship to his own legacy and the abiding enigma of his own final testament. In instructing Max Brod to destroy the archive of his unpublished writings, Kafka appointed as his literary executor the one person that he knew perfectly well would never follow his directions.[17]

The "sickness"—or, rather, "sickening" (*Erkrankung*)—of tradition has nothing to do with homesickness or nostalgia; rather, it is a viral contagion in which what is being contracted is precisely virality or contagiousness. We are being infected with infectability. The sickness of tradition is essentially the *traditio*, the transmission, of sickness—the transmission of transmissibility itself. (Benjamin describes a similar logic in "The Task of the Translator" when he argues that the ultimate goal of every translation is to secure *translatability*. Translation allows language to lurch towards its own potentiation; it raises language itself to the second power.)[18] This transfer of potentiality releases a reservoir of unbound negativity in excess of every determination.[19] This could be regarded as a kind of destruction. Benjamin comments that the destructive character—the one that smashes everything to bits without an "image" of the future, without a program or agenda for what comes after—"stands in the front line of traditionalists."[20] Why? Precisely because in reducing everything to rubble he opens up unprecedented passages for transmission: "Some people pass things down to posterity, by making them untouchable and thus conserving them; others pass on situations, by making them practicable and thus liquidating them. [. . .] What exists he reduces to rubble—not for the sake of the rubble, but for that of the way leading through it."[21] By destroying things the destructive character makes them handy.

It is in this sense that Benjamin speaks, in his second thesis on history, of a *geheime Verabredung*—a "secret agreement," covenant, rendezvous, assignation, or appointment (timing is crucial)—between the dead and the living.[22] *Secret* here means unconscious. In other words, we are circling around the theme of transgenerational trauma. "Our coming was expected."[23] The past presents itself as a time-lapse document—unveiled posthumously, unsigned and undated, but all the more binding in the exorbitance of its demand. This deferred coming-to-legibility is not an empirical contingency; the delay is not an accident of composition; it is not a defect in the technologies of transmission or a provisional error of reception; and this is not just a cliché about the clarity of hindsight. Rather, the delay corresponds to a structural torsion and distortion—a traumatic *Nachträglichkeit*—that Benjamin has been thinking about incessantly since his earliest reflections upon language.

"[L]ike every generation that preceded us, we have been endowed with a *weak* messianic power, a power on which the past has a claim."[24] This power is weak for several connected reasons. It is hostage to antecedent claims; its outcome is far from certain; and it has already been tested repeatedly and found lacking. Benjamin emphasizes that there is nothing unique or novel about "our" assignation. *Every* generation has been endowed with the very same power—and to little avail. It is an ineffectual power that needs incessantly to keep reasserting itself and a strange messiah that needs constantly to be returning.

In his twelfth thesis Benjamin famously reorients the political act: He reverses the direction of the revolutionary gaze from the future towards the past. Revolution is inspired not by "the ideal of liberated grandchildren" but by "the image of enslaved ancestors."[25] Benjamin is here not only reproducing the standard Marxist admonitions against utopian socialism, although this is part of his point. He is also extending the rebuke to include all the progressivisms, reformisms, and pragmatisms of his day, from the mollifications of social democracy to the forced march of the Second International. Any future envisaged from the vantage point of the present unfailingly reinforces and embellishes this present. The future vanishes the moment we turn to look at it—Orpheus and Eurydice in reverse.

Benjamin is here registering the retroactive force of testation. The heir generates his own inheritance: Every image that is not seized at the "dangerous, critical moment," every demand that is not acknowledged, threatens to vanish forever.[26] In other words, *inheritance* must be understood in its strictly unfinished or gerundive aspect. The past is not a patrimony handed down from generation to generation; it does not precede the act of inheritance but is forged in this act and has no significance beyond it. This implies that the heir becomes testator to his own testator. In generating his own inheritance, he becomes the ancestor of his own ancestor; he bequeaths past generations with the power of bequeathing. The intentions of the past become legible only retroactively; a promise can be grasped as such only belatedly in the light of its eventual betrayal; a possibility is registered as such only in the light of its nonrealization; a hope becomes palpable only in its shattering. The intentions of past generations are charged as expectations—they become anticipations—only retroactively and from the perspective of their ruination.

This is Benjamin's version of Immanuel Kant's "Copernican revolution."[27] The past is not a frozen lump of positivity. Rather, it becomes significant *as* past, it acquires its *pastness,* only "heliotropically"—only in the light of the catastrophe of its aborted futures. It is for this reason that history is not a stockpile of accomplishments but a reservoir of possibilities: not a heritage but a demand. Every moment that is congealed as heritage is stripped of its potentiality and thus surrenders its historicity. In relinquishing its counterfactual pressure upon the present, it becomes ossified and inert. This ossification does not apply exclusively to the victory monuments of the winners. Failure too can be reified, becoming beautiful (when it inspires our empathy) or sublime (when it reinvigorates us with a renewed sense of our own moral purpose). Ancient suffering then becomes embalmed and mythical, inspiring legends of eternal victimhood and producing ledgers of competing trauma.

***

We can regard Benjamin's whole corpus as an enormous testamentary project—a time capsule, a message in a bottle, a writing from beyond the grave. This may shed light upon a peculiar feature of Benjamin's own writing. He never stopped cataloguing. It is amazing, all things considered, just how much of this paperwork has actually survived. Alongside the other heaps of things Benjamin was continually amassing (collections of toys, postcards, children's books, books of the insane), there is an endless proliferation of lists—meticulous lists of every book he read since high school graduation, acquisition lists of every book he was given, purchased or otherwise acquired, lists of his own publications, lists of works in progress, reading lists for unfinished projects, bibliographies for finished ones, lists of words and phrases, lists of every malapropism and cute saying pronounced by his son Stefan throughout childhood, lists of correspondents and correspondences.[28] There are lists of his cardboard file boxes, described by color and contents, lists of the desk drawers and cupboards in his apartment in which the other things were stored. And, finally, there are lists of lists—tattered envelopes, labeled upon the outside with a list of all the slips folded inside it, each slip in turn containing more lists (reading lists, lists of essay topics, outlines and annotations for works both unwritten and finished).

Benjamin's method of composition is itself an infinite process of self-archiving. He never stopped self-annotating, self-encapsulating, self-reviewing. Essays are perpetually broken down into their own abridgments, condensations, and projections; even after being finished, they would be turned back into their own sketches or metabolized into their digested remainders. Publication did not put an end to this process of abbreviation and condensation: Published offprints kept getting cut up into separate sections, the fragments glued onto other pieces of papers, corrected in the margins, the collage functioning both as a stockpile of disposable resources and as a kind of ruin and memorial, at once raw material and remnant. Finished works would transform into their own drafts and summaries, simultaneously precursors and survivors of themselves—a perfect literary enactment of the genealogical reversal they would never stop exploring. In its incessant self-revision and self-anticipation, Benjamin's own writing presents a snapshot (or, more precisely, moving image) of the dialectical image.

This drive to self-encapsulation and self-miniaturization became literal in Benjamin's crazy, microscopic handwriting, sometimes as tiny as one millimeter high. Inspired by the example of the grain of wheat in the Musée Cluny in Paris upon which a scribe had managed to write an entire prayer, Benjamin's ambition was to squeeze an entire essay onto a single sheet of paper.

This reduction also produces a kind of strange nominalization. Paragraphs are shrinking into sentences, sentences into words, essays into titles. Everything is contracting, everything is being indexed, language is turning into compulsive, onomastic enumeration: an acquisitions list, a row of lines on a tombstone, an inventory, a bureaucratic registry—or, alternatively, which may, in the end, prove to be not all that different, a series of proper names, where the name not only kills but also generates the thing it nominates, like Adam naming the animals, every moment a new one, in the limbo where sketch meets ruin.

Every list points simultaneously in two opposite temporal directions. You can think about the list melancholically and retrospectively: an inventory, a litany, an *ubi sunt*, a catalogue of the dead. You can also think about it fetishistically and futurally: a wish list, a shopping list, an agenda, an ever-receding to-do list. I suspect it is both at once.

This drive to condensation raises a basic set-theoretical question: Does the list necessarily include itself as one of its own items? This brings us, finally, to the abiding enigma of Benjamin's own last, unfinished project, *The Arcades Project*, namely, what is it? Must the collection eventually include itself within one of its own convolutes? Is the book an arcade, a collection, a wax museum, a morgue, a catacomb, a department store, a construction site, a ragpicker's gleanings, an overstuffed interior?

What was Benjamin looking for as he sifted through the detritus of the Second Empire? There was a lot of garbage generated in that uncertain period between two revolutions—that long hiatus between the crushing of the worker's revolution of 1848 and the crushing of the Paris Commune some two decades later. Whatever he was doing in the library all those years during his Paris exile—foraging through reading lists, copying and recopying passages, organizing and arranging, amassing all of those heaps of paper (sometimes these piles would get so large that they threatened to fall out of the book altogether and break away to form the torso of a new one), alphabetizing, enumerating, summarizing, classifying, cross-referencing, color-coding, adding more and more folders (some would remain conspicuously empty and even unlabeled), developing his increasingly bizarre system of classification—whatever he was doing, he was not scrambling after treasures, diving for coral, or singing requiems to a dead city. It might look as if Benjamin was scavenging, stockpiling, or hoarding. It might look as if he was gambling upon some kind of alchemical conversion along cultural studies lines—expanding the canon, upgrading minor into major, converting mud into gold. Nothing could be further from the truth.

In drafting *The Arcades Project* Benjamin was registering the testament of the Revolution. It had ended up as a pile of paperwork.

Notes

1. See Jacques Derrida, "Envois," in *The Post Card: From Socrates to Freud and Beyond*, trans. Alan Bass (Chicago: University of Chicago Press, 1987), 1–256.

2. Walter Benjamin, "On the Concept of History," in *Selected Writings, 1938–1940*, ed. Howard Eiland and Michael W. Jennings, trans. Harry Zohn, vol. 4 (Cambridge: Belknap Press, 2003), 394.

3. See Hannah Arendt, "Preface: The Gap between Past and Future," in *Between Past and Future: Six Exercises in Political Thought* (New York: Viking, 1961), 3–15; *On Revolution* (New York: Penguin, 1990), 215, 281; and *The Life of the Mind* (New York: Harcourt, 1978), 12.

4. See René Char, *Feuillets d'Hypnos*, in *Oeuvres complètes* (Paris: Gallimard, 1983), 190. All translations of the text appearing here are my own.

5. Ibid., 222.

6. Ibid., 182.

7. Ibid., 232.

8. Arendt, *On Revolution*, 216.

9. Ibid., 275.

10. Benjamin, "Letter to Gershom Scholem on Franz Kafka," in *Selected Writings, 1935–1938*, ed. Howard Eiland and Michael W. Jennings, trans. Edmund Jephcott, vol. 3 (Cambridge: Belknap Press, 2002), 326.

11. Ibid.

12. Benjamin, "Franz Kafka: On the Tenth Anniversary of His Death," in *Selected Writings, 1931–1934*, ed. Michael W. Jennings, Howard Eiland, and Gary Smith, trans. Harry Zohn, vol. 2, part 2 (Cambridge: Belknap Press, 1999), 810.

13. Theodor W. Adorno, "Notes on Kafka," in *Prisms*, trans. Samuel and Shierry Weber (Cambridge: MIT Press, 1997), 259–60.

14. Franz Kafka, "The Judgment," in *The Complete Stories*, ed. Nahum N. Glatzer, trans. Willa and Edwin Muir (New York: Schocken, 1971), 88.

15. See, for example, Kafka, "October 19, 1921" and "January 28, 1922," in *The Diaries, 1910–1923*, ed. Max Brod, trans. Martin Greenberg with Hannah Arendt (New York: Schocken, 1976), 393–94, 407–8.

16. See Kafka's famous catalogue of impossibilities: "The impossibility of not writing, the impossibility of writing German, the impossibility of writing differently. One might also add a fourth impossibility, the impossibility of writing." Kafka to Max Brod, June, 1921, in *Letters to Friends, Family, and Editors*, trans. Richard and Clara Winston (New York: Schocken, 1977), 289.

17. In the postscript to the first edition of *The Trial*, Brod cites the following letter found among Kafka's papers after his death: "Dearest Max, my last request: Everything I leave behind me [. . .], in the way of diaries, manuscripts, letters [. . .], sketches, and so on, to be burned unread; also all writings and sketches which you or others may possess; and ask those others for them in my name. Letters which they do not want to hand over to you, they should at least promise faithfully to burn themselves. Yours, Franz Kafka." Kafka, "Postscript to the First Edition," in *The Trial*, trans. Willa and Edwin Muir (New York: Schocken, 1984), 265–66. Brod provides several compelling reasons for not complying with his friend's request,

the most striking of which is that he apparently told Kafka explicitly in 1921 that he would never destroy his unpublished work. See also Max Brod, *Franz Kafka: A Biography*, 2nd ed., trans. G. Humphreys Roberts (New York: Da Capo, 1995), 198.—Eds.

18. See Benjamin, "The Task of the Translator," in *Selected Writings, 1913–1926*, ed. Marcus Bullock and Michael W. Jennings, trans. Harry Zohn, vol. 1 (Cambridge: Belknap Press, 1996), 253–63.

19. I am here inspired by Samuel Weber's wonderful *Benjamin's -abilities* (Cambridge: Harvard University Press, 2008).

20. Benjamin, "The Destructive Character," in *Selected Writings, 1931–1934*, vol. 2, part 2, 542.

21. Ibid.

22. Benjamin, "On the Concept of History," in *Selected Writings, 1938–1940*, vol. 4, 390.

23. Ibid.

24. Ibid.; emphasis in original.

25. Ibid., 394.

26. Benjamin, "N," in *The Arcades Project*, ed. Rolf Tiedemann, trans. Howard Eiland and Kevin McLaughlin (Cambridge: Belknap Press, 1999), 463; translation modified. See also "On the Concept of History," 390.

27. See Benjamin, "K," in *The Arcades Project*, 388–89.

28. For a lovely sampling, see Benjamin, *Walter Benjamin's Archive: Images, Texts, Signs*, ed. Ursula Marx, Gudrun Schwarz, Michael Schwarz, and Erdmut Wizisla, trans. Esther Leslie (New York: Verso, 2007).

CHAPTER 8

"We" and "They"

Animals behind Our Back

Oxana Timofeeva

The question of community is a question of a definition lost in scholarly paradigms. The question of what the community should be is a question of value and what ought to be. Any attempt to answer it leads us to discordant models of social organization, to an ideological quarrel about how to rebuild humanity. The community appears as a gathering of people, large or small, but it is certainly different from a group, collective, or society in terms of its density, the character of its objectives, anatomy, and teleology.

The question of community—so we are told—is a question about the essence of democracy, the limits of human coexistence, the common, and what we share with one another beyond everything that links us to a group, a collective, a nation, and a people, as well as to the crowd and the masses. It is as if there was, between us, a place for some kind of common "in general," some general-in-commonality, but without ever being total, much less "totalitarian." This is a specific modality of resisting totalization, resisting the unification of an imaginary gathering under a common flag. The community, so we are told, will not march in step to the victory of any one transcendental principle. As an indeterminate and immanent multiplicity of singularities, the community is indistinguishable from the absence of community: It is unrepresentable, but nothing is possible without it. It is just like the air we breathe—common to all and belonging to no one. No one can appropriate the air.[1]

The specter of communism hangs in the common and unappropriated air. The very name swears an oath of allegiance to the idea of community.

Communism is the society of the community, of what is common and belongs to no one, but we will never agree about whether or not this principle coincides with or opposes democracy. Thus, the specter of communism, having appeared out of the air, disperses into it as well. The name *communism* is hurriedly stuffed with the noise of discussions about the general horizon of the future, and these discussions are filled with the noise of other discussions about the past and the burden we collectively drag together toward the horizon, making it seem all the more frightening. Communism is humanity's memory of what has not yet happened. In this way, it resembles a dream—one never knows when the idyll may turn into a nightmare.

The moment an idyll turns into a nightmare is one of those moments in a dream when the real of desire tries to speak. It speaks in the language of the unconscious, a language difficult to translate and belonging to no one. There is no "I" in this language; it is prepersonal and preindividual, and it is with this language that the unrepresentable, anonymous multiplicity expresses itself. It is not so much an "it" or "id," in the Freudian sense, as a "they" that has not yet appeared as a gathering of people. The inhabitants of this world are animals; the dream's navel joins "me" with "them," with those who have no faces.

The question of what a community is or should be, a question of definition and necessity, is a question about people, calculable gatherings of people, by whose efforts the original matter of democracy or communism is, in the end, subordinated to the forms of national or totalitarian states—or at least this is what concrete, historical experience teaches us. But a "they" is not a "we"—only at the level of the real of desire, the level of affect, does the uncountable multiplicity of beasts first come into rights. The question of community as desire, the question of utopia, brings us back to the uncountable multiplicity of beasts, that is, the animal unconscious. Here, there is nothing primary, original, organic, or native; following "them," the paths of beasts, we return not to the origin but to that which has never been.

The idyll of the community (communism) never existed before its reality became a nightmare. The real of our desire never existed before we began to translate it from the language of the unconscious—an inarticulate language, like a beast's cry. We only know this language in translation, but indeed it only arises at the moment of translation; the original (forgotten or lost) arises through the process of translation. "They" do not exist before us by themselves, but as soon as "we" arrive, "they" are always already there; "they" were always already here—a paradoxical retrospection. The question of "we," of the community (and, with them, the question of communism, democracy, and utopia), in this way, becomes a question of the animal multiplicity (the unconscious), and this is precisely how we will raise it here.

According to Jacques Lacan, the unconscious is structured like a language,[2] and it speaks (*ça parle*).[3] The unconscious is the speech of the Other, a form of speech not ruled by the ego. Human subjectivity, as Lacan understands it, is the result of an appropriation of what lies beyond speech, namely, the outside. A human being is born prematurely, awkward, fragmented, ill-prepared. But when a small child, just having learned to walk, looks into the mirror and sees his or her reflection, suddenly he or she guesses that what he or she sees is "me." The miracle of recognizing oneself in the mirror is something like a compensation for our premature appearance in the world.[4]

According to Lacan, animals do not have language, and this means that, for them, there is no unconscious nor speech of the Other to appropriate from the outside with which to build integrity and individuality. What does Lacan's pigeon see in the mirror? Another pigeon, a potential sexual partner. Lacan refers to a biological experiment that

> acknowledges that it is a necessary condition for the maturation of the female pigeon's gonad that the pigeon see another member of its species, regardless of its sex; this condition is so utterly sufficient that the same effect may be obtained by merely placing a mirror's reflective field near the individual. Similarly, in the case of the migratory locust, the shift within a family line from the solitary to the gregarious form can be brought about by exposing an individual, at a certain stage of its development, to the exclusively visual action of an image akin to its own, provided the movements of this image sufficiently resemble those characteristic of its species.[5]

In his essay "And Say the Animal Responded?" Jacques Derrida groups Lacan in with René Descartes, Martin Heidegger, and Emmanuel Levinas—philosophers who draw a clear line between the human and the animal. For Derrida, the very possibility of such a distinction is highly problematic; it is one of a series of metaphysical, binary oppositions that reduces the multiplicity of beasts to a certain generic figure of the "animal," against the background of which the identity of the human is organized. This is how he discusses the passage quoted above about the pigeon: "Lacan speaks of movement from the 'solitary' to the 'gregarious' form, and not to the social form, as though the difference between *gregarious* and *social* were the difference between animal and human."[6]

Of course, for Derrida, this is a question of a particular kind of politics—an unresponsive, speechless, herd-like animality that turns out to be that point, at first glance marginal, from which all the viciousness of the repressive, totalitarian, philosophical tradition appears as the viciousness of the circle that marks the human, logos, and being.[7] Giorgio Agamben calls the mechanism of the production of this distinction the "anthropological machine," which not only separates human beings from animals but also anthropologizes animals and bestializes humans.[8]

Both Agamben and Derrida are concerned with this border and the violence that occurs upon its approach—racist violence or the violence of the apparatus toward life and the body. Both base their analysis of animality—an analysis of difference and borders—upon a deconstruction or criticism of Heidegger's project and, in particular, Heidegger's critique of humanism (according to Heidegger, humanism is not sufficiently radical because it recognizes the animality of the human, which may be superior in some ways, including with respect to thinking, but which is still animal).[9] The deconstruction of Heidegger's Destruktion follows the tracks left by beasts that are excluded from the human community. We can live with them in one house, Heidegger says, but we cannot coexist with them and share being with them, just like we cannot share sense with them—after all, only language is the authentic house of being, while they are homeless, do not understand our language, and produce only senseless noise.[10]

While I agree with Derrida, Agamben, and other contemporary philosophers that the classic idea of the human's superiority over the animal is far from innocent and that its sustained unraveling is a matter of principal importance, I cannot deny the constitutive role of binary oppositions and their ambivalent consequences—in particular, for a nonhuman theory of the community, in the name of which this essay will risk a brief sketch. Of course, Derrida's attacks upon traditional metaphysics and its reduction of the irreducible multiplicity of the animal world to one simple category of "the animal" are fair, but at the same time, as Slavoj Žižek affirms in a somewhat Hegelian vein, "the violent reduction of such a multiplicity to a minimal difference is the moment of truth."[11] Žižek's idea, to put it briefly, is that this minimal, theoretical binary gives birth to the truth of the human—not the truth that is officially pronounced upon its side of the opposition (rational, thinking, and so on), but another truth about the nonhuman core of humanity. We would never have learned about this other side without animals, which we think we are not and that loom upon the horizon of our knowledge about ourselves.

Yes, such animals *have* no unconscious; they *are* the unconscious (not so much the darkness of instincts and drives but the language of the Other—not the possession of language but its being, which is carried to us either as noise or a cry). They *have* no being; they *are* being (the human is the shepherd of being,[12] according to Heidegger, and this means that being is a herd; the call that comes from it is indistinguishable from noise or a cry). They *have* no community; they *are* community (an irreducible, noisy multiplicity).

To begin, I will attend to another distinction Heidegger makes between the animal and the human: Animals are incapable not only of language but also of counting.[13] This thesis brings us back to Lacan's pigeon, which cannot count to one. The pigeon is a real narcissist, naively believing in the reality of its reflection in the mirror. In fact, the animal world has no mirrors—in contrast to gatherings of people, animal multiplicities are not formed from singularities or egos. The pigeon and its reflection are already a couple, hinting at coitus: a visual effect is enough. People come together into gatherings—and they come one by one. By contrast, animals multiply, looking at one another. Yes, they do not know how to count; they are uncountable. Pigeons—"rats with wings" and grey bastards of the city—block the sky with their bodies, fill city squares, and shit on monuments of the most noble and respected people.

One can, within a certain margin of error, count all of the people living upon the planet. But one could never count all of the animals. Only some limited groups of specific animals can be counted, provided they are integrated into the economic activity of human beings (pets, livestock, examples of rare or disappearing species). True, the economic activity of human beings spreads across the entire living world, but to determine the number of beasts, as a whole, is impossible—not because there are too many of them but because they have no number. There is no number that can be calculated, rationally enumerated, and inventoried. The human being's economic control of the animal world, for this reason, replaces the count of classifications, parsing this motley, humming multiplicity into types, species, and families.

Thus, the book of Numbers is a kind of census of the Jewish population, a broad calculation of gatherings of people. Leviticus, which precedes it, contains, among other things, a classification of animals. The God of Leviticus tells the Jews which animals can be eaten or sacrificed and which are clean and unclean. We learn about one particularly radical biblical attempt at counting the animals in Genesis, the story of Noah's ark. Regretting what he has created (since humanity has fallen into sin), God decides to exterminate all living things—the flood waters are meant to wipe all living beings from the face of the earth, apart from those taken aboard the rescue boat.

Turning to Noah, God gives his first command about the animals—take "two of every kind of flesh," "male and female": "Of fowls after their kind, and of cattle after their kind, of every creeping thing of the earth after his kind, two of every sort shall come unto thee, to keep them alive."[14] Here, the count is a question of life and death; only those that have been counted will survive. What is disturbing about this command? Whole species remain beyond the field of the ark creator's vision. All animals that lack sexual difference—hermaphrodites, homosexual animals, and those who reproduce asexually—will not make it on board.

However, later, God issues a new command: "Of every clean beast thou shalt take to thee by sevens, the male and his female: and of beasts that are not clean by two, the male and his female. Of fowls also of the air by sevens, the male and the female; to keep seed alive upon the face of all the earth."[15] Why should clean animals be taken aboard in sevens and the unclean only in couples? Noah, of course, does not ask God about this, but we would have liked to ask if we had had the opportunity. Perhaps the answer was obvious for the people of the Old Testament. The selection of animals for the ark is the most serious and important household activity with which Noah and his family are entrusted, and classification, here, serves as the foundation for a headcount of cattle. Clean animals are those that can be, first, eaten, and, second, sacrificed. Most likely, besides one couple, intended for the maintenance of the species, two extra couples (and, perhaps, their offspring) formed a kind of food supply. One member of each group of seven—a single animal, with no mate, as if agamic—will be sacrificed to God as a sign of gratitude when the floodwaters recede and the boat reaches dry land.

And so the preparations are complete: "[A]ll the fountains of the great deep were broken up, and the windows of the heavens were opened. And the rain was upon the earth forty days and forty nights."[16] Only one couple or one group of seven of every species is aboard. All of the rest—that have not been counted and are uncountable—are abandoned to the deep. Is it not from this abyss that the animal unconscious is called to our memory? Is it not from there that we inherit?

Another pertinent Bible story comes from the New Testament. In the legend of the exorcism of the Gerasene demoniac, Jesus and his disciples sail to the country of Gadara and meet a man who is possessed by devils, wears no clothes, and lives not in a house but in tombs. The unclean spirits torture the possessed man; people bind him in chains, but he tears them off and flees into the desert. Jesus asks his name and the man answers: "My name is Legion: for we are many."[17] The legion of devils asks Jesus not to send them into the abyss but into a herd of pigs grazing nearby. Jesus allows them to enter the bodies of the pigs after leaving the man, and the herd throws itself into a lake and drowns.

Pigs are unclean animals. Another meaning of the word *unclean* is "devil," an evil spirit. The unclean, evil spirits—the number of which fits their name, Legion—find, in the final analysis, a refuge (and death) in the bodies of beasts. The herd of sheep, carrying away the devils inside, recall the famous "ship of fools," particularly Michel Foucault's description of it in *History of Madness*.[18] Foucault refers to the medieval tradition of gathering all madmen, putting them aboard a boat, and sending them off on an endless voyage in the open sea. Thus, the community—the gathering of people—heals its body by excluding the dangerous, heterogeneous elements that do not participate in economic activity and do not submit to calculation. The ship of fools is Noah's ark in reverse. Here, safety is only upon land, and the sea, together with the ship, is a symbol of the abyss (and, as Foucault reminds us, a symbol of madness).

Abandoned by the crowd of devil-beasts, man is left alone. This is the meaning of the healing procedure; now he is given his name and a home, now he can recognize himself again in the mirror and return to the society of other people. The possession that tortured him—his mental illness or madness—has abated; the legion of devils has retreated and gone into the small abyss of the lake; "they" have fallen silent; and the unclean animal multiplicity has given up its place for the unity of the human "I."

There is something in this biblical miracle of healing akin to psychoanalysis, the science of the unconscious, which Sigmund Freud linked to the repressed animal element in the human, and Lacan linked to language and the unruly speech of the Other. In 1910, a Russian patient, Sergei Pankejeff, later known as the Wolf Man, came to Freud in order to complete a course of therapy and cure himself of his psychical malady. During one of the sessions he tells Freud of his childhood nightmare. It is nighttime and the boy (the patient) is lying in his bed. Suddenly, the window of his bedroom swings open and he sees a tree, and upon its branches sit wolves—several (six or seven) white wolves with bushy tails, like fox tails. The wolves sit motionless and stare fixedly at the boy. After this terrifying vision (he is afraid of being eaten by the wolves), the boy wakes.

The patient notes that the only movement in this dream about motionless wolves is the window opening before him. This is a rather significant detail, which allows the patient to understand all at once that it was not the window but his own eyes that suddenly opened before something terrible. In the course of analysis, by means of an inversion, the idea comes up that the fixed stare of the wolves is in fact the boy's own gaze. According to Freud, it is he, the boy, who is looking with wolf's eyes at something frightening in the place where he is supposed to be: "The attentive looking, which in the dream was ascribed to the wolves, should rather be shifted on to him."[19]

Interpreting this narrative, Lacan again uses the metaphor of the mirror. The subject's gaze coincides with the place toward which it is directed: "The subject passes beyond this glass in which he always sees, entangled, his own image."[20] Lacan links this unique experience provided by the navel of the dream with some ultimate real, emphasizing the fact that the unconscious is not some kind of supplement to the subject but its dissociation, disintegration, and disruption. The human subject carries its rupture within. The multiplicity of animals, evil spirits, and the abyss is now no longer in some other place but in the human subject itself. The boy is the wolves staring at him with their fearsome eyes. To be precise, they stare at him from the outside, the anonymous multiplicity of the unconscious.

While trying to describe his dream, the patient cannot remember exactly how many wolves were sitting in the tree. He hesitates—were there seven, six, or even five? Freud has an explanation for this uncertainty. No doubt the patient heard from his nanny the popular Russian fairy tale "The Wolf and the Seven Kids." The mommy-goat left her seven kids alone one day and went off for milk. While she was gone the wolf got into the house. The kids had time to hide in different places, but the wolf found them anyway and ate them. Only one of them managed to survive—the one hiding in the wall clock. The seventh child hid and watched the scene of devouring from his hiding place against the wall. And this child, as we can guess, is the boy himself, as if watching the others (who have now turned into strange wolves, as if they were bitten by a vampire). What follows is an extensive interpretation, upon the basis of which Freud concludes that a traumatic episode lies at the root of this wolf fantasy—a scene of his parents copulating that the patient happened to observe in very early childhood.

Freud's conclusion has become the butt of endless jokes. For Gilles Deleuze and Félix Guattari, for instance, who dedicate the second chapter of *A Thousand Plateaus* to the Wolf Man, "1914: One or Several Wolves?" Pankejeff's dream is the call of the pack, the animal multiplicity of the dreamer's unconscious: "Freud tried to approach crowd phenomena from the point of view of the unconscious, but he did not see clearly, he did not see that the unconscious itself was fundamentally a crowd. He was myopic and hard of hearing; he mistook crowds for a single person."[21]

With their silence the wolves call the boy to join the pack—to which he may have always already belonged. Their gaze is a call to become one of them, a becoming-wolf into which the boy was already being drawn, until his vision turned into a nightmare. Freud, according to Deleuze and Guattari, performs an unforgiveable reduction, substituting the wolves with kids, sheep, sheep-dogs—in a word, domestic animals—and then the parental couple, and, finally, the father. He substitutes the singularity of family history for the wild multiplicity of the pack, step by step reducing the indeterminate number of wolves to one, and then zero, in order to construct the false unity of what is, in fact, an irreducible schizoid multiplicity. Wolves always travel in packs, as Deleuze and Guattari remind us. Everyone knows this, even a little child, but Freud does not:

> We witness Freud's reductive glee; we literally see multiplicity leave the wolves to take the shape of goats that have absolutely nothing to do with the story. Seven wolves that are only kid-goats. Six wolves: the seventh goat (the Wolf-Man himself) is hiding in the clock. Five wolves: he may have seen his parents make love at five o'clock, and the roman numeral V is associated with the erotic spreading of a woman's legs. Three wolves: the parents may have made love three times. Two wolves: the first coupling the child may have seen was the two parents *more ferarum*, or perhaps even two dogs. One wolf: the wolf is the father, as we all knew from the start. Zero wolves: he lost his tail, he is not just a castrater but also castrated. Who is Freud trying to fool? The wolves never had a chance to get away and save their pack.[22]

Unlike Freud, Deleuze and Guattari know that a pack cannot be counted. They are fascinated by the beauty and multiplicity of the wolf pack, and they have no concern for family drama or the kid-goats. We cannot agree with these authors, however, when they say that the kids have nothing to do with the story. The biblical tradition—which we all, analysts and patients alike, continue to inherit—does not allow us to agree with them. In this tradition, goats are specific animals, linked to evil spirits and even the cult of Satan. What Deleuze and Guattari call a reduction, in slightly different language, could sound like the miracle of the psychoanalytic cure. Turning the wolves into fairy-tale kids, Freud literally drives out the demonic wolves that had possessed the patient, sending them into a herd of goats (comparable to the herd of pigs "feeding nigh"), in order to make both the demons and the beasts disappear. There is no place for the animal multiplicity in human society, and one of the tasks of analysis is its integration. The ship of fools must sail off without the Russian boy aboard.

How many wolf-kids can fit upon this boat? Since the ship of fools is Noah's ark in reverse, nothing prevents us from assuming that seven animals climb aboard. Freud's seven kids are not the ones taken onto Noah's ark but the ones sent away upon the ship of fools or cast into the abyss, along with the demonic wolves. The seventh kid (suspended, hiding in the wall clock or upon the other side of the bedroom window) is the one who must be sacrificed (perhaps as the cost of success in the psychoanalytic treatment).

We recall that goats are traditionally sacrificed, and these goats are called "scapegoats" or expiatory sacrifices. All of the sins of a given community are laid upon them, and then they are driven away.

The little wolf-man is not only a man and a wolf (wolves) but also a scapegoat, torn to pieces by the sins (desires and fears) he embodies. He is also a little kid, peeking out of his hiding place at all of these sins (starting with the famous Freudian primal scene and ending with the devouring of the other kids by the papa-wolf). He is a little boy whose gaze not only meets but also suddenly coincides with the gaze of the uncountable beasts, which must be driven out, cast into the abyss, into oblivion, if he is to achieve, in exchange, the unity of human life. This expiatory sacrifice, described in the language of psychoanalysis in terms of repression, is the cost of being born into the individual and adult world. From such units is formed the gathering of people. However we try to build humanity, there must always be the miracle of exorcizing demons—or, what amounts to the same thing, the nightmare of repression.[23]

Here, I understand the thesis of how repression turns the animal (herdness or pack-ness) into the human (the social, adding one by one) only in a very narrow sense. The animal multitude (the unconscious) does not exist immediately by itself before and unrelated to the act of repression; instead, it arises in this mediating act as what immediately returns. As Lacan says,

> [t]he trauma, in so far as it has a repressing action, intervenes *after the fact* [*après coup*], *nachträglich*. At this specific moment, something of the subject's becomes detached in the very symbolic world that he is engaged in integrating. From then on, it will no longer be something belonging to the subject. The subject will no longer speak it, will no longer integrate it. Nevertheless, it will remain there, somewhere, spoken, if one can put it this way, by something the subject does not control.[24]

According to Lacan, repression and the return of the repressed are one and the same thing. What returns has never been. Repression transforms what has never been into a kind of active nonbeing. I am speaking about the negativity of the wolf pack; with this Deleuze and Guattari would never agree, since they put the animal multiplicity of the unconscious into the plane of immanence, which knows no nonbeing (it is well known that the theoreticians of schizoanalysis had a negative attitude toward negativity, the servant of dialectics).

The wolf pack (the crowd, the animal multiplicity of the unconscious) is not so much a naive, wild predecessor as it is an ambiguous fellow traveller of the human, which condemns it to nonbeing. These monsters are engendered by the sleep of reason, and this sleep should not be understood metaphorically as a pause or deactivation of the waking work of thought but as what Freud called the other scene (*eine andere Schauplatz*)[25]—something that thinks instead of us. There are no original, natural wolves calling the boy to return to the pack. It was not just simple wolves that came for him but cultured, sexual, political wolves. They are complexly organized. "They" think.

Yet, how should one relate to Deleuze and Guattari's assertion that wolves always travel in packs? Is it not an exaggeration to examine the heritage of the animal unconscious exclusively in terms of a multiplicity? Our mythology is filled with lone wolves and she-wolves. The wolf is a veritable symbol of solitude—proud, romantic solitude; the solitude of the strongest; or the solitude of an overdriven beast. Wolves travel in packs; at night flashes a multiplicity of evil, yellow eyes, but for some reason our cultural imagination stubbornly rips out a single wolf from the pack. How can a given, concrete, and singular individual be a part of a pack? Deleuze answers this question with the words of a girl named Franny: "How stupid, you can't be one wolf, you're always eight or nine, six or seven. Not six or seven wolves all by yourself all at once, but one wolf among others, with five or six others."[26]

Let us turn our attention to this "we" of wolves that we are in the schizophrenic experience of the pack. Here, there is no I-wolf; we are in a composition of wolves, always immediately the entire pack; and we are only ever together with others, among their number. Offering another example, Franny recounts her dream—"a very good schizo dream," as Deleuze and Guattari characterize it—about the desert: "There is a teeming crowd in it, a swarm of bees, a rumble of soccer players, or a group of Tuareg. *I am on the edge of the crowd, at the periphery; but I belong to it, I am attached to it by one of my extremities, a hand or foot.* I know that the periphery is the only place I can be, that I would die if I let myself be drawn into the center of the fray, but just as certainly if I let go of the crowd."[27]

In this description another interesting quality, peripherality, is added to the impossibility of being alone in a pack (Franny is bound to the desert crowd by her hands and legs, her oneiric "I" is inseparable from the "we"—bees, footballers, or Tuareg people). We are both in the pack and at its edge. Let us compare this with Elias Canetti's description of the pack (this time a human one—for example, a hunting pack or war party), which Deleuze cites so as to emphasize the distinction between a pack and a mass. A person in a mass presses toward the center; he or she is completely dissolved, submitting to the leader of the mass, to its tasks and goal. The pack, by contrast, is characterized by decentralization—or, in Deleuze and Guattari's words, "is

constituted by a line of flight or of deterritorialization."[28] Each individual in
Canetti's pack "will again and again find himself at its edge. He may be in
the centre, and then, immediately afterwards, at the edge again; at the edge
and then back in the centre. When the pack forms a ring round the fire, each
man will have neighbours to right and left, but no-one behind him; his back
is naked and exposed to the wilderness."[29]

From Deleuze and Guattari's perspective, the question of one wolf in
the pack does not make any sense at all, since the wolf is not some individual collection of characteristics but a name for the affect of becoming-wolf;
every animal is already a pack. An irreducible multiplicity is not a gathering
of individual beasts, taken one by one. An irreducible multiplicity means
that every animal is a pack, among its number.

Nonetheless, Deleuze and Guattari do have a place for the lone wolf—
the one who runs alongside and, at the same time, a bit apart from the main
pack. He can be the leader of the pack or an outcast. Deleuze and Guattari
call such an animal, which exists in every pack, a demon, an exceptional
individual or anomaly. And, here, the theme of the periphery or the border takes on a special significance. The exceptionalness of the individual is
determined by its position at the border of the pack (sorcerers, for example,
"have always held the anomalous position, at the edge of the fields or woods
[. . .] at the borderline of the village, or *between* villages,"[30] where they enter
into a secret alliance with various animals and demons).

The anomaly is not simply at the border; it is also the phenomenon of the
border itself, of "bordering."[31] In other words, the border of the pack runs
through the exceptional individual: "[B]eyond the borderline, the multiplicity changes nature,"[32] crossing over into another dimension. As Catherine
Malabou notes, the role of the anomaly is "to mark out the end of a series
and the imperceptible move to another possible series, like the eye of a nee-
dle of affects, the point of passage by means of which one motif is stitched to
another."[33] This extremely dynamic world of multiplicities and series is measured by intensities of becoming—upon the borders of the pack anomalous
individuals form alliances and blocks of becoming and transition.

One should also not forget about sorcery—metamorphoses that occur at
the border of the pack, metamorphoses of certain types of animals into others, including monsters. At a certain moment the lone wolf appears not only
upon the horizon but also as a werewolf or wolf in sheep's clothing. Let us
return to the Wolf Man and have a look at this, using the optics of becoming
and transition in order to better understand how the metamorphosis from
one animal series into another takes place in Freud's interpretation. What

follows is significant for its bringing psycho- and schizoanalysis, Freud and Deleuze, together into a paradoxical and unnatural alliance.

So, once again, the seven wolves are the kid-goats (eaten by the wolf). There are six of them because the seventh hid in the wall clock. I have already drawn a comparison with the vampire bite—the kids eaten by the wolf turn into wolves themselves (contagion is one of the characteristics of a pack). It is clear that the dreamer himself should have been eaten first. But he was able to hide—at the cost of having to observe the bloody massacre of the others.

At this original stage of his interpretation, Freud seems to perform a reverse movement, again drawing the little bodies of the kids out of the belly of the demonic wolves—or, more precisely, the belly of one demonic wolf (this time we remember another fairy tale, Little Red Riding-Hood, in which a woodsman kills the wolf and frees the little girl and her granny, whom the wolf had eaten). Later, we learn that the wolf, having eaten everyone else, is, in fact, the boy's father, some kind of strange universal father-mother who, in order to give birth to the boy from his belly, must first eat him (or vice versa—the sequence does not matter in the world of the unconscious). Here, the patient's recollection of a book illustration with which his sister used to scare him in childhood plays a significant role: a wolf standing upon its hind legs and reaching out a forelimb. Note the extraordinary position of this wolf; it is a pose uncharacteristic of his species, standing upon the border between two packs, animal and human.

Thus, before us there are at least three borders between packs, three anomalies: between the wolves and the kids, between the wolf and the human, and between the monstrous multiplicity of wolf-kids, which Freud reduces to the lonely figure of the father, and the boy himself, who meets and exchanges gazes with it (there are also intermediary borders, involving sheep, sheep-dogs, the spread legs of the mother, and even the wall clock). Upon which border does the patient find himself? All three.

However, we should not allow for simple confusion at these borders. It is not just an undifferentiated animal multiplicity before us, where the fantasies of the child and the hypotheses of the analyst allow easy transformations from one thing into another. The animal multiplicity is not primordial chaos but the complexly constructed and difficult-to-translate language of the Other. Thus, between the wolves and the kids runs a line of tension that separates two animal multiplicities—not just one pack from another but, let us be clear, a pack from a herd. Deleuze and Guattari are not very interested in this aspect of the situation. In principle, they are indifferent to

what parameters, besides intensities and affects, real animals use to organize themselves, namely, packs, herds, crowds, and colonies—all of these
are nothing more than scientific abstractions, "ridiculous evolutionary
classifications."[34]

Meanwhile, I insist that the appearance of herd animals in Freud's interpretation is not an accident (although it does seem like one). The difference
between a herd and a pack is the difference between those who devour and
those who are devoured. It is precisely devouring in the given case that facil-
itates the transition from one condition into another. The wolf in sheep's
clothing is not merely an interloper. There will come a time when he will
stand up, straighten his legs, and throw off the sheepskin; at the last moment
of their lives, the sheep will encounter the naked king, the father-devourer.
The alliance between the wolf, the sheep (the kid-goats), and the father, god,
or leader who runs along the borders between the pack and the herd, and
between the human and the animal, remains outside Deleuze and Guattari's
field of vision. For us, however, it is of fundamental importance.

At the beginning of his seminar dedicated to the sovereign and the beast,
Derrida puts together a fantastic series of different cultural representations
of the wolf, setting the stage for his quotation from Jean-Jacques Rousseau's
The Social Contract: "It is doubtful, then, according to Grotius, whether the
human race belongs to a hundred or so men, or if that hundred or so men
belong to the human race [. . .]. So, here we have the human race divided
into herds of cattle, each one with its chief who keeps it in order to devour
it."[35] This is one of the most exhaustive descriptions of human communities,
where the exceptional position belongs, as Derrida says, precisely to the wolf
(who, we should note, intentionally runs across the border between the pack
and the herd):

> [H]e, the chief, does not keep the beast *by devouring* it, while devour-
> ing the beast (and we are already in the space of *Totem and Taboo*
> and the scenes of devouring cruelty that are unleashed in it, put
> down, repressed in it and therefore displaced in it into symptoms;
> and the devouring wolf is not far away, the big bad wolf, the wolf's
> mouth, the big teeth of Little Red Riding Hood's Grandmother-Wolf
> ("Grandmother, what big teeth you have"), as well as the devouring
> wolf in the Rig Veda, etc., or Kronos appearing with the face of Anu-
> bis devouring time itself).[36]

This Kronos with the face of Anubis, whom Derrida mentions, was time
itself, devouring his children. To say that he devours time is an inversion,

making time appear to devour itself. He devours his children when they are still infants, fearing the prophecy that one of them will destroy him. In the end, of course, this is what happens: Kronos eats five infants (according to the myth, they are Hestia, Demeter, Hera, Hades, and Poseidon); the sixth, Zeus, manages to survive (his mother Rhea goes to Crete and gives birth to Zeus in a cave, slipping Kronos a stone in his place); then, Zeus overthrows (and, in some versions, castrates) his father and releases the other devoured children from his belly.

Thus, we have five devoured children; the sixth survived (hidden in a cave). If we are speaking of the same story, dealing with different versions, then there should be a seventh. Who is this seventh? It is Kronos himself. He is also part of the pack, part of the herd, a member of the family. He is one of us, just like the leader, who worries about the herd in order to devour it; he is a member of this herd, just like the wolf-father—one of the wolves sitting in the tree in Pankejeff's dream. The one who devours and the ones who are devoured or sacrificed are reflected in one another.

What is the bloody drama enacted at this border, a drama of our cultural heritage, narrated in the different languages of legends, fairy tales, and the dreams of little Russian schizophrenics? The drama can take different names: the exorcism of demons, the miracle of healing, the nightmare of repression (or, in Freud's words, "organic repression"),[37] the birth of the one out of the multiple (which has never existed), the child becoming an adult, and the formation of human society. And here is the moral of the story—the road to the human runs through the wolf.

The fact is that, on the level of social being, we can always determine who is the oppressor and the devourer and who is the oppressed and the devoured. Our ideas about justice, equality, and liberty, which, for this reason, lay the foundation for our version of how to rebuild humanity, are all upon the surface. That is, we can act in solidarity with the oppressed, the repressed, and the devoured. We speak about repression in the context of violent state apparatuses, for example. But what should we do with the other type of repression, the repression each of us enacts upon an individual level even before we are aware of it—perhaps, at that very moment, unlike pigeons, we recognize ourselves in the mirror? When, by appropriating the image of the other, we relegate the animal multiplicity that we inherit into nonbeing? The multiplicity, which never abandons its nonbeing, has its nonbeing actualized, acquiring meaning retrospectively in the very act of repression.

Deleuze and Guattari reject the negativity, retrospection, and reflexivity of the pack. They populate the plane of immanence with packs, where one series crosses over into another along the borderlines, guaranteeing ontological continuity. But, for them, the violence practiced in the process of normalization, at the entrance to human society, is clear—the wolves are not allowed to speak. However, for Deleuze and Guattari, it is Freud who is to blame for all of this, who resembles the papa-wolf and embodies the repressive apparatus of psychoanalysis, founded upon the reduction of multiplicity. I contend that psychoanalysis plays a somewhat different role here, pinpointing transformations that occur upon the border of human society, giving them narrative structure, and thus forcing a certain constitutive act of violence to speak. "They" speak—but "we" do not like it. The analyst is not so much the subject of this act (which Deleuze sees as discursive violence against the patient) but rather its medium, if one can put it this way, the one who translates it into the language of symptoms. It is not immanent borders that divide the Freudian packs but a painful, traumatic rupture. The rupture was there from the beginning—before the one appeared upon this side and multiplicity upon the other. It is something like a psychoanalytic Big Bang, from which "we" and "they" emerge every time. We cannot simply get up and return to the wolves that call to us with their silent gaze, since there is no authentic, primordial pack waiting for the schizophrenic at the end of his journey—every pack has a border and this border is us, not another wolf. We should speak of the exceptional position occupied not by certain individuals but by everyone in the pack—recall how Canetti tells us that one's back is only exposed to something outside of us. From there, behind our back, we hear the inarticulate speech of the Other.

It is not as if there are some separate, lonely wolves running in the distance that are exceptional ("anomalous," to put it in Deleuze's terms) with regard to the rest, the regular individuals in the pack. All individuals are exceptional, only some, to paraphrase George Orwell, are more exceptional than others:[38] the fathers of families, leaders, gods, wolf-devourers in sheep's clothing—these are illustrative models of how each of us integrates into normal human society. In order to get into this society, it is necessary first to become some of it, to complete organic repression, to drive out, devour, or annihilate. All of us perform this complex sacrifice with natural ease. We have to go through all of the stages of becoming at once: the scapegoat, the son, and the wolf-father driving off the pack and devouring the herd (strictly speaking, the pack of other predators is driven off in order to master one's own herd and devour it). Simultaneously, there is the return of the repressed, the pack, which must first be driven out in order to return to us again, because we are still among its number, or the return of the herd, which must first be eaten in order to be born again from the belly of the predator. Our pack and our herd—the animal, multiple, heritage of the unconscious—will always run after and frighten us with their silent call.

But how, then, it must be asked, can we rebuild a community based upon such human material, in which organic repression, at the individual level, entails oppression and violence, at the level of the social? Is a human community ever possible without immediately turning into a nightmare? It is clear that without the presence of repressed elements no separate adult human and no separate society are possible. But repression means the return of the repressed; in gatherings composed of people one by one, each, in the final analysis, is anxious, tortured, and haunted by the whole pack of those who have been devoured, driven out, crushed, or not taken aboard the ark—because each remains a part of this pack.

Let us now go back to the point where we began, with the formulation of the question of community as a question of the unconscious and the real of our desire. We did not invent this desire in order to desire it consciously; something desires for us, behind our back. The pack that runs after us wants something from us. "They" speak, addressing us with a call that we interpret as either infantile drives, the unformed, abnormal child sexuality beyond the ego, or the inarticulate animal cry, howl, or silent call. The theory of community that I am suggesting here revolves around these shadows that follow us, trying to look behind our back. "Unconscious desire for communism" is probably not the best name for it, but I have not thought of anything better. Between us, all three of these words are dubious—*unconscious*, *desire*, and *communism*. All three are problematic, ambivalent. In any case, this triad is preferable to, say, *consciousness*, *interest*, and *capitalism* (or various others), since it hints at a nonhuman community. It reminds us of what has not yet been and returns us to a future we inherit from nowhere.

As Jodi Dean writes, "[t]he communist horizon is not lost. It is Real,"[39] while also, by the way, associating the desire for communism with the unconscious. It is precisely in this sense that she calls it "Real": not real communism (as we are accustomed to speak, for example, of "really existing socialism"), but communism as the real, in the Lacanian sense, as a certain traumatic excess that resists symbolization, which can in no way be confused with reality. The real of desire does not coincide with those desires that we recognize in ourselves; it stands behind us, just like the horizon of communism, which has never been. It stands directly behind our back, right there, forming a border between what has been and what has not. It is as if we have grown into this horizon with our backs and we are the border ourselves.

Like Dean, I speak of the real of the horizon and the desire for communism, but I want to follow this desire all the way to the level of the unconscious and the animal. One might object that animals do not have an unconscious and, thus, cannot have the real of desire—they only have instincts. That is just the point. They—our pack and our herd—live, in principle, for *being* rather than *having*; in other words, they are the unconscious and the desire for communism, which exists nowhere in nature—not in the plane of immanence and not among real wolves. This "not," precisely, indicates the negative character of desire; in this "not" we hear the "not yet" and "still not yet" that troubles us so (incidentally, in Pankejeff's second dream about wolves, which Freud's student Ruth Mack Brunswick analyzes, these animals, again scaring the dreamer, are associated with the Bolsheviks).[40]

If we replace the plane of immanence with the plane of retrospection, our desire will be there, in that forgotten pack, which arose along with us and, immediately, stuck to us. What they want from us is the real of our desire, and this is where we should begin when we ask the question of community. "You send sailors / onto the sinking ship, / where / a forgotten / kitten meows," writes Vladimir Mayakovsky about the revolution,[41] and I cannot imagine a better image for the program of communism with a non-human face. The community is not for us but for them; it is redemption and a turn, a reactivation of animal negativity. This is a task absurd enough to be discussed seriously.

Translated by Jonathan Brooks Platt
A version of the essay published here was originally published as "Unconscious Desire for Communism," *Identities: Journal for Politics, Gender and Culture* 11 (2015): 32–48.

Notes

1. I am referring here, in particular, to the idea of community as it was developed in twentieth-century French philosophy. See, for example, Jean-Luc Nancy, *The Inoperative Community*, trans. Peter Connor, Lisa Garbus, Michael Holland, and Simona Sawhney (Minneapolis: University of Minnesota Press, 1991); and Maurice Blanchot, *The Unavowable Community*, trans. Pierre Joris (Barrytown: Station Hill Press, 1988).

2. See, for example, Jacques Lacan, "The Function and Field of Speech and Language in Psychoanalysis," in *Écrits: The First Complete Edition in English*, trans. Bruce Fink (New York: W. W. Norton, 2006), 223; "Science and Truth," in *Écrits:*

The First Complete Edition in English, 737; and *The Seminar of Jacques Lacan, Book XI: The Four Fundamental Concepts of Psychoanalysis*, ed. Jacques-Alain Miller, trans. Alan Sheridan (New York: W. W. Norton, 1998), 149, 203.

3. See Lacan, "The Freudian Thing, or the Meaning of the Return to Freud in Psychoanalysis," in *Écrits: The First Complete Edition in English*, 344; and *The Seminar of Jacques Lacan, Book VII: The Ethics of Psychoanalysis, 1959–1960*, ed. Jacques-Alain Miller, trans. Dennis Porter (New York: W. W. Norton, 1992), 206.

4. See Lacan, "The Mirror Stage as Formative of the *I* Function as Revealed in Psychoanalytic Experience," in *Écrits: The First Complete Edition in English*, 75–81.

5. Ibid., 77.

6. Jacques Derrida, "And Say the Animal Responded?" in *The Animal That Therefore I Am*, ed. Marie-Louise Mallet, trans. David Wills (New York: Fordham University Press, 2008), 121; emphasis in original.

7. See, for example, Derrida, "The Ends of Man," in *Margins of Philosophy*, trans. Alan Bass (Chicago: University of Chicago Press, 1982), 109–36.

8. See Giorgio Agamben, *The Open: Man and Animal*, trans. Kevin Attell (Stanford: Stanford University Press, 2004), 33–38.

9. See Martin Heidegger, "Letter on Humanism," in *Basic Writings: From "Being and Time" (1927) to "The Task of Thinking" (1964)*, ed. David Farrell-Krell, rev. ed. (New York: Harper and Row, 1977), 213–65.

10. See, for example, Susanna Lindberg, "Heidegger's Animal," in *Phänomenologische Forschungen* (Hamburg: Felix Meiner Verlag, 2004): 57–81. See also Oxana Timofeeva, "Koni v zakone: Kratkii nabrosok k filosofii zhivotnogo," *Sinii divan* 10/11 (2007): 80–95; "Bednaia zhizn: Zootekhnik Visokovskii protiv filosofa Xaideggera," *Novoe literaturnoe obozrenie* 106 (2010): 96–113; and *History of Animals: An Essay on Negativity, Immanence and Freedom* (Maastricht: Jan van Eyck Academy, 2012), 119–30.

11. Slavoj Žižek, *Less Than Nothing: Hegel and the Shadow of Dialectical Materialism* (New York: Verso, 2012), 409.

12. See Heidegger, "Letter on Humanism," 234, 245.

13. See, for example, Stuart Elden, *Speaking against Number: Heidegger, Language and the Politics of Calculation* (Edinburgh: Edinburgh University Press, 2006).

14. Gen. 6:19–20. All biblical references are to the King James Version.

15. Gen. 7:2–3.

16. Gen. 7:11–12.

17. Mark 5:9.

18. See, in particular, Michel Foucault, "*Stultifera Navis*," in *History of Madness*, ed. Jean Khalfa, trans. Jonathan Murphy and Jean Khalfa (New York: Routledge, 2006), 3–43.

19. Sigmund Freud, "From the History of an Infantile Neurosis," in *The Standard Edition of the Complete Psychological Works of Sigmund Freud* (hereafter *SE*), ed. and trans. James Strachey et al. (London: Hogarth Press, 1953–1974), 17:34.

20. Lacan, *The Seminar of Jacques Lacan, Book II: The Ego in Freud's Theory and in the Technique of Psychoanalysis, 1954–1955*, ed. Jacques-Alain Miller, trans. Sylvana Tomaselli (New York: W. W. Norton, 1988), 177.

21. Gilles Deleuze and Félix Guattari, *A Thousand Plateaus: Capitalism and Schizophrenia*, trans. Brian Massumi (Minneapolis: University of Minnesota Press, 2005), 29–30.

22. Ibid., 28.

23. On the problem of counting beasts in the context of an analysis of these two stories and the case of the Wolf Man, see Timofeeva, "Chislo zverei," *Lakanaliia* 6 (2011): 118–22.

24. Lacan, *The Seminar of Jacques Lacan, Book I: Freud's Papers on Technique, 1953–1954*, ed. Jacques-Alain Miller, trans. John Forrester (New York: W. W. Norton, 1988), 191; emphasis in original.

25. See Freud, *The Interpretation of Dreams*, in *SE* 5:536.

26. Deleuze and Guattari, *A Thousand Plateaus: Capitalism and Schizophrenia*, 29.

27. Ibid.

28. Ibid., 33.

29. Elias Canetti, *Crowds and Power*, trans. Carol Stewart (New York: Continuum, 1981), 93.

30. Deleuze and Guattari, *A Thousand Plateaus: Capitalism and Schizophrenia*, 246; emphasis in original.

31. Ibid.

32. Ibid., 245.

33. Catherine Malabou, "Who's Afraid of Hegelian Wolves?" in *Deleuze: A Critical Reader*, ed. Paul Patton, trans. David Wills (Cambridge: Blackwell Publishers, 1996), 128.

34. Deleuze and Guattari, *A Thousand Plateaus: Capitalism and Schizophrenia*, 239.

35. Jean-Jacques Rousseau, *Du contrat social* (Paris: Classiques Garnier, 1954), 237, quoted in Derrida, *The Beast and the Sovereign*, ed. Michel Lisse, Marie-Louise Mallet, and Ginette Michaud, trans. Geoffrey Bennington, vol. 1 (Chicago: University of Chicago Press, 2009), 11–12.

36. Derrida, *The Beast and the Sovereign*, vol. 1, 12; emphasis in original.

37. See Freud, "A Case of Obsessional Neurosis," in *SE* 10:248; and *Civilization and Its Discontents*, in *SE* 21:99–107.

38. See George Orwell, *Animal Farm: A Fairy Story* (New York: Mariner, 2007), 192.

39. Jodi Dean, *The Communist Horizon* (New York: Verso, 2012), 11.

40. See Ruth Mack Brunswick, "A Supplement to Freud's 'History of an Infantile Neurosis,'" in *The Wolf-Man by the Wolf-Man*, ed. Muriel Gardiner (New York: Basic, 1971), 289.

41. Vladimir Mayakovsky, "Ode to the Revolution," in *Selected Poems,* trans. James H. McGavran III (Evanston: Northwestern University Press, 2013), 71.

CHAPTER 9

F. O. Matthiessen

Heir to (American) Jouissance

Donald E. Pease

[*J*]*ouissance* [is] a kind of inheritance we can use, but not use
up; something that can never be titled to us. [. . .] It is not
ours alone even if it is the most intimate part of who we are.
What every individual inherits is not an identity or identifying property, but a potentiality, a capacity, which does not
prescribe in advance what it is a potential for.

— Joan Copjec[1]

The publication of F. O. Matthiessen's 1941 masterwork *American Renaissance: Art and Expression in the Age of Emerson and Whitman* continues to
be acclaimed as a watershed event in the advancement of the field of American studies.[2] A key founding text of the American studies movement, *American Renaissance* inspired the growth of American studies in the United
States and abroad. Indeed, Matthiessen's *American Renaissance* and the
Salzburg Seminar brought American literature to postwar Europe. When it
was tethered to the consensus view of the field in the late forties, *American
Renaissance* fostered the multiplication of American studies courses across
Europe and the United States, complete with programs of study, periodicals,
theses, dissertations, conferences, national associations, and a slate of distinguished scholarly authorities, including graduates of the Salzburg Seminar.[3]
    However, Matthiessen's motives for writing *American Renaissance* lie
deeper than adding courses to the university curriculum. *American Renaissance* was important for its canonization of examples of American writing

sufficiently accomplished in craft and vision to justify comparison with the finest works in other national literatures. It figured as the most sophisticated effort to turn forms of life from the American past into a resource available for use in the politics of the present. It also served as a timely affirmation of the values of American democracy as the nation was about to enter the Second World War.[4]

Before World War II, Nazi totalitarianism threatened to dissever Western civilization's ties to democratic values. To resist this threat, Matthiessen put classic texts from America's past into the service of articulating and representing the political consensus forged within the Popular Front. Matthiessen's *American Renaissance* consolidated these classic texts into a coherent national tradition, representing a heritage of democratic values to defend against European fascism and National Socialism.[5]

"True scholarship," as Matthiessen (quoting Louis Sullivan) claims in the conclusion to the opening essay of *American Renaissance*, must prove that it "has been applied for the good and enlightenment of all the people, not for the pampering of a class. [. . .] In a democracy there can be but one fundamental test of citizenship, namely: Are you using such gifts as you possess for or against the people?"[6] In order to authorize a canon of American authors, Matthiessen articulated a political discourse comprised of a nationalist approach to literature, underwritten by Emersonian self-reliance, an organicist aesthetic, buttressed by an ideology of liberal democracy, and a heteronormative social order, sustained by a progress-oriented teleology, that corroborated a Popular Front consensus, rather than his own values.[7] After World War II, however, Matthiessen found it necessary to reaffirm his allegiance to socialist aspirations that Popular Front imperatives obliged him to leave unrepresented within the pages of *American Renaissance*.

When Matthiessen directed his six-week seminar in the summer of 1947, American studies lacked the consensual logic that would thereafter lend coherence to this field of study.[8] Although it would soon be dubbed the "Marshall Plan of the mind," the Salzburg Seminar did not originate as an instrument of US Cold War policy. At the time of its founding in 1947 by the Harvard University Student Council, the Salzburg Seminar was not yet under US state control.[9] In the summer of 1947, Matthiessen, Alfred Kazin, Margaret Mead, and Walt Rostow joined seven other scholars to teach American literature, culture, and social sciences at Schloss Leopoldskron to a European student body consisting of displaced persons (DPs), antifascists, and former Nazis.

From the Heart of Europe was written from within sites quite literally surrounded by problems of military occupation and reeducation. Matthiessen had to pass through camps for Jewish refugees and political prisoners upon opposite sides of the street, leading from Schloss Leopoldskron to the center of the city of Salzburg. Hitler's "Eagle's Nest" hideaway was visible from his bedroom window, as were the heavily armed US GIs patrolling the streets surrounding the schloss. Matthiessen correlated the *American Renaissance* figures he discussed within his seminar to questions concerning the relationship between American literature and the more encompassing projects of military occupation and the Americanization projects taken up by US cultural diplomats in Salzburg.[10] Rather than promoting the political agendas of the State Department officials who monitored the work of scholars at the Salzburg Seminar, Matthiessen, in his welcoming address, reassured the participants that "none of our group has come as imperialists of [P]ax Americana to impose our values upon you."[11]

The itinerary Matthiessen recounted in *From the Heart of Europe*—his travel from Salzburg, by way of London and Paris, to Prague, Brno, Bratislava, and Budapest—carried him behind what Churchill described as the "Iron Curtain," establishing the contested border between East and West in the advent of the Cold War. The devastated postwar landscapes and vast DP camps in which Schloss Leopoldskron was situated in 1947 brought Matthiessen face to face with the catastrophic effects of the war. It was within this melancholic topography that he encountered the limitations to the national tradition he had fashioned in *American Renaissance*. Matthiessen understood his work in Europe less as part of a broader de-Nazification campaign than as an opportunity to contest emerging Cold War dynamics from the standpoint of the Europeans who were its targets. "Europe has always had the effect of making me take stock of my political opinions," he remarks in the context of refusing to participate in or sanction ideologically charged conversations that forced discussants into reductive positions "for" or "against" American hegemony.[12] At Salzburg, he began to realize that intellectuals were getting conscripted into the cause of aligning their teaching and scholarship with a culturally pervasive false choice. In this "moment of danger," Matthiessen sought to articulate a radical rethinking of the literary and political coordinates of the American cultural tradition that *American Renaissance* helped to codify.[13]

Writing against the Cold War consensus from within the historical conjuncture in which it was being forged, Matthiessen witnessed firsthand the violent dissolution of the cultural ways of life and political utterances to which he had been and continued to be committed.[14] In his view, *American Renaissance* remained too parochially within the American exceptionalist paradigm that was ushering the entirety of Europe to the precipice of disaster. He undertook the work of constructing intertextual relays between *American Renaissance* and *From the Heart of Europe* that would enable him to rededicate himself to the political imperatives that *American Renaissance* would not pass on:

> So far as American politics are concerned, progressives can no longer allow themselves to be deflected into delaying actions, into supporting the lesser of two evils. If you believe in democratic socialism you must act accordingly, and work for it. Many of the positions you take will be the same as those taken by the Communists, and you will of course be vilified for that. But however bad the odds, the final stakes are international co-operation or a war that will, at the very least[,] complete the destruction of Europe, the heart of our civilization.[15]

Matthiessen felt chiefly obliged to work for the accomplishment of a democratic socialism under threat of extinction in the United States and Europe. He aspired to articulate political aspirations that he had allowed "to be deflected into delaying actions" within the symbolic order that *American Renaissance* authorized. To realize this aspiration, Matthiessen positioned himself within a site of enunciation that lacked a position in the American Renaissance tradition. But through what subjective agency could Matthiessen now inherit the political prerogatives that the symbolic identity he took up in *American Renaissance* had precluded him from representing?

Inheritance Anxieties: The Double's Share

In the remarks that follow I intend to respond to this question through an interpretation of *From the Heart of Europe* as Matthiessen's staging of the reception of an impossible inheritance from the tradition of American Renaissance scholarship that he inventively codified in 1941. My understanding of what renders the reception of this impossible inheritance possible draws upon Jacques Derrida's account of the dual responsibility of the heir.[16] To clarify the significance of the figure that does the inheriting, I will draw upon Slavoj Žižek's notion of the fantasmatic specter.[17]

Matthiessen situated *From the Heart of Europe* astride what Derrida names the "dual responsibility" of the literary heir—a responsibility, on the one hand, to continue *American Renaissance*'s already established literary heritage and, on the other hand, to fulfill the demands issuing from a coming (socialist) democracy that were utterly inassimilable within that heritage.[18] These contradictory injunctions situated the Matthiessen who would perform the inheriting within a relentlessly contradictory position. He could not inherit socialist democracy without restoring representations of persons and events whose suppression enabled *American Renaissance* to achieve its coherence. Paradoxically, Matthiessen's commitment to the socialist democracy *American Renaissance* had excluded now seemed the only way to inherit what had inspired him to write *American Renaissance*: "the good and enlightenment of all the people."

From the moment of its publication, *American Renaissance* had served as an instrument of rule determinative of who would or could be excluded from the literary canon. Matthiessen published *American Renaissance* just prior to the United States' entry into the Second World War. In composing this masterwork, Matthiessen performed the socially symbolic action of constructing a national, cultural heritage to defend against Nazi totalitarianism. That act required that he suppress, in the name of his adherence to Popular Front aims, the figures, events, and passages in these works that reflected his genuine political commitments.[19]

Matthiessen's travel across postwar Salzburg's devastated cultural terrain evoked an uncanny specter within him through which he encountered the dark underside to the literary nationalism *American Renaissance* had fostered. Nothing seemed more revealing of the US occupation's potentially fatal effect upon Europe's mental and cultural landscape than a road sign reading "Death Is So Permanent" that Allied commanders had posted across Salzburg to caution GIs of the danger of reckless driving. To Matthiessen, the road sign was a signal, part of the procedures of systematic destruction that had rendered the entire city of Salzburg a vast DP camp: "Salzburg is for me, in a special sense, a city of ghosts."[20] Ironically, it was Matthiessen's experience of himself as a specter in communication with the undead ghosts haunting the living that supplied him with the condition of belonging proper to the "city of ghosts."

Rather than reeducating Nazis and inducting displaced Europeans into the American way of life, Matthiessen aspired, in the work he took up in *From the Heart of Europe*, to animate the figures, characters, events, and political dispositions that lie dormant within the pages of *American Renaissance*. However, before he could release these figures from the condition of representational latency, he had to incite the nonsynchronous potentiality inherent to the American Renaissance tradition.[21] In restoring a democratic, socialist past that was not actualized in the triumphal unfolding of US history that *American Renaissance* was understood to represent, Matthiessen correlated US history's nonactualized potential with the democratic, socialist futurity emanating from within the pages of *From the Heart of Europe*.

When Matthiessen took up the task of passing on this not-yet-actualized heritage, he restaged potentially revolutionary scenes, events, and relationships from within *American Renaissance* so as to enable political aspirations that lacked representation in 1941 to become resources for political activity in 1947. Overall, *From the Heart of Europe* interrupted, derailed, and undid *American Renaissance*'s procedures of literary governmentality. It changed the criteria for the selection of canonical authors as well as the mode of valuing them. Matthiessen put this counterhistory to the work of proleptically resisting the narratives of Cold War nationalism poised to achieve ideological dominance.[22]

At Salzburg, Matthiessen witnessed and participated in a vital tradition of democratic socialism whose systematic eradication in the US inspired him to reaffirm the political convictions that his Popular Front allegiances had muted. "Whatever objective reasons compelled toward socialism in the nineteen-thirties," he writes, "seem even more compelling now, and it is the responsibility of the intellectual to rediscover and rearticulate that fact."[23] In following through on this responsibility, Matthiessen adopted an increasingly public, radical stance. Throughout the pages of *From the Heart of Europe*, he openly championed the causes of trade union activists, the rights of minorities, Labor Party candidates, antiwar dissidents, migrant laborers, pacifists, and non-American Americans.[24]

However, in his efforts to promote aspects of the political and literary past whose representation *American Renaissance* had disallowed, Matthiessen had to subjectivize an enunciative position that had played no avowable part in the representation, selection, interpretation, and transmission of the tradition of the American Renaissance. The figure that pronounces the ringing imperatives in *From the Heart of Europe* occupied a site of enunciation from which he desired an American past that would realize "the good and enlightenment of all the people" but nonetheless lacked a position within the American Renaissance tradition. When he inhabited this site, Matthiessen found himself between two deaths—the death of an American, socialist tradition and the death of the symbolic identity in whose name *American Renaissance* had authorized its dissolution.

This "spectral presence" that Matthiessen occupied within the symbolic order was the uncanny double of the symbolic identity he personified when he authorized *American Renaissance*'s order of literary governmentality.[25]

The fantasmatic specter through which Matthiessen composed *From the Heart of Europe* gave body to that which *American Renaissance* perforce excluded from its system of representations, yet it also inhered in those representations as what was more real than their symbolic reality.

Upon embodying this subject position, Matthiessen added what his literary persona had formerly elided from the repertoire of *American Renaissance* representations. He supplanted nationalist with internationalist imperatives, Emersonian self-reliance with Whitmanian solidarity, liberal democracy with Christian socialism, and the historical epic with democratic tragedy. He infused each of these reconfigurations with the affective intensities emanating from his twenty-year relationship with Russell Cheney. To comprehend the consequences of these addenda, we need simply recall what Matthiessen's best readers and interpreters have claimed he left out of the composition of *American Renaissance*—socialist politics and his relationship with Cheney and Walt Whitman's "Calamus" poems, in other words, "a sexual politics [. . .] that could allow him to connect his many kinds of work and the life he led with Russell Cheney."[26]

Art and Expression in the Age of Whitman and Socialism: An American Renaissance Masque

The seminar in American literature that Matthiessen directed at Salzburg did not endorse *American Renaissance*'s consensual understanding of America's past and future. He had come to Salzburg to profess what he could not say in the pages of *American Renaissance*. To do so, he took up the position of the legatee of an inheritance that *American Renaissance* did not pass on and of which the State Department would soon dispossess him.

In *From the Heart of Europe*, Matthiessen turned *American Renaissance* into a revisable work whose themes he purported to describe from the perspective of previously marginalized characters and scenes. To disrupt *American Renaissance*'s social efficacy, he had to undermine the cultural power of the writer who buttressed the symbolic identity through which Matthiessen authorized his masterwork's hegemonizing power. Ralph Waldo Emerson occupied the dramatic center of *American Renaissance*. Rather than ratifying Emerson's grandeur, however, Matthiessen brought Emerson down in stature by exposing the European sources and "analogues" for the Concord Sage's most compelling portrayals of self-reliance.[27] Matthiessen then reinterpreted key scenes and characters in *American Renaissance* from the viewpoint of Whitman's "solidarity" rather than Emerson's solitude.

Captain Ahab had been the primary focus of Matthiessen's attention in the *Moby-Dick* chapter of *American Renaissance*, where he describes Ahab's will to power as a prefiguration of Nazi totalitarianism. But, in *From the Heart of Europe*, after castigating Ahab for his subordination of the *Pequod*'s crew to appendages of his self-destructive will, Matthiessen concludes that "no more challenging counterstatement to Emerson's self-reliance has yet been written."[28]

In *From the Heart of Europe*, Matthiessen designates Whitman rather than Emerson as the central figure of the age. Matthiessen's undermining of Emerson's thematic dominance implemented his celebration of the ecstatic bonds of fellowship that Whitman communicated through his poetry. After refashioning his interpretation of Ahab into a critique of Emerson, Matthiessen assigns the novel's primary significance to Ishmael's interactions with Queequeg, which he exalts as a fusion of Christian socialism and democratic brotherhood. He then connects Ishmael-Queequeg's intense intermingling with Whitman's representative act of giving expression to the "unshackled, democratic spirit of Christianity in all things."[29]

Upon toppling Emerson from his standing as America's "Representative Man," Matthiessen felt moved to describe his allegiance to Whitman's tradition as that of a socialist who lacked a party:

> Whitman knew, through the heartiness of his temperament, as Emerson did not, that the deepest freedom does not come from isolation. It comes instead through taking part in common life, mingling in its hopes and failures, and helping to reach a more adequate realization of its aims, not for one alone, but for the community. [. . .] So, trying to clarify my own American politics that have carried me now from Paris to London to Prague, I reaffirm my allegiance to the Whitman tradition. I am a socialist, though still without a party.[30]

The Matthiessen who inherited Whitman's tradition of democratic socialism within *From the Heart of Europe* was an aspect of his writing self that had been denied identification within the discourse of *American Renaissance*. When Matthiessen performatively accomplished the inheriting of this alternative past through the restagings of key scenes of interpretation within his masterwork, he became part of an order of reference and event that had no part in *American Renaissance*. The Matthiessen who described himself as a "socialist, though still without a party" now felt himself to be a specter dwelling within the space between the dissolution of a viable socialist party and the death of the companion whose surplus relationality had filled this absence.

F. O. Matthiessen's Dual Inheritance:
The Immortal Share

In postwar Europe, Matthiessen no longer wrote under the constraints imposed upon his political proclivities by the Popular Front. He nonetheless wrote with implacable grief over the loss of Russell Cheney, whose death on July 12, 1945 made him feel dispossessed of the gifts he had exalted in a letter he posted two years before the publication of *American Renaissance*: "I remember that early phrase from a letter of yours from Venice, of how our gifts of love to each other enabled all our other relationships to share in 'largesse from our unknown wealth, untold wealth of love.'"[31]

We have seen how Matthiessen's retrieval of the figures of thought and speech elided from *American Renaissance* had transmuted him into the subject position of a fantasmatic specter that brought his European students into a vital relationship with the unactualized potentiality of the United States' past. Matthiessen invoked the ghost of Cheney to explain what entitled his bringing the unlived past to life. Having instructed Matthiessen in "how to see life" with "more vividness [. . .] than [he] had ever felt,"[32] Cheney now stirred Matthiessen to bring not-yet-actualized forms of political and social life across the boundary separating the postwar present from this undead past.

Matthiessen described his bedroom at the schloss as the place where he felt most at home in Salzburg because of the uncanny resemblance of its high ceiling, pink calcimine plaster walls, green tiled stove, and wide floorboards to the bedroom he had shared with Cheney in their Kittery, Maine cottage. But Cheney's visitations were not restricted to Matthiessen's bedroom. Recollection of the journey they took through Salzburg a decade earlier impelled Matthiessen to remark that "[w]hen I notice something new or changed here, I find myself speaking it in my mind to him. [. . .] This is the only sense in which immortality has a meaning which I have experienced."[33]

Since the entirety of *From the Heart of Europe* attests to a change in Matthiessen's orientation to the literary and political questions he took up in *American Renaissance*, it can be described as a continuation of his posthumous conversation with Cheney. We, its readers, are, in effect, overhearing Matthiessen speak to Cheney about this potential change in America's ethical and political coordinates from within the place in his mind that he has described as reserved for the meaningful experience of immortality. The figure of Cheney that Matthiessen evokes in this passage personifies the sublime excess of relationality that would interconnect what has not yet taken place in America's past to America's democratic, socialist future, which, like the nonsynchronous past it heralds, awaits actualization.

In the letters between them that Louis Hyde edited under the title *Rat and the Devil*, Matthiessen and Cheney frequently discuss the significance of their relationship as granting them access to this disjointed temporality. In an unpublished letter addressed to Cheney on November 20, 1924, Matthiessen associates the affective excess inflooding their relationship with the contradictory temporal logics that his specter straddled:

> But I don't wonder at all about what a certain seven weeks is going to do for me. It's going to give me the actual experience of love that I had never imagined until September, and that it has taken me since then to fully grasp. But I guess we come close to understanding what has happened to us now, don't we . . . ? At least we know how it feels to love and be loved with the whole reach of the soul.[34]

Throughout this passage, Matthiessen situates himself between, on the one hand, a past eventfulness ("the actual experience of love that I had never imagined until September") whose potential for actualization exceeded the capacity of the writing "I" to "fully grasp," and, on the other hand, a futurity to come ("a certain seven weeks is going to do for me") that would retroactively endow what had been imagined in September with the actuality it lacked as of November 20 ("It's going to give me the actual experience of love I had never imagined until September"). If it is this surplus relationality that suffuses the fantasmatic specter interconnecting what aspired to actualization from within the precincts of *American Renaissance* to the socialist futurity through which it will have been accomplished, Whitman was the American Renaissance figure through whom Matthiessen and Cheney attested to this event. Whitman becomes a sign, medium, and, in some instances, the expressive revelation of "how it feels to love and be loved with the whole reach of the soul."

Indeed, whenever rifts posed threats to the wholeness of his lifelong bond with Cheney, Matthiessen would inflood the breach with lines from Whitman's poetry. At a crucial juncture in the early years of their relationship, Cheney expresses the wish to extirpate sexuality as an unwanted manifestation of their love:

> I'm sorry, Dev, sorry, if it is true, as I believe, that the base of our love is not physical but intense understanding of a mutual problem. [. . .] [I]t is the pressure of opinion that has showed up what I have

glimpsed off and on, but dodged—that the only possible life is one, every part of which can be acknowledged. I have been nothing but a big bluff, and it's been a hell of a wrench to admit that and say I am through—that if there is something in my life I cannot acknowledge, out it comes.[35]

Matthiessen formulates his rejection of Cheney's wish as a gloss upon lines from Whitman's "I Sing the Body Electric":

You say that our love is not based on the physical, but on our mutual understanding, and sympathy, and tenderness. And of course that is right. But we both have bodies: "if the body is not the soul, what then is the soul?" [. . .] [I]t would mean that there would no longer be the same abundant joyous lack of restraint, and that the dim corners of our hearts where physical desires lurked would no longer be wholly open to each other.[36]

Despite this expression of his faith in the absolute acknowledgment of their relationship's "abundant joyous lack of restraint," however, Matthiessen vents a comparable complaint about the effects of their sexual intimacy upon the truth of his public identity in a letter he sent Cheney five years later:

My sex bothers me, feller, sometimes when it makes me aware of the falseness of my position in the world. And consciousness of that falseness seems to sap my confidence of power. Have I any right in a community that would so utterly disapprove of me if it knew the facts? I ask myself that and then I laugh; for I know I would never ask it at all if isolation from you didn't make me search into myself. I need you, feller; for together we can confront whatever there is. But damn it! I hate to have to hide when what I thrive on is absolute directness.[37]

Cheney's need for a relationship grounded in the complete acknowledgment of every part of his life could never be gratified in the community that "would so utterly disapprove of [Matthiessen] if it knew the facts." According to Matthiessen, it was the intensity of their mutual affection—the "absolute directness," the "complete acknowledgment," and the "abundant joyous lack of restraint" in their infinitely immanent sense of relationality—that attached Matthiessen and Cheney to each other and the work that connected them both to the world.

Matthiessen may have stipulated that the "untold largesse" of his relationship with Cheney supplied the creative resources through which their worldly projects became expressible. But he nonetheless excluded representation of the significance of their relationship from the pages of *American Renaissance*, whose organic unity was, in part, constituted out of its exclusion. Was Matthiessen afraid that knowledge of their relationship would falsify or invalidate the statements about American art and political culture to which he gave expression in *American Renaissance*? Did he fear that if the community of readers ("all the people") he wanted to address knew the truth about his relationship with Cheney they would not only deny him the "right" to authorize the symbolic order *American Renaissance* promoted but also remove him from it?

Such speculations might seem far-fetched were it not for the fact that, on January 4, 1939, two years before the publication of *American Renaissance*, Matthiessen recorded his experience of feeling quite literally cast out of its composition by a force that seemingly overrode his control:

> I don't know how to begin a record of this experience [. . .] I can trace, and have traced to various friends the genesis of my condition. At Kittery, this fall, instead of riding my work, it began without precedent to ride me. [. . .] I was hauled out of sleep by the fantasy it would be better if I jumped out the window. And during the succeeding week in Kittery I was recurrently filled with the desire to kill myself. Why?[38]

Why should the experience of feeling overtaken by his work in such a way that he felt driven by *it*, rather than by the work's driving animus, give rise to the fantasy that "it would be better if I jumped out of the window"? In response to this question about the cause of his hallucinated suicide, Matthiessen comes up with an answer that takes the form of an even more perplexing question: "At once I raised the question of whether I could face life without Russell."[39]

The question as to whether Matthiessen could live without Cheney does not emerge as the declarative cause of his hallucinated suicide. Whether he could survive without Cheney instead *appears* to be a question that only imagining his own suicide allowed him to consider. Does his projection of this imagined disconnection from his lover give him reason to believe he would be better off if he killed himself? If it does, such imagining would appear to be in response to a reciprocal question: "Can Russell Cheney live without me?"

In the interim between the thoughts gathering around the fantasy of jumping out the window and acting upon it, Matthiessen's thoughts turn to a seemingly consoling resolution: "Russell is not dead, and my present confused misery can only serve to dishearten and bring nearer the very event that I fear."[40] But this reasonable resolve immediately dissolves into Matthiessen's ceding control yet again to that overriding defenestration fantasy that will have rendered the event of Cheney's death all the more proximate, "though it seemed a much longer interval, since having once glimpsed the image of suicide, my mind and emotions galloped so violently down the corridors of that temptation."[41]

As Matthiessen galloped through this portal, he voided his subject position of any image other than that of the impossible conjoining of his suicide with his lover's reciprocal death—to infinity. Matthiessen's fantasy opens up a space in the finite temporal order itself wherein he can subjectively experience the unconditional relationality immanent to their love that, in exceeding the restraints of death, "infinitizes" even his finite bodily being.

But who or what brought Matthiessen to this fantasy? And how is this fantasy related to the dynamism in the work that began "to ride" Matthiessen out of its pages? This fantasy emerged while Matthiessen was in the throes of completing the literary project that would constitute the US national community from out of the exclusion of any signs of homoerotic relationality. As he neared completion of a work that he originally intended to entitle *Man in the Open Air*, did Matthiessen write with increased awareness of the fact that representations of his relationship with Cheney could not be integrated within the discourse that he described as addressed to "all the people"? Is the command "it would be better off if [you] jumped out the window" construable as an ethical demand emanating from within the symbolic order *American Renaissance* authorized? Does the phrase "it would be better off" enunciate the decision of the work's (Emersonian) ego-ideal that, "it," the social-symbolic order that *American Renaissance* represents, would be better off if Matthiessen were cast out of its framework? Or has this superegoic demand been rerouted through the id, reemerging as Matthiessen's obtaining access to the joyous lack of restraint in his relationship with Cheney through his leaping out into the infinite openness of the air?

No matter how we respond to these questions, the material outcome of the fantasy is unmistakable. In his projective identification with the absolute loss of Cheney, Matthiessen materially acted out the literal voiding of signifiers of their relationship within *American Renaissance*. The fantasmatic specter Matthiessen embodies in *From the Heart of Europe* will have learned how to turn the force that impelled this voiding into the means of inheriting what

remains of Cheney as an inextricable portion of the unactualized potentiality of *American Renaissance*.

(American) Jouissance: Russell Cheney's Impossible Legacy to F. O. Matthiessen

In my remarks thus far, I have been intent upon showing how Matthiessen
wrote *From the Heart of Europe* to accomplish three interrelated aims: first,
to situate himself astride two incompatible ethical demands (the obligation
to acknowledge the value of the literary tradition he had codified in *American Renaissance* and to affirm the tradition of "Christian socialism" that
had been disallowed within *American Renaissance*); second, to turn this site
of contradictory demands into the place for the inheritance of an alternative tradition; and, third, to discern, extract, represent, valorize, and render
inheritable the unactualized potentiality of the tradition of Christian socialism as what will have become the future of American socialist democracy
from within the pages of *American Renaissance*.

My effort to accomplish these aims has resulted in my describing the
surplus relationality that inhered in Matthiessen's lifelong bond with Cheney
as a salient figuration of the unactualized potentiality he wrote *From the
Heart of Europe* to inherit. I also proposed that the fantasmatic specter that
Matthiessen embodied to inherit this legacy was itself a placeholder for
what, perforce, had to remain nonsymbolizable within the symbolic order
regulated by the norms and rules of *American Renaissance*.

In naming the heir of this disavowed tradition a fantasmatic specter, I
intend to call attention to the unusual status of the subject that inherits this
potentiality as what, perforce, remains nonsymbolizable within *American
Renaissance*. Jacques Lacan named the *plus-de-jouir* (surplus-jouissance) I
argue suffused Matthiessen's relationship with Cheney (and that drove him
to restore the unactualized futurity of *American Renaissance*) the object
a.[42] The excess over satisfaction and signification flooding through the "joy
without restraint" that circulated around, through, and within Matthiessen's
relationship with Cheney also instantiated the objective cause of Matthiessen's need to actualize Christian socialism.

Although it is more real than the symbolic reality of *American Renaissance*, however, the jouissance immanent to what Matthiessen wrote *From
the Heart of Europe* to inherit is irreducible to either his Christian-socialist
allegiances or his homoerotic bond with Cheney. That is why the jouissance passing through the intertextual relays interconnecting *American*

Renaissance and *From the Heart of Europe* remains a vital, if unactualized, site of inheritance.

Notes

1. Joan Copjec, "The Inheritance of Potentiality: An Interview with Joan Copjec," *E-rea: Revue électronique d'études sur le monde Anglophone* 12, no. 1 (2014), http://erea.revues.org/.

2. Sacvan Bercovitch convincingly describes *American Renaissance* as the foundational text, and the Salzburg Seminar as the site of origin, for American studies as an international movement in "The Problem of Ideology in American Literary History," *Critical Inquiry* 12, no. 4 (1986): 631–33.

3. In "Closet, Coup, and Cold War: F. O. Matthiessen's *From the Heart of Europe*," Arthur Redding provides what I consider the definitive account of the significance of *From the Heart of Europe*, characterizing it as Matthiessen's effort to reactivate the radical, socialist agenda that lies encrypted within *American Renaissance*. Redding's interpretation of *From the Heart of Europe* as a critique of the Cold War consensus with which *American Renaissance* has incorrectly been affiliated has deepened my understanding of both works. My sole reservation pertains to Redding's assumption that the figure that inherited this radically progressive tradition was compatible with the Matthiessen who authored *American Renaissance*. See Redding, "Closet, Coup, and Cold War: F. O. Matthiessen's *From the Heart of Europe*," *boundary 2* 33, no. 1 (2006): 171–201.

4. Randall Fuller offers a splendid account of Matthiessen's critical achievement in "Aesthetics, Politics, Homosexuality: F. O. Matthiessen and the Tragedy of the American Scholar," *American Literature* 79, no. 2 (2007): 363–65. Fuller is especially perceptive about the role Emerson played in Matthiessen's feeling uncannily disinherited of the social authority to transmit the themes and aims of *American Renaissance*.

5. This aspect of Matthiessen's project has engaged my research from the time that I, along with the other participants in the 1982 and 1983 English Institute, invoked Matthiessen as a tutelary presence. In "*Moby Dick* and the Cold War," I argue that Matthiessen's *American Renaissance* performs the symbolic function of constructing a national, cultural heritage to defend against Nazi totalitarianism. See Donald E. Pease, "*Moby Dick* and the Cold War," in *The American Renaissance Reconsidered*, ed. Walter Benn Michaels and Donald E. Pease (Baltimore: Johns Hopkins University Press, 1985), 113–55. In "New Americanists: Revisionist Interventions into the Canon," I claim that, as an instrument of canon formation, *American Renaissance* plays a crucial role in the formation of the Cold

War consensus. See Pease, "New Americanists: Revisionist Interventions into the Canon," *boundary 2* 17, no. 1 (1990): 1–37.

6. F. O. Matthiessen, *American Renaissance: Art and Expression in the Age of Emerson and Whitman* (New York: Oxford University Press, 1941), 18.

7. Jonathan Arac has provided an illuminating account of the discursive and psychosocial structures through which Matthiessen achieved this suppression and its psychological and political cost in "F. O. Matthiessen: Authorizing an American Renaissance," in *The American Renaissance Reconsidered*, 90–112.

8. Eric Cheyfitz discusses the ways in which *American Renaissance* performed the work of consolidating a Cold War consensus in "Matthiessen's American Renaissance: Circumscribing the Revolution," *American Quarterly* 41 (1989): 341–61. Geraldine Murphy elaborates upon the psychosocial dynamics informing the construction of this consensus in "Romancing the Center: Cold War Politics and Classic American Literature," *Poetics Today* 9, no. 4 (1988): 737–47. Bercovitch describes the role *American Renaissance* played in arriving at a consensual account of American literary history in "The Problem of Ideology in American Literary History," 631–33.

9. Henry Nash Smith published an authoritative account of the foundational work of the Salzburg Seminar in "The Salzburg Seminar," *American Quarterly* 1 (1949): 30–37. For an official record of the event, see Timothy W. Ryback, "The Salzburg Seminar—A Community of Fellows," http://www.sjsu.edu/salzburg/docs /thesalzburgseminaracommunityoffellows.pdf.

10. Redding supplies numerous examples of Matthiessen's adamant resistance to emergent geopolitical hegemonies throughout "Closet, Coup, and Cold War: F. O. Matthiessen's *From the Heart of Europe*," 171–201.

11. Matthiessen, *From the Heart of Europe* (New York: Oxford University Press, 1948), 14.

12. Ibid., 74.

13. Matthiessen considered this revisionist engagement with the nonsynchronous potential of the past as the critic's chief responsibility: "Today we can take no tradition for granted, we must keep repossessing the past for ourselves if we are not to lose it altogether." Matthiessen, "Responsibilities of the Critic," *Michigan Alumnus Quarterly Review* 55 (1948): 285.

14. See Redding, "Closet, Coup, and Cold War: F. O. Matthiessen's *From the Heart of Europe*," 171–201.

15. Matthiessen, *From the Heart of Europe*, 193–94.

16. See Jacques Derrida and Elisabeth Roudinesco, *For What Tomorrow . . . : A Dialogue*, trans. Jeff Fort (Stanford: Stanford University Press, 2004), 5–6.

17. See Slavoj Žižek, "Between Symbolic Fiction and Fantasmatic Spectre: Toward a Lacanian Theory of Ideology," in *Interrogating the Real*, ed. Rex Butler and Scott Stephens (New York: Continuum, 2006), 229–48.

18. See Derrida and Roudinesco, *For What Tomorrow . . . : A Dialogue*, 8–15.

19. See Pease, "*Moby Dick* and the Cold War," 113–55. See also Redding, "Closet, Coup, and Cold War: F. O. Matthiessen's *From the Heart of Europe*," 171–201.

20. Matthiessen, *From the Heart of Europe*, 22.

21. Jean-Luc Nancy describes similar tactics as *désoeuvrement*. See *The Inoperative Community*, ed. Peter Connor, trans. Peter Connor, Lisa Garbus, Michael Holland, and Simona Sawhney (Minneapolis: University of Minnesota Press, 1991), 154n23.

22. See Pease, "Pip, *Moby-Dick*, Melville's Governmentality," *Novel: A Forum on Fiction* 45, no. 3 (2012): 327–42. "Governmentality" is a term Michel Foucault invented to describe the encompassing processes linking the way in which individual subjects conduct themselves ("ethics") with the forms of power and domination through which states regulate the conduct of national populations. See Foucault, "Governmentality," in *The Foucault Effect: Studies in Governmentality*, ed. Graham Burchell, Colin Gordon, and Peter Miller (Chicago: University of Chicago Press, 1991), 93–94. National literary formations constitute the form that governmentality assumes when it targets the modalities of expression, political proclivities, schemata of perception, affective dispositions, and embodied beliefs through which governing rules and norms are internalized to supply, secure, and maintain readers' forms of conduct and programs of self-governance. Because of their capacity to take hold of the processes of behaving, thinking, and feeling immanent to their readers' conduct and to create structures of desire and affective protocols that introduced, secured, and valorized new forms of life, national literary metanarratives, such as *American Renaissance*, implement both registers of governmentality. *American Renaissance* participates in the global hegemonization of Americanist values. It provides American literary studies with a discourse organized out of the norms and assumptions of the American public sphere. This discourse rationalizes the liberal values of freedom and individual autonomy that Americanists describe as responsible for the progressive movement of world history.

23. Matthiessen, *From the Heart of Europe*, 79.

24. See ibid., 68–91.

25. This argument draws upon Žižek's notion of spectral presence in "Between Symbolic Fiction and Fantasmatic Spectre: Toward a Lacanian Theory of Ideology," 229–48.

26. Michael Cadden, "Engendering F. O. M.: The Private Life of *American Renaissance*," in *Engendering Men: The Question of Male Feminist Criticism*, ed. Joseph A. Boone and Michael Cadden (New York: Routledge, 1990), 34. See also Cheyfitz, "Matthiessen's *American Renaissance*: Circumscribing the Revolution," 341–61; Arac, "F. O. Matthiessen: Authorizing an American Renaissance," 90–112;

and Jay Grossman, "The Canon in the Closet: Matthiessen's Whitman, Whitman's Matthiessen," *American Literature* 70 (1998): 799–832.

27. "In talking about Emerson, the dramatic center became, to a degree that it had not previously been for me, his own voyage of self-discovery to Europe at twenty-nine. It was the best kind of year for him. It freed him from the constrictions of his ministerial background and it freed him from the awe of Europe by giving him instead the intimacy of knowledge. What was most exciting in discussing Emerson here was the sense of closeness to his European sources and analogues." Matthiessen, *From the Heart of Europe*, 24.

28. Ibid., 37.

29. Ibid., 35.

30. Ibid., 90.

31. Matthiessen to Russell Cheney, July 12, 1945, in *Rat and the Devil: Journal Letters of F. O. Matthiessen and Russell Cheney*, ed. Louis Hyde (Hamden: Archon, 1978), 244.

32. Matthiessen, *From the Heart of Europe*, 22.

33. Ibid.

34. Matthiessen to Cheney, November 20, 1924, Matthiessen Papers, Beinecke Library, Yale University. See also David Bergman, "F. O. Matthiessen: The Critic as Homosexual," *Raritan* 9 (1990): 62–82.

35. Cheney to Matthiessen, February 5, 1925, in *Rat and the Devil: Journal Letters of F. O. Matthiessen and Russell Cheney*, 80.

36. Matthiessen to Cheney, February 7, 1925, in *Rat and the Devil: Journal Letters of F. O. Matthiessen and Russell Cheney*, 86–87.

37. Matthiessen to Cheney, January 30, 1930, in *Rat and the Devil: Journal Letters of F. O. Matthiessen and Russell Cheney*, 200.

38. Matthiessen to Cheney, January 4, 1939, in *Rat and the Devil: Journal Letters of F. O. Matthiessen and Russell Cheney*, 245–46.

39. Ibid., 246-47.

40. Ibid., 247.

41. Ibid.

42. See, in particular, Jacques Lacan, *The Seminar of Jacques Lacan, Book XVII: The Other Side of Psychoanalysis*, ed. Jacques-Alain Miller, trans. Russell Grigg (New York: W. W. Norton, 2007), 19.

CHAPTER 10

A Mortimer Trap

The Passing of Death in *The Real Life of Sebastian Knight*

Sigi Jöttkandt

Through the agency of the "family plot," the postwar films of the 1940s and 1950s register a danger to the state in the form of an internal threat. In classics, such as Orson Welles's *The Stranger* and Alfred Hitchcock's second *The Man Who Knew Too Much*, as well as lesser-known Hollywood films, such as *Mystery of the 13th Guest* and *Murder by Invitation*, the peril comes not from the outside world but from within the home itself. A common feature of this genre is the conceit of the extra, uncounted "guest" in a family drama of succession. In the latter films, death stalks in the form of a mysterious killer who invites seeming strangers to an isolated house. But they are not strangers after all; it turns out they are members of the same family. By knocking all of them off, the killer stands to inherit the family fortune. The villain thus interrupts the rightful transmission of the estate, but the inheritance is a pretext that masks what is really being passed down. For, as it turns out, this is not so much about items of monetary value as much as it is about the "wealth" of a certain representational and conceptual order supported by the right relation to a first cause. Inheritance, in the final analysis, implies the legitimate relation of descendants to an original that is the source of their riches.

Concealed in secret compartments hidden within the walls, the killer in these films short-circuits the "natural" train of succession. Secretly, he interferes with how events unfold in time. He removes and then replaces objects from his position offstage. He kills off family members and leaves their corpses in cupboards, only to make them disappear again in a darkly comic game of *fort/da*.[1] Joan Copjec has suggested that the key to the detective genre is the paradox of an excess in a representational system.[2] In whodunits of the "thirteenth guest" variety, this excess registers in the figure of a family member who is also a foreign body, a trespasser in his own family.

Vladimir Nabokov's work is filled with such guest figures, carriers of the "aurelian sickness" that, in his real life, threatened more than once to derail his literary career, as he tells us in his autobiography, *Speak, Memory*.[3] The love of butterflies appears here as the expression of a masculine gene, typically passed down asexually through a line of tutors.[4] In his fiction, Nabokov expands upon this idea of an alternative, nonbiological parentage to encompass a medley of "lepi-adoptive" tutelary figures whose influence steers his heroes towards different fates.[5] Garbling their literary history like Nabokov's young tutor from Volga who "informed me that Dickens had written *Uncle Tom's Cabin*,"[6] what links them is the "cinematic" threat they pose to the established representational order of literature, whose tropes they imitate only to deflect from their usual course. Accordingly, the legacy these tutelary figures bequeath to Nabokov is counterfeit from the outset, riddled with impersonations, ventriloquism, and repetitions. Collectively, they represent an inheritance in *letters* where, like the "Muscovite muskrats"[7] of the tutor Lenksi's tongue-twisting dictation, meaning "scrambles out" laterally from Nabokov's writing, instead of waiting its turn to unfold in an orderly manner over time.

This ongoing contest of competing claims by cinema and literature within Nabokov's writing has largely escaped critical notice. When it is remarked upon, one tends to read it through its refraction as a narrative topos: Nabokov's dual- or multiple-worlds theme. But this spatial thematization lends itself too easily to recapture by theotropic paradigms. Nabokov criticism is saturated with discoveries of a ghostly "otherworld" of the sort that Nabokov himself was always so quick to satirize in his novels as a wrong turn. It is a world populated by supervising spirits; whether malevolent or benign is irrelevant, for behind their shadow play lies the most controlling figure of all—the specter of Vladimir Nabokov, their God-like Creator. However, if we were to divest our interest in Nabokov from the overworked question of authority, with its outworn programs of selfhood, what would we find? One's reading would trip, precisely, over the jutting outlines of a family plot, one concerning two related but separate representational strands devolving from the same "paternity." In *The Real Life of Sebastian Knight*, Nabokov allegorically projects the twinned heritage of literature and cinema as half brothers, variants of a single generative, reproductive power that will silently reach into and upend all identificatory models.

The Real Life of Sebastian Knight is the first of Nabokov's novels written in English. When the story begins, the narrator's half brother, Sebastian Knight, has just died, leaving a number of questions about his life open. In an attempt to solve the mystery, the narrator, V, embarks upon a literary biography of the famous novelist. V's text, *The Real Life of Sebastian Knight*, would be the putatively true-life account of Sebastian—*real*, as opposed to the comically inaccurate version written by Knight's former secretary, the ironically named Mr. Goodman. Parodying the genre of the detective quest, *The Real Life of Sebastian Knight* accordingly recounts the events pertaining to the short life of the young novelist. The author of six novels, he was evidently also unhappily involved with a Russian femme fatale, for whom he left his long-time mistress, Clare Bishop. As several critics have noted, Sebastian's life history thus demonstrably reflects Nabokov's own youthful biography up to the point of his writing *The Real Life of Sebastian Knight*, albeit without mention of the disastrous affair with Irina Yurievna Guadanini, for whom Nabokov almost left his wife, Vera. The ostensible plot of *The Real Life of Sebastian Knight* revolves around V's search for the identity of Sebastian's secret lover, who, after playing a cat-and-mouse chess game involving impersonation, turns out to be the darkly mysterious Nina Rechnoy. However, the real object of V's quest is a different Black Queen—Death—who outwits V in the novel's final scene. In a parody of our novelistic desire for resolution, the narrator, at the close of the novel, sits at the bedside of the one whom he believes is the dying Sebastian, but, in this instance too, it turns out to be a case of mistaken identity. The endgame resolves nothing; death's stealth operation remains intact—V's deathbed vigil is at the side of a stranger, not Sebastian Knight but a certain Mr. Kegan, whose name has been bungled in a comic scene of linguistic *méconnaissance*:

> "[T]he English Monsieur is not dead. K, K, K . . ."

> "K, n, i, g . . ." I began once again.

> "C'est bon, c'est bon," he interrupted. "K, n, K, g . . . n . . . I'm not an idiot, you know. Number thirty-six."[8]

If, however, the soporific satisfaction of narrative resolution proves off limits for Nabokov, this is not because of any error in perception, whose implication is that it could be righted. It is because the fundamental premise of identity, as being the exclusive *property* of one individual, turns out to be faulty. "The soul is but a manner of being," V realizes from his vigil at the mis-shuffled bedside, "not a constant state."[9] For this is the mystery the story of Sebastian's "real life" finally reveals to his half brother: "I am Sebastian Knight," V announces at the novel's end.[10]

> I feel as if I were impersonating him on a lighted stage, with the people he knew coming and going—the dim figures of the few friends he had [. . .]. They move round Sebastian—round me who am acting Sebastian. [. . .] Sebastian's mask clings to my face, the likeness will not be washed off. I am Sebastian, or Sebastian is I, or perhaps we both are someone whom neither of us knows.[11]

The individual person, it transpires, is merely a disguise, masking a more far-reaching exchangeability among selves: "[A]ny soul may be yours, if you find and follow its undulations. The hereafter may be the full ability of consciously living in any chosen soul, in any number of souls, all of them unconscious of their interchangeable burden."[12]

I.

V begins his account with the biographer's traditional conceit, regaling us with certain incontrovertible "facts" about his half brother's life. In the first sentence, we learn that Sebastian was born on December 31, 1899. And thanks to the chance finding of an old lady's diary, we even know the meteorological conditions on that day: "a fine windless one,"[13] twelve degrees below zero, as it happens. However, such realist details quickly dissolve into a lyrical rhapsody about the "delights of a winter day" in St. Petersburg. Here, V mocks the prosaic details of the biographical real, offering in its place the superior virtues of memory. "Her dry account," he sniffs, "cannot convey to the untravelled reader the implied delights of a winter day such as she describes in St. Petersburg":

> the pure luxury of a cloudless sky designed not to warm the flesh, but solely to please the eye; the sheen of sledge-cuts on the hard-beaten snow of spacious streets with a tawny tinge about the middle tracks due to a rich mixture of horse-dung: the brightly coloured bunch of toy-balloons hawked by an aproned pedlar; the soft curve of a cupola, its gold dimmed by the bloom of powdery frost; the birch trees in the public gardens, every tiniest twig outlined in white; the rasp and tinkle of winter traffic . . . [.][14]

V's passage is a virtuosic flight of poetic description, a tribute to the literary power of words to transport us to an unknown or forgotten place. However, this reanimated St. Petersburg has not been brought back by the agency of literary memory but by an *image*, specifically an image of an old picture postcard snapped by an anonymous photographer in the previous century, which now lies upon the narrator's desk: "every tiniest twig outlined in white; the rasp and tinkle of winter traffic . . . and by the way how queer it is when you look at an old picture postcard (like the one I have placed on my desk to keep the child of memory amused for a moment)."[15] From the outset, it is a *cinematic* memory that directs V's biographical project, as indeed we ought to have suspected from the very beginning of this passage. The photograph of the old Russian capital floats before us as if conjured by the circular, repeating Os of the old female diarist's name, whose "egglike alliteration," the narrator confesses, would have "been a pity to withhold." "Her name was and is Olga Olegovna Orlova."[16] And, in fact, when we look (or listen) more closely to the descriptive passage, V's language similarly bristles with repeating vowels and consonants:

> the *sheen* of *sledge*-cuts on the hard-beaten *snow* of *spacious streets* with a *tawny tinge* about the middle tracks due to a *rich mixture* of horse-dung: the brightly coloured bunch of toy-balloons hawked by an aproned pedlar; the soft *curve* of a *cupola*, its gold *dimmed* by the *bloom* of powdery frost; the birch trees in the public gardens, every *tiniest twig* outlined in white; the rasp and *tinkle* of winter *traffic* . . . and by the way how queer it is when you look at an old *picture post-card* (like the one I have placed on my desk to keep the child of memory amused for a moment).

If, in this opening gambit, the real of biography is set in opposition to an apparently more "real" memory, memory, too, suddenly finds itself divided between two forms: a lived memory versus a cinematic "memory." There seems to be a hidden, forking maneuver at play at each turn in the dialectic of life and its representation, intimating the presence of another power of artistic generation secretly at work in the attempt to represent the "real life" of Sebastian Knight. What is this other power?

One could describe it in shorthand as a tendency towards self-replication that exists in the representational impulse that escapes or exceeds the conscious intention of the representing subject. From the outset, V's account of Sebastian's "real life" documents a narrative "fate" driven not by fidelity to biographical facts but to the shapes and sounds of linguistic patterns.

Another protocol of representation is simultaneously set loose by the literary biographer's impulse to portray the real, a protocol founded upon different representational "necessities" than those of fact, event, and information. These other "necessities"—the exigencies of sound and letter—secretly direct V's sentences away from their documentary goal. In accordance with this discovery, Sebastian's birthdate now registers with its full cinematic import: Born at the very *turn* of the twentieth century, that is, the cinematic century, it is through its double zeros that Sebastian's short life will be thrown as if through the rotating reels of a film projector.

Even from this short account, one quickly sees how Nabokov sabotages the mimetic model that governs the art/life opposition, inserting into its dialectic a third, "cinematic" actor that fatally interferes with the mirror reflection. In this respect, Nabokov is classically Platonic. In *The Republic*, Plato claims that art is not twice but "thrice removed" from the real.[17] As Socrates explains in his famous allegory of the cave in book 7, what we perceive are merely shadows cast by firelight upon the wall to which our eyes are forcibly turned. Art, as mimesis, would be the imitation not of the real but of another *appearance*, which is itself only a poor reflection of a truth that lies elsewhere, beyond the cave, in the realm of ideal forms. When Alain Badiou (re)writes *Plato's "Republic,"* it will be precisely this "cinematic" dimension of the cave allegory that becomes the centerpiece of his philosophical intervention.[18]

In *The Real Life of Sebastian Knight*, Nabokov similarly cautions us to beware the trap of dualistic paradigms. "Remember," V forewarns, "that what you are told is really threefold: shaped by the teller, reshaped by the listener, concealed from both by the dead man of the tale."[19] In V's formulation, both the biographer and his reader appear cut off from the real of Sebastian's truth, which, in the form of death, escapes the grasp of representation. But a little later, death itself reveals something about Sebastian's life. Projecting the figure of a reflecting pool, V marvels at the "occult resemblance between a man and the date of his death. Sebastian Knight d. 1936 . . . This date to me seems the reflection of that name in a pool of rippling water. There is something about the curves of the last three numerals that recalls the sinuous outlines of Sebastian's personality."[20] Let us pause here for a minute to take in the import of this strange statement. If V remains circumspect about representation's ability to convey the truth about Sebastian's life, it seems this is not due to something "ineffable" about the real. A Neoplatonic ruse smuggled into Plato's "obscure chamber"[21] by Plotinus, the concept of the Ineffable shuts down Plato's nascent arche-cinema with the fiction of an inexpressible One located beyond all language. The Ineffable wraps itself around the poetic impulse as a stalling tactic, a last resort intended to secure a strict chain of relations between an original and its imitation, strategically promoting a final link in the representational chain to the status of a nonlink that proves, paradoxically, to be the most powerful link of all.

V posits here, on the one hand, a similarity between Sebastian's name, his date of death, and his personality and, on the other hand, a relation between the real and its representation that is radically different from that proposed by other representational forms, such as the novel, theater, or even the visual arts—different, that is, from the dual captivations of fiction and representation offered, respectively, by diegesis and mimesis. As V halts before the collusion between Sebastian's life and death, he fixes upon the relation between Sebastian's name and the date of his demise. He finds Sebastian's "personality" aligning along the expressive coils of the numbers 9, 6, and 3. Making a mockery of Ferdinand de Saussure's dictates regarding the arbitrariness of the sign, V proposes a nominal determination for Sebastian that would see name, self, and date coalesce, the name transforming to number and spreading stain-like to absorb all of the technologies of "fate" and "character," the usual preserve of the "literary."

What remains as yet unanswered is whether or not V is caught up in a Cratylic fantasy in which name and thing are the same. Recall how, in Plato's *Cratylus*, Socrates elicits Hermogenes's assent that names have "by nature a truth":[22] "[A]s his name, so also is his nature,"[23] they agree. Their discussion, however, quickly converges upon farce, for, by this logic, each letter of the name should similarly be expected to share a prior relation of likeness to what it represents, and so on, down to each mark or inscription. The specter of this mise en abyme is quickly put to rest by Cratylus. How do we know, Socrates asks, whether the name really is like the thing it describes? "How can we suppose that the givers of names had knowledge, or were legislators before there were names at all, and therefore before they could have known them?"[24] Cratylus's answer is that names originate from a power "more than human."[25] True names come from a divine source.

Accordingly, *Cratylus* proves the wrong reference point for the kind of likeness V is getting at, which, upon closer inspection, has more in common with Walter Benjamin's concept of nonsensuous similarity. In his 1933 essay "Doctrine of the Similar," Benjamin broaches a similar question to Plato's regarding the relation of words to things.[26] Like Plato, Benjamin traces what he calls the "mimetic faculty" to an onomatopoetic quality present in all language.[27] And yet, if there appears to be a similarity between the word and what it names, this likeness must necessarily also traverse the differences of languages. To account for linguistic differences, Benjamin suggests that whatever "similarity" obtains between the thing and its linguistic sign must inhere as a relation among languages. Nonsensuous similarity emerges as a crosslinguistic relation of all languages to each other. Its privileged location is the written sign:

> [L]anguage is the highest application of the mimetic faculty—a medium into which the earlier perceptual capacity for recognizing the similar had, without residue, entered to such an extent that language now represents the medium in which objects encounter and come into relation with one another. No longer directly, as they once did in the mind of the augur or priest, but in their essences, in their most transient and delicate substances, even in their aromas. In other words: it is to script and language that clairvoyance has, over the course of history, yielded its old powers.[28]

Interestingly, Benjamin will also turn to a cinematic figure—the image—to render more concretely his concept of a nonsensuous similarity. Whereas V discerns Sebastian's "personality" secreted in the coils of his death date, likewise, for Benjamin, writing discloses "picture puzzles" of its writer that silently run parallel to what he calls the "semiotic or communicative element of language."[29] Writing, Benjamin claims, records and preserves an "archive" of such nonsensuous similarities and correspondences, each deriving not from a one-to-one mapping of word to thing held together by the divine but by way of a third route, a detour through an indirect relation *among* languages as they circle the real:[30]

> For if words meaning the same thing in different languages are arranged about that signified as their center, we have to inquire how they all—while often possessing not the slightest similarity to one another—are similar to the signified at their center. [...] It is thus nonsensuous similarity that establishes the ties not only between what is said and what is meant, but also between what is written and what is meant, and equally between the spoken and the written. And every time, it does so in a completely new, original, and underivable way.[31]

In Benjamin, the resemblance in play in language is thus radically different from Plato's hierarchies of appearances that summit at the real of truth, beauty, and the good. Re-semblance, in fact, is a misnomer for a likeness that has no memory or "recollection" of a first cause. We would thus be dealing with a similarity or semblance without an original, a sort of ductile, floating similitude or "-esqueness" (SK-ness) capable of straddling several different formal systems at once. Writing, speech, letter, and number, hence, diverge from their usual task of representing the "semiotic" and "communicative" elements of language to form moving images. What name could we give to this representational force? Here, the legacy of Nabokov's "aurelian sickness" gives us a hint in the shapes of one of the natural world's more mysterious adaptations, namely, mimicry.

Mimicry is normally thought of in terms of the self-preservative functions of disguise, camouflage, and imitation in the natural world. However, as the French sociologist Roger Caillois has noted, there are cases (particularly among butterflies, no less) when certain adaptations seem inexplicable in such purely functional terms. This leads Caillois to posit the idea of mimicry as an independent, autonomous aesthetic principle. Writing in 1958, he comments that, "[r]eluctant as one may be to accept this hypothesis [. . .], the inexplicable mimeticism of insects immediately affords an extraordinary parallel to man's penchant for disguising himself, wearing a mask, or playing a part."[32] Twenty years earlier, in the 1935 essay "Mimicry and Legendary Psychasthenia," he writes, "[m]imicry would [. . .] be accurately defined as *an incantation fixed at its culminating point* and having caught the sorcerer in his own trap."[33] Releasing itself into the world as a pure semblance, without an original, mimicry suggests a mode of representation that has shed the responsibility of representing a real. Possessing the fundamental characteristic of the lure, mimicry marks the point at which representation emerges as something other than what it had formerly seemed to be, constituting, as Mladen Dolar has suggested, a sort of anamorphosis of the natural world.[34]

Mimicry thus offers Nabokov a model of "biography" that does not rely upon the tropes of literary realism, this time as *bio-graphein*, literally a "living writing." In fact, this is precisely how V describes the effects of Sebastian's last novel, *The Doubtful Asphodel*. It was as if, in reading it,

> [t]he answer to all questions of life and death, "the absolute solution" was written all over the world he had known: it was like a traveller realising that the wild country he surveys is not an accidental assembly of natural phenomena, but the page in a book where these mountains and forests, and fields, and rivers are disposed in such a way as to form a coherent sentence; the vowel of a lake fusing with the consonant of a sibilant slope; the windings of a road writing its message in a round hand, as clear as that of one's father; trees conversing in a dumb-show, making sense to one who has learnt the gestures of their language . . . Thus the traveller spells the landscape and

its sense is disclosed, and likewise, the intricate pattern of human life turns out to be monogrammatic, now quite clear to the inner eye disentangling the interwoven letters.[35]

In the earlier passage, Sebastian's "personality" undulated in the curves of number. Here, the world itself coils around the linguistic sign. Mimesis's famous divide, stretching back to the Greeks, is a MacGuffin, Nabokov implies. In an anamorphic twist, "life" and "art" are not the mirror reflections envisaged by the mimetic model but different "personalities," half brothers sprung from the same wellspring of inscription. As for Henri Bergson, the key distinction emerges through the image.[36] Both art and life are equally *images* for Nabokov, twin illusions forged in the flickering of a mercurial, pan-graphematic line.

II.

If, in *The Real Life of Sebastian Knight*, being is disclosed as fundamentally anamorphic, this implies that neither "art" nor "life" possess the rights and privileges of a first cause or origin. In Dolar's phrasing, to say that subjectivity is anamorphic means "we never have an initial zero situation where [the] subject would confront being out there, where the subject would be essentially established in a subject-object relation, in a correlation."[37] But if the core distinction lies not in the diremption of representation and the real but in a shared inscriptive ancestry always preceding that divide, what causes the split that sees representation run along two parallel paths such that an entire metaphysical tradition has misread it as ontological? In Nabokov's novel, if V's and Sebastian's mutual identities only become visible to us when cast through the twists of the detective plot—the surrogate for the "turns" of literary figuration per se—it is because, while inhabiting the same space, "art" and "life" coexist in different temporalities. Time produces a ripple in the representational manifold and travels out into space-time in different directions and at different velocities. It is time, then, that produces the illusion of a difference between self and other, initiating being's partition into the standard categories of appearance and its "real" beyond.

When one encounters this difference in temporality in Nabokov's novel it is troped in terms of V's perpetual belatedness with respect to Sebastian's life, culminating in his comically missed appointment at Sebastian's deathbed. For not only does he mistake the two Mr. K's, he is also, apparently, too late anyway: "'Oh-la-la!' [the nurse] exclaimed getting very red in the face.

'Mon Dieu! The Russian gentleman died yesterday, and you've been visiting
Monsieur Kegan . . . [.]'"[38]

Certainly, Sebastian's own experience of time is deeply idiosyncratic. As
V tells us, for Sebastian, time

> was never 1914 or 1920 or 1936—it was always year 1. [. . .] He could
> perfectly well understand sensitive and intelligent thinkers not being
> able to sleep because of an earthquake in China; but, being what he
> was, he could not understand why these same people did not feel
> exactly the same spasm of rebellious grief when thinking of some
> similar calamity that had happened as many years ago as there were
> miles to China. Time and space were to him measures of the same
> eternity.[39]

Statements such as these have lent support to the earlier-mentioned image
of Nabokov as an arch-Designer, a God-like Creator who transcends time to
reveal the underlying pattern of all things. Samuel Schuman, for example,
suggests that "Nabokov's ideal reader is the mirror of the author, and the
author stands as an all-knowing, all-seeing God in relation to his work."[40]
This common "topos" of Nabokov criticism is buttressed by Nabokov's own
self-projections in essays and interviews as a despotic figure, a "haughty aris-
tocrat" bent upon controlling every aspect of his art.[41] However, such readings clearly imply mimetic models, such as that of a "Vladimir Nabokov"
who, as all-powerful auteur, stamps his name anagrammatically across his
work like Hitchcockian cameos, thus securing for himself the stabilities of
authorship as, in Richard F. Patteson's words, the "self-conscious artificer of
his created world."[42]

But the suggestion here is that such fantasies of authorial control are neutralized, made redundant in advance by a cinematic power of replication that
reads as a broader refusal of any metaphor of self- or personhood that could
supply the final halting link in the representational chain. As we have seen,
V's investment in the literary "real" of biography is undercut in advance by
an uncanny cinematic mimicry, which destabilizes and absorbs into itself all
concept of self as something separate or autonomous, sloughing it off as a
false face or detachable tail, a mask for a writing system that always precedes
the "fall" of representation into its consolidated categories of alphabet, number, figure, and trope, even as it anticipates and deforms them.

If the mimetic paradigm fails to account for what is involved in what
one might call Nabokov's "signature-effect," what other ways are there for
understanding what is in play? How else, in other words, might one read

Sebastian's strange atemporal vision if not as the expression of a totalizing authorial vision? In Sebastian's own novels, Nabokov offers us a surrogate for how one might think time outside of mimetic models and their implacably teleological apparatuses.

The Prismatic Bezel is Sebastian's first novel. The word *bezel* evidently means "edge," although we also learn that Sebastian's first working title for the novel is "Cock Robin Hits Back," giving us our clue—it is a counterpunch to death, a refusal to lie back and allow literature to pacify us with its mourning dirges from the nursery.[43] Sebastian's book treats an already familiar "cinematic" theme, a detective mystery centered upon a group of strangers at a boarding house, one of whom has been murdered. And sure enough, all of the twelve guests turn out to be related to one another, and as their individual stories start to blossom, the tale, says V, "takes on a strange beauty": "The idea of time, which was made to look comic (detective losing his way . . . stranded somewhere in the night) now seems to curl up and fall asleep. Now the lives of the characters shine forth with a real and human significance and G. Abeson's sealed door is but that of a forgotten lumber-room."[44] The illusion, however, is brought to an abrupt halt by a "grotesque knocking" that admits the detective, a "shifty fellow" who "drops his h's."[45] But the dead body has disappeared and the joke is on us; old "Nosebag," the seemingly most harmless of the lodgers, removes his disguise, disclosing the face of G. Abeson: "'You see,' says Mr. Abeson with a self-deprecating smile, 'one dislikes being murdered.'"[46]

We should look past the tired plot through which Sebastian parodies the clichés and "decay"[47] of the modern novel, V tells us. The novel's real interest lies in how it brings to the fore what he calls "methods of literary composition": "It is as if a painter said: look, here I'm going to show you not the painting of a landscape, but the painting of different ways of painting a certain landscape, and I trust their harmonious fusion will disclose the landscape as I intend you to see it."[48] In his next book, *Success*, Sebastian continues his experiment, focusing this time upon exposing the "methods of human fate":

> The author's task is to find out how this formula [the meeting of his two heroes] has been arrived at; and all the magic and force of his art are summoned in order to discover the exact way in which two lines of life were made to come into contact [. . .]. [F]ate is much too persevering to be put off by failure. And when finally success is achieved it is reached by such delicate machinations that not the merest click is audible when at last the two are brought together.[49]

What Sebastian makes in these and his later books (whose titles ring strangely and suspiciously as close cousins of Nabokov's own) is what one would call now a "metarepresentational gesture." He takes his reader "behind the scenes," so to speak, to demonstrate the "mechanical" engineering behind the seemingly "natural" trajectories of diegesis and mimesis. Yet, as the narrative circles back each time to the novel's opening reality, Sebastian (and, by extension, in layered fashion, Nabokov himself) performs a topologization of form and content. The gesture, then, is not so much that of an all-powerful Creator who, winking slyly at us, reveals the workings of his puppetry from a position outside the representational universe. Rather, it offers the paradox of an "edge" in a representational system that, giving the illusion of leading into a dimension beyond its coordinates, surreptitiously returns us, Escher-like, to the opening framework from which we began.

This is surely what V means when he describes *The Prismatic Edge* as "somewhat allied to the cinema practice,"[50] for this is the cinematic gesture par excellence, according to Gilles Deleuze. In *Cinema 2: The Time-Image*, Deleuze quotes Jean-Louis Schefer as saying that cinema "is the sole experience where time is given to me as a perception."[51] The temporal equivalent of an anamorphic effect, cinema's "time-image" gives access to an incommensurability in the coordinates of space and time by seeming to achieve not "a real as it would exist independently of the image" but "a before and an after as they coexist with the image, as they are inseparable from the image."[52] This "temporalization of the image" is accomplished in different ways by the different directors to which Deleuze refers, such as the characteristic tracking shots of Alain Resnais and Luchino Visconti, and Orson Welles's use of depth of field.[53] Most relevant to the discussion here, however, is what Deleuze identifies as the "crushing" of the image's depth in the films of Carl Theodor Dreyer. Dreyer's "planitude" of the image "directly open[s] the image on to time as fourth dimension."[54] In flattening the image, by shearing it of the illusion of depth, Dreyer takes apart the mechanics of the movement-image to give us nothing but the interval "between" each moment itself. In the time-image, "[t]he interval is set free," as Deleuze puts it later on: "[T]he interstice becomes irreducible and stands on its own."[55]

The cinematic time-image would thus provide a means of going "backstage" of representation much in the way performed by Sebastian's (and Nabokov's) novels. By presenting the interval between the succession of instants, the time-image exhibits the necessarily repressed gap that secretly sustains the cinematic illusion of movement. In this sense, it is similar to Sebastian's vision of space and time as "measures of the same eternity"—not in the sense of seeing from a position outside representation but by showing us, anamorphically, the "eternal" but necessarily occluded moment of time's beginning and end *from within time itself.*

Consequently, if something comparable to the flattened time-image is possible in written form, its closest counterpart may be the elongated, slow-motion stretching of sentences found in Sebastian's first drafts. V describes

> the queer way Sebastian had—in the process of writing—of not striking out the words which he had replaced by others, so that, for instance, the phrase I encountered ran thus: "As he a heavy A heavy sleeper, Roger Rogerson, old Rogerson bought old Rogers bought, so afraid Being a heavy sleeper, old Rogers was so afraid of missing to-morrows. He was a heavy sleeper. He was mortally afraid of missing to-morrow's event glory early train glory so what he did was to buy and bring home in a to buy that evening and bring home not one but eight alarm clocks of different sizes and vigour of ticking [. . .] which alarm clocks nine alarm clocks as a cat has nine which he placed which made his bed-room look rather like a."[56]

In these repetitions, it is hard not to think of the stuttering of a string of letters threading through a projector that has not quite caught. What Nabokov draws attention to here are the secret workings of the representational sleight-of-hand that are normally unseen or repressed in ordinary discourse. All representation, Nabokov reminds us, is subject to time and space, but lurking within its categories is something that proves more archaic than both, something that, as Bernard Stiegler has said, still "remains unthought," namely, speed.[57] It is speed that quietly stitches together the images that Nabokov suggests are the raw materials of both art and life, giving the illusion of movement to each.[58]

III.

In Sebastian's novel *The Prismatic Bezel*, a living old Nosebag revivifies the dead G. Abeson through an anagrammatic rematerialization. Something in the apparatus of language seeks to redefine life and death, proving them as pregnable to one another as representation is to the real. This redefinition is repeated in *The Real Life of Sebastian Knight*. Despite its opening victory in the novel, death fails to adequately secure its territories, which, in the course of the novel, become infiltrated by a "real life," a reproductive power that sidesteps and emerges unscathed from the necessities of any natural process.[59] Whatever name we give to this power, it is proof that something lives on beyond the individual and his or her particular death, suspending the category of the self in favor of something that undoes identity protocols, along with the accompanying logics of time that support them. In this, Nabokov finds an unlikely ally in Sigmund Freud. In *The Ego and the Id*, Freud claims that the id harbors the "residues" of countless egos. The id alone is capable of being "inherited."[60]

Freud's comment comes at the close of his discussion of the emergence of so-called morality in man. The preserve of the superego, morality emerges in Freud's discussion as something that has its origins in totemism. Freud says that what we usually think of as "the highest in the human mind" has its source in what belonged "to the lowest part of mental life," the id.[61] What intrigues me about Freud's discussion is his description of how the id came by the experiences that, in the murky origins of the human's phylogenetic development, led to the formation of the superego. "Reflection at once shows us," he comments, "that no external vicissitudes can be experienced or undergone by the id, except by way of the ego, which is the representative of the external world to the id. Nevertheless it is not possible to speak of direct inheritance in the ego."[62] Freud goes on to explain that, although nothing in the ego can be directly passed down to successive generations, if experiences are repeated "often enough and with sufficient strength in many individuals in successive generations, they transform themselves, so to say, into experiences of the id, the impressions of which are preserved by heredity."[63]

According to Freud, then, we carry within ourselves the traces of multiple egos, whose "memories" pulse through us as the drive: "[W]hen the ego forms its super-ego out of the id, it may perhaps only be reviving shapes of former egos and be bringing them to resurrection."[64] This is an astounding claim, but one that Sebastian and—surprisingly, given his well-known antipathy to all things Freudian—Nabokov appear to endorse in *The Real Life of Sebastian Knight*. The id threads its way through each individual as a super-sleuth, carrying the "riches" of an inheritance that can never be diluted, squandered, or otherwise lost. Spanning multiple generations, it gathers up the memories it will pass on in toto through a transmission process Jacques Lacan calls a "direct line," in contradistinction to the signifier's normally circuitous operation.[65] It comes as no surprise to readers of Nabokov, then, that the figures Lacan reaches for to illustrate how the signifier "short-circuits" the pathways of thought to arrive at the subject's "truth" should appear as a flexing V-shape, in which we also recognize the characteristic initials of one of literature's most consummate cryptocrats. As Lacan explains, "[y]ou have only to remind yourselves of the figure of the Roman five, for example, insofar as it is involved and reappears everywhere in the outspread legs of a woman, or the beating of the wings of a butterfly, to know, to comprehend that what is involved is the handling of the signifier."[66] Smuggled into the literary drawing-room, along with the after-dinner mints and crossword puzzles as a harmless game of anagrams, or sheathed in the "childish" clothing of what Tom Cohen, speaking of Hitchcock, calls "cinememes,"[67] an uncanny VN signature zigzags through Nabokov's works as an extra, "thirteenth" guest at literature's table d'hôte. It comes into view in *The Real Life of Sebastian Knight* as Sebastian's initials, which have meanwhile sharpened into focus. The curves of Sebastian's S taper into points and, with the K, perform a quarter turn to line up beside their siblings: <u>NVNVNVN</u>.[68] Is this the final calling card of Nabokov the Creator, or something more singular? An immortal, wandering "guest," perhaps, at the heart of the human family narrative, which secretly draws back all exigencies of "thought"—including, especially, the twists and turns of the pleasure principle's desiring quest— toward what is neither living nor dead but older than both? You decide.

Notes

1. See Sigmund Freud, *Beyond the Pleasure Principle*, in *The Standard Edition of the Complete Psychological Works of Sigmund Freud* (hereafter *SE*), ed. and trans. James Strachey et al. (London: Hogarth Press, 1953–1974), 18:12–17.

2. See Joan Copjec, "Locked Room/Lonely Room: Private Space in Film Noir," in *Read My Desire: Lacan against the Historicists* (Cambridge: MIT Press, 1994): 163–200.

3. [*Aurelian* is an archaic word for a lepidopterist, someone who studies or collects butterflies.—Eds.] See Vladimir Nabokov, *Speak, Memory*, in *Novels and Memoirs, 1941–1951* (New York: Library of America, 1996), 459–79.

4. Although not exclusively, as Nabokov "inherited" it from his biological father who caught the "bug" from his German tutor. See Brian Boyd, *Vladimir Nabokov: The Russian Years* (Princeton: Princeton University Press, 1993), 69.

5. A quick rundown of such figures would include Valentinov, Luzhin's "chess father" in *The Luzhin Defense*, Ivan Black in *Look at the Harlequins!*, Kinbote in *Pale Fire*, Van in *Ada or Ardor: A Family Chronicle*, and many others. See *The Luzhin Defense*, trans. Michael Scammell in collaboration with the author (New York: Vintage, 1990); *Look at the Harlequins!*, in *Novels 1969–1974* (New York: Library of America, 1996), 563–747; *Pale Fire*, in *Novels 1955–1962* (New York: Library of America, 1996), 437–667; and *Ada or Ardor: A Family Chronicle*, in *Novels 1969–1974*, 1–485.

6. Nabokov, *Speak, Memory*, 504.

7. Ibid., 506.

8. Nabokov, *The Real Life of Sebastian Knight*, in *Novels and Memoirs, 1941–1951*, 156.

9. Ibid., 159.

10. Ibid.

11. Ibid., 159–60.

12. Ibid., 159.

13. Ibid., 3.

14. Ibid.

15. Ibid.

16. Ibid.

17. See Plato, *Republic*, in *Plato: Complete Works*, ed. John M. Cooper, trans. G. M. A. Grube (Indianapolis: Hackett, 1997), 597e2–4.

18. See Alain Badiou, *Plato's "Republic": A Dialogue in 16 Chapters*, trans. Susan Spitzer (New York: Columbia University Press, 2012), 212–18. In Badiou's version, an astute Glaucon discerns that the impression the audience perceives in the theater masquerading as the real is in fact a projected, "digital" copy of the analogue copies parading down the moving walkway, which double for "life" in representation's darkened auditorium.

19. Nabokov, *The Real Life of Sebastian Knight*, 40.

20. Ibid., 143.

21. Christian Metz, "The Imaginary Signifier," *Screen* 16, no. 2 (1975): 52.

22. Plato, *Cratylus*, in *Dialogues of Plato*, trans. Benjamin Jowett, vol. 1 (New York: Cambridge University Press, 2010), 391a4.

23. Ibid., 395a4.

24. Ibid., 438b3–5.

25. Ibid., 438c2.

26. See Walter Benjamin, "Doctrine of the Similar," in *Selected Writings, 1931–1934*, ed. Michael W. Jennings, Howard Eiland, and Gary Smith, trans. Michael W. Jennings, vol. 2, part 2 (Cambridge: Belknap Press, 1999), 694–98.

27. Ibid., 694.

28. Ibid., 697–98.

29. Ibid., 697.

30. Note too that, for Benjamin, the perception of similarities must always travel through this *third* path that he likens to the figure of an astrologer who is able to read off in the conjunction of two stars a similarity to a human being. Ibid., 696.

31. Ibid., 696–97.

32. Roger Caillois, *Man, Play and Games*, trans. Meyer Barash (Urbana: University of Illinois Press, 2001), 20.

33. Caillois, "Mimicry and Legendary Psychasthenia," *October* 34 (1984): 27; emphasis in original.

34. See Mladen Dolar, "Anamorphosis," *S: Journal of the Circle for Lacanian Ideology Critique* 8 (2015): 131.

35. Nabokov, *The Real Life of Sebastian Knight*, 139.

36. Recall how, for Bergson, the proper dividing line is not between appearances and the real but between images and memory. As he writes in *Matter and Memory*, "[h]ere I am in the presence of images, in the vaguest sense of the word, images perceived when my senses are open to them, unperceived when they are closed." Henri Bergson, *Matter and Memory*, trans. Nancy Margaret Paul and W. Scott Palmer (New York: Zone, 1991), 17.

37. Dolar, "Anamorphosis," 125.

38. Nabokov, *The Real Life of Sebastian Knight*, 149. Sebastian and V will thus only infrequently intersect with each other in the narrative. Nonetheless, although they are "traveling" at different speeds, V does have a vague presentiment of the "common rhythm" that inheres between himself and Sebastian, which he likens to the two fraternal tennis champions who, despite the difference in their strokes, followed the same essential pattern, "so that had it been possible to draught both systems two identical designs would have appeared." Ibid., 25.

39. Nabokov, *The Real Life of Sebastian Knight*, 50.

40. Samuel Schuman, "Hyperlinks, Chiasmus, Vermeer and St. Augustine: Models of Reading *Ada*," *Nabokov Studies* 6 (2000/2001): 127.

41. See Nabokov's comments in *Strong Opinions* (New York: Vintage, 1990). See also his foreword to *Lolita: A Screenplay*:

> [I]f I had given as much of myself to the stage or the screen as I have to the kind of writing which serves a triumphant life sentence between the covers of a book, I would have advocated and applied a system of total tyranny, directing the play or the picture myself, choosing settings and costumes, terrorizing the actors, mingling with them in the bit part of guest, or ghost, prompting them, and, in a word, pervading the entire show with the will and art of one individual—for there is nothing in the world that I loathe more than group activity.
> Nabokov, *Lolita: A Screenplay*, in *Novels 1955–1962*, 673.

42. Richard F. Patteson, "Nabokov's *Bend Sinister*: The Narrator as God," *Studies in American Fiction* 5, no. 2 (1977): 241.

43. The well known nursery rhyme ends, "All the birds of the air / Fell sighing and sobbing, / When they heard the bell toll / For poor Cock Robin." See Blanche Fisher Wright, "The Death and Burial of Poor Cock Robin," in *The Real Mother Goose* (New York: Scholastic, 1994), 124–25.

44. Nabokov, *The Real Life of Sebastian Knight*, 72.

45. Ibid.

46. Ibid., 73.

47. Ibid., 70.

48. Ibid., 73.

49. Ibid., 74–75.

50. Ibid., 71.

51. Gilles Deleuze, *Cinema 2: The Time-Image*, trans. Hugh Tomlinson and Robert Galeta (Minneapolis: University of Minnesota Press, 1989), 37.

52. Ibid., 38.

53. Ibid., 39.

54. Ibid.

55. Ibid., 277.

56. Nabokov, *The Real Life of Sebastian Knight*, 30.

57. Bernard Stiegler, *Technics and Time, 1: The Fault of Epimetheus*, trans. Richard Beardsworth and George Collins (Stanford: Stanford University Press, 1998), 15.

58. As Benjamin similarly comments, "tempo, that swiftness in reading or writing which can scarcely be separated from this process, would then become, as it were, the effort, or gift, or mind to participate in that measure of time in which similarities flash up fleetingly out of the stream of things only in order to sink down once more." Benjamin, "Doctrine of the Similar," 698.

59. In Sebastian's novel *Lost Property*, Nabokov obliquely references the chess opening called the Mortimer trap. Named after the nineteenth-century chess player James Mortimer, it entails Black making a false move in the hope of drawing White into making a mistake. This is just one of many chess references in *The Real Life of Sebastian Knight*, including, of course, the names of key characters.

60. Freud, *The Ego and the Id*, in *SE* 19:38.

61. Ibid., 36.

62. Ibid., 38.

63. Ibid.

64. Ibid.

65. Jacques Lacan, *La logique du fantasme* (1966–1967), unpublished seminar, lesson of December 7, 1966, http://gaogoa.free.fr/; my translation.

66. Ibid.

67. Such cinememes include the Nabokovian petting zoo of small dachshunds, rabbits, mice, tortoises, monkeys, squirrels, parrots, wax dummies and mechanical dolls, furred moths and spiders, and small items of "lost property," such as the matches, stray chess pieces, letters, tennis balls, buttons, marbles, and broken china shards that are littered throughout his works, which one consumes without

really noticing, along with the chocolate, colored jujubes, and other *boules de gomme* Nabokov sells us from his refreshment stand during brief intermissions. See Tom Cohen, *Hitchcock's Cryptonymies: Secret Agents*, vol. 1 (Minneapolis: University of Minnesota Press, 2005), 221.

68. In case we missed it the first time, the letters S and K are each just *three* steps away from V and N in the alphabet.

CHAPTER 11

Freud Fainted

or, "It All Started 1000s of Years Ago in Egypt . . ."

Lydia R. Kerr

I.

Sigmund Freud came to the United States only once, in 1909, to deliver a series of lectures at Clark University and to secure a certain legacy for American psychoanalysis. Ishmael Reed conjures a more nefarious reason for this visit in his 1972 novel *Mumbo Jumbo*. In the novel, Freud is dispatched by a secret society known as the Atonist Path because he coins the terms it needs to diagnose, control, and contain a strange psychical outbreak sweeping the nation, "eating away at the fabric of our forms our technique our aesthetic integrity," and threatening to bring an end to "Civilization As We Know It."[1] In Reed's brutal send-up, the square and squeamish father of psychoanalysis does not hold a cigar but drinks from a sanitary Dixie Cup as his party sails "into the hinterland of the American soul" and confronts "the Thing" itself, "the Something or Other that led Charlie Parker to scale the Everests of the Chord," "that touched John Coltrane's Tenor; that tinged the voice of Otis Redding and compelled Black Herman to write a dictionary to Dreams that Freud would have envied."[2] There, face to face with "the festering packing Germ,"[3] Freud fainted.

The story is recounted by Reed's main character, a "jacklegged detective of the metaphysical"[4] named PaPa LaBas, who runs "a Neo-HooDoo therapy center"[5] known by its critics as the Mumbo Jumbo Kathedral. He plays no part in the ongoing Atonist conspiracy in which Freud had been enlisted to secure "America, Europe's last hope, the protector of the archives of 'mankind's' achievements."[6] For those unfamiliar with the novel, the main plot concerns LaBas's endeavor, in 1920s Harlem, to solve the mystery of the "plague" the Atonists now call "Jes Grew." Since LaBas "carries Jes Grew in him like most other folk carry genes,"[7] he figures that it did not, in fact, just grow—that it is not at all without a history, nor is it external to the history of Civilization As We Know It. Jes Grew's symptoms, like ragtime and jazz, only appear as inassimilable excesses—spontaneous and senseless diversions with respect to the aesthetic integrity of America and its entrusted European inheritance—because the record is being "doctored" to misrepresent such manifestations (in Congo Square in 1890s New Orleans and now again during the Harlem Renaissance) as "flair-up[s]"[8] [*sic*] that therefore could be mistaken for mere entertainment or as derivative of some other tradition. In fact, LaBas suggests, Jes Grew is at least as old as civilization itself. The intensity of its repeated and divisive return indicates for him that "[i]t's up to its Text"; it is no plague but an "anti-plague" "yearning for The Work of its Word"[9] here in America. This same yearning compels LaBas to find and disclose the name of this Text and how it will ensure the inheritance of the "Jes Grew Carriers" within, and despite, the Atonist history that conspires to exclude and destroy it.

Reed's United States is thus internally divided, and apparently along lines that one might neatly demarcate in terms of black and white. But *Mumbo Jumbo* complicates this. By playing upon the tensions between, for instance, the Jazz Age and the literature of the Harlem Renaissance, it suggests that this internal division is not a matter of racial difference. In any case, Reed is not treating the 1920s as a discrete historical setting for the narrative's action; instead, and by characterizing this era as "that 1 decade which doesn't seem so much a part of American History as the hidden After-Hours of America struggling to jam,"[10] *Mumbo Jumbo*, he claims, is an effort to reveal how the events of the 1920s move across time and sync up with the present. Reed thus asks us to explore race relations in the United States through a division that is historical and textual—discursive—in that history is read as a whitewashing of the past; but this division also indicates something about race in America that struggles—by way of another, "hidden" means of communication—against being reduced to a transparent "part" or mere byproduct of history or discourse. In what follows, I shall argue that what we encounter here is thus not an idea of race or racial difference but, despite Reed's provocations toward psychoanalysis, something like the transmissions of unconscious inheritance that Freud himself detected in the hidden after hours of Civilization As We Know It.

For Reed, writing is not simply the act of typing but a strategy of transmitting "voices" from the past so that they may "comment on the present."[11]
The notion of inheritance we find in *Mumbo Jumbo* thus crucially informs
his "Neo-HooDoo" aesthetic and his use of writing as a sabotage of history.
This is perhaps why he has been pressed to respond to persistent interview
questions about race and American literature; about his African and European influences; how he distinguishes himself from experimental white
authors; and what inherent thing or quality gives the African American literary tradition its particular flair, what holds it together, in spite of all that
differentiates, say, the slave narrative from the passing trope, or his own aesthetic from the Black Arts Movement, and so on. Here is Reed:

> Chester Himes has said that the black people in this country are
> the only new race in modern times and I think that's probably true.
> Nothing in history quite happened like it happened here. I think that
> the young black writer draws from this experience instead of looking
> over his shoulder [. . .] as white writers do, at least many of them.
> [. . .] A black writer sitting down doesn't have all of Europe looking
> over his shoulder [. . .] a bunch of dead people [. . .] like Henry James
> and Chekov. I think that blacks got over that and are trying to set up
> their own stuff.[12]

We can gather a lot from this perhaps initially jarring response to such
inquiries. To begin with, *Mumbo Jumbo's* formal experimentalism is part
of Reed's endeavor to participate in the invention of new literary forms not
subordinated to European aesthetic values and traditions. Yet, in the same
interview, Reed says that this is not a departure from tradition but rather
"has all the stuff that you find in a traditional novel."[13] So his endorsement
of Himes's observation does not suppose his "own stuff" to be without or
beyond inheritance (as if, like Topsy from *Uncle Tom's Cabin*, it "jes grew"),
for this would exempt some fixed, ahistorical racial or cultural essence from
the unique *historical experience* of the writer he describes. Rather, Reed
suggests that this experience, which is constitutive of the literary tradition
in which he includes himself, engages inheritance as something other than
indebtedness to an idealized past that lurks over one's shoulder and man-
dates its repetition in and as the present. As Reed says, "[n]othing in history
quite happened like it happened *here*."[14] What thus inheres in this history
and tradition, what we might imagine the writer *carries in him* like *most
other folk carry genes*, is the experience and repetition of a fundamental *difference within* America and the inscription of this inheritance through an

indefinite, heterogeneous multitude of expressions. While Reed organizes works of Euro-American literature according to their similarities—according to a homogeneous and homogenizing ancestry—he includes himself as a member of Himes's "new race"[15] and a part of its literary tradition; at the same time, however, if, indeed, Reed can speak of either of these things at all, it is because of the very differences that constitute them.

These repetitions of difference have nothing to do with maintaining some idealized heritage, which would be just as constraining as the anxiety of influence just described. Reed appropriately figures them in the novel not only through Jes Grew's disruption of the monocultural Atonism, which seeks to repress it, but also along the gaps and contradictions within and between the aesthetic traces—the music, art, and literature—that Jes Grew animates. At the same time, however, I do not think that *Mumbo Jumbo* promotes the pluralism and revelry in the free play of signification that many readers have seen as a consummate alternative to the monotheistic determinacy of Western history and reason. In highlighting the failure of some determinate limit, in other words, Reed does not presume to liberate a multitude of experiences, cultures, or truths from beyond or before the writing of Civilization As We Know It, so that they might express themselves in a veritable "celebration" of indeterminacy.[16] We will see that, far from envisioning this sort of idealistic multicultural alternative, *Mumbo Jumbo* actually warns against it in the way it treats what might be called the mystery of inheritance. At least since Freud's horrified reaction in *Civilization and Its Discontents* to the Christian imperative to "Love thy neighbor," psychoanalysis, too, is deeply suspicious of this brand of multiculturalism.[17] This apprehension is at the horizon of my dispute with the pluralistic understanding of Reed's aesthetic strategy as well as the explanation for Freud's fainting spell in *Mumbo Jumbo*. Freud's fainting will moreover help us glimpse that, in pluralistic free play, difference can only be tolerated as an ideal if real self-difference is evacuated of its inherently and radically disruptive potential.

Earlier I suggested that, for Reed, inheritance is discursive but illegible as a mere product of discourse. In terms closer to the novel, we can now say that Jes Grew names not just the plague and failure of language in the quest to protect inheritance as an entrusted ideal but also the surplus of language in the search to recite inheritance as an intimate mystery. While it is true that the field of social relations in America cannot be regulated exhaustively by any one discourse or historical perspective, because there is always some excess, something more than language can diagnose, "bring into focus or categorize,"[18] the impotence of language simultaneously generates, in the very instance of its failure, a profusion of signifiers that inevitably say too much. Every failed effort to grasp the whole truth of inheritance, to deprive it of its mystery, therefore also adds something more to the discursive field: a citational chain in which inheritance is inscribed not as a venerated ideal but as a mystery, thus as that which marks history's difference from itself. We will find that this difference indicates the *internal limit of language as such*—the limit that constitutes it and ensures the interminability of both the failure and surplus of meaning. With Reed and Freud we will pursue the notion of inheritance as internal difference, one within language, not just because it is what prevents the subject's ownmost indeterminacy from becoming fixed as an ideal but also because it is perhaps only this that keeps difference from blurring into tolerant indifference.

II.

So PaPa LaBas's response to the conspiracy of an all-consuming ideal threatening from beyond will not look like the one that progresses with failed diagnoses, as in Reed's caricature of American psychoanalysis. His investigation into this whitewashing will rather culminate in a strange fiction that nevertheless serves a particular function in the novel and in relation to the history it reconstructs. As Jacques Lacan describes the function of myth, we will see that it articulates "a signifying system or scheme" that designates the way the subject "suffers from the signifier."[19] For Lacan and for us, this "passion of the signifier" is central to Freud's *Moses and Monotheism*, the text toward which Reed is leading us. LaBas's myth, a dizzying confabulation that traces the mysteries of inheritance in America to the trauma of an ancient Egyptian fratricide, has acute resonances with Freud's.

In response to demands that he "explain rationally and soberly" his charges against the conspirators, LaBas commences his narrative: "Well if you must know, it all began 1000s of years ago in Egypt."[20] If it was not composed in three parts over several years, *Moses and Monotheism* might have started the same way, since ancient Egypt was also the setting for this "historical novel" in which Freud sought to demystify the question of Jewish inheritance, not by recovering some "material truth" from beyond the archive of Western history and reason but rather through the discovery of another kind of truth, a "historical truth" that haunts it from within. A first clue to the peculiar, ghostly quality of this truth lies in the Hebrew preface to *Totem and Taboo*, where Freud asks about his own inheritance, given his complete estrangement from "the religion of his fathers"—he does not know Hebrew, engage in Judaic ritual, believe in any of the precepts of the religion, and "cannot take a share in nationalist ideals." What remains of his Jewishness after all these characteristics have been set aside? "A very great deal," he answers, "and probably [the] very essence."[21] *Moses and Monotheism* clarifies that this intransigent essence is neither a natural, material truth immune to the vicissitudes of history, nor an immutable, transcendental beyond of either nature or culture. Like Jes Grew and the new American race to which Reed refers, it resides within culture and the language that transmits it, yet at the same time seemingly outside the network of signifiers that articulates and sustains all of the positive traits with which Freud does not identify.

This notion of a beyond of language that is nevertheless within language is decisive, for it will guarantee two simultaneous but incompatible orders of inheritance. On the one hand, the contents of the archive—the scriptural account of the Exodus, archaeological record of migration and settlement, history of survival in the face of profound adversity, and so on—transmit the story of a chosen people, guardians of a sacred truth delivered to them by Moses their protector and an *eternal* truth directly entrusted to Moses by God. On the other hand, there is the order of unconscious or phylogenetic inheritance, where Freud famously locates the repressed murder of an original, Egyptian Moses, who was later confused in several convenient ways with the Biblical Moses by way of a tendentious doctoring of the record, not unlike the one we find in Reed's account. By following the "noticeable gaps, disturbing repetitions and obvious contradictions—indications which reveal things to us which it was not intended to communicate," Freud determines the effects upon the archive of an unavowed trauma, an unconscious remainder, which clings to it.[22] So the "essence" of Jewishness cannot be counted among its contents except as that remainder that disturbs its claims to coherence and completeness. It is there where history, whether the history of the individual or the group, will never coincide with itself. Situated alongside his remarks from *Totem and Taboo*, we find that inheritance is not merely a matter of consciously and willingly identifying with the values and ideals of a supposedly noble heritage but can be detected only in the experience of being gripped by what that heritage has tried and failed to repress. More precisely, it is the particular way in which one manages the return of the repressed—the specificity of the symptom—that determines the essence of one's ancestry.

This symptom pertains to the repressed murder of Moses, a crime that ultimately ensured the continuation and intensification of the precepts he imposed upon his people: the absence of an afterlife, belief in a single God, and, most importantly, the prohibition against any imaginary representation of the divine. According to Freud, God is equated with absolute truth in the same breath that forbids any material referent for this truth or any access to it after death. "From that time on," Freud writes, "the Holy Writ and the intellectual concern with it were what held the scattered people together."[23] The religion we know today—with its absence of iconography, its placement of the Torah at the center of its rituals of worship, the exacting litany of laws and regulations found in the holy scriptures, and so forth—is composed of the lasting effects of the Mosaic prohibition; these hallmarks of modern Judaism bear witness, we might say, to an originary interdiction against venturing outside the text, a refusal of the possibility of any metalanguage through which one might apprehend holy truth.

Freud's origin of monotheism finally also has nothing to do with any positive attributes of religious doctrine. The truth and unicity of God, the impossibility of returning to him after death, and his unrepresentability are all bound together within Moses's original "No," a negation signifying nothing other than the prohibition of any beyond. Of what? Precisely of what Lacan will call the symbolic. Once divested of any material content, God becomes nothing but a hole around which religious discourse perpetually circulates, which generates this discourse and inaugurates its historical trajectory but can never be (ful)filled without effacing the sacred truth it contains. Freud's insight, finally, which Lacan calls the "affirmation of [a] discovery,"[24] is that modern history, the history of Civilization As We Know It, hinges upon the assumption not of some external limit to the truth—one that could be imposed from out of the flames of a burning bush or the thunder clouds atop Mount Sinai—but of a limit that is *internal* to language: the hole in the symbolic of which the Mosaic prohibition is but one iteration. A prohibition, it is worth noting again, that Freud insists issued from a historical figure, the murder of whom underlies the intensity with which a historical people cleave to their textuality. It is therefore the *intellectual investment* in the Holy Book, not the particularities of its contents, that Freud emphasizes as the key effect of the dematerialization of the divinity. What holds the people together, what constitutes them as a people, is the shared bequest of the "No" that limits their relation to God—to truth—as only to a text in which the truth never appears.

This negation, which I have been calling language's internal limit, has two implications for inheritance for which Reed has already prepared us. It ensures that in speaking about our inheritance we will always say too little of the truth. But this is not because there is always more to be had, as if it resides outside the symbolic and can be progressively assimilated through an infinite expansion of its parameters. The fact that this historical truth inheres *within* the symbolic as an empty center beyond the system of exchange in which signifiers operate means that language says too much, always exudes a certain sense or trace of this unconscious inheritance. Both this failure and surplus of signification result from the lack in the symbolic indexed by the "No" of the Mosaic prohibition.

III.

We are now prepared to see how Reed formulates the encounter with this internal limit in a narrative that resonates with Freud's construction, not merely in terms of setting and theme, but more importantly in how it dislocates inheritance from any conscious material truths of cultural identification and relocates it in the historical truth of a trauma specific to Civilization As We Know It in the United States. After mounting his case against the conspiracy of history—meaningfully but dizzyingly assembled throughout the novel from signifiers appropriated from the history, myths, legends, and literature that compose the idealized inheritance he aims to condemn—LaBas begins his lengthy explanation of the crimes.

To evoke the other myth of which even the murder of Moses was but a repetition, let us say that, in Reed's United States, the primal father was already murdered in a revolution by which the rebellious sons declared themselves independent and equal.[25] LaBas's construction thus begins in medias res, and, like Freud's, presumes this internal limit imposed by the negation at the heart of the symbolic—except, in his version, one of the sons considers himself an exception. At the outset of the story, he is busy using "the death of their father as an excuse for invading foreign countries," while his brother "became known as the man who did dances that caught on"[26] at home. One of LaBas's clues, the horoscope "America is born [...] on the 4th of July, Gemini Rising,"[27] conjures the twinned or paired conception of the two brothers: There is Set, who is connected with discipline, militarism, death, and containment; and Osiris, who is associated with a theater of dance, agriculture, procreation, and dissemination known as the "Black Mud Sound."[28] LaBas explains that Osiris recorded "The Book of Thoth" to give the people a means to transmit and "determine what god or spirit possessed them as well as learn how to make these gods and spirits depart."[29] Set—"arrogant jealous egotistical"[30]—meanwhile, paused his imperialist endeavors to organize a violent conspiracy against his brother's contagious popularity. Despite his own desire to participate in the song and dance rites of the Black Mud Sound, he had Osiris murdered and established a new religion in opposition to his brother's, a system that would be inherited as the Atonist Path. But the dismemberment of Osiris's corpse only ended up reanimating his spirit everywhere a fragment of his body was found, constituting a proliferation of variations upon his original litany or Text. Set's renunciations, attempts to control that within him that he could not control, nevertheless continued in the form of prohibitions that included Dancing, Singing, Fucking, and eventually Life itself. And even as Set "went down as the 1st man to shut nature out of himself," calling it "discipline,"[31] Atonism was not fully established until after a latency period, when he appeared to Moses in the form of a burning spirit bearing crude instructions for stealing the Book of Thoth from Isis. Book in hand, Moses (himself an Egyptian prince) demanded sanity and reason from the populace, but his misuse of the Work accidentally caused a sort of nuclear explosion. Thus began the decisive rift in the uses of the Text with which we are concerned. In addition to providing Jes Grew with the litany for its liturgy, it had now been appropriated by those who "didn't know when to stop"[32] with the powers it held.

LaBas's fratricidal myth thereby traces the origin of the interminable failure and surplus of the signifier, as well as the two forms of inheritance to which this corresponds in the American discursive terrain. The Atonist mode of inheritance projects the limit, which Freud demonstrates is internal to language, into an external beyond, where it appears either as a cherished ideal or an enemy to be destroyed. Treating self-difference in this way is doomed to failure, just as the ego inevitably fails to command and control that which it has excluded in its efforts to fit into an established history and social scene. For the function of the limit, as Lacan says, is "to make man always search for what he has to find again, but which he will never attain."[33] This failure, this persistence of an internal mysteriousness, despite all attempts to dispel and make it transparent and exchangeable, like an object of knowledge among others, is also what persists in the form of uncanny repetitions as Jes Grew, what Freud calls the return of the repressed. The alternative mode of inheritance, the one also endorsed by Reed, is to admit the mystery and search for its solution interminably without imagining that it can ever finally be found. Since, as Lacan also notes, the prohibition of the Thing "doesn't only have a negative side, it also has a positive side."[34]

Let us first address the problem of Set's inheritance. According to LaBas, ideals of cultural and civilizational progress and the physical and representational violence they enable and endorse—colonialism, slavery, endless imperial expansion—are nothing more than a proliferation of strategies of repression, increasingly and interminably endeavoring to rectify a failure to destroy what Set originally tried to both appropriate to and excise from himself: what he saw as his brother Osiris's sensual nature. The writing of

Civilization As We Know It, finally, is a manipulation of the powers of the Text and a protracted repetition of Set's original crime. In Reed's rendition of the early twentieth century, this manifests in several ways: the invasion and colonial occupation of Haiti (a major backdrop to the events in Harlem); the theft of cultural relics from across the globe and their incarceration within American Centers of Art Detention (museums); the pathologization of Jes Grew, which labels it an "infestation"; the characterization of its music and dance "symptoms" as meaningless "coon mumbo jumbo";[35] and the effort to depict its textual manifestations as derivative, pandering, rhetoric, verbal gymnastics, and so on. LaBas's construction reveals that these are all attempts to resolve the mystery of inheritance. Atonism devalues all forms of thought that do not conform to its own hyperrationalism (whence its militant racism); it appropriates traces of these other forms of thought and reduces them to artifacts and curiosities; and it accomplishes all of this by establishing certain external—that is, ahistorical, "God-given," self-evident—ideals with which it orients its narrative of civilizational progress and attempts to fill the hole in the symbolic with final, determinate meaning.

Against this destructive idealism, Reed offers another form of relation to inheritance *as mystery*, one internal to American history, literature, and discourse, to the traumatic foundations of America as such. At the conclusion of LaBas's reconstruction, when his audience again demands evidence, hard proof, for his incredible account, he presents a box supposed to contain the Book of Thoth, Jes Grew's original Text. Upon opening it, however, he finds it "empty!!"[36] At first surprised, LaBas later reflects that its absence is precisely what ensures its survival: "They will try to depress Jes Grew but it will only spring back and prosper. We will make our own future Text. A future generation of young artists will accomplish this."[37] This is the Osirian side of inheritance, the irrepressible drive to construct one's relation to history, not as an ideal but as a mystery for which there is never a final solution.

Like the notion of inheritance Freud established in terms of a people's relation to language's internal limit, Reed's has nothing to do with a repressed content of Civilization As We Know It. It is not some buried memory that just needs excavating before it can take its proper place among the avowed, conscious contents of history. Though LaBas does all he can to explain the conspiracy, the real mystery of inheritance is always improper to the archive, that is, out of place within it, out of time with the rhythm of history, a remainder of history's difference from itself, unconscious. Its bequest is only an empty box where its Text ought to have been. It is the task of the Jes Grew Carriers to pose a limit to the Atonist injunction to realize an abstract, external ideal, and instead to inscribe the Text, to generate an interminable multitude of iterations, each of which, like a piece of Osiris's fragmented corpse, is a re-membering of the inheritance against which history has been built as a symptomatic defense. The purpose of these inscriptions is not to dispel the trauma but to carve new channels for its expression as mystery, as a kernel of a truth that engenders a future that is more and other than an ever-failing repetition of the past. This is also why Reed insists that inheritance must be sought in the immanent historical experience of a "new race," a new textual tradition that is constituted according to its internal gaps, contradictions, and repetitions—according to its experience of history as difference.

IV.

Situating LaBas's account alongside *Moses and Monotheism* reveals how it performs the same mythical function Lacan recognized in the passion of the signifier, bestowed by the negation at the heart of the symbolic. Neither Freud's primal patricide nor LaBas's primal fratricide in ancient Egypt are true—at least not according to the weak sense of truth as a mere description of an actual historical event—but nor are they false. As Lacan tells us, this truth "has the structure of fiction,"[38] not because it is untrue but because it cannot be attached to any referent within language's structure of exchange; it is the internal limit of that structure, the gap in meaning that sustains its functioning and produces the twinned phenomena of failure and surplus in signification we have been pursuing.

Since, for Freud, construction was first of all an analytic technique, we may clarify the function of the myth in *Mumbo Jumbo* by returning to Reed's comments upon his own Neo-HooDoo writing strategy:

> [O]ne can speak more accurately of the psychological history of a people if one knows the legends, the folklore, the old stories which have been handed down for generations, the oral tales, all of which tells you where you came from, which shows the national mind, the way a group of people looks at the world. I think you can ascertain that by going and reconstructing a past which I call Neo-HooDoo in my work [. . .] because you can have your own psychology rather than someone else's. [. . .] I think that although we can go to science to prove our common ancestry—the one cell amoeba or some distant primate or whatever—we are different and it's wrong for one group of people to impose their psychology on another. [. . .] That's what

> I mean when I say we have to create our own fictions. [. . .] We've
> been lied to in this country. [. . .] A few hundred years of American
> history have been given wrong interpretations so now what we have
> to do is to provide another side, another viewpoint. And that's what
> I try to do in my novels.[39]

Echoing Freud, Reed insists that the "psychological history" of a people,
their "national mind," can be found in their "old stories," but he moreover
charges that American history is one of misinterpretation, in other words, a
fiction. To redress this psychological oppression it is not enough merely to
recover marginalized traditions or to posit new interpretations, correcting
the record with recuperated content. This is the basis for the celebratory
pluralistic approach that supposes cultural differences to be positive traits
with which individuals consciously identify and against which Freud's sub-
tractive examination of his own Jewish inheritance is already a strong rebut-
tal.[40] But Freud also addressed this question through the transmission of a
modern myth; and so too does Reed call for "our own fictions," subversive
counter-fictions that reconstruct the traumatic past and determine its pull
upon the present. HooDoo, which Reed names as a sort of precedent for
his Neo-HooDoo practice, was, he explains, "always open to the possibility
of the real world and the psychic world intersecting. They have a principle
for it: *LegBa* (in the U.S., 'LaBas')." As he continues, "[t]here were sections
of *Mumbo Jumbo* which were written in what some people call 'automatic'
writing, or the nearest thing to it. Writing is more than just the act of typing.
I think you get a lot of help from heritage—you know, 'voices.'"[41] For Reed,
as I mentioned earlier, writing is a conduit for the transmission of ancestral
voices. He furthermore suggests that this does not take place in the order of
consciousness but through a kind of possession. There where the real and
psychical worlds intersect are the crossroads of present and past, living and
dead, and ultimately conscious and unconscious. PaPa LaBas's grand narrative of the Egyptian origins of Jes Grew and the Atonist Path performs
precisely this intersectional function. It is a counter-fiction to the official
fictions of Western and American history, a primal crime divined from the
echoes of the past. And Reed insists that there is nothing "occult" about it;
writing is simply the site where history possesses him, where the past syncs
up with itself and with the present in previously unrecorded ways.

    The assertion that Neo-HooDoo means "you can have your own psy-
chology rather than someone else's"[42] is thus crucial to Reed's sense of the
relation between ancestry and writing. Through this evocation of old stories
or ancestral voices, Reed is not aiming to enrich the imaginary framework

of the cultural archive but to reanimate and re-member a repressed *form of thought*. The repressed trauma of Set's original fratricide haunts the 1920s as well as the present because it is the origin of the very structure in which history takes place: the form of thought that inaugurates and governs the relations among its inhabitants.[43] Both Reed and Freud therefore endorse an ethical orientation toward the repressed historical truth at the foundation of Western reason; *Moses and Monotheism* and *Mumbo Jumbo* each respond to an address issuing from what civilization imagines it had left in the dust of ancient Egypt but which was inscribed in its history from the very beginning.

If, in the passion of the signifier, truth has the structure of fiction, Reed helps us recognize that, when this passion is played in the theater of inheritance, fiction can have the structure of truth. In "Constructions in Analysis," Freud claims that the effect of his technique of construction inhered in a conviction about the truth it articulates, a conviction that could supplement a repressed memory and return that piece of historical truth impinging upon the present "back to the point in the past to which it belongs."[44] Note how this resonates with the etymology of the term "mumbo jumbo" Reed provides: "Mandingo *mā-mā-gyo-mbō*, 'magician who makes the troubled spirits of ancestors go away': *mā-mā*, grandmother + *gyo*, trouble + *mbō*, to leave."[45] As with the analytic construction, Reed's Neo-HooDoo aesthetic examines fiction—the literature, legends, myths, and signifying schemes that comprise the United States—not in order to disabuse American history of its inaccuracies but in order to discover the truth it contains and to reconstruct that truth in the form of yet another fiction. This is why he figures inheritance as that "anti-plague" that "enlivened its host" and portrays the Book of Thoth as a Text that must continually be written as a means of determining, exorcising, and transmitting spiritual possessions. In the end, the mystery of inheritance is not dispelled, any more than Freud's construction dispels the unconscious; rather—as Reed also says of the African American literary tradition—the gap that sustains history's noncoincidence with itself is transformed into a site of variation, difference, and potential.

If we lose sight of this mystery we miss the radical challenge *Mumbo Jumbo* poses to our collective relation to the past. Instead of that which enjoins us to produce ever-more iterations of our unconscious history, pushing us into an indeterminate future, inheritance becomes nothing but a trove of precious objects to be protected within an indifferent network of imaginary identifications and interminably circumscribes the future with what has already been. Freud himself noted that "[t]he present cultural state of America would give us a good opportunity for studying the damage to civilization which is [. . .] to be feared" when our social bonds are grounded upon such imaginary identifications, but he stopped short of criticizing "American civilization" because he did not "wish to give an impression of wanting [. . .] to employ American methods."[46] Reed's novel gives us a clue as to what these American methods might be.

V.

By now, the Freud whom Reed sought to make into a kind of founding father of American myth bears little resemblance to the Freud who led us into and out of ancient Egypt. Let us return to the former, the one who fainted when he confronted the Thing that internally divides *Mumbo Jumbo*'s "Egypt of America":

> What he saw must have been unsettling to this man accustomed to the gay Waltzing circles of Austria, the respectable clean-cut family, the protocol, the formalities of "civilization." [. . . His] followers [have] not seen such an outburst since [he] waxed all "paranoid" when someone awarded him a medal upon which was etched the Sphinx being questioned by the traveler. Or [. . .] when Carl Jung confronted him with the fable of the fossilized corpses of peat moss. [. . .]
>
> What did this clear-headed, rational, "prudish" and "chaste" man see? "The Black Tide of Mud," he was to call it. "We must make a dogma . . . an unshakeable bulwark against the Black Tide of Mud," [by which, according to Jung, h]e meant occultism. [. . .] Freud [. . .] was in no position to make a diagnosis. [. . .] Later Jung travels to Buffalo New York and [. . .] discovers what Freud saw. Europeans living in America have undergone a transformation. Jung calls this process "going Black." This chilly Swiss keeps it to himself however.[47]

Since he is not in any protected position outside of Civilization As We Know It, we cannot expect "Freud" to be different from "Moses" or any other signifier deployed in Reed's strategy. Our venerated ancestor, and other citations from the psychoanalytic archive, is submitted here to Reed's American Edition of history, where he is complicit with the whole apparatus of psychiatric power that pathologizes and diagnoses the effects of the unconscious and strives to normalize the ego. In the United States, according to Reed, psychoanalysis is on the side of repression. It is to this misuse of Freud as an

"Atonist compromise"[48] that *Mumbo Jumbo* directs us in its association of race and racism in America with Freud's dogmatic misdiagnosis of the Black Mud Sound as a Black Tide of Mud. And there is really nothing here with which we can disagree, since it is all a matter of historical record.[49]

But there is, of course, a remainder that does not coincide with this American history of psychoanalysis. Just as Freud's reconstruction of history produced two Moseses, Reed has confronted us with an uncanny double. For there is also the other father of psychoanalysis, with whom Lacan fought in order to salvage its inheritance. And it was often from American ego psychology that he rescued this Freud, the one who, as Carl Jung recorded in his autobiography, wished to establish psychoanalysis as a bulwark against the "black tide of mud of occultism."[50] The immediate context for this comment was a popular spiritualism that Freud had encountered during his 1909 stay in Boston, which made free use of two great resistances to analysis, hypnotism and religion, and Jung noted that the bulwark with which Freud meant to oppose it was his libido theory. Jung argued that Freud insisted upon this theory as one clings to a faith "for all time," whereas a "scientific truth" should be a "hypothesis" adequate only "for the moment."[51] In fact, what Freud supposed as a truth "for all time" was nothing but the experience of history's repeated return. Jung mistook for religious dogma Freud's lasting commitment to a reading of history as that which never neatly coincides with itself. This is why Lacan calls libido "the effective presence as such of desire." It is "not some archaic relation, some primitive mode of access of thoughts, some world that is there like some shade of an ancient world surviving in ours," like Jung's archetypes.[52] Libido rather names the effects of the past upon the present *as* desire. We can think of it precisely as a bulwark against such forms of relation to history that imagine the past as some kernel beyond or outside its immanent effects, something that survives history and lurks over one's shoulder at the typewriter, or visits one like a spirit in a séance, or commands religious obedience to a shared concept of the good or the true, or defines cultural belonging according to some transparent and communicable identification. Against these modes of relation to inheritance, Lacan opposes the ethics of psychoanalysis, "for which we, the inheritors of Freud, are responsible."[53] Our responsibility to this inheritance entails, first and foremost, an ethical opposition to anything that effaces the hole in the symbolic that marks the subject's noncoincidence with its history and itself.

With *Moses and Monotheism* and *Mumbo Jumbo*, we see that only in this way can the future be something other than a dogmatic repetition of the past; only in the gap that marks the mystery of inheritance does the future remain open. History *is* only insofar as it is different from itself. Inheritance is not some residue of history; it is the experience of history in the present—as uncanny repetitions, coincidences, and remainders—that compels and sustains our desire for the future.

Notes

1. Ishmael Reed, *Mumbo Jumbo* (New York: Scribner, 1996), 17, 4.

2. Ibid., 211.

3. Ibid., 208.

4. Ibid., 212.

5. Ibid., 211.

6. Ibid., 15.

7. Ibid., 23.

8. Ibid., 4, 208, 213, 215.

9. Ibid., 33.

10. Ibid., 16.

11. This is how Reed describes his Neo-HooDoo writing strategy in "The Writer as Seer: Ishmael Reed on Ishmael Reed," in *Conversations with Ishmael Reed*, ed. Bruce Dick and Amritjit Singh (Jackson: University Press of Mississippi, 1995), 62, 61.

12. Reed made these comparisons during the composition of *Mumbo Jumbo* in an interview with John O'Brien. Reed, "Ishmael Reed," in *Conversations with Ishmael Reed*, 39.

13. Ibid., 34.

14. Ibid., 39; emphasis added.

15. Ibid.

16. I borrow this idea from Henry Louis Gates Jr., who argues that "[i]t is indeterminacy, the sheer plurality of meaning, the very play of the signifier itself, which *Mumbo Jumbo* celebrates" in his seminal treatment of the African American vernacular and literary traditions. Gates, *The Signifying Monkey: A Theory of African-American Literary Criticism* (New York: Oxford University Press, 2014), 252. Though Gates himself does not explicitly articulate this multicultural reading of Reed's novel, his poststructuralist analysis elides the immanent, here and now, crossroads experience of unconscious inheritance that *Mumbo Jumbo* foregrounds, instead tracing the indeterminacy of black vernacular Signifyin' to willfully and consciously transmitted ancestral systems that survived despite the "dangerous fiction" that the Middle Passage founded a "tabula rasa of consciousness." Ibid., 4. To my mind, Gates thus has initiated several such pluralistic interpretations. See, for example, Roxanne Harde, "'We will make our own future Text':

Allegory, Iconoclasm, and Reverence in Ishmael Reed's *Mumbo Jumbo*," *Critique* 43, no. 4 (2002): 361–77; W. Lawrence Hogue, "Postmodernism, Traditional Cultural Forms, and the African American Narrative: Major's *Reflex*, Morrison's *Jazz*, and Reed's *Mumbo Jumbo*," *NOVEL: A Forum on Fiction* 35, 2/3 (2002): 169–92; Michael Rothberg, "Dead Letter Office: Conspiracy, Trauma, and *Song of Solomon*'s Posthumous Communication," *African American Review* 37, no. 4 (2003): 501–16; and Joe Weixlmann, "Culture Clash, Survival, and Trans-Formation: A Study of Some Innovative Afro-American Novels of Detection," *Mississippi Quarterly: The Journal of Southern Cultures* 38, no. 1 (1984/1985): 21–32.

17. See Sigmund Freud, *Civilization and Its Discontents*, in *The Standard Edition of the Complete Psychological Works of Sigmund Freud* (hereafter *SE*), ed. and trans. James Strachey et al. (London: Hogarth Press, 1953–1974), 21:108–16.

18. Reed, *Mumbo Jumbo*, 4.

19. Jacques Lacan, *The Seminar of Jacques Lacan, Book VII: The Ethics of Psychoanalysis, 1959–1960*, ed. Jacques-Alain Miller, trans. Dennis Porter (New York: W. W. Norton, 1992), 143.

20. Reed, *Mumbo Jumbo*, 160.

21. Freud, *Totem and Taboo*, in *SE* 13:xv.

22. Freud, *Moses and Monotheism*, in *SE* 23:43.

23. Ibid., 115.

24. Lacan, *The Seminar of Jacques Lacan, Book VII: The Ethics of Psychoanalysis, 1959–1960*, 66. Here, Lacan refers to the "primordial law, [. . .] where culture begins in opposition to nature," the prohibition of incest, which the Mosaic prohibition repeated. Ibid., 66–67. Lacan's point is that Freud discovered, in both laws and both murderous transgressions, the way the signifier installs both a limit to desire and a desire to transgress that limit.

25. Here, I am referring to the murder of the father of the primal horde, the myth that Freud situated at the inauguration of civilization and culture as such. See Freud, *Totem and Taboo*, in *SE* 13:100–61.

26. Reed, *Mumbo Jumbo*, 162.

27. Ibid., 16.

28. Ibid., 161.

29. Ibid., 164.

30. Ibid., 162.

31. Ibid.

32. Ibid., 91,186.

33. Lacan, *The Seminar of Jacques Lacan, Book VII: The Ethics of Psychoanalysis, 1959–1960*, 68.

34. Ibid.

35. Reed, *Mumbo Jumbo*, 4.

36. Ibid., 196.

37. Ibid., 204.

38. Lacan, *The Seminar of Jacques Lacan, Book VII: The Ethics of Psychoanalysis, 1959–1960*, 12. See also Lacan, "Psychoanalysis and Its Teaching," in *Écrits: The First Complete Edition in English*, trans. Bruce Fink (New York: W. W. Norton, 2006), 376; "The Youth of Gide, or the Letter and Desire," in *Écrits: The First Complete Edition in English*, 625; and "The Subversion of the Subject and the Dialectic of Desire in the Freudian Unconscious," in *Écrits: The First Complete Edition in English*, 684.

39. In this 1979 interview with Peter Nazareth, Reed aligns the idea of a "common ancestry," which for him is one of the "wrong interpretations" provided by the West, with the absurd but dangerous ideological fiction of a "pure race." Reed, "An Interview with Ishmael Reed," in *Conversations with Ishmael Reed*, 186–87. He also clarifies that his Neo-HooDoo strategy is only "multi-cultural" insofar as it has allowed him to "link up" meaningfully with authors, publishers, and critics from other backgrounds who also consider the relationship between inheritance and writing as a matter of directing the influences of the past toward the critical evaluation of the present and the creation of future texts. Ibid., 195.

40. Along these same lines, but in the context of experimental theater, Ryan Anthony Hatch provides a particularly astute and contemporary problematization of the multiculturalist attempt to reclaim and celebrate a supposedly authentic and idealized racial experience in "postrace America." See Hatch, "First as Minstrelsy, Then as Farce: On the Spectacle of Race in the Theater of Young Jean Lee," *CR: The New Centennial Review* 13, no. 3 (2013): 89–114.

41. Reed, "The Writer as Seer: Ishmael Reed on Ishmael Reed," 62.

42. Reed, "An Interview with Ishmael Reed," 186.

43. Joan Copjec offers an intricate analysis of this distinction between the form of thought in which history takes place and the contents of history, as well as what it means for the question of inheritance qua psychoanalysis. See Copjec, "Moses the Egyptian and the Big Black Mammy of the Antebellum South: Freud (with Kara Walker) on Race and History," in *Imagine There's No Woman: Ethics and Sublimation* (Cambridge: MIT Press, 2002), 82–107; and "The Censorship of Interiority," *Umbr(a): Islam*, no. 1 (2009): 165–86.

44. Freud, "Constructions in Analysis," in *SE* 23:268.

45. Reed, *Mumbo Jumbo*, 7.

46. Freud, *Civilization and Its Discontents*, in *SE* 21:116.

47. Reed, *Mumbo Jumbo*, 208–9.

48. Ibid., 172.

49. Against Freud's vehement wishes, the American branch of the International Psychoanalytic Association agreed to retain its membership only upon the condition that the practice of psychoanalysis in the United States be confined to

medical practitioners. See, in particular, Bruno Bettelheim, *Freud and Man's Soul* (New York: Vintage, 1984), 31–49. Badia Sahar Ahad complicates this history of American psychoanalysis's complicity with racism in the twentieth century, arguing that while "the influence of psychoanalytic culture in the shaping of black lives" is undeniable, there has also always been a "black intellectual and literary response to, or influence on, the culture of psychoanalysis in the United States." Ahad, *Freud Upside Down: African American Literature and Psychoanalytic Culture* (Urbana: University of Illinois Press, 2010), 12. For another reading of the history of psychoanalysis that emphasizes the inherently and radically anticonservative potential of the Freudian discovery by locating its origin not in Europe but in mesmerism's place within the Haitian Revolution, see Nathan Gorelick, "Extimate Revolt: Mesmerism, Haiti, and the Origin of Psychoanalysis," *CR: New Centennial Review* 13, no. 3 (2013): 115–38.

50. C. G. Jung, *Memories, Dreams, Reflections*, ed. Aniela Jaffé, trans. Richard and Clara Winston (New York: Vintage, 1989), 155.

51. Ibid., 151.

52. Lacan, *The Seminar of Jacques Lacan, Book XI: The Four Fundamental Concepts of Psychoanalysis,* ed. Jacques-Alain Miller, trans. Alan Sheridan (New York: W. W. Norton, 1981), 153.

53. Lacan, *The Seminar of Jacques Lacan, Book VII: The Ethics of Psychoanalysis, 1959–1960,* 182.

The Inheritance of Psychoanalysis

CHAPTER 12

Freud's Lamarckian Clinic

Daniel Wilson

In a 1917 letter to Karl Abraham, Sigmund Freud describes his planned project, with Sándor Ferenczi, to bring together psychoanalysis and Lamarckian evolution:

> The idea is to put Lamarck entirely on our ground and to show that his "need," which creates and transforms organs, is nothing but the power of *Ucs.* [unconscious] ideas over one's own body, of which we see the remnants in hysteria, in short the "omnipotence of thoughts." This would actually supply a ψα [psychoanalytic] explanation of [biological] expediency; it would put the coping stone on ψα [psychoanalysis].[1]

While this shared project never materialized, Freud developed, through his correspondence with Ferenczi, a Lamarckian metapsychology that links the "power of *Ucs.* ideas over one's own body"—that is, the transformation, in conversion hysteria, of "psychical excitation into chronic somatic symptoms"[2]—to an inheritance from the prehistory of humanity. As Freud writes in *Introductory Lectures on Psychoanalysis*, "[t]he prehistory into which the dream-work leads us back is of two kinds—on the one hand, into the individual's prehistory, his childhood, and on the other, in so far as each individual somehow recapitulates in an abbreviated form the entire development of the human race, into phylogenic prehistory too."[3] It is because of this shared prehistory that the dreamwork, which deciphers the unconscious logic of the symptom, reveals a universal truth beyond the singularity of individual experience.

Freud gives his fullest articulation of the phylogenic history that structures individual experience in his twelfth so-called lost metapsychological paper, "Overview of the Transference Neuroses," which was written in 1915 and rediscovered by Ilse Grubrich-Simitis in 1983.[4] In "Overview," Freud takes up Ferenczi's argument—from his 1913 article "Stages in the Development of the Sense of Reality"[5]—that the structure of experience is determined by real events that took place during the last ice age. Freud proposes that the conditions of the Ice Age forced early humans to limit reproduction and that, to manage the energy of the drive, which no longer found its object in the instinctual satisfaction of reproduction, humans developed the symptom. Once the energy of the drive was bound in the symptom, humans invented language and established the primal father to protect the group. Eventually, they rebelled and murdered the primal father, then later resurrected him as a figure of the moral law. The second part of this history has been well rehearsed, and, in texts from *Totem and Taboo* to *Moses and Monotheism*, Freud reconstructs the historical conditions that led to the invention of religion and the establishment of the law. "Overview" adds an additional logical moment to this story, namely, the spontaneous response of the body to the excess of the drive before the invention of language.

Grubrich-Simitis suggests that Freud did not publish the paper because he was "dealing with fantasies that trouble[d] him":

> [Freud] declares in a letter to Ferenczi sent only three days after the draft, "I maintain that one should not make theories—they must fall into one's house as uninvited guests while one is occupied with the investigation of details." A few months earlier, [. . .] Freud had concisely and memorably described to Ferenczi the "mechanism" of scientific creativity as the "succession of daringly playful fantasy and relentlessly realistic criticism." We can assume that the daringly, all too daringly, playful fantasy in the second part of the twelfth metapsychological paper did not stand up to the subsequent relentlessly realistic criticism.[6]

While "Overview" is undoubtedly speculative, it brings together ideas that appear throughout Freud's writings. The idea that individuals can transform their bodies dates to *Studies on Hysteria*, and Freud fervently maintained his belief in Lamarckian recapitulation in some of his most canonical texts, returning to his theory of the phylogenetic effects of the Ice Age in *The Ego and the Id*, where he writes that the "Oedipus complex [is] a heritage of the cultural development necessitated by the glacial epoch."[7] In the terms that Grubrich-Simitis proposes, Freud's Lamarckian metapsychology is an "uninvited guest" that refuses to be turned out. As Freud writes to Georg Groddeck in 1917, "Lamarck's theory of evolution coincides with the final outcome of psychoanalytical thinking."[8] Freud's Lamarckism is perhaps a fantasy, but it is a fundamental fantasy that organizes the clinic by providing a universal structure of human experience.

Much of the attention paid to Freud's Lamarckism focuses upon his late *Moses and Monotheism*, in which he acknowledges that "the present attitude of biological science [. . .] refuses to hear of the inheritance of acquired characters by succeeding generations," yet, he continues, "I cannot do without this factor in biological evolution."[9] Many critics sympathetic to Freud's work attempt to save him from Lamarck, as if Freud's "serious" thought could be separated from his Lamarckian eccentricities.[10] It is, perhaps unsurprisingly, critics who have no deep commitment to psychoanalytic theory or the clinic—such as Frank J. Sulloway and Patricia Kitcher[11]—who are the best readers of the deep entanglement between Freud's Lamarckism and his metapsychology. Kitcher, who works to dissect the theoretical foundations of Freud's thought, argues that, "if the support provided by Lamarckianism and recapitulationism were withdrawn from psychoanalysis, central parts of its theoretical structure would collapse."[12] As Kitcher continues, while "[t]he proper response to the crises in recapitulationism and Lamarckianism that threatened the foundations of psychoanalysis was to go back to the home discipline of evolutionary biology and fight the battle there," Freud did not abandon his Lamarckism "but continued to build higher."[13]

Yet, Freud's psychoanalysis is by no means applied Lamarckism. Psychoanalysis is a practice, not a theory, and the question is not why Freud did not return to evolutionary biology to rebuild psychoanalysis as a neo-Darwinian psychology—a project that both Sulloway and Kitcher are invested in—but rather why and how Freud uses Lamarck to cultivate and sustain a clinical practice. In what follows, I begin by sketching out the logic of Lamarckian evolution as well as the tradition of psycho-Lamarckian thought. I then turn to Freud's metapsychology to examine both the logic of recapitulation in Freud's texts in general and the Lamarckian biology of the death drive in *Beyond the Pleasure Principle* in particular. I end by examining the stakes of Freud's Lamarckism in both Freud's own clinic and Jacques Lacan's. During the same period that Freud developed his Lamarckian metapsychology he wrote "From the History of an Infantile Neurosis," in which he situates the Wolf Man's symptom—the hysterical transformation of his intestines to express an unconscious idea—within a logic of experience determined by a phylogenic inheritance. While Lacan had no interest in Freud's Lamarckism, his reading of the Wolf Man locates the same three structural moments—a trauma, a response in the body, and the entrance into language—that Freud describes as a phylogenic inheritance. Freud's Lamarckian metapsychology centers the psychoanalytic clinic upon the body's spontaneous response to a trauma and the ethical position of the subject divided between the singular fantasy at work in the body and the shared space of language.[14]

Psycho-Lamarckism before Freud

In *Zoological Philosophy*, Jean-Baptiste Lamarck proposes that species evolve, in part, through the needs of individuals: "If an animal, for the satisfaction of its needs, makes repeated efforts to lengthen its tongue, it will acquire a considerable length (ant-eater, green-woodpecker); if it requires to seize anything with this same organ, its tongue will then divide and become forked."[15] According to Ernst Haeckel's theorization of Lamarckian evolution, acquired characteristics are passed on through the logic of recapitulation. In Haeckel's influential formulation, "ontogeny recapitulates phylogeny": The embryonic development of the individual recapitulates the phylogenic development of the species. At a certain moment in the development of a human embryo, the embryo has gill slits, while at a later moment it grows a tail and is covered with hair. Stephen Jay Gould writes that, "in Haeckel's evolutionary reading, the human gill slits *are* (literally) the adult features of an ancestor."[16] As Gould continues, "all evolutionary recapitulationists accepted a mechanism based on two laws: first, 'terminal addition'—evolutionary change proceeds by adding stages to the end of ancestral ontogeny; second, 'condensation'—development is accelerated as ancestral features are pushed back to earlier stages of descendent embryos."[17] If the body of an individual is modified "for the satisfaction of its needs," then its offspring will pass through this latest modification as the final moment of embryonic development.

When Freud replaces Lamarck's notion of need—the anteater's desire to reach the ant—with "the power of unconscious ideas," he situates himself within a psycho-Lamarckian vocabulary that was common in late nineteenth-century biology. In an 1870 lecture entitled "On Memory as a Universal Function of Organized Matter," Ewald Hering—who was Josef Breuer's teacher and colleague—links recapitulation to the idea of "unconscious memory." In recapitulation the individual "remembers" the development of the species, and "unconscious memory" is thus both the logic that organizes matter in the individual and the mechanism through which newly acquired traits, sustained in and through unconscious memory, are passed on:

> An organised being, therefore, stands before us a product of the unconscious memory of organised matter, which, ever increasing and ever dividing itself, ever assimilating new matter and returning it in changed shape to the inorganic world, ever receiving some new thing into its memory, and transmitting its acquisitions by the way of reproduction, grows continually richer and richer the longer it lives.[18]

An "organized being" is the unconscious memory of the phylogenic history that determines its form, and the Lamarckian transformation of the body, based upon individual need, is the continual modification of this unconscious memory. Hering argues that it is not only the body but also the psyche that is organized by unconscious memory. The coherence of inner life, "[b]etween the 'me' of to-day and the 'me' of yesterday," comes through unconscious memories hidden from view:

> Who can hope after this to disentangle the infinite intricacy of our inner life? For we can only follow its threads so far as they have strayed over within the bounds of consciousness. We might as well hope to familiarise ourselves with the world of forms that teem within the bosom of the sea by observing the few that now and again come to the surface and soon return into the deep.[19]

For Freud, however, unconscious memory does not present an infinite task, insofar as individual experience recapitulates specific events in the prehistory of humanity. The prehistory of humanity reveals the "world of forms" hidden in individual experience as a universal inheritance.

Freud's Lamarckian Metapsychology

In the 1914 preface to *Three Essays on the Theory of Sexuality*, Freud modifies Haeckel's law by adding an important caveat: "Ontogenesis may be regarded as a recapitulation of phylogenesis, in so far as the latter has not been modified by more recent experience."[20] Freud does not theorize evolution as an ongoing process but rather as a specific phylogenic heritage that has not been modified by "recent events." Freud originally planned for "Overview of the Transference Neuroses," in which he gives this history, to be published in the same collection of metapsychological essays as "The Unconscious."[21] In the former paper, Freud describes the historical process through which the metapsychological structure of the latter came into existence. Understanding the stakes of Freud's "Overview" therefore requires entering briefly into the metapsychology of "The Unconscious."

"The Unconscious" returns to the language of *Project for a Scientific Psychology*, in which *das Ding*—the missing object—is at the center of human desire. In *Project for a Scientific Psychology*, Freud writes that all "perceptual complexes are divided into a constant, non-understood, part—the *thing*—and a changing, understandable, one—the attribute or movement of the thing."[22] The complexity of psychology comes from the fact that "the 'thing-complex' recurs linked with a number of 'attribute-complexes.'"[23] The subject looks for a "thing" that is missing from experience. In "The Unconscious," Freud asks how das Ding, the missing object, comes to inhabit perceptual experience. Freud proposes that the psyche is composed of three systems—the unconscious, the preconscious, and consciousness—that each present das Ding differently. The unconscious is the presentation of the "thing" alone. The preconscious links the presentation of the "thing" to the "word," and some of these links between the "thing" and the "word" become conscious, while others are repressed. "Consciousness" is thus a subset of the preconscious links between the word and the "thing." As Freud writes, "the conscious presentation comprises the presentation of the thing plus the presentation of the word belonging to it, while the unconscious presentation is the presentation of the thing alone."[24] Between each of these systems there is a specific mode of censorship. In attaching the "thing" to the word, the preconscious censors the unconscious presentation of the "thing." Within the field of language, there is a secondary mode of censorship, as certain things named in language are excluded from consciousness. The function of conscious experience is to present the "thing" as if it were an object in the environment. As Lacan explains, "[t]he world of perception is represented by Freud as dependent on that *fundamental hallucination* without which there would be no *attention available*."[25] In "Overview," Freud argues that the origin of humanity is unconscious and that language and consciousness are constructed only after the unconscious presentation of das Ding has been organized in the symptom.

In "Overview," Freud's prehistory begins as the Ice Age descended, and the "hitherto predominantly friendly outside world, which bestowed every satisfaction, transformed itself into a mass of threatening perils."[26] One of these perils was a shortage of food, which forced early humans to limit the size of the "human hordes."[27] Because of "narcissistic" mothers' resistance to "the killing of newborn infants," it became a "social obligation to limit repro-duction."[28] As Freud continues, "[p]erverse satisfactions that did not lead to the propagation of children avoided this prohibition, which promoted a cer-tain regression to the phase of the libido before the primacy of the genitals."[29] The loss of an object for the instincts introduces the problem of the missing object of the drive. Confronted with this loss of a reproductive aim for the instincts, early humans had to find something else to do with the energy of the libido. Freud writes that "[t]his whole situation obviously corresponds to the conditions of conversion hysteria": "From its symptomatology we con-clude that man was still speechless when, because of an emergency beyond his control, he imposed the prohibition of reproduction on himself, thus also had not yet built up the system of the Pcs. over his Ucs."[30] Through conversion hysteria early humans developed the symptom to manage the energy of the drive. After the energy of the drive was organized through the perverse satisfactions of conversion hysteria, man "developed himself under the sign of energy [and] formed the beginnings of language."[31] Once lan-guage was invented, the primal father was established to protect the group. He was eventually murdered and then preserved as a religious symbol.

Freud argues that each of these logical moments corresponds to, and is recapitulated in, one of the transference neuroses. The difficulty of the Ice Age (anxiety hysteria) leads to the transformation of the body through the production of a symptom (conversion hysteria), the invention of language, and the establishment of the primal father (obsessional neurosis). The expe-rience of being subject to the whims of the primal father (dementia praecox) resulted in the formation of secret alliances (paranoia) that resulted in the murder of the primal father, who was then preserved as a religious sym-bol (melancholia). The transference neuroses describe possible structures of experience. While all modern humans pass through these various stages, certain neurotic illnesses are marked by regressions to specific moments in this phylogenically determined structure.

The first two moments of this history—anxiety hysteria and conversion hysteria—are by definition unconscious, inasmuch as consciousness is a system that exists with language, and these phenomena, which Freud will suggest are recapitulated around the primal scene, occur before language exists. The sequence of neuroses that follow—from "obsessional neurosis" to "melancholia"—are all inscribed within the traversal of Oedipus and trace the entrance into language and the installation of the law. Freud's phylogenic history thus resolves into three distinct moments: a trauma that produces anxiety; the body's response to this trauma; and the entrance into language. In the metapsychological terms of "The Unconscious," the unconscious presents the "thing"—the missing object—by producing a symptom. The entrance into language, under the threat of castration from the primal father, allows the energy that had been organized in the "perverse satisfactions" of the symptom to be sublimated into the quest for the prohibited object. The threat of castration that ends the child's Oedipal relationship to his or her mother installs a principle of censorship within language so that the missing object—das Ding—can be represented as the inaccessible object. The law, as Lacan puts it, functions to raise the object to the dignity of das Ding.[32]

From the Ice Age to the Signifier

Lacan has no patience for Freud's evolutionary speculations. As Michael Lewis writes, "for Lacan [. . .] the very definition of 'evolution' implies a *continuous* development."[33] Whereas in evolutionary discourse the being evolves in response to environmental conditions, for Lacan, humanity begins with the intrusion of the signifier that opens up a breach in natural meaning by introducing something that is not in the environment. As Lacan states, "the fashioning of the signifier and the introduction of a gap or *hole in the real* is identical."[34] From the moment the human is exposed to this "hole in the real," human desire aims at something—das Ding—that is missing from the environment. One difficulty in reading Freud comes from the fact that Freud does not have a concept of the signifier as the cause of this originary rupture. In order to explain the fact that the human is motivated by the missing object, he must therefore find an environmental cause that introduces something that is not in the environment.

Freud's phylogenic history in "Overview" begins with an anxiety that comes when the difficult conditions of the Ice Age turn the world into a "mass of threatening perils."[35] This originary phylogenic experience of anxiety finds its ontogenic correlate in the trauma of birth. As Freud writes in 1910, "[b]irth is both the first of all dangers to life and the prototype of all the later ones that cause us to feel anxiety, and the experience of birth has probably left behind in us the expression of affect which we call anxiety."[36] In *Inhibitions, Symptoms and Anxiety*, Freud seems to revise his position on anxiety, writing that each experience of anxiety cannot be understood as a repetition of a birth anxiety, but that anxiety is rather a signal of a "situation of danger."[37] Freud, however, by no means abandons the idea that the trauma of birth is related to a fundamental loss. In his late *Civilization and Its Discontents*, he writes of "the mother's womb, the first lodging, for which in all likelihood man still longs, and in which he was safe and felt at ease."[38]

The mother's womb, like the world of plenty before the Ice Age, is a scene of absolute loss. Anxiety does not refer back to an original trauma but is rather a signal that the lack introduced by this trauma persists, regardless of the barriers that have been built up against it.

For Lacan, the origin of the human is likewise related to an anxiety. The signifier introduces a "hole in being" and Lacan speaks of anxiety as "where the subject stands in relation to his lack."[39] While Lacan will eventually replace the trauma of birth with the intrusion of the signifier, he writes in his 1938 article "Les complexes familiaux" that the prototype of anxiety "appears in the asphyxia of birth."[40] The trauma of the signifier is a technical innovation introduced by Lacan to theorize the fact that the human is oriented towards something that is missing from the environment. It is through the trauma of the Ice Age, itself recapitulated in the trauma of birth, that Freud theorizes the absolute loss of environmental satisfaction to understand how the human is oriented towards something that is missing from the environment. Freud's Ice Age, like Lacan's theorization of the primordial intrusion of the signifier, is a construction that allows him to approach both the problem of the missing object and the creativity of the symptom that responds to the loss of a natural object for the instincts.

Primary Masochism and the Structure of the Symptom

In one of the stranger passages in *Beyond the Pleasure Principle*, Freud stages an argument with August Weismann about whether or not single-cell organisms are immortal. As Freud writes, "the question may well arise in our minds whether any object whatever is served by trying to solve the problem of natural death from a study of the protozoa."[41] Weismann was an influential late nineteenth-century evolutionary biologist whose germplasm theory gave an early refutation of Lamarckian inheritance. In what follows I want to suggest that, in his critique of Weismann, Freud develops the Lamarckian logic through which the body transforms itself to respond to the lack of an object for the instincts. Freud argues that a single-cell organism uses its own biological processes to lead itself to its death. Read through his theory of recapitulation, the logic of the death drive at work in the single-cell organism describes the structure of the symptom that compensates for the loss of natural satisfaction. In these terms, the metapsychological stakes of Freud's biologism do not have to do with "the problem of natural death" but rather with the moment that Freud identifies as "conversion hysteria" in his phylogenic history.

According to Weismann's germplasm theory, there is both a "germ" and a "soma" in an organism. The germ stores the hereditary information that is passed on to offspring, while the soma is the body that is constructed upon the basis of this information. Germplasm theory aimed to refute Lamarckian inheritance, for although hereditary information moves from germ to soma, such information never moves from soma to germ. As Keith A. Francis writes, "[t]he germ plasm was the basic reproductive unit of the parents that created the progeny, but the parents simply passed on the germ plasm to the next generation without changing it: any changes in the parents' structure caused by external conditions of use and disuse were not passed on to the progeny."[42] Richard Dawkins, who writes that his idea of the "selfish gene" "was foreshadowed by A. Weismann in pre-gene days," makes the point succinctly: The hereditary information wants to perpetuate itself and "it does this by helping to program the bodies in which it finds itself to survive and to reproduce."[43] Freud clearly grasps the consequences of this position, writing that, according to Weismann, "germ-cells [. . .] are potentially immortal, in so far as they are able, under certain favourable conditions, to develop into a new individual, or, in other words, to surround themselves with a new soma."[44]

Whereas, in the case of Weismann's organism, the individual is reduced to a means for the germ to reproduce itself, Lamarckian evolution is motivated by the individual's need in excess of what is given in its biology. In the case of the Lamarckian animal—for example, the giraffe whose neck becomes longer as it stretches to reach higher branches—the individual's desire to reach the object of its instincts drives evolution. The animal is motivated by the pleasure principle and transforms its body to reach a possible object that exists in the environment. Freud, however, uses Lamarck to theorize a response to a need that is beyond the pleasure principle, given that there is no way for the organism to modify itself to attain das Ding, the missing object. In response to the fact that there is no object for the drive in the environment, the organism uses its body to produce a hostile environment that explains this lack.

While multicellular organisms are composed of both germplasm and soma, in unicellular organisms "the individual and the reproductive cell are [. . .] one and the same."[45] Freud thus turns to the unicellular organism to examine the desire that motivates life. If Weismann is correct and reproduction is the only objective of life, then the unicellular organism will be immortal; if Freud is correct, the organism—which is motivated by something other than reproduction—will die. In a laboratory in which organisms are grown in a dish, as long as the researcher "provide[s] each generation with fresh nutrient fluid,"[46] they will reproduce over thousands of genera-tions. Yet, if the "nutrient fluid" is not replaced, the organisms eventually die, "injured by the products of metabolism which they extruded into the surrounding fluid."[47] Freud thus concludes that "[a]n infusorian, therefore, if it is left to itself, dies a natural death owing to its incomplete voidance of the products of its own metabolism."[48] While Freud turned to the unicellular organism as a special case, he ends by generalizing to all animal life, pro-posing that "it may be that the same incapacity [the incomplete voidance of metabolic products] is the ultimate cause of the death of all higher animals as well."[49] Freud introduces a rudimentary structure of the address through which the organism's own biological processes are received back—by the organism—as if they originated in the environment. The protista finds its "natural death" through a masochistic address.

This argument takes on metapsychological weight insofar as Freud's uni-cellular organism theorizes the logic of the drive at work in the human. In the language of Freud's metapsychology, the masochistic address that leads to the organism's death is the unconscious presentation of das Ding. The organism does not look for something in the environment but rather trans-forms the environment in order to compensate for the fact that there is no object for the drive. In his phylogenic history Freud proposes that the Ice Age cuts the instincts from their object. In the case of the protista, the organ-ism produces by a hostile environment. The protista stages an environmen-tal trauma that repeats a phylogenetic trauma. The difference between the environmental trauma of the Ice Age and the environmental trauma staged by the organism is one of register. The phylogenic loss of an object is the universal condition of experience, and the phylogenic loss of environmental satisfaction has nothing to do with the environmental conditions of one's actual life. Because each human inherits this loss, there is no Other that can be held responsible for this loss. The fantasy at work in the symptom, however, theorizes the loss as contingent, as if the Other of the fantasy—the persistent hostility of the environment in the case of Freud's protista—were responsible for the excess of the drive over any object of satisfaction.

In Freud's phylogenic history the moment of "conversion hysteria" that produces a symptom is followed by a sequence of events—the invention of language and the establishment and then murder of the primal father—that establish the moral law. It is thus no surprise that, in *The Ego and the Id*, Freud describes the attitude of "moral masochism" on the model of the protista: "In suffering under the attacks of the super-ego or perhaps even succumbing to them, the ego is meeting with a fate like that of the protista which are destroyed by the products of decomposition that they themselves have created."[50] Freud's analogy suggests that the moral masochism through which the ego situates itself with respect to superegoic ideals is constructed upon the basis of a primary masochism at work in the symptom, which subverts the biology of the organism in order to produce the fantasy of an Other. The first relationship to the Other comes through the unconscious response of the body to the excess of the drive. The entrance into language both opens a space where the missing object of the drive can be pursued in the symbolic and cuts the subject off from the singularity of the Other at work in the body. The clinical stakes of Freud's Lamarckism will turn around the tension between the singular fantasy at work in the symptom and the shared space of the symbolic order.

The Lamarckian Clinic

In "Overview," Freud writes that "anxiety hysteria, conversion hysteria, and obsessional neurosis [are] regressions to phases that the whole human race had to go through at some time from the beginning to the end of the Ice Age."[51] These structures are not mutually exclusive, and at the center of the Wolf Man's case is a "small trait of hysteria which is regularly to be found at the root of an obsessional neurosis."[52] Freud writes that the Wolf Man's "principal subject of complaint was that for him the world was hidden in a veil [. . .]. This veil was torn only at one moment—when, after an enema, the contents of the bowel left the intestinal canal; and he then felt well and normal again."[53] When Freud invites the "hysterically affected organ" to "join in the conversation,"[54] he is led into the Wolf Man's past. When the Wolf Man was a small child, he saw his parents having sex, a tergo, one afternoon. His father, who is later related to the devouring wolf, at once enjoys his mother and introduces something deadly into her body, and when his mother develops dysentery, the Wolf Man understands the illness as the effect of his father inserting his penis into his mother's anus, as if "his mother had been made ill by what his father had done to her."[55] The Wolf Man seizes upon this scene of inexplicable enjoyment to interpret the drive at work in his body, linking the image of copulation to the "'cannibalistic' or 'oral' phase" of sexual organization, "during which the original attachment of sexual excitation to the nutritional instinct still dominates the scene."[56] Like the protista that addresses itself to a lethal Other, this moment of hysterical conversion serves to organize the drive through a fantasy of the Other that is responsible for the deadly excess at work in the body. The Wolf Man identifies with the position of his mother, who is the object of the Other's jouissance. This initial inscription of the primal scene in his intestines—through the "phenomena of conversion"[57]—determines the modalities through which he will search out and encounter jouissance throughout his life. His fear of wolves, attitude towards money, and sexual predilections are all organized by a fantasy at work in his symptom.

Lacan notes that "[t]he patient was never able to evoke, to remember, this scene directly, and it is reconstructed by Freud."[58] Freud himself writes that, while he would be "glad to know whether the primal scene in [the Wolf Man's] case was a phantasy or a real experience [. . .], the answer to this question is not in fact a matter of very great importance," for the primal scene is "an inherited endowment, a phylogenic heritage."[59] In Freud's phylogenic history the body transforms itself in order to bind the energies of the drive, through a fantasy of the Other, before the subject enters into language. Because this first relation to the Other, staged through a spontaneous response in the body to the experience of the primal scene, is necessary to the structure of experience, "a child catches hold of this phylogenic experience where his own experience fails him. He fills in the gaps in individual truth with prehistoric truth; he replaces occurrences in his own life by occurrences in the life of his ancestors."[60]

In his reading of the Wolf Man's experience Lacan finds the same logical structure that Freud argues is an "inherited endowment."[61] Whereas Freud, however, presents this structure as a sequence of neuroses, Lacan interprets it as the effects of distinct traumas in the registers of the real, imaginary, and symbolic. A trauma in the real—the introduction of the signifier that introduces das Ding as the missing object—produces the body of the drive in excess of the instinctual logic of the organism; the energies of the drive respond to a trauma in the imaginary—as Freud notes, the primal scene is the experience of "looking"[62]—by transforming the body to stage a fantasy of the Other; and the entrance into the symbolic both opens the space of the Other, beyond the solitude of the symptom, and censors the singular fantasy at work in the body.

In order to theorize the primal scene as a trauma in the imaginary, Lacan "borrow[s] a term from the theory of instincts such as it has been developed in recent times, in a manner that is certainly more meticulous than in Freud's day, especially for birds, [namely,] the *Prägung*—this term possesses resonances of *striking*, striking a coin—the *Prägung* of the originating traumatic event."[63] Konrad Z. Lorenz developed the idea of imprinting—the Prägung—to describe the process through which, at a specific moment in the bird's development, a perceptual experience determines the other to which the animal will address its instinctual behavior.[64] In the same way a visual experience determines the other to whom the bird will address its instincts, the infant constructs the imaginary Other through the imprint of the primal scene.

There is, however, an important difference between the bird and the infant. The bird cannot be traumatized by the imprint, and its instinctual response to perceptual experience is so overdetermined that it is possible "to direct the imprinting of some reaction to a substitute object"[65]—whether to another species of bird, a researcher who imitates a bird, or even, if it occurs "at exactly the right moment," boats.[66] The instincts find their mark, regardless of the object that is presented, and the imprint determines the bird's social behavior. The situation is more complicated for the child, since the child responds to the Prägung of the primal scene in the imaginary but will live his or her life in the symbolic. In response to the "imaginary break-in" of the primal scene, the child constructs a fantasy that will remain in conflict with his or her life in the shared space of the social.

Freud proposes that the Wolf Man observed his parents having sex when he was one and a half years old. Lacan suggests, however, that it "happened at six months,"[67] thus situating the primal scene at the very beginning of the mirror stage, when "that which will be $i(a)$ [the ideal ego] lies in the disorder of the objects a in the plural and it is not yet a question of having them or not."[68] The child responds to the Prägung of the image before the body has achieved an imaginary coherence, before the mirror stage "situates the agency known as the ego, prior to its social determination, in a fictional direction."[69] The primal scene inscribes itself into the fragmented body and provides the material for a fantasy of the Other that is responsible for the disorder, the excess, at work in the body. This unconscious relationship to the Other, articulated in response to the "imaginary break-in" of the primal scene, will continue to exist in tension with the scene of the ego.

In Freud's metapsychological language, the primal scene takes place before the preconscious has been built up over the unconscious, and the unconscious presentation of the "thing" thus persists in discordance with the scene of linguistic experience within which consciousness is established. As in Freud's phylogenic history, where the symptom organizes the drive before language exists, the fantasy of the primal scene accounts for the excess of the body before the child comes into the symbolic. The entrance into the symbolic will be traumatic precisely because the singular fantasy of the primal scene at work within the body has no place in the symbolic order, which "universalises significations."[70] As Lacan explains, "something of the subject's becomes detached in the very symbolic world that he is engaged in integrating. From then on, it will no longer be something belonging to the subject. The subject will no longer speak it, will no longer integrate it."[71] And yet, this censored experience, cut off from consciousness, will "remain there, somewhere, spoken, if one can put it this way, by something that the subject does not control."[72] As in the Wolf Man's symptom, it seems the "world was hidden in a veil"[73] and that the veil is only torn when he discharges his bowels after an enema.

Freud's phylogenic history describes a series of events that are recapitulated in each individual's life. There is a trauma that produces the drive in excess of any possible object of satisfaction, a symptom that stages a masochistic address to the Other of the fantasy that is responsible for the excess of the drive, and the entrance into language that replaces the singularity of the imaginary Other with the universal laws that situate the ego within the social link. The task of psychoanalysis begins where this phylogenic history ends, taking the side of the signifier to submit the fantasy at work in the body to the rigor of symbolic articulation, in order to open a space in which the subject can confront the loss of jouissance as the inheritance of a shared humanity, rather than as a personal loss. Freud's Lamarckian metapsychology thus leads to an ethical choice that is not itself determined by phylogenic history: to take refuge in the fantasy of an imaginary Other, or to take responsibility for the unconscious position at work in the body by finding a way to act upon the basis of an impossible object within the shared space of language.

Notes

1. Sigmund Freud to Karl Abraham, November 11, 1917, in *The Complete Correspondence of Sigmund Freud and Karl Abraham, 1907–1925*, ed. Ernst Falzeder, trans. Caroline Schwarzacher, with the collaboration of Christine Trollope and Klara Majthényi King (New York: Karnac, 2002), 361.

2. Freud and Josef Breuer, *Studies on Hysteria*, in *The Standard Edition of the Complete Psychological Works of Sigmund Freud* (hereafter *SE*), ed. and trans. James Strachey et al. (London: Hogarth Press, 1953–1974), 2:86.

3. Freud, *Introductory Lectures on Psycho-Analysis*, in *SE* 15:199.

4. See Freud, "Overview of the Transference Neuroses," in *A Phylogenetic Fantasy: Overview of the Transference Neuroses*, ed. Ilse Grubrich-Simitis, trans. Axel Hoffer and Peter T. Hoffer (Cambridge: Belknap Press, 1987), 1–20.

5. See Sándor Ferenczi, "Stages in the Development of the Sense of Reality," in *First Contributions to Psycho-Analysis*, trans. Ernest Jones (New York: Karnac, 2002), 213–39.

6. Ilse Grubrich-Simitis, "Metapsychology and Metabiology: On Sigmund Freud's Draft Overview of the Transference Neuroses," in *A Phylogenetic Fantasy: Overview of the Transference Neuroses*, 83.

7. Freud, *The Ego and the Id*, in *SE* 19:35.

8. Freud to Georg Groddeck, June 5, 1917, in *Letters of Sigmund Freud*, ed. Ernst L. Freud, trans. Tania and James Stern (New York: Basic, 1960), 317.

9. Freud, *Moses and Monotheism*, in *SE* 23:100.

10. Ernest Jones, who knew from Freud's letters of the plan to write "Overview of the Transference Neuroses," writes that Freud "wisely dropped the whole train of thought," perhaps hoping to sweep the whole business of Freud's Lamarckism under the carpet. Ernest Jones, *The Life and Work of Sigmund Freud: The Last Phase, 1919–1939*, vol. 3 (New York: Basic, 1957), 330. Lacan writes of the "embarrassment" he imagines Freud felt when referring to Ferenczi's Lamarckian theories. Jacques Lacan, *The Seminar of Jacques Lacan, Book I: Freud's Papers on Technique, 1953–1954*, ed. Jacques-Alain Miller, trans. John Forrester (New York: W. W. Norton, 1988), 127. Richard J. Bernstein writes with regret that "Freud bases his understanding of the dynamics of a religious tradition on a 'discredited' Lamarckism." Bernstein, *Freud and the Legacy of Moses* (New York: Cambridge University Press, 1998), 49. Others read Freud's Lamarckism as a metaphor of sorts. Yosef Hayim Yerushalmi, for example, suggests that Freud's Lamarckism can be taken as a metaphor for Jewishness, since, "[d]econstructed into Jewish terms, what is Lamarckism if not the powerful feeling that, for better or worse, one cannot really cease being Jewish." Yerushalmi, *Freud's Moses: Judaism Terminable and Interminable* (New Haven: Yale University Press, 1991), 31. Jacques Derrida proposes that what Freud understands through Lamarckian inheritance "could well follow (Freud would certainly not say it here in this form) quite complicated linguistic, cultural, cipherable, and in general ciphered transgenerational and transindividual relays." Derrida, *Archive Fever: A Freudian Impression*, trans. Eric Prenowitz (Chicago: University of Chicago Press, 1996), 35.

11. See Frank J. Sulloway, *Freud, Biologist of the Mind: Beyond the Psychoanalytic Legend* (Cambridge: Harvard University Press, 1992); and Patricia Kitcher, *Freud's Dream: A Complete Interdisciplinary Science of Mind* (Cambridge: MIT Press, 1992).

12. Kitcher, *Freud's Dream: A Complete Interdisciplinary Science of Mind*, 175.

13. Ibid., 179.

14. This line of thought owes a great debt to Willy Apollon, who developed the concept of the "letter of the body" to name the spontaneous response in the body—well before the child's entrance into the symbolic order—that determines the subject's position in jouissance. See Willy Apollon, "The Letter of the Body," in *After Lacan: Clinical Practice and the Subject of the Unconscious*, by Willy Apollon,

Danielle Bergeron, and Lucie Cantin, ed. Robert Hughes and Kareen Ror Malone (New York: State University of New York Press, 2002), 103–15.

15. Jean Baptiste de Lamarck, *Zoological Philosophy: An Exposition with Regard to the Natural History of Animals*, trans. Hugh Samuel Roger Elliott (New York: Cambridge University Press, 2011), 120.

16. Stephen Jay Gould, *Ontogeny and Phylogeny* (Cambridge: Harvard University Press, 1977), 7.

17. Ibid.

18. Ewald Hering, "On Memory as a Universal Function of Organised Matter," in *Unconscious Memory*, by Samuel Butler (London: Jonathan Cape, 1922), 80–81.

19. Ibid., 71.

20. Freud, *Three Essays on the Theory of Sexuality*, in *SE* 7:131.

21. Freud wrote to Ferenczi that his article was "the draft of the XII [paper]." Freud to Sándor Ferenczi, July 28, 1915, in *The Correspondence of Sigmund Freud and Sándor Ferenczi: 1914–1919*, ed. Ernst Falzeder and Eva Brabant, with the collaboration of Patrizia Giampieri-Deutsch, trans. Peter T. Hoffer, vol. 2 (Cambridge: Belknap Press, 1996), 73. Grubrich-Simitis notes that, "[f]rom November 1914 until the summer of 1915[,] Sigmund Freud worked on a series of papers that he originally intended to publish in book form under the title *Zur Vorbereitung einer Metapsychologie* (Preliminaries to a metapsychology)." Grubrich-Simitis, "Preface to the Original Edition," in *A Phylogenetic Fantasy: Overview of the Transference Neuroses*, xv. While Freud planned twelve metapsychological papers, only five were published: "A Metapsychological Supplement to the Theory of Dreams," "Mourning and Melancholia," "Instincts and their Vicissitudes," "Repression," and "The Unconscious."

22. Freud, *Project for a Scientific Psychology*, in *SE* 1:383.

23. Ibid.

24. Freud, "The Unconscious," in *SE* 14:201.

25. Lacan, *The Seminar of Jacques Lacan, Book VII: The Ethics of Psychoanalysis, 1959–1960*, ed. Jacques-Alain Miller, trans. Dennis Porter (New York: W. W. Norton, 1992), 53; emphasis added.

26. Freud, "Overview of the Transference Neuroses," 14.

27. Ibid.

28. Ibid., 14–15.

29. Ibid., 15.

30. Ibid.

31. Ibid.

32. See Lacan, *The Seminar of Jacques Lacan, Book VII: The Ethics of Psychoanalysis, 1959–1960*, 112.

33. Michael Lewis, *Derrida and Lacan: Another Writing* (Edinburgh: Edinburgh University Press, 2008), 48; emphasis in original.

34. Lacan, *The Seminar of Jacques Lacan, Book VII: The Ethics of Psychoanalysis, 1959–1960*, 121; emphasis added.

35. Freud, "Overview of the Transference Neuroses," 14.

36. Freud, "A Special Type of Choice of Object Made by Men," in *SE* 11:173.

37. Freud, *Inhibitions, Symptoms and Anxiety*, in *SE* 20:161.

38. Freud, *Civilization and Its Discontents*, in *SE* 21:91.

39. Lacan, *The Seminar of Jacques Lacan, Book X: Anxiety*, ed. Jacques-Alain Miller, trans. A. R. Price (Malden: Polity, 2014), 235.

40. Lacan, "Les complexes familiaux dans la formation de l'individu: Essai d'analyse d'une fonction en psychologie," in *Autres écrits*, ed. Jacques-Alain Miller (Paris: Éditions du Seuil, 2001), 33; my translation.

41. Freud, *Beyond the Pleasure Principle*, in *SE* 18:49.

42. Keith A. Francis, *Charles Darwin and "The Origin of Species"* (Westport: Greenwood Press, 2007), 71.

43. Richard Dawkins, *The Selfish Gene* (New York: Oxford University Press, 2006), 11, 88.

44. Freud, *Beyond the Pleasure Principle*, in *SE* 18:46.

45. Ibid.

46. Ibid., 48.

47. Ibid.

48. Ibid.

49. Ibid., 48–49.

50. Freud, *The Ego and the Id*, in *SE* 19:56–57.

51. Freud, "Overview of the Transference Neuroses," 13.

52. Freud, "From the History of an Infantile Neurosis," in *SE* 17:75.

53. Ibid., 74–75.

54. Ibid., 76.

55. Ibid., 78.

56. Ibid., 106.

57. Ibid., 113.

58. Lacan, *The Seminar of Jacques Lacan, Book I: Freud's Papers on Technique, 1953–1954*, 189.

59. Freud, "From the History of an Infantile Neurosis," in *SE* 17:97.

60. Ibid.

61. Ibid.

62. Ibid., 34.

63. Lacan, *The Seminar of Jacques Lacan, Book I: Freud's Papers on Technique, 1953–1954*, 190.

64. See Konrad Z. Lorenz, "The Companion in the Bird's World," *The Auk* 54, no. 3 (1937): 245–73.

65. Ibid., 267.

66. Ibid., 269, 268.

67. Lacan, *The Seminar of Jacques Lacan, Book I: Freud's Papers on Technique, 1953–1954*, 189.

68. Lacan, *The Seminar of Jacques Lacan, Book X: Anxiety*, 118.

69. Lacan, "The Mirror State as Formative of the *I* Function as Revealed in Psychoanalytic Experience," in *Écrits: The First Complete Edition in English*, trans. Bruce Fink (New York: W. W. Norton, 2006), 76.

70. Lacan, *The Seminar of Jacques Lacan, Book I: Freud's Papers on Technique, 1953–1954*, 191.

71. Ibid.

72. Ibid.

73. Freud, "From the History of an Infantile Neurosis," in *SE* 17:75.

CHAPTER 13

Freud against Oedipus?

Philippe Van Haute

There is a popular story, even among scholars, that tells us that Freudian psychoanalysis was founded at the very moment Sigmund Freud wrote to Wilhelm Fliess in 1897 to reveal that he no longer believed in his *neurotica*: "*Ich glaube an meine Neurotica nicht mehr*."[1] The story reads this declaration as follows: I no longer take the traumatic stories of my patients at face value but rather interpret them as distorted expressions of Oedipal fantasies. In other words, this declaration is understood as the result of the following reasoning: What my patients tell me is not factually true; nothing "really" happened; consequently, the different psychopathological syndromes cannot be caused by traumatic (especially sexual) events and, thus, my seduction theory is mistaken; instead, we have to lay bare the true meaning of these narratives by restoring the unconscious (Oedipal) themes and the instinctual mechanisms of which they are the expression, and this is done in the free association that is the fundamental method of psychoanalytic treatment. It is clear that this version of the genesis of psychoanalytic thinking implies that Freud had already introduced the Oedipus complex in 1897 and that the latter is, in the strictest sense, the shibboleth of psychoanalytic metapsychology from the very beginning. If this were true, however, it would mean that Freud understood psychopathology *from the outset* as the result of the vicissitudes of the development of the (psychosexual) relations of the little child with its parents and the Oedipus complex that characterizes these relations as the most fundamental determining factor of human subjectivity.

This history is defended by both psychoanalysts and hard-core critics of psychoanalytic theory. I limit myself here to one (telling) example. Ernst Kris, in the introduction to the 1952 edition of Freud's letters to Fliess and *Project for a Scientific Psychology*, writes the following: "In his letters [*Briefe an Wilhelm Flieβ*], we learn that Freud's insight into the structure of the Oedipus complex, i.e. the core problem of psychoanalysis, was made possible by his self-analysis, which began in the summer of 1897 during his stay in Aussee."[2] Even Jeffrey Masson, who regards the abandonment of the seduction theory as an "assault on truth,"[3] does not dispute the fact that the abandonment of the seduction theory coincides with the discovery of the Oedipus complex. "Kris is correct: Freud had altered the direction of his thinking. Earlier, he had recognized the aggressive acts of parents against their children—for seduction was an act of violence. Now Freud had a new insight, that children had aggressive impulses against their parents."[4]

In this essay I will show that this narrative about the history of Freudian psychoanalysis is highly questionable. I will illustrate this through a close reading of some passages from the Dora case and through an analysis of some aspects of the 1905 edition of *Three Essays on the Theory of Sexuality*. This analysis will also make it possible to explain in what sense these early texts contain a "pathoanalysis of existence" in which the Oedipus complex plays no role whatsoever.[5] On the contrary, Freud only introduces the Oedipus complex—or, at least, a fundamental aspect of it, namely, the ambivalence towards the father—in his 1909 study of the Rat Man ("Notes upon a Case of Obsessional Neurosis"). On top of that, the clinical arguments he uses to justify this introduction are far from self-evident. In discussing these arguments I will try to identify the logic that is at the basis of the "Oedipalization" of Freudian theory and briefly suggest some aspects of Freudian thinking that could have protected Freud against the Oedipal pitfall.

The Case of Dora

As I have already indicated, the traditional story about the historical origins of Freudian psychoanalysis implies that the Oedipus complex was part of Freudian theory from the very beginning. However, when we look at the texts that Freud published in the decade after 1897—at least when we make the effort to look at the original editions of these texts—we find no reference whatsoever to the Oedipus complex.[6] Both *The Interpretation of Dreams* and *Three Essays on the Theory of Sexuality*, which were published in 1900 and 1905 respectively, were republished with substantial additions in later years, and it is these later editions that we find in both *Gesamtausgabe* and the

Standard Edition.[7] In both collected editions these texts do indeed contain Oedipal explanations and references to the central role of the famous complex of psychopathology, but all of these references were introduced into later editions. In the 1905 edition of *Three Essays*, for example, there is not one reference to the Oedipus complex. Rather, all of the references to this complex were introduced in 1920, and then only in the footnotes. Whatever we think of the historiographical account I am questioning here, its defenders have some explaining to do. More importantly, if my argument is accepted, there seems to be a Freudian psychoanalysis that is not at all Oedipal.

Before discussing the central role of *Three Essays* in the context of a non-Oedipal psychoanalysis, I will first illustrate my point with a short analysis of some passages from the Dora case study (*Fragment of an Analysis of a Case of Hysteria*), which was also published in 1905 and which one can, without exaggeration, claim as a crucial link between *The Interpretation of Dreams* and *Three Essays*. In this case study Freud intended to show the importance of the analysis of dreams for the treatment of hysterical patients (hence its initial projected title, *Traum und Hysterie*). It is at the same time a kind of clinical complement to *Three Essays*, which takes hysteria *expressis verbis* as its basis of reflection. Although it was published in 1905, Freud wrote it in 1901. The reasons for the delay in its publication are obscure. But, whatever we make of this, both its conception and publication date from after Freud's alleged abandonment of the seduction theory in 1897. Hence, it may come as a surprise that the text begins with an extremely positive reference to the 1895 text *Studies on Hysteria*, where we find the formulation and defense of this very theory. Freud confirms at the beginning of *Analysis of a Fragment of a Case of Hysteria* that the psychical conditions for hysteria described in his and Josef Breuer's *Studies on Hysteria*—psychical trauma, conflict between the affects, and a disturbance in the sphere of sexuality[8]—are present in Dora. This passage seems to indicate that Freud is still defending here, in one (reformulated) way or another, his classical theory of seduction, but this has not received much attention from his interpreters, or, for that matter, Freud scholars. The latter turn more eagerly to other passages in Dora's case history that concern Oedipal themes. As these passages seem to contradict my claim that the Oedipus complex was not yet part of Freudian theory in 1905, I shall now examine them closely.

Dora's case history is structured around two dreams. Dora's first dream occurs a few days after an incident at a lake in which Dora slaps Herr K, a friend of the family, after he declares his love for her. In this dream, Dora is awoken by her father, their house on fire. Her mother does not want to leave the house without saving her jewelry box, but Dora's father objects: "I refuse to let myself and my two children be burnt for the sake of your jewel-case."[9] When asked about this dream, Dora tells Freud of a fight between her parents about a piece of jewelry. Her mother wanted teardrop pearls to wear as earrings, but her father gave her a bracelet instead. Freud, then, introduces a link between the "jewel-case" (and jewelry more generally) and female genitals. Freud further remarks that Dora's mother is a former rival for her father's affections, and that she might want to "give" her father what her mother refuses, that is, her jewelry.[10] The Oedipal theme is clearly present in this dream; as Freud writes, "I have shown at length elsewhere at what an early age sexual attraction makes itself felt between parents and children, and I have explained that the legend of Oedipus is probably to be regarded as a poetical rendering of what is typical in these relations."[11] According to Freud, it follows from all of this that the dream expresses a revival of "germs of feeling in infancy"[12] that have an Oedipal character. But is an Oedipal theme the same as providing an Oedipal explanation? What is the exact status of these Oedipal references?

Freud links the idea that Dora's father was trying to save her from a burning house with the fact that he used to wake her up as a child in the middle of the night to prevent her from wetting her bed.[13] He suggests that, apart from their obvious meaning, "fire" and "burning" have sexual connotations. According to Freud, Dora's father replaces Herr K, for whom Dora burns with desire.[14] It is against this "fire" that Dora's father must protect her in the same way that he protected her before against bed-wetting. As Freud concludes, "[m]y interpretation was that she had at that point summoned up an infantile affection for her father so as to be able to keep her repressed love for Herr K in its state of repression."[15] So the affection for her father, which goes back to an "Oedipal" attachment in her youth, is a "reactive symptom" in service of repression.[16] Freud views the Oedipus myth as a poetic expression of something typical in relations between parents and children. However, at no point does he claim that "Oedipal relations" lie at the origin of Dora's *petite hystérie*. On the contrary, the memory of this affection is only revived to help repress Dora's desire for Herr K (and, more fundamentally, Frau K). At the center of Dora's problematic—and Freud is quite clear about this—we find an *actual love* (for either Herr or Frau K, or both) and not an infantile one for her father. At this point, then, Freud is still far removed from the theory of an Oedipus complex as the *nuclear* complex of all neuroses that, in principle, can provide insight into the fundamental dynamic of the entire field of pathology.[17]

Sexual Disposition and Pathoanalysis

We should not conclude from all of this that the famous letter of 1897 has
no special importance for the development of Freudian thinking. Having
explained why he no longer believes in his neurotica—the disillusioning fact
that no analysis could be brought to a satisfactory end; the absence of a reality index in the unconscious; the incredibly high number of perverts among
the Viennese population that the truth of the theory would require; and the
fact that the unconscious memory of childhood traumas does not surface,
even during the most extreme conditions of psychotic confusion[18]—Freud
writes that giving up seduction as the exclusive cause of psychopathology in
general (and hysteria in particular) brings a new factor to the fore: the idea
of a constitutional disposition.[19] In this Freud looks back to an old Charcotian idea, but with one crucial difference. In "My Views on the Part Played
by Sexuality in the Aetiology of Neuroses," Freud characterizes the change
in his thought after the abandonment of the seduction theory as follows:
"Accidental influences derived from experience having thus receded into the
background, the factors of constitution and heredity necessarily gained the
upper hand once more; but there was this difference between my views and
those prevailing in other quarters, that on my theory the 'sexual constitution' took the place of a 'general neuropathic disposition.'"[20] In 1897, a transition occurs in Freud's thinking from trauma to disposition, but the primacy
of sexuality remains untouched. Henceforth, this disposition is *a libidinal
(sexual) constitution*. This allows us to understand at least one crucial aspect
of the importance, meaning, and status of the first edition of *Three Essays*: It
articulates a general—typically human—sexual disposition, which is at the
basis of hysteria.

What is this "disposition"? What is its content? This "hysterical disposition" is roughly composed of three elements: a strong version of bisexuality,
both upon the side of the object and the side of the subject (and we may
recall that Freud's original title for what was to become *Three Essays on the
Theory of Sexuality* was *Human Bisexuality* [*Die menschliche Bisexualität*]);
the need to overcome (through idealization and repression) the permanent
threat of contamination of the sexual by the excremental function; and the
need to cope with the perverse (and homosexual) tendencies (that is, the
partial drives) that intrinsically belong to human sexuality. Oedipal conflict,
this much is clear, plays no part in this libidinal disposition.

But this is not the whole story. Freud arrives at the idea of a *universal* human disposition through the study of hysteria; in this way, hysteria
turns out to be, as it were, the "royal road" to understanding humankind as

such. Freud understood the symptoms of his hysterical patients to be the disguised expression of perverse fantasies. Neurosis (hysteria), he writes, is the negative of perversion.[21] This also means—and this is essential to what we could call Freud's philosophical "methodology"—that the sexual disposition at the basis of hysteria can only be studied properly from the perspective of the pathological variations of sexuality. This is why the first of Freud's three essays on the theory of sexuality focuses upon the so-called sexual aberrations (homosexuality and the traditional "paraphilias"). On the one hand, these aberrations demonstrate that sexuality has no natural object of its own. This insight further makes it possible for him to break away from the functional interpretation of sexuality that characterized sexology at the end of the nineteenth century.[22] On the other hand, it was only by breaking away from this functional interpretation that Freud could consider the tendencies—the partial drives—that underlie the different perversions as the building blocks of the sexual life of all human beings. In other words, Freud regards the partial drives, which he discovers through the study of the perversions, as the constitutive elements of human sexuality as such.

The "organic" repression of the partial drives[23] (the development of the reaction formations of shame and disgust) and the constitutive threat of contamination of the sexual by the excremental function are at the basis of hysteria; at the same time, they can also be said to characterize human sexuality as such. This seems to suggest that the argument of *Three Essays* concerns not just the primacy of sexuality but, even more so, the primacy of the pathological for the study of the human being. Freud's claim for the primacy of sexuality is based upon the discovery that sexuality confronts us with a number of unsolvable problems and conflicts rooted in our biological constitution that are at the basis of psychopathology. But this biological constitution can only be studied properly *starting from* pathology. The primacy of sexuality and the primacy of the pathological for understanding human existence are thus, for Freud, two sides of the same coin. This means that Freud's idea of a "hereditary disposition" should not be understood as a genetic determination in the contemporary sense of the word but rather as a complex field of problematics—a question or questions, rather than an answer or answers—that we all share as human beings and that determines our existence. Its intensity—or, better, urgency—is subject not only to individual variation but also to change in the course of our lives.

Freud's "hysterical disposition" consists of a field of forces with which we all have to deal and for which there are no "good" or "ultimate" solutions, let alone a solution inscribed into the very nature of this disposition. When it comes to psychosexuality, the early Freud is profoundly anti-Aristotelian:

There is no intrinsic norm (inscribed into the very nature of our sexual existence) that would allow us to determine, once and for all, what the outcome
of (psycho)sexual development should be. We should rather understand the
sexual body in Deleuzian terms as a "disjunctive synthesis"; the interactions
between the different partial drives that are inscribed into it do not themselves aim at a predetermined goal to which they should (at least ideally)
all be subordinated.[24] The (sexual) body is, on the contrary, a constitutive
field of forces with an ever-changing strength and intensity that, in principle,
never gives us any rest. This "disposition" is the topic of Freud's *Fragment of
an Analysis of a Case of Hysteria*, a disposition upon which psychoanalysis
has no grip and which it cannot change. We can, according to Freud, resolve
the symptoms of our patients but not the disposition as a consequence of
which these symptoms find their origin. Humans, so much is clear, are first
and foremost "sick animals."

From Hysteria to Psychosis and Obsessional Neurosis

As long as Freud used hysteria as the sole paradigm to understand human
existence, the Oedipus complex played no role in psychoanalytic thinking.
But even in *Three Essays*, where the exclusive emphasis upon hysteria falls
away, Freud is still far removed from the idea of an Oedipus complex that, at
least in principle, shows us what the outcome of psychosexual development
ought to be. The first edition of *Three Essays*, together with the Dora case
history, was a culminating point in the development of Freudian thinking.
Things changed soon afterwards. And quite drastically! Dora is Freud's last
case study of a hysterical patient. After 1905 Freud turned his attention to
psychosis and obsessional neurosis. There are many reasons—both internal and external—for this shift. The external reasons concern us less here. I
will simply point out that Freudian psychoanalysis constantly resonates in
many complex ways with the history of psychiatric thought and that, after
1905, hysteria, at least in the Charcotian sense, quickly disappeared from
the psychiatric agenda. Its symptoms were redistributed among other new
categories, such as schizophrenia.[25] More interesting are the internal reasons
for this change in Freud's interest.

The first edition of *Three Essays* left open some important problems
that still needed to be solved. In Freud's early theory, infantile sexuality is
considered to be autoerotic, which, for Freud, means "without an object"
(*Objektlos*).[26] Infantile sexuality is, in this way, reduced to pleasurable bodily
experiences that can be described in purely physiological terms.[27] As a result,

infantile sexuality is also not fantasmatic. For Freud, fantasmatic scenarios essentially imply a relation to an object. According to the early Freud, fantasmatic activity starts only at the beginning of puberty, when sexuality finds its object. In the first edition of *Three Essays*, the sexual drive's discovery of an object at the beginning of puberty is not considered to be a special problem. The sexual drive finds its object by leaning upon (*Anlehnung*)[28] the drives of self-preservation. At the beginning of puberty the sexual drive almost automatically and unproblematically invests in parental figures, which until then took care of the child.[29]

But Freud soon realized that things may be much more complicated. Psychotic experience showed him that the affective ("libidinal") relation to the external world, together with the ego that supports it, can be absent from the beginning or destroyed later on in life, and that such a relation is far from guaranteed. But if this is the case, the question of how sexuality finds an object becomes much more urgent than Freud had previously realized.[30] This question is intrinsically linked to another: How does the subject or the ego—Freud does not distinguish between the two here—find its unity, if the original situation is one of random bodily objects and partial drives? In order to solve these problems—and in complete agreement with a pathoanalytic approach—Freud now turns to the study of psychosis and obsessional neurosis.

I will first concentrate upon psychosis, since it is the pathology in view of which the problem of (the genesis of) the relation between a unified ego and the external world is dramatized to the extreme. Freud's theory of the ego is, at least in some respects, the mirror image of his reflections upon sexuality in 1905. As in the case of sexuality, Freud breaks with a functional understanding of the ego. Just as with sexuality, the ego should not be understood from a functional (and, more specifically, adaptive) point of view. Even if the ego informs us about the reality in which we live and allows our adaptation to it, this is not the perspective according to which Freud wants to understand and conceptualize the ego at this stage of his thinking. Hence, for instance, in "My Views on the Part Played by Sexuality in the Aetiology of Neuroses," Freud introduces the ego exclusively as a defensive instance.[31] Generally, Freud's reflections upon psychosis and, more particularly, his reflections upon narcissism lead to a "deconstruction" of the ego that, in a certain sense, repeats his early deconstruction of sexuality. More concretely, just as sexuality in the early texts is rethought as a conflictual field of opposing forces (in contradistinction to a function with a clear and determined goal), so the ego now appears to be built up by conflicting identifications, so that it can no longer be reduced to an adaptive function.

A detailed analysis of Freud's texts on narcissism, which were published between 1910 and 1915, would lead us too far astray. But a brief examination of a passage in Freud's discussion of the case of Daniel Paul Schreber, in which he introduces narcissism in an extensive way, shows that the analogy above between sexuality and the ego, in the final analysis, has some serious limitations. Freud writes, for instance, "[t]here comes a time in the development of the individual at which he [. . .] begins by taking himself, his own body, as his love-object, and only subsequently proceeds from this [. . .] half-way phase between auto-eroticism and object-love [. . .] to hetero-sexuality."[32] This passage can teach us many things. First, it clearly indicates in what respect the introduction of narcissism is meant to show (infantile) sexuality its way to the object. As a result, infantile sexuality is no longer without an object. Second, this introduction goes along with a developmental perspective that was almost completely absent from the 1905 edition of *Three Essays*. Indeed, in that edition Freud mentions only two "developmental phases"—infantile masturbation and its return when the child is three years old—and he does not attribute much value to either of them. Third, and most importantly, the reference to a structural and invincible bisexuality, which was central to the hysterical disposition, is replaced by an opposition between hetero- and homosexuality in such a way that it is difficult to avoid the conclusion that heterosexuality is the "normal" (normative) outcome of the evolution at hand. The only thing Freud now needs to explain is how the homosexual position gives way to a heterosexual one. This is the role of the Oedipus complex.

The Introduction of the Oedipus Complex

Freud introduces the Oedipus complex for the first time in his study of the Rat Man in 1909. More precisely, Freud articulates in this case study (and in the study of Schreber published in 1911) what he calls the *father complex*, the ambivalent relationship to the father, which is an essential element of what will become, in later years, the Oedipus complex.[33] It is only at this point of his intellectual development that Freud puts the problem of the law—of the father who says "No" to the autoerotic pleasures of the infant—and the opposition between love and hatred that goes along with it, at the center of his thought.[34] Indeed, according to Freud, this dynamic opposition, which is an essential aspect of an "obsessional disposition," plays a crucial role in the pathogenesis of obsessional neurosis in general and in the study of the

Rat Man in particular.[35] What does this mean, and, more importantly, is it as self-evident as Freud himself suggests?

One no doubt remembers the fits of anger that structure the Rat Man's history from his early childhood onwards. Whenever the Rat Man cannot satisfy his libido he falls prey to an extreme anger, which he directs towards the object that causes it: his father who forbids masturbation; the old professor who got the room in the sanatorium next to the room of a nurse whom the Rat Man fancied; and the grandmother of his fiancée after the latter went to visit the former. Freud understands these events in the clinical part of the case study of the Rat Man consistently in terms of *anger*.[36] He writes, for instance, that the outbursts show "a tremendous feeling of rage, which was inaccessible to the patient's consciousness and was directed against some one who had cropped up as an interference with the course of his love."[37] But anger is not hate. Anger is an affect that can occur whenever one feels treated unjustly or when we cannot have something we think we are entitled to. This anger can be abreacted against any object that is at hand. Anger is an acute condition that passes once it has been abreacted. Its object is (like the object of the sexual drive?) completely subordinate to its goal. It can easily be replaced by another. The object has no value in itself. This is not the case with hatred (or, for that matter, love). Hatred is a *passion* that has a permanent object that cannot be replaced easily by another one. Hatred against one person cannot be satisfied by destroying an object or another person, as is the case with anger. But this obvious difference does not prevent Freud, in the theoretical part of his case study on the Rat Man, from requalifying what he first called anger in terms of sadism and hatred. So Freud writes, for instance,

> the sadistic components of love have, from constitutional causes, been exceptionally strongly developed, and have consequently undergone a premature and all too thorough suppression, and [. . .] the neurotic phenomena we have observed arise on the one hand from conscious feelings of affection which have become exaggerated as a reaction, and on the other hand from sadism persisting in the unconscious in the form of hatred.[38]

As a result, the Rat Man's anger against his father, the old professor, and his fiancée's grandmother can now be rethought as expressions of one and the same passion, a permanent hatred. In addition, the objects of this anger are now reinterpreted as replacements of the same object: the Rat Man's father.

The reasons for this confusion between hate and anger should not occupy us here, but it is clear that it has important consequences. As long as Freud considered infantile sexuality as essentially autoerotic, the Oedipus complex, as the formative complex of subjectivity in early childhood, was literally unthinkable. The study of psychosis made Freud give up the idea that infantile sexuality has no object. His (problematic) interpretation of obsessional neurosis taught him, in addition, that the father (and the parental figure in general) plays a crucial and predominant role in the development of the infantile libido towards its objects. From now on, all elements are in place to understand psychopathology (and, for that matter, the construction of subjectivity) as dependent upon the libidinal relations of the little child with its parents—the Oedipus complex.

There is not enough space to articulate all of the consequences of this change in perspective on both metapsychological and clinical levels. Instead, I will limit myself to a general hypothesis: From 1909 onwards, the sexual body as a constitutive field of forces, with an ever-changing strength and intensity, which, in principle, never gives us any rest, progressively becomes inscribed in an Oedipal logic that concretizes the reference to the law (of the father) just mentioned. The partial drives, for instance, are now thought of as phases in a development that—at least ideally—aims at their integration in a heterosexual relation (which is, furthermore, claimed to be based upon the evolutionary history of humankind). The different psychopathologies, including hysteria, are conceived as failed attempts to overcome the Oedipal problematic. It is not always clear whether this failure has a structural or contingent character, but, whatever the case may be, the problematic of the Oedipus complex shows us the ideal (heterosexual) outcome of our psychosexual development. In this way, Freud reintroduces a normative element, which was not present in his theories between 1897 and 1909. Indeed, in these theories there was no intrinsic norm that would allow us, in any way whatsoever, to "judge" the outcome of our psychosexual history. This outcome itself could not be anything but the contingent result of the interaction between our "hysterical" disposition and the contingent encounters through which this disposition takes concrete shape.

Freud against Oedipus

The original 1905 version of Freud's *Three Essays* articulates a nonOedipal psychoanalysis. As such it still has a definite "emancipatory" potential. Freudian psychoanalysis is not Oedipal in its very nature. It is only from 1909 onwards (that is, roughly speaking, starting with the study on the Rat Man and through the introduction of the law of the father and the Oedipus complex) that psychoanalysis tends to become a sophisticated defense of what Freud first called the "popular opinion" about sexuality.[39] It was precisely this popular opinion that psychoanalysis was originally meant to deconstruct. Is there a Freudian escape—that is, an escape that remains not so much within Freudian orthodoxy as within its inspiration—from this impasse?

There is. Freudian psychoanalysis is a pathoanalysis. According to Freud, we can only understand the human being through the study of psychopathology. Indeed, according to Freud, psychopathology shows us in an exaggerated way the fundamental problematics—the hysterical and obsessional dispositions discussed above—that characterize human existence as such. This idea implies, at least in principle, that *different* pathologies illustrate *different* problematics. But Freud does not really remain faithful to this idea. Over and over again, Freud privileges one particular pathology in order to understand human existence in general and human pathology in particular. His turn towards psychosis and obsessional neurosis did not lead to the articulation of a new disposition *next to* the hysterical disposition; instead, it led to the articulation of a new universal "key" to understanding human nature as such. The fundamental elements of the hysterical disposition were redefined and neutralized in the process; the partial drives and erogenous zones were reintegrated into a developmental scheme and the bisexuality that was crucial to understanding hysteria reappeared in the positive and negative versions of the Oedipus complex that was itself supposed to install a heterosexual relationship. As a result, hysteria itself progressively became understood according to an Oedipal—that is, obsessional—paradigm. If Freud had stuck to his original pathoanalytic credo, he would have realized that the problematic that is at the basis of obsessional neurosis—important as it may be—is only one among others and that it only plays a predominant role in one particular pathology. At best, it is this pathology and this pathology alone—obsessional neurosis—that can be understood upon the basis of our relation to the law (and, hence, at least according to Freud) in Oedipal terms.

If Freud had respected his own pathoanalytic inspiration more systematically, the Oedipus complex would never have become the shibboleth of psychoanalysis. Obviously, my pathoanalytic rereading of Freud does not solve all of the problems regarding the status of the Oedipus complex in Freudian metapsychology. For one thing, it is far from clear why the law has to be the law of the father. This identification of the law with the father seems to be the result of another "original sin" that consists in situating (a particular type of) the family "before" culture.[40] Here, too, Freud might have thought differently if he had taken seriously the lessons from hysteria, instead of covering them up with the Oedipus complex. Freud's early theories of sexuality do not imply that, *in sexualibus*, "anything goes." Quite the contrary, his understanding of the reaction formations (shame, disgust, guilt) explains why the experience of sexuality is never without inherent limitations and why it is essentially conflictual. Does this not also imply that sexuality is inevitably subject to a historical and contingent law? Indeed, Freud says that experiences of shame, guilt, disgust, and so on not only belong to the very nature of sexuality but also that the content of these experiences—what it is exactly we consider to be disgusting or shameful—depends to a high degree upon the social and cultural prohibitions that structure our lives.[41] This implies that every culture is confronted with the inevitable task of providing concrete content to these experiences. But nowhere does Freud state that this culture is essentially patriarchal, as the theory of the law of the father and the Oedipus complex teach us. What exactly will be forbidden and the status of the law that forbids both depend upon ever-changing cultural circumstances. It seems that Freud's texts are less Oedipal than is generally believed, even containing the necessary elements for thinking a nonOedipal psychoanalysis. Freud against Oedipus? Yes, indeed.

The text printed here was originally delivered as a talk on April 25, 2014, at a symposium at the University at Buffalo (SUNY), organized by the Center for the Study of Psychoanalysis and Culture, entitled "What Is Sex?" A modified version was subsequently published in *Radical Philosophy* 188 (2014): 39–46.

Notes

1. Freud writes "I no longer believe in my *neurotica* (theory of the neuroses)" (*Ich glaube an meine Neurotica nicht mehr*) and not "I no longer believe my neurotic patients" (*Ich glaube meine neurotische Patienten nicht mehr*). Sigmund Freud, "Extracts from the Fliess Papers," in *The Standard Edition of the Complete Psychological Works of Sigmund Freud* (hereafter *SE*), ed. and trans. James Strachey et al. (London: Hogarth Press, 1953–1974), 1:259. Since *neurotica* is a Latin ablative, it is clear that Freud is referring here—as Strachey rightly points out in the *Standard Edition*—to his seduction theory of neurosis and not to the stories his patients told him (as one finds in recent French translations). So what Freud no longer believes in 1897 is that psychopathology is inevitably *caused* by traumatic (sexual) events. This

does not come as a surprise when we realize that hardly any of Freud's patients spontaneously came up with stories about sexual traumas. Freud always had to go—quite insistently—in search of these traumas. Freud did so because he was convinced—for *theoretical* reasons—that he would find them if only he looked for them. For more on this problematic, see Tomas Geyskens, *Our Original Scenes: Freud's Theory of Sexuality* (Leuven: Leuven University Press, 2005); and Allen Esterson, "The Mythologizing of Psychoanalytic History: Deception and Self-Deception in Freud's Accounts of the Seduction Theory Episode," *History of Psychiatry* 12 (2001): 329–52.

2. Ernst Kris, "Einleitung zur Ertausgabe," in *Briefe an Wilhelm Flieβ*, by Sigmund Freud (Frankfurt am Main: Fischer, 1985), 545; my translation.

3. Jeffrey Masson argues that Freud obscured real assaults of children by adults when he abandoned the seduction theory. See Masson, *The Assault on Truth: Freud's Suppression of the Seduction Theory* (New York: HarperCollins, 1992).

4. Ibid., 112–13.

5. The notion of a "pathoanalysis"—or what amounts to a clinical anthropology that seeks to understand human existence in terms of its psychopathological variations—is derived from the work of Jacques Schotte. See, for example, Schotte, *Szondi avec Freud: Sur la voie d'une psychiatrie pulsionelle* (Brussels: Editions De Boeck-Université, 1990); and Philippe Van Haute and Geyskens, *A Non-Oedipal Psychoanalysis? A Clinical Anthropology of Hysteria in the Works of Freud and Lacan*, trans. Joey Kok (Leuven: Leuven University Press, 2012).—Eds.

6. But the same is true for the texts of this period that were published posthumously. One thinks here of *Briefe an Wilhelm Flieβ*. See Freud, *The Complete Letters of Sigmund Freud to Wilhelm Fliess, 1887–1904*, ed. and trans. Jeffrey Moussaieff Masson (Cambridge: Harvard University Press, 1985).

7. Not only do the last editions of Freud's texts appear in *Gesamtausgabe* and the *Standard Edition* but also these last editions appear in the volume that should contain the original edition. Hence, for example, we find the last edition of *Three Essays*, which is almost twice as long as the original and which was published in 1924, in the volume that contains Freud's texts from 1905, the date of publication of the original version of this text.

8. See Freud, *Fragment of an Analysis of a Case of Hysteria*, in *SE* 7:24.

9. Ibid., 64.

10. Ibid., 69.

11. Ibid., 56.

12. Ibid.

13. Ibid., 72.

14. Ibid., 73–74.

15. Ibid., 86.

16. Ibid., 58.

17. I cannot comment here upon the references to the Oedipal myth in *The Interpretation of Dreams*, except to say that it is clear that even if the Oedipal theme is considered to have a universal character in this book it is by no means thought to be the universal key for understanding pathology and accessing culture. See Miriam Leonard, "Freud and Tragedy: Oedipus and the Gender of the Universal," *Classical Receptions Journal* 5, no. 1 (2013): 63–83.

18. See Freud to Wilhelm Fliess, September 21, 1897, in *The Complete Letters of Sigmund Freud to Wilhelm Fliess, 1887–1904*, 264–65.

19. Ibid., 265.

20. Freud, "My Views on the Part Played by Sexuality in the Aetiology of the Neuroses," in *SE* 7:275–76.

21. See Freud, *Three Essays on the Theory of Sexuality*, in *SE* 7:165.

22. See Arnold Davidson, *The Emergence of Sexuality: Historical Epistemology and the Formation of Concepts* (Cambridge: Harvard University Press, 2001).

23. See Freud, "My Views on the Part Played by Sexuality in the Aetiology of the Neuroses," in *SE* 7:269–79.

24. See Paul Moyaert, "Seksualiteit is niet te integreren: Hoe Freud over de 'conditio humana' nadenkt," in *Freud als Filosoof: Over seksualiteit, psychopathologie en cultuur*, ed. Philippe Van Haute and Jens De Vleminck (Kalmthout: Pelckmans, 2013), 67–89.

25. See Mark S. Micale, "On the 'Disappearance' of Hysteria: A Study in the Clinical Deconstruction of a Diagnosis," *Isis* 84, no. 3 (1993): 496–526.

26. Freud, *Analysis of a Phobia in a Five-Year-Old Boy*, in *SE* 10:25.

27. It is true that Freud also writes in 1905 that the breast is the initial object of infantile sexuality. However, it is clear from the context that infantile sexuality is not directed towards this object as such. The object only plays a role insofar as it is instrumental for bodily pleasure. The image that best expresses infantile sexuality—Freud leaves no doubt about this—is of lips kissing each other. For a more detailed explanation of this problem, see Van Haute and Geyskens, *Confusion of Tongues: The Primacy of Sexuality in Freud, Ferenczi, and Laplanche* (New York: Other Press, 2004).

28. See, for example, Freud, *Three Essays on the Theory of Sexuality*, in *SE* 7:182.

29. This also explains why, in the first edition of *Three Essays*, Oedipal themes— which, I repeat, are not the same as an Oedipus complex—belong to puberty and not to childhood, as will be the case once Freud introduces the Oedipus complex.

30. We would have to explain here why Freud considers the relation to reality that is lost in psychosis "libidinal" (and, hence, sexual). We know that in psychosis the relation of self-preservation can continue to exist while, at the same time, the affective ("meaningful") relation to the external world is destroyed. But the logic of Freud's dualistic drive theory forces him to consider every relation to reality or

towards the other (or loss thereof) that cannot be reduced to self-preservation to be sexual in its very nature. This is, of course, far from self-evident. Suffice it to say here that Freud does not have a convincing theory of attachment. For more on this point, see Van Haute and Geyskens, *From Death Instinct to Attachment Theory: The Primacy of the Child in Freud, Klein, and Hermann* (New York: Other Press, 2007).

31. Indeed, it is difficult to conceptualize repression, for example, without an ego.

32. Freud, "Psycho-Analytic Notes on an Autobiographical Account of a Case of Paranoia (Dementia Paranoides)," in *SE* 12:60–61.

33. The Oedipus complex will receive its most complete formulation in Freud, *The Ego and the Id*, in *SE* 19:1–66.

34. The reason for this shift is, in a certain sense, straightforward. This problematic characterizes obsessional neurosis, which, together with psychosis—and at the expense of hysteria—is at the center of Freud's reflections between 1908 and 1915.

35. We leave out a discussion of the exact status of aggressivity (whether or not it is of a sexual nature), which plays a crucial role in Freud's texts we are discussing here. On this question, see Jens De Vleminck, *De schaduw van Kaïn: Freuds klinische antropologie van de agressiviteit* (Leuven: Universitaire Pers, 2013).

36. Freud, "Notes upon a Case of Obsessional Neurosis," in *SE* 10:182.

37. Ibid., 189.

38. Ibid., 240.

39. See Freud, *Three Essays on the Theory of Sexuality*, in *SE* 7:135.

40. See Freud, *Totem and Taboo*, in *SE* 13:1–162.

41. See Freud, *Three Essays on the Theory of Sexuality*, in *SE* 7:151.

CHAPTER 14

Plastic Sex? The Beauty of It!

Patricia Gherovici

What is sex? What is not sex? I am a psychoanalyst. I belong to a profession that is supposed to consider *everything* sexual. All right, maybe I exaggerate. But, "[i]n psycho-analysis," as Theodor Adorno quips, "nothing is true except the exaggerations."[1]

It is well known that Sigmund Freud's first patients presented symptoms that he later revealed to be sexual in origin. Freud's *Studies on Hysteria* could have been called *Essays on Sexuality*. But do we still think psychoanalytic symptoms are *sexual*?

We may, as some people have argued, be entering a postsexual era. In a "society of the spectacle,"[2] the body has become a commodity and sex has lost its intimacy; sex is no longer private and taboo, as it was in Freud's time. In our day of Internet connectivity, Tinder, OkCupid, and the myriad of other mobile dating apps, a sexual mate can be found with the swipe of a finger. Hookups are casual and instantaneous. Dating and courting are relics of a bygone era. In our day of "selfies," filters, and Photoshop, we are rapidly becoming serialized versions of copies of a copy of a lost original. Or at least our ideals are.

Our celebrities are look-alikes. The women on our magazine covers look like lanky pubescent boys with oversized breasts. The man on the cover of *GQ* is a clone of a clone, so made up that he comes across as feminine. The taboo of Freud's time may have been airbrushed to the curb, but has sexual difference disappeared as well?

For the beautiful hysterics of yesteryear—the Lucys, Elisabeths, and Annas of the late nineteenth and early twentieth centuries[3]—sex was a repressed destiny. Hysterical symptoms and crises were often described as pantomimes of scenes of sexual pleasure. The paralyses did not follow the anatomy of nerves and muscles but the imaginary mapping of an erotogenic body. As Charcot observed and reluctantly confessed to Freud, "it's always a question of the genitals—always, always, always" (*c'est toujours la chose génitale, toujours . . . toujours . . . toujours*).[4] However, Charcot did not act upon this insight; instead, he left it to Freud to pursue the clinical promise of this great discovery.

For Charcot, the neurologist, the thing (*la chose*) was always the genitals, not the brain, and it had the overwhelming determination of an "always, always, always." By contrast, for Freud, the psychoanalyst, sex may have been *always* but it was also *everywhere*—the brain, or any other body part, for that matter, could behave like the genitals. As Freud writes, "I have been led to ascribe the quality of erotogenicity to all parts of the body and to all the internal organs."[5] If, in 1905, genital and sexual pleasure were synonymous, as Tim Dean has noted, by 1915, genitality, for Freud, was a subset of sexuality; the genital was always sexual, although sexuality was not always genital. This is how Freud queered sexuality: He distinguished it from genitality and thereby separated it from gender and reproduction.[6]

What people found most irritating about Freud's early sexual theories was not what he claimed about infantile sexuality but the nonessentialism of his definition of sexuality. Freud's later notion of the drive (*Trieb*) was also not gender-specific. And this was the true scandal; these were ideas that clashed with a Victorian sensibility. Thereafter, the post-Freudians repressed the scandal.

During this same period, leading sexologists and pioneer activists, like Magnus Hirschfeld, sparked controversy with their discoveries. They worked closely with Freud upon what seemed to promise a fruitful collaboration between sexology and psychoanalysis. Hirschfeld's classic book of 1910, *Die Transvestiten: Eine Untersuchung über den erotischen Verkleidungstrieb*, was perhaps so ahead of its time that it was not translated into English until eight decades later in 1991. It was published under the title *Transvestites: The Erotic Drive to Cross-Dress*.[7]

Note the word *drive*; it belongs to a psychoanalytic nomenclature. The choice of this word, even if it is used here in a different sense, reveals an engagement with psychoanalysis. In fact, Hirschfeld made the publication of a number of psychoanalytic texts possible. Freud's own article "Hysterical Phantasies and Their Relation to Bisexuality" appeared in the very first issue of Hirschfeld's new journal *Zeitschrift für Sexualwissenschaft* (Journal of Sexology), which was exclusively devoted to the science of sexology.[8] Subsequent issues published original work by Alfred Adler, Karl Abraham, and Wilhelm

Stekel.[9] However, Hirschfeld's contribution to psychoanalysis was not limited to his activity as a publisher. As a founding member of the second-ever psychoanalytic society, he played a key role in the creation of the international psychoanalytic movement. In August 1908, Hirschfeld cofounded, with Karl Abraham, the Berlin Psychoanalytic Society.[10] The society was started by six members, three of whom were sexologists, including the two other founders of modern sexology, Albert Moll and Iwan Bloch.[11]

The strong presence of sexologists within the burgeoning psychoanalytic movement was not a coincidence. Freud believed in the benefits of an alliance between the two emerging disciplines. He wrote to Jung about Hirschfeld, expressing how happy he was that such a prominent sexologist was joining the psychoanalytic movement: "He is moving close to us," he told Jung, "and from now on will take our ideas into account as much as possible."[12] Freud was resolute about the advantages of the collaboration between sexology and psychoanalysis, and he urged Abraham to support Hirschfeld and disregard the existing social prejudice against the political advocacy of homosexual rights.[13]

At the third international Weimar congress of psychoanalysts, which convened in 1911, Freud greeted Hirschfeld as an honored guest and a Berlin authority on homosexuality.[14] Nevertheless, despite such recognition, and Abraham's efforts of persuasion, Hirschfeld left the Berlin Psychoanalytic Society shortly after the Weimar meeting.[15]

Hirschfeld's departure had been precipitated by "an external cause," which Abraham described as "a question of resistances."[16] It seems that Jung had objected to Hirschfeld's homosexuality.[17] Unlike Jung, however, Freud did not mind Hirschfeld's political activism or openness about his sexual orientation; in fact, Freud saw Hirschfeld's advocacy of homosexual rights as a positive development. From the beginning, Freud encouraged Abraham to work with Hirschfeld.[18] After losing Hirschfeld, the Berlin Psychoanalytic Society decided, at Abraham's instigation, to work collectively upon Freud's *Three Essays on the Theory of Sexuality*. The irony here is that *Three Essays* owes a lot to Hirschfeld's research (on the first page Freud credits the "well-known writings" of Hirschfeld, along with eight other authors on sexology, ranging from Krafft-Ebing to Havelock Ellis, each of whom published in *Jahrbuch für sexuelle Zwischenstufen* [Yearbook for Sexual Intermediary Stages], the journal under Hirschfeld's direction).[19]

Hirschfeld's empirical data revealed that transvestites include both men and women who were homo-, bi-, or, contrary to popular belief, heterosexual. He observed that some transvestites were asexual (or, to use his term, "automonosexual"); this eventually led to the 1950s classification "transsexual." Hirschfeld broke new ground when he proposed that trans-vestism was a sexual variation distinct from fetishism and homosexuality.

Let us note, however, that, as a clinician and researcher, Hirschfeld never wavered in his belief in a biological (endocrinological) basis for sexuality. Thus, he was not opposed to Eugen Steinach's experimental testicular trans-plants to "treat" male homosexuality.

Despite the conflict, Hirschfeld continued working with psychoanalysts. In 1919, when he opened his legendary *Institut für Sexualwissenschaft* (Insti-tute for Sexology), he did so with his close collaborator Arthur Kronfeld (who later became a psychoanalyst to Harry Benjamin, the endocrinologist, sexologist, and "father" of the clinical treatment of transsexualism in the United States). Hirschfeld's story bears unmistakable witness to the ambiv-alence and tensions between psychoanalysis, psychology, psychiatry, and sexology. Benjamin, for example, established the protocol for the treatment of transsexualism, which gives the mental health professional the power to determine potential candidates for surgery. The mental health professional, and not the sexologist, according to this protocol, has the final word on the course of treatment.

Let us move beyond Hirschfeld. In matters of sex, not much has changed since Freud. His major revelation that the unconscious is sexual at root is confirmed in our current practice. The chief complaint one hears is that something is wrong with sex. Sex happens too early or too late; it happens too much or not enough. The permutations of this underlying complaint are numerous. "All they talk about is bad fucking."[20] Without much innu-endo, this is how Jacques Lacan crudely encapsulates what people talk about when lying upon the couch. Analysands continually suffer because sex never seems to go as expected. The couch appears to guarantee "satisfaction or your money back." But that damned sex thing.

"Sex will never be simple or nice in the ways we might like it to be," as Alain de Botton puts it succinctly in his neat self-help book *How to Think More about Sex*: "[Sex] is not fundamentally democratic or kind; it is bound up with cruelty, transgression and the desire for subjugation and humiliation. It refuses to sit neatly on top of love, as it should."[21] How can psychoanalysts talk about *normal* sexuality when the presumption is that "normal" is syn-onymous with "heterosexual"? Only a century ago, Freud observed that the mutual interest of men and women is "a problem that needs elucidating and is not a self-evident fact."[22] As I have proposed elsewhere, psychoanalysts have a sex problem and, indeed, psychoanalysis is overdue for a "sex change."[23]

Dean and Christopher Lane have noted that one of the paradoxes in the history of psychoanalysis is that its institutions have, in the course of their development, normalized moralistic and discriminatory practices antithetical to psychoanalytic concepts.[24] This is sad because psychoanalysis could make a valuable contribution to the field. To truly listen to the unconscious is to deal with sex, sexual identity, and sexuality. Analytic work entangles us in the complex relationship between the body and the psyche; it teases out the precariousness of gender, the instability of the opposition between male and female, and the fragility of the construction of sexual identity. This work calls attention to the uncertainties of sexuality, the challenges of making a sexual choice, and the difficulties of assuming a sexual position. Ultimately, this work throws us into a confrontation with the conundrum of sexual difference. Each of these pivotal issues, which analysts deal with on an everyday basis, could have important implications for gender theorists, activists, and transgender individuals. When confronted they have the potential to enrich current debates about gender and sexuality.

Sex Driven

Freud's concept of the drive exiles the subject from the certainties a sexual instinct would otherwise grant. The drive is a force without a predetermined goal, save for its own satisfaction. It is nonadaptive, incomprehensible within a simple tension-discharge model, and incompatible with the goal of harmony or equilibrium. This is why Freud presents the attraction between the sexes as a problem to be elucidated rather than a conclusion to be accepted.

Freud's provisional answer to the problem of the attraction between the sexes is the Oedipus complex. Lacan rephrases Freud's answer and proposes that anatomical sexual differences pass through the sieve of language and are ultimately reduced to having or not having the phallus. Both sexes must assume castration; that is, they must renounce the fantasy of being the mother's phallus. For the boy, the transaction is simple: He barters the mother for the promise of exogamy in order to save his phallus. For the girl, the transaction is less seamless: Why would she love men and not her mother? Freud is left with an unanswered question: "What does woman want?"[25] The construction of the Oedipus complex may explain masculine sexuality, but it does not account for feminine sexuality.

There is no signifier of sexual difference in the unconscious. Only the phallus, which does not have a feminine equivalent, signifies sexual difference. Thus, there is a fundamental asymmetry; we have only the phallus to define two sexual positions. As such, we fail to account for the opposition between masculine and feminine. The unconscious seems unable to recognize this elaborate system of difference we call gender.

Lacan pushed Freud's conception of human sexuality further when he put forward the notion of *sexuation*.[26] Whereas Freud's conception held that sexuality is a process by which each person makes a choice and adopts a sexual orientation, regardless of anatomical differences, psychical consequences, or social conventions, Lacan's conception of sexuation accounts for the unconscious sexual choice this process entails. For Lacan, the anatomical contours of our bodies do not constrain this unconscious sexual choice. The rules, roles, and restrictions a particular society inscribe for each gender may determine this choice. But they also may not. One ultimately assumes his or her orientation by dealing with sexual difference, which is determined neither by sex (anatomy) nor by gender (social construction). One's choice, then, is ultimately subjective and unconscious.

Lacan's model of sexuation, which he proposed in 1972, marked an important step forward in the debate about sexual difference. It established a division based upon two forms of being—masculine and feminine—which corresponded to two forms of jouissance, phallic and Other. Lacan located phallic jouissance upon the male side and gave it the force of necessity (all men), which relies upon the exclusion of one man, the primal father, who is incapable of jouissance. According to this model of sexual division, there are two positions: the phallic One ("man"), limited by the father exempt from castration (the exception to the phallic rule that provides its support), and the "not all" ("woman"), able to access unlimited jouissance, free from phallic constraints. Lacan's model established sexual difference as the opposition of two logics: phallic, for men, and not-all phallic, for women. Furthermore, it established two modalities of jouissance: phallic and supplementary.

It is well known that Freud's contemporaries accused him of placing too much emphasis upon sex. If his contemporaries wanted the pendulum to swing back the other way, toward less sex, well, swung it has. Today, psychosexuality tends to be thought of as concealing nonsexual objects and self-related conflicts. This is the case to the chagrin of psychoanalyst Peter Fonagy, who longs for the Freudian days when sex was central to the understanding of symptoms. In 2006, Fonagy urged his colleagues to restore sex to psychoanalysis.[27]

Object relations, self-psychology, and intersubjective relational approaches focus upon affective developmental object-attachments, not sexuality. Noting the reduced presence of sexuality in psychoanalytic publications, Fonagy offered as explanation a widening gap—Freud's drive theory is anathema to a developmental theory. Domesticated, psychosexuality is reduced to early developmental libidinal stages because drive theory is incompatible with an object-relations theory based upon mother-infant interaction. Today, subscribers to attachment theory and relational psychoanalysis consider psychosexuality a behavioral system concealing nonsexual objects and self-related conflicts. Sexual material is reduced to an underlying, "primitive," and relationship-based pathology. This shift has desexualized sex. Relational theorist Stephen A. Mitchell, for example, views sex as an expression of a wish to establish contact and intimacy.[28] For Mitchell, sex is a manifestation of sociability. Such a sanitized notion of sex is a far cry from the experience of radical dissolution. And such a sanitized notion of sex does not sit well with Fonagy, who concludes that sex has left psychoanalysis (or have psychoanalysts left sex?) because psychoanalysis has not been able to provide a persuasive model of psychosexuality.[29]

Etymologically, *sex* means division (from the Latin *sexus* and *secāre*, "to divide"). It is ironic that analysts should feel tarred by the accusation of pansexualism because the unconscious sex does not know sex. If sex represents division, Freud discovered that the unconscious knows only one side of the divide. The unconscious is thus homosexual—that is, same-sexual—since the phallus does not have a corresponding female signifier. How does a sexed subject come into being? Precariously. Most people express concern about how well they conform to the standards of their sex. Many of my patients who identify as female wonder about their femininity by asking themselves "Am I straight or bisexual?" Then there is the patient who identifies as transsexual. This patient speaks of an "error"; despite her anatomy, she belongs to the other sex. Such patients are right to talk about an error—the error of taking an organ to be a signifier of sexual difference.

The Plasticity of Gender

In my clinical practice, many of my trans patients wonder aloud "Am I a man or a woman?"—the classic hysterical question about sexual identity. "I am a man trapped in a woman's body," one patient may claim, or "Despite my male organs, I always knew I was a woman." Some patients may identify as trans; some may take hormones; some may have had surgery; and some may have changed sex. But all are preoccupied with their gender presentation. They mean to assert or diffuse it, or to catch the puzzled gaze of a bystander. As Freud remarks, the first thing one wonders when meeting someone in the street is "male or female?"[30] Most of the time, we make this distinction instantaneously and without any information about the person's genital configuration. Every day we attribute a gender to the people around us based upon differences in clothing, manners, behavior, and style, not genitals.

One's face plays perhaps the most important role as a body-marker of gender. To reiterate, in most social interactions, we see each other's faces, not genitals. Emmanuel Levinas suggests as much when he defines ethics as the rapport of two faces.[31] Such a phenomenological approach sees the face as a structure. What distinguishes transsexuals, though, is that the almost infinite distance between the face and the Other can be crossed within a single person.

When one changes sex, one—by definition—embodies a gender different from the one with which one was born. Such a transformation implies that the materiality of the body is not immediately given. Therefore, both hysterics (by questioning their gender) and transgender people (by answering it) demonstrate the disjunction between the subjective sense of one's sexual body and its material reality. Yet, for hysterics and transgender people alike, it is indeed sexual difference that appears as a conundrum. Technology and market rules play a crucial role in any sexual transformation. After all, contemporary transsexual transformations depend upon a surgeon and an endocrinologist.[32] This type of medicalized transformation reduces the subject to a body, a malleable, natural entity, and its plasticity extends to sexuality.

We now live in a world in which love, sex, gender, and appearance are commodities. We find ourselves in a time when the free market promises relief from the burden of old-fashioned hang-ups. This is the illusion I intend to expose when I argue that transgenderism has been "democratized."[33] In a free market, one should be free to choose one's preferred commodity, this illusion supposes. What could be more democratic than giving everyone the choice of changing one's gender upon demand?

But only if we are dealing with a plastic organism and not a body, as Charles Shepherdson has noted, does medical science offer the possibility of transformation.[34] In many cases, the idea of gender as a malleable construct glosses over an escape from the conundrum of sexual division. Both the medical community, providing corrective treatment, and the transsexual, demanding a sex change, forego such an escape. "[T]he transsexual phenomenon," as Colette Chiland claims, "is surely a product of our technology-based, individualistic culture, a token of its contradictions."[35] In other words, transsexualism has been made trivial. In the United States, to undergo a sex change is akin to becoming a vegetarian or moving to a suburban community—it is yet another consumer lifestyle choice. For Jennifer Finney Boylan, however, this is exactly what the transsexual experience is not:

What it's emphatically *not* is a "lifestyle," any more than being male or female is a lifestyle. When I imagine a person with a *lifestyle*, I see a millionaire playboy named Chip who likes to race yachts to Bimini, or an accountant, perhaps, who dresses up in a suit of armor on the weekends.

Being transgender isn't like that. Gender is many things, but one thing it is surely not is a *hobby*. Being female is not something you do because it's clever or postmodern, or because you're a deluded, deranged narcissist.[36]

In my clinical experience, I have encountered people whose entire being is consumed by this central question. "But your sample size is hardly representative," one might say: "Your analysands, if not pathological, are at least experiencing some significant distress, enough for them to seek professional help." This concern is valid. But research supports my clinical experience. In a survey, Jay Prosser finds that, across the transgender community, transitioning is not a minor pursuit but a major endeavor that takes over subjects' lives: "As the insider joke goes, transitioning is what transsexuals do (our occupation, as consuming as a career)."[37]

One of my patients, a trans man, told me recently, "Transitioning is complicated. It is the most amazing and horrific experience one can go through." He then added, "This chance of being who you are, of having your body match how you feel, is amazing but can also be horrifying. You do not really know what is going to happen." He paused, smiled, and, nodding in astonishment, continued, "When I started my transition 10 years ago, I did not know what was going to happen. It was a harrowing experience. Now it may be more common. There are kids who start transitioning at age 17, 18. I am 35. I do not know what it would have been if I had transitioned earlier, at age 18 or 20."

I noticed a look of surprise in his face:

But I have to tell you, I have friends of friends who identify as women, who transitioned at 18, took T, had mastectomies, and now they are feminine, oh, very feminine, they say: "I had to become a man to know I wasn't one." My process was so intense, so internal, so agonizing. I did not know how to think about it. I thought I was going mad, I felt sick, alone, isolated. It was a big deal. It was the transformation of the whole of adolescence in just a couple of months.

I have heard this kind of narrative a lot in my experience. It is a rather common account in our practice, even if it seems exceptional to the public.

Remember when, in 2014, Angelina Jolie candidly disclosed that she carried a rare genetic mutation that predisposed her to reproductive cancers? The public was shocked. Facing the prospect of staring down cancer, haunted by the fear of death, she decided to have a preventive double mastectomy. Jolie made the choice to amputate healthy body parts, with the hope that she would steer clear of her genetic destiny. She took control of her body. Jolie underwent surgery to reconstruct her breasts with implants. Soon she will lack hormone-producing ovaries. Will she not be the same as many transsexual women? Is Jolie's sexual identity really the sum of her body parts? Are any of our sexual identities really the sum of our body parts?

Sexual identity cannot be determined by quantities of hormones or the artful work of a surgeon with a scalpel. There is a lesson to be learned from Jolie's story—sexual identity transcends anatomy and remains a mystery.

Can we understand Jolie's transformation—her mastectomy and subsequent reconstructive surgery—and that of my analysand in the same context? Are both transformations *plastic*?

Plastic sexuality is a concept the sociologist Anthony Giddens developed in 1992 in order to account for the malleability of erotic expression in both individual choice and social norms. Fixed sexuality, by contrast, stands in opposition to the binaries of hetero- and homosexual, marital (legitimate) and extramarital (illegitimate), committed and promiscuous, and "normal" (coital) and "perverse" (anal, autoerotic, sadomasochistic). For Giddens, effective contraception, in tandem with the social and economic independence women have achieved, "liberates" men from the constraints of traditional gender expectations. Plastic sexuality, according to Giddens, is a result of this shift: "Plastic sexuality is decentred sexuality, freed from the needs of reproduction. It has its origins in the tendency, initiated somewhere in the late eighteenth century, strictly to limit family size; but it becomes further developed later as the result of the spread of modern contraception and new reproductive technologies. Plastic sexuality [. . .] frees sexuality from the rule of the phallus."[38] Thus, Giddens claims that plastic sexuality represents a shift in value. Sex is no longer a means to an end; it involves more than reproduction, kinship, and generational continuity. Nor is sex still bound up with death—today, women rarely die during childbirth.

Some Brazilian women, in fact, set out to erase any trace of childbirth and lactation altogether. Alexander Edmonds has observed the cultural prevalence of plastic surgery in Brazil, where, across social classes, in glitzy clinics and free public hospitals, Brazilians are lining up to get surgery, or *plástica*, as it is called there.[39] Brazilian women want a body that looks young and toned, not a body that looks worn of sexual reproduction. Fundamentally, perhaps, these women want to deny their own mortality—"I know very well that I am mortal, but nevertheless. . . ."[40]

AIDS, however, has reintroduced the connection between sex and death, as Giddens has noted.[41] Indeed, AIDS forces us to rethink sexuality because, as Dean has shown, it can lead to an exchange of life for sex—a dramatic, literal relationship between the two thereby emerges.[42] This relationship is a complex one. Here, I will focus upon the "return" of the death drive because I see the drive as a limit to the promise of plasticity. One may recall in this context Judith Butler's conception of gender as performative, a promise of endless plasticity.[43] Is the transsexual not the most radical example of the "plastic" drive, or, as G. W. F. Hegel may have suggested, the desire to work against nature?

Beautiful Darlings

Gender transformation often aims to achieve a beautiful, stable form. The wonderfully tender and intimate documentary *Beautiful Darling: The Life and Times of Candy Darling, Andy Warhol Superstar* explores this aim. The 2010 feature-length film focuses upon the life of Candy Darling, the moving transgender muse, who appeared in several of Andy Warhol's films and inspired a number of Lou Reed's songs. The documentary includes a clip from another documentary, *Warhol*, in which the artist explains the difference between "drag queens" and his stars. Drag queens, Warhol says, "just dress up for eight hours a day. The people we use really think they are girls and stuff, and that's really different." Warhol may have even suggested to Candy that she have a sex change operation. But Candy demurred: "I'm not a genuine woman [. . .], but I'm not interested in genuineness. I'm interested in being the product of a woman." Thus, she dosed herself with the same female hormones that very likely caused her death from lymphoma in 1974. She was twenty-nine years old. Candy was not preoccupied with her genitalia; she had a beautiful face—it was "eye candy" or, rather, "I, Candy." Her face was extraordinary; it was spellbinding, pale, and luminous, always impeccably made-up. Candy had the face Roland Barthes sees when he looks at Greta Garbo—a face "descended from a heaven where all things are formed and perfected in the clearest light."[44] To Barthes, Garbo's beauty "represented a kind of absolute state of the flesh, which could be neither reached nor renounced."[45]

Candy was supremely beautiful. Her majestic face, though, did not allow her to reconcile the limits imposed upon her by her corporeal, sexual being.

"I feel like I'm living in a prison," Candy wrote. She noted how she could not do certain things—swim, visit relatives, get a job, or have a boyfriend. Her sex life remains a matter of speculation. As she lay dying upon her hospital bed, Candy posed for Peter Hujar, who snapped a black and white portrait, later entitled *Candy Darling on her Deathbed*. Death was not far from the lens; Candy died soon after the picture was taken.

She left a note:

To whom it may concern

By the time you read this I will be gone. Unfortunately before my death I had no desire left for life. Even with all my friends and my career on the upswing I felt too empty to go on in this unreal existence. I am just so bored by everything. You might say bored to death. It may sound ridiculous but is true. I have arranged my own funeral arrangements with a guest list and it is paid for. [. . .] Goodbye for Now

Love Always

Candy Darling[46]

"Peter Hujar knows that portraits in life are always, also, portraits in death," Susan Sontag writes of this last image.[47] Photography "converts the whole world into a cemetery," Sontag writes in her introduction to *Portraits in Life and Death*, the single book Hujar published during his life.[48]

The tension between beauty and death is what I would like to underline here. More specifically, I would like to explore beauty as a denial of death and a limit to the promise of plasticity and endless permutation. In the early 1900s, Bakelite, the first fully synthetic thermoset, was created; in 1933, polyethylene was discovered; in 1939, at the World's Fair in New York City, the DuPont Corporation introduced nylon, the first purely synthetic fiber; and, in the 1940s and 1950s, mass production of plastics began. Significantly, as Joanne Meyerowitz has explained, the 1950s marked the beginning of the mediatic popularization of transsexualism.[49]

A press frenzy erupted in 1952 after Christine Jorgensen underwent sex reassignment surgery in Denmark; *sex change* became a household term: "[T]he press discovered Christine Jorgensen and inaugurated an era of comprehensive, even obsessive, coverage. In the history of sex change in the United States, the reporting on Jorgensen was both a culminating episode and a starting point."[50] In the United States, Jorgensen's tremendous public presence was emblematic of a growing cultural preoccupation with the intertwining domains of science and sexuality. It was as if, all of a sudden, Jorgensen herself embodied the crucial question "What is a man and what is a woman?"

The 1960s brought the contraceptive pill and a sexual revolution. The word *plastic* has roots in both Greek and German. It derives from the Greek πλαστικός (*plastikos*), which means "capable of being shaped or molded"; *plastikos* derives from πλαστός (*plastos*), which means "molded," in reference to the malleability of forms, allowing them to be cast, pressed, or extruded into a variety of shapes. And *plastic* derives from the German *Plastik*, meaning "classical sculpture," the intention to present beautiful forms or a harmonious arrangement of visual stimuli.

In her groundbreaking meditation *The Future of Hegel*, Catherine Malabou pivots from Hegel's discussion of Greek art and sculpture in *Aesthetics* as "the plastic art par excellence":[51]

> This sense for the perfect plasticity of gods and men was pre-eminently at home in Greece. In its poets and orators, historians and philosophers, Greece is not to be understood at its heart unless we bring with us as a key to our comprehension an insight into the ideals of sculpture and unless we consider from the point of view of their plasticity not only the heroic figures in epic and drama but also the actual statesmen and philosophers. After all, in the beautiful days of Greece, men of action, like poets and thinkers, had this same plastic and universal yet individual character both inwardly and outwardly.[52]

Malabou understands "philosophical plasticity" as a philosophical attitude, the behavior of the philosopher; to her, "philosophical plasticity" applies to philosophy, to the rhythm with which the speculative content is unfolded and presented.

In the preface to the 1831 edition of *The Science of Logic*, Hegel states,

> [a] plastic discourse demands, too, a plastic sense of receptivity and understanding on the part of the listener; but youths and men of such a temper who would calmly suppress *their own* reflections and opinions in which "the need to think for oneself" is so impatient to manifest itself, listeners such as Plato imagined, who would attend only to the matter at hand, could have no place in a modern dialogue; still less could one count on readers of such a disposition.[53]

I will not engage fully with the nuance of Malabou's argument here; I will simply note that she has chosen to emphasize the idea of a continuous productivity of forms, namely, *plasticity*, whereas *plastic*, by itself, hesitates awkwardly between a certain concept of beauty and the technical possibility of transforming matter according to the canons of beauty—hence, *plastic surgery*.

Plastic surgery aims to reshape or move tissue, to fill a depression, cover a wound, or improve an appearance. Let us note that, today, among the most popular surgical interventions—tummy tucks, chin and breast implants—is vaginal plastic surgery. Labiaplasties and vaginoplasties are among the fastest growing cosmetic procedures, as the quest for a "designer vagina" intensifies. Curiously enough, most vaginal reshaping aims to create the kind of symmetrical vagina produced by sexual reassignment surgery for male-to-female sex changes.

Giddens assumes that plastic sexuality is freed from "the rule of the phallus, from the overweening importance of male sexual experience."[54] I was quite surprised by something I discovered in doing research about intersex people. Androgen Insensitivity Syndrome, or Testicular Feminization Syndrome, is a genetic condition suffered by male XY fetuses unresponsive to testosterone during gestation. It results in babies that look like girls, with a standard looking vagina—although the vagina is shorter than usual, with no uterus, fallopian tubes, or ovaries. This syndrome is often detected during adolescence, when these girls do not have menstrual periods. All medical descriptions converge upon this observation: Women with this syndrome tend to be exceptionally beautiful. They have wonderful skin complexion (the lack of androgen prevents the development of acne), are extremely tall, with lean bodies and long arms and legs (a possible effect of the masculinization of the skeleton), have generous breasts, and have no pubic hair. What is surprising is that they seem to embody the current ideal of female beauty in Western society, and many women with this syndrome pursue careers, such as modeling or acting, in which beauty is prized.

Sexual identity is not the sum of body parts; the genitals may or may not play a central role in its construction. We can be confident of this conclusion in light of the intersex and transgender experience. "I cannot be defined by what I have between my legs" is a common refrain. Remember when actress Laverne Cox flawlessly shut down Katie Couric's invasive questions about genitalia during a 2014 TV interview? Cox turned Couric's attention to the staggering rate of violence against trans people in the United States.

Consider the most famous scene in Neil Jordan's film *The Crying Game*, in which a man, Fergus, is about to have sex with a beautiful woman, Dil, when she undresses and reveals she has a penis. Fergus vomits and attacks

Dil. We know from the experience of treating hysteria that the other side of revulsion is desire and that violence may be a reaction to its awareness. Fergus's attraction to Dil unsettles his gender identity and causes him to question his sexual orientation. He is shaken with disgust upon discovering that his desire for Dil has veered him away from a heterosexual aim.

Freud observes that disgust "interferes with the libidinal overvaluation of the sexual object but can in turn be overridden by libido. Disgust seems to be one of the forces which have led to a restriction of the sexual aim. These forces do not as a rule extend to the genitals themselves. [...] The sexual instinct in its strength enjoys overriding this disgust."[55] In a later section of *Three Essays* headed "Fixations of Preliminary Sexual Aims," which introduces the notion of sublimation for the first time, Freud writes,

> [v]isual impressions remain the most frequent pathway along which libidinal excitation is aroused; indeed, natural selection counts upon the accessibility of this pathway—if such a teleological form of statement is permissible—when it encourages the development of beauty in the sexual object. The progressive concealment of the body which goes along with civilization keeps sexual curiosity awake. This curiosity seeks to complete the sexual object by revealing its hidden parts. It can, however, be diverted ("sublimated") in the direction of art, if its interest can be shifted away from the genitals on to the shape of the body as a whole. It is usual for most normal people to linger to some extent over the intermediate sexual aim of a looking that has a sexual tinge to it.[56]

A footnote added in 1915 reads as follows:

> There is to my mind no doubt that the concept of "beautiful" has its roots in sexual excitation and that its original meaning was "sexually stimulating." [There is an allusion in the original to the fact that the German word *Reiz* is commonly used both as the technical term for "stimulus" and, in ordinary language, as an equivalent to the English "charm" or "attraction."] This is related to the fact that we never regard the genitals themselves, which produce the strongest sexual excitation, as really "beautiful."[57]

Is sublimation and the interest in art a strategy to avoid the ugliness of the genitals?

Is Sex Nature's Joke?

Perhaps nature has a sense of humor. "Nature," as Hegel explains, "combines the organ of its highest fulfillment, the organ of generation, with the organ of urination."[58] Slavoj Žižek uses Hegel's comment, along with his critique of phrenology, as a point of departure for reading *Phenomenology of Spirit*. He does so by referring to what he describes as Augustine's "theory of the phallus," according to which sexuality is not the sin for which humans are punished but rather a punishment for "man's pride and his want of power."[59] The phallus embodies this punishment, "the point at which man's own body takes revenge on him for his false pride."[60] Man may be able to master the movement of all parts of his body, but there is one notable exception—the phallus acts on its own, has its own volition and will.

Žižek reverses this paradox with reference to a vulgar joke: "What is the lightest object on earth?—The phallus, because it is the only one that can be elevated by mere thought."[61] In this divine levitation any punishment can be dialectically overcome. The phallus is less the way in which the flesh is humbled than it is the way in which the signifier of the power of thought over matter is made manifest. Thought, words, and images can be mobilized and avoid the sad fate defined by anatomy.

Recall that Freud avoided the trap of having to choose between anatomy and social convention. For psychoanalysis, sex is never a natural event, nor can it be reduced to a discursive construction. Sex or gender is a false alternative. Sexual difference is neither sex nor gender, because gender needs to be embodied and sex needs to be symbolized. There is a radical antagonism between sex and sense, as Joan Copjec has argued persuasively.[62] Sex is a failure of meaning, a barrier to sense. Is sexual difference a category comparable to other forms of difference at play in the construction of identity—social, racial, class? Or is sexual difference a different—allow me—type of difference?

Let us return to the clinic. The patient I mentioned above—whom I will call Stanley—is a transsexual man in his early forties. He speaks easily of his mother and her desire. He was raised by his grandmother, who, he told me, was the only person who loved him. Stanley's grandmother rejected her daughter—Stanley's mother—because she "only loved boys." Nevertheless, when, as a child, Stanley was sent to live with his grandmother, she warmly embraced the little girl.

Stanley's mother, Marika, left home at fourteen to marry Robert, who was fifteen. Marika was already pregnant when she moved out. Stanley's father was Polish-American; Robert was the sort of muscular, fun-loving, heavy-drinking man Marika's mother, Gilda, who was also of Polish descent, preferred. When Marika moved in with Robert's family she became very close with her new husband's family.

They were all very poor. Some worked (on the mother's side), whereas others were continually unemployed (on the father's side). Both of Stanley's parents died young. Robert died in a car crash, but Stanley suspects he committed suicide. Marika died of an accidental drug overdose.

In Marika's teenage marriage, Stanley's mother refashioned Claude Lévi-Strauss's formula, "I take a wife and give a daughter":[63] Marika gave herself to her husband Robert's family as a daughter and, in turn, gave her own daughter to her mother. My analysand says he was a tomboy growing up. His grandmother would tell him "Do not get pregnant," and Stanley would answer, "I will never be pregnant."

Stanley admits that being a man today has a lot to do with not being pregnant; not getting pregnant as a teenager, like his mother did, has allowed him to avoid repeating a destiny he claims most girls in his school followed. Today, Stanley is a married man. His wife is a heterosexual woman who never dated anyone queer before meeting him. They have a daughter conceived by artificial insemination. They are a normal couple whose current problem is that Stanley's wife wants a second child.

My analysand fears that he will have a son and, thus, opposes the idea. He thinks it would be difficult to be the "father of a boy." A revealing slip of the tongue follows: "I cannot be a trans father." But Stanley is already a trans father; he has a daughter. He thinks that raising a son will expose an insufficiency—his lack of knowledge about masculinity. Stanley regards himself as a "feminist man"—a label in which the other sex is already written in its identity. He is not, he says, like a biological man; he feels at ease among men but also feels different (this is important because he is not psychotic).

Recently, Stanley described a dream: "I was making love with a man. He does not know I am trans. I am anxious. I touch his penis but find a weird translucent plastic thing with a red rod in it." He added, as if to explain, "A transparent plastic thing." I stopped the session, but not before repeating, "trans parent plastic thing."

The most radical discovery of psychoanalysis is that sex is tied to the death drive. Stanley's "castration" has to do with his acceptance of his own mortality, a fact not unrelated to his conflicted desire to become a parent. Reproduction proves the mortality of the individual. One does not "duplicate" in sexual reproduction, as we often think. We do not buy a share of immortality by having children; on the contrary, as Lacan puts it, sexual reproduction means that "the living being, by being subject to sex, has fallen under the blow of individual death."[64] Reproduction does not guarantee immortality through replication but rather shows the uniqueness (and death) of each individual. In Stanley's case, this is made absolutely clear—his wife will get pregnant using sperm from an anonymous donor. And Stanley is aware of this fact. He is quite relieved that, thanks to artificial insemination, his offspring will not carry the "defective, addiction-prone" genes in his family. For Stanley, the cut of castration or mortality with which he is struggling to come to terms is also an expression of his singularity as a subject and a feminist man, a "trans parent."

For Freud and Lacan, sexual reproduction and death are two sides of the same coin. Sexual reproduction requires more than one individual; one person or partner alone simply cannot produce a new being. In principle, the sexed, living being implies the death of the immortal individual. Sexual difference and sexual reproduction account for the constitutive lack in the subject—a lack Lacan ascribes to "reproduction, through the sexual cycle."[65] As we have seen, there is no preprogrammed "biological" dictate in the psyche that determines why somebody will situate him- or herself, independent of his or her body, as a man or a woman; further, there is no "biological" dictate that seeks a "fitting" complement.

Here we see that to occupy a sexual orientation is to accept a primal loss. Again, sex needs to be symbolized and gender needs to be embodied. The major signifiers at work in Stanley's unconscious—*trans*, *parent*, *plastic*—may perhaps reknot themselves in a *sinthome*.[66] We shall see; this is a case in progress.

This feminist man is at ease in the world because he can pass in his masculine persona. His being a man is never questioned. He is tall, lean, muscular, and good-looking, and he has all the markers of what, in our society, is seen as virile masculinity. Once more, he is obviously not psychotic. Stanley often says in session that it is "weird" to be a trans man and that his transition is hard to explain, even to himself, but that he needs to invent something to survive. In the years preceding his transition he was drinking heavily and ruminating about suicide.

I rely upon Lacan's concept of the *sinthome* to make sense of such cases and especially to distinguish them from pathological structures. With his invention of the sinthome Lacan did not just put forward a new technical key term but opened a revolutionary theoretical avenue. I would like to highlight that the coining was made apropos of a gifted artist, James Joyce, whom Lacan claimed personified the sinthome. Lacan's theory of the sinthome applied above all to the singularities of Joyce's art but could be generalized somewhat. Taking Joyce for a "case," Lacan constructed a clinical example upon the art of the sinthome. His idea was that Joyce's writing was a corrective device to repair a fault, a slip of the knot. According to Lacan, Joyce's enigmatic writing undid language; it became his sinthome, made him a name, produced a new ego through artifice, and became his signature, a mark of his singularity as an artist.

My main contention links the peculiar meaning Lacan gives to the concept of *art* in his interpretation of Joyce's works with what I have discovered in my clinical practice treating trans patients. In Joyce's case, his art was able to compensate for a defect in his subjective structure, saving him from insanity. The sinthome-art grants access to a know-how with which he repairs a fault in the psyche, working as a supplement that holds together the registers of the real, the symbolic, and the imaginary in such a way that it fastens the subject in place.

I want to emphasize the strong drive to beauty within the transsexual transformation. I have encountered many trans individuals who hope to be seen or read according to the gender with which they identify. They talk about passing or not passing. I cannot help but wonder if this is a purely imaginary beauty or one like Antigone's, in which Lacan sees a sheer radiance or "unbearable splendor,"[67] that is, a beauty purified of the imaginary? In his description of Antigone, Lacan regards Antigone's beauty as a protective "barrier" that "forbids access to a fundamental horror."[68] For Lacan, her beauty is a screen that offers protection from the destructive power of the impossible, which he calls the real.[69] Beauty can be a limit to reckless jouissance and an intermediary site between two deaths. This may lead to the conclusion that transgender individuals want to be recognized in their being. When they say "I am beautiful" the stress is upon *I am* more than *beautiful.* Theirs is an ethical as well as aesthetic concern.

The text printed here was originally delivered as a talk on April 25, 2014, at a symposium at the University at Buffalo (SUNY), organized by the Center for the Study of Psychoanalysis and Culture, entitled "What Is Sex?"

Notes

1. Theodor Adorno, *Minima Moralia: Reflections on a Damaged Life*, trans. E. F. N. Jephcott (New York: Verso, 2005), 49.

2. See Guy Debord, *The Society of the Spectacle*, trans. Donald Nicholson-Smith (New York: Zone, 1995).

3. See Sigmund Freud and Josef Breuer, *Studies on Hysteria*, in *The Standard Edition of the Complete Psychological Works of Sigmund Freud* (hereafter *SE*), ed. and trans. James Strachey et al. (London: Hogarth Press, 1953–1974), 2:1–311.

4. See Freud, "On the History of the Psycho-Analytic Moment," in *SE* 14:14.

5. Freud, *Three Essays on the Theory of Sexuality*, in *SE* 7:184n1.

6. See Tim Dean, *Beyond Sexuality* (Chicago: University of Chicago Press, 2000), 65.

7. See Magnus Hirschfeld, *Transvestites: The Erotic Drive to Cross-Dress*, trans. Michael Lombardi-Nash (Buffalo: Prometheus, 1991).

8. See Freud, "Hysterical Phantasies and Their Relation to Bisexuality," in *SE* 9:155–66.

9. See Vern L. Bullough, *Science in the Bedroom: A History of Sex Research* (New York: Basic, 1994), 68.

10. See Peter Gay, *Freud: A Life for Our Time* (New York: W. W. Norton, 1998), 181.

11. See George Makari, *Revolution in Mind: The Creation of Psychoanalysis* (New York: HarperCollins, 2008), 237.

12. Freud to Carl Jung, April 14, 1908, in *The Freud/Jung Letters: The Correspondence between Sigmund Freud and C. G. Jung*, ed. William McGuire, trans. Ralph Manheim and R. F. C. Hull (Princeton: Princeton University Press, 1974), 138.

13. See Gay, *Freud: A Life for Our Time*, 181.

14. See Bullough, *Science in the Bedroom: A History of Sex Research*, 64.

15. See Karl Abraham to Freud, October 29, 1911, in *The Complete Correspondence of Sigmund Freud and Karl Abraham, 1907–1925*, ed. Ernst Falzeder, trans. Caroline Schwarzacher, with the collaboration of Christine Trollope and Klara Majthényi King (New York: Karnac, 2002), 139–41.

16. Ibid., 139, 140.

17. Ibid., 141n2.

18. See Gay, *Freud: A Life for Our Time*, 181.

19. Freud, *Three Essays on the Theory of Sexuality*, in *SE* 7:135n1.

20. See Colette Soler, *La maldición sobre el sexo*, trans. Horacio Pons (Buenos Aires: Ediciones Manantial, 2000), 9; my translation.

21. Alain de Botton, *How to Think More about Sex* (New York: Picador, 2012), 5.

22. Freud, *Three Essays on the Theory of Sexuality*, in *SE* 7:146n1.

23. On November 16, 2011, Gherovici delivered a talk at the University at Buffalo (SUNY) entitled "Psychoanalysis Needs a Sex Change."—Eds.

24. See Dean and Christopher Lane, "Homosexuality and Psychoanalysis: An Introduction," in *Homosexuality and Psychoanalysis*, ed. Tim Dean and Christopher Lane (Chicago: University of Chicago Press, 2001), 5.

25. See Ernest Jones, *The Life and Work of Sigmund Freud: Years of Maturity, 1901–1919*, vol. 2 (New York: Basic, 1963), 421; and Gay, *Freud: A Life for Our Time*, 501.

26. See Jacques Lacan, *The Seminar of Jacques Lacan, Book XX: Encore, On Feminine Sexuality, the Limits of Love and Knowledge, 1972–1973*, ed. Jacques-Alain Miller, trans. Bruce Fink (New York: W. W. Norton, 1999).

27. See Peter Fonagy, "Psychosexuality and Psychoanalysis: An Overview," in *Identity, Gender, and Sexuality: 150 Years after Freud*, ed. Peter Fonagy, Rainer Krause, and Marianne Leuzinger-Bohleber (London: Karnac, 2009), 1–19.

28. See Stephen A. Mitchell, *Can Love Last? The Fate of Romance over Time* (New York: W. W. Norton, 2002), 59–60.

29. See Fonagy, "Psychosexuality and Psychoanalysis: An Overview," 6.

30. Freud, *New Introductory Lectures on Psycho-Analysis*, in *SE* 22:113.

31. See Emmanuel Levinas, "Ethics and the Face," in *Totality and Infinity: An Essay on Exteriority*, trans. Alphonso Lingis (Pittsburgh: Duquesne University Press, 2007), 194–219.

32. See, for example, Bernice L. Hausman, *Changing Sex: Transsexualism, Technology, and the Idea of Gender* (Durham: Duke University Press, 1999), 75; and Catherine Millot, *Horsexe: Essay on Transsexuality*, trans. Kenneth Hylton (New York: Autonomedia, 2005), 17.

33. See Gherovici, "The Democratizing of Transgenderism," in *Please Select Your Gender: From the Invention of Hysteria to the Democratizing of Transgenderism* (New York: Routledge, 2011), 23–40.

34. See Charles Shepherdson, *Vital Signs: Nature, Culture, Psychoanalysis* (New York: Routledge, 2002), 95–100.

35. Colette Chiland, *Transsexualism: Illusion and Reality*, trans. Philip Slotkin (Middletown: Wesleyan University Press, 2003), 2.

36. Jennifer Finney Boylan, *She's Not There: A Life in Two Genders* (New York: Broadway, 2003), 22; emphasis in original.

37. Jay Prosser, *Second Skins: The Body Narratives of Transsexuality* (New York: Columbia University Press, 1998), 4.

38. Anthony Giddens, *The Transformation of Intimacy: Sexuality, Love and Eroticism in Modern Societies* (Stanford: Stanford University Press, 1992), 2.

39. See Alexander Edmonds, *Pretty Modern: Beauty, Sex, and Plastic Surgery in Brazil* (Durham: Duke University Press, 2010).

40. See Octave Mannoni, "I Know Well, but All the Same . . . ," in *Perversion and the Social Relation*, ed. Molly Anne Rothenberg, Dennis Foster, and Slavoj Žižek (Durham: Duke University Press, 2003), 68–92.

41. See Giddens, *The Transformation of Intimacy: Sexuality, Love and Eroticism in Modern Societies*, 27.

42. See Dean, *Beyond Sexuality*, 20–21.

43. See Judith Butler, *Gender Trouble: Feminism and the Subversion of Identity* (New York: Routledge, 1990).

44. Roland Barthes, *Mythologies*, trans. Annette Lavers (New York: Hill and Wang, 1972), 57.

45. Ibid., 56.

46. Candy Darling, *Candy Darling: Memoirs of an Andy Warhol Superstar*, ed. James Resin (New York: Open Road Integrated Media, 2015), 144.

47. Susan Sontag, "Introduction," in *Portraits in Life and Death*, by Peter Hujar (New York: Da Capo Press, 1976), v.

48. Ibid.

49. See Joanne Meyerowitz, *How Sex Changed: A History of Transsexuality in the United States* (Cambridge: Harvard University Press, 2004).

50. Ibid., 51, 49.

51. Catherine Malabou, *The Future of Hegel: Plasticity, Temporality and Dialectic*, trans. Lisabeth During (New York: Routledge, 2005), 9. See also G. W. F. Hegel, *Aesthetics: Lectures on Fine Art*, trans. T. M. Knox, vol. 2 (Oxford: Clarendon Press, 1975), 709: "[T]he classical form is the genuinely plastic one."

52. Ibid., 9–10. See also Hegel, *Aesthetics: Lectures on Fine Art*, vol. 2, 719.

53. Ibid., 10; emphasis in original. See also Hegel, *The Science of Logic*, ed. and trans. George Di Giovanni (Cambridge: Cambridge University Press, 2010), 20: "A plastic discourse requires a plasticity of sense also in hearing and understanding; but youths and men of such a temper who would calmly suppress *their own* reflections and opinions in which *original thought* is so impatient to manifest itself, such listeners attentive to the facts as Plato portrayed them, could hardly be imagined in a modern dialogue; and even less could one count on readers of similar disposition."

54. Giddens, *The Transformation of Intimacy: Sexuality, Love and Eroticism in Modern Societies*, 2.

55. Freud, *Three Essays on the Theory of Sexuality*, in *SE* 7:152.

56. Ibid., 156–57.

57. Ibid., 156.

58. Hegel, *Phenomenology of Spirit*, trans. A. V. Miller (Oxford: Oxford University Press, 1977), 210.

59. Slavoj Žižek, *The Sublime Object of Ideology* (New York: Verso, 1989), 222.

60. Ibid., 223.

61. Ibid.

62. See Joan Copjec, *Read My Desire: Lacan against the Historicists* (Cambridge: MIT Press, 1994), 204.

63. See, for example, Claude Lévi-Strauss, *The Elementary Structures of Kinship*, ed. Rodney Needham, trans. James Harle Bell, John Richard von Sturmer, and Rodney Needham (Boston: Beacon Press, 1969).

64. Lacan, *The Seminar of Jacques Lacan, Book XI: The Four Fundamental Concepts of Psychoanalysis*, ed. Jacques-Alain Miller, trans. Alan Sheridan (New York: W. W. Norton, 1998), 205.

65. Ibid., 199.

66. See Lacan, *Le Séminaire de Jacques Lacan, Livre XXIII: Le sinthome, 1975–1976*, ed. Jacques-Alain Miller (Paris: Éditions du Seuil, 2005).

67. Lacan, *The Seminar of Jacques Lacan, Book VII: The Ethics of Psychoanalysis, 1959–1960*, ed. Jacques-Alain Miller, trans. Dennis Porter (New York: W. W. Norton, 1992), 247.

68. Lacan, "Kant with Sade," in *Écrits: The First Complete Edition in English*, trans. Bruce Fink (New York: W. W. Norton, 2006), 654.

69. See, for example, Lacan, *The Seminar of Jacques Lacan, Book XI: The Four Fundamental Concepts of Psychoanalysis*, 167; and *The Seminar of Jacques Lacan, Book XVII: The Other Side of Psychoanalysis*, ed. Jacques-Alain Miller, trans. Russell Grigg (New York: W. W. Norton, 2007), 123.

CHAPTER 15

The Autistic Body and Its Objects

Éric Laurent

What Is an Autistic "Object"?

The field of disability studies has emerged, within the last forty years, from the political activism of disabled people. By engaging with current disability research, in order to ensure a firm conceptual and empirical footing, and with the questions this field raises in terms of identity politics, I will present a psychoanalytic approach to subjects with autism, a category of subjects that, in France, has recently acquired a number of rights.[1] The psychoanalytic approach I will develop here stresses that people with autism have a particular skill and they usually have a favorite chosen object that accompanies them and that they will not relinquish. This object has been spoken of as the autistic "object," which is very particular; such an object does not exist in other fields of psychopathology. One may be tempted to associate this object with bad behavior and so try to separate it from the child; however, we maintain, on the contrary, that this object must be taken as a point of departure with which to complexify the world of the child. The contact psychoanalysis inspires with the autistic subject does not recommend a stimulus-repetition approach, wherein one size fits all, but a way of soliciting the child that is tailor-made.

Consider the following example, in which a child's sole object of interest was a stick he dragged and waved around. The initial approach was a behavioral one that sought, at all costs, to get him to let it go, which provoked anguish and screaming. With a psychoanalytic-inspired approach, we took the existence of this chosen object as a starting point and made it more complicated. In this case, an encounter took place between the stick and the clapper of a neighboring church bell that gave rise to the child's fascination with this big voice, which then led him to take an interest in the hours when the bell rang and the hands of the clock. From there, we transitioned the child to learning about figures, at first addressed concretely—twelve hours, then twenty-four hours, then sixty minutes in an hour. Finally, we transitioned the child to learning arithmetic at school. In this way, the child's interests were allowed to grow from his object, taken not as an obstacle to but as a support for his inventions. The psychoanalytic orientation accompanies autistic children upon the detours they take to access learning. This orientation is compatible with a variety of mixed approaches that seek to move away from rigid techniques so as to make it possible to solicit the particularities of the child, whereas, by contrast, the results of intensive, rigid learning are poorly maintained beyond the artificial framework of learning. Methods are currently being developed with great diversity. In Canada, for example, particular attention is being paid to the speech of high-level autists. It is not therapies that are being proposed but methods of training normotypes upon autistic particularities:

> Several other autistic adults write books, give interviews and lectures explaining their view of the world, their difficulties, but also to speak of their pride in what they are, claiming a difference that should not have to be corrected but celebrated. [. . .] Convinced that most therapies focus too much on correcting the visible symptoms of autism, notably the difficulties in communication and socialization, [the practitioners of these methods] strive [. . .] to provide autistic people with the key to their own functioning.[2]

A Non-psychoanalytic Approach to the Autistic Object

The autistic object can be described as the passion of the subject—or, alluding to Johann Wolfgang von Goethe, his or her elective affinity[3]—for a specific object. Cornelia and Ron Suskind, parents of an autistic child named Owen, chose the term *affinity* and the term *affinity therapy* for the inventive battle their whole family came to wage, inventing a language and method based upon Owen's specific interest. Ron provides an account of this struggle in *Life, Animated: A Story of Sidekicks, Heroes, and Autism.*[4] This book has found many echoes and has given rise to a number of revealing interviews. I will recall just a few key moments from this account that particularly struck me. First of all, I was struck by Cornelia's first interpretation, after the onset in the mid-1990s, about the time the family moved to Washington, DC, where Ron had taken a job as a national affairs reporter for *The Wall Street Journal.* "Our son disappeared," Ron explains, figuratively. "He cried, inconsolably. Didn't sleep. Wouldn't make eye contact. His only word was 'juice.'"[5] In an interesting and moving article in *Slate*, Hanna Rosin, another journalist and writer who is also the mother of an autistic child, draws attention to this crucial moment: "One day, while watching *The Little Mermaid*, Owen said the first word he'd said in a while: 'juicervose.'"[6] His mother, Cornelia, figured out that he was saying "just your voice," which are lyrics from a song Ursula, the sea witch, sings to Ariel, the mermaid. The family took this as a sign that Owen was looking for a way to get his voice back. At an international conference in March 2015 at Université Rennes 2, entitled "Affinity Therapy: Recherches et pratiques contemporaines sur l'autisme," Cornelia told the audience that her guide towards this interpretation was the body-event, the excitation that invaded Owen's body while he watched this scene from *The Little Mermaid* again and again.

"From then on," Rosin reports, "Disney scripts became the language the Suskind family used to communicate with Owen, literally, speaking to each other in the voice of various characters to address real-life problems." "As he got older," she continues, "Owen began to use the voice of various Disney sidekicks to understand the world around him. Speaking in his own voice, he could sometimes seem confused or shut down, but when he mimicked one of his favorite characters he could access insights about people and situations that were 'otherwise inaccessible to him,' his father wrote."[7]

Another account of Owen's use of these Disney dialogues puts a moment of caesura in a new light: "One day, at his brother Walter's ninth birthday party, Walter became a bit teary. 'Walter doesn't want to grow up, like Mowgli or Peter Pan,' Owen said. Comparing his brother to Disney characters was the most sophisticated thing Owen, then 6, had uttered in years."[8] "Eventually," Rosin explains, "the family began working with therapist Dan Griffin (a *Slate* contributor) to help Owen use the scripts more creatively. He stayed in character but began to improvise, developing a comfortable way to express his inner thoughts."[9] We see here the way in which a new use of strict repetition can be favored. This approach, however, nevertheless introduces the fear of being trapped in repetition.

Rosin, who has also met Griffin, describes the dilemma parents of autistic children face:

> As it happens, my son Jacob has also seen Griffin, who is based in Maryland. And while Jacob has a much milder form of autism than Owen, he's certainly had his affinities over the years, starting at a

very young age with letters and graduating lately, at age 10, to *Mine-craft*. I spend a lot of evenings talking to my son about *Minecraft*, and I get caught up in the same worry as many parents in my situation: Am I helping or hurting him by indulging this obsession? Should I connect with my son over his favorite subject or let him know that soliloquies about *Minecraft* strategy are not usually a successful path to friendship?[10]

Keith Stuart, another father of an autistic child, published an article in the *Guardian* in which he explains how he has also found the use of *Minecraft* interesting for a communication dynamic:

> But most important was the way in which, after talking to each other while playing, they came to talk to us. Zac never really tells us much about what he does at school; his short-term memory isn't great and a lot of it doesn't seem to filter through. Or perhaps he doesn't want us to worry. We know he doesn't play with other children at break times or lunch, he sits by himself—the other kids grew tired of the fact that he couldn't deal with team games. But he talks to us about *Minecraft*. He talks and talks. We were getting bored of it, to be brutally honest, but then my wife read an article that said if you listen to your children when they're young, they'll tell you more when they're older. It's sort of an investment of care. So we always listen, even though we don't really get what the ender dragon is, or why it matters.[11]

Stuart also appears in Charlie Booker's documentary *How Videogames Changed the World*: "I talked about how it was being used in schools to help teach kids everything from physics to architecture, but most of all I talked about how it created a safe and creative space for a lot of children who may struggle to find safe and creative spaces elsewhere. 'I'd love to shake the hand of the guy who designed that game,' I said."[12] At the conference at Université Rennes 2, Valerie Gray, the mother of an eleven-year-old autistic boy, spoke of the crucial importance of this game in enabling him to build a game world that allowed him to understand the world he was in.

I would like to stress here the tension between the behavioral logic, on the one hand, and the logic of interchange in the therapy, on the other, in order to understand what happens in these moments that allow the therapist to use repetition to go beyond its limits. From the behavioral point of view, we see how Yale researchers who want to establish a standardized therapy upon the basis of the intuition at work in affinity therapy accept its

surprising results, provided, however, that the Disney dialogues are understood to function as a form of "role play" reinforced by a reward system:

> Autism researchers have known for a long time to use children's
> interests as a means of teaching social skills and increasing develop-
> ment, said Fred Volkmar, chair of the Yale Child Study Center and
> autism researcher.
>
> Volkmar said a paper he, Ventola, and seven others published in
> 2012 showed brain changes in two autistic children who underwent
> PRT [Pivotal Response Treatment]. The treatment is a behavioral
> approach that facilitates the development of social skills. An example
> of PRT on the website of Autism Speaks, an autism science and advo-
> cacy organization, is that of a child requesting a stuffed animal. If the
> child "makes a meaningful attempt"—if he or she uses full sentences
> and eye contact, for example—he or she will get the stuffed animal.[13]

Besides this behavioral point of view, we have the point of view of therapist
Dan Griffin, who isolates the breakthrough moment when Owen was able to
invent a new use of the dialogues:

> Dan Griffin: I remember it to the day. We took a break from therapy.
> Usually Owen hightails it out of the office, and this time he stayed.
> And you guys did a scene, with Iago [from *Aladdin*], I think. And
> suddenly there was this whole ionic charge in the room. You were
> much more engaged. He was much more engaged. It seemed like
> anything was possible. There was pure connection and pure joy, and
> it hit me pretty quick, we've got to be able to exploit this!

> Ron: I'll tell you what it was. It was the scene where Iago says, OK,
> "So you marry the princess and you become the chump husband."
> Owen did that one. And I'd say, as Jafar, "I love the way your foul
> little mind works!"[14]

What Griffin sees as an "ionic charge in the room" seems to capture this
point where the recuperation of Owen's voice allows him to push beyond the
limit of the exchange and enlarge his world. Beyond that, it is worth noting
that both Ron and Owen take the functioning of the "mind" of the other
into account. This is a dialogue upon the "theory of the mind" of the other.

Owen's mother provides her own description of this moment when
things go beyond their limit: "All of these kids do have obsessions and

affinities. The difference is, we used his affinity as a tool, to not only reach him by singing songs, watching movies together, playing with characters and being the characters, but then we took it further and started to use it to help him with academics and social growth."[15] Ron also describes the reverse of these moments of "ionic charges," the way in which Owen tames the huge emotional charge of the dialogues by the treatment of repetition:

> These movies have powerful themes going back to the Brothers Grimm and thousand-year-old myths. But it wasn't until the arrival of the VCR for domestic use that kids like Owen could rewind and hyper-systemize to learn, at their own pace, from these emotionally rich narratives the things that they couldn't get from human interactions.
>
> Owen used the movies to understand himself and his place in the world. He viewed himself as a sidekick. He told us, "A sidekick helps the hero fulfill his destiny." These are very deep ideas. He would give sidekick identities to other kids at school and say, "I am the protector of sidekicks. No sidekicks left behind."[16]

Judith Warner, writing for the *New York Times*, draws attention to the changes in context that the uses and interpretations of the therapy make possible:

> The results are extraordinary: Helped by Disney credits, Owen learns to read. He hones his writing skills by reworking classic Disney scripts. Talking through the voices of wise or protective Disney sidekicks like Rafiki, a supporting mandrill-like monkey from "The Lion King," he feels his way through stories set up by his therapist to cover territory like "being lost or confused, being tricked, being frustrated, or losing a friend."
>
> The costs are huge: $90,000 a year, Mr. Suskind estimates, plus the hours and effort expended by Cornelia, who runs "Team Owen," the stable of professionals who guide them. She tries to help him make friends, with limited success, and even home-schools him for a time.[17]

The results, after all these years, are clear:

> Owen is at a school out on Cape Cod. It's a school for folks, some are on the autism spectrum, other kids with different kinds of challenges. He'll be graduating in two weeks, after three years there. It's

been a great time there, for him. As soon as he got there he started Disney Club, of course, to meet people like him, he says, and to find answers, whatever that means. And first year there's 12 kids, this year there's 35 kids in it and they all speak Disney. They do that and meditate on it like philosophers, little social connections are forming in Disney Club, several boyfriend-girlfriend mixes, including Owen, who's had a steady girlfriend for the last two years. Walt is his main adviser on romance.[18]

In addition to these "socializing" results, Owen addressed the five hundred people at the conference at Université Rennes 2 to explain, in a moving testimony, how he could use the Disney dialogues to understand the world and his place within it. He explained how *Beauty and the Beast* allowed him to think about France, where the film is set. He also added that, thanks to the film, he could think of himself growing old and being a man. This point is crucial. Recall that, at six years old, he began to speak about his brother Walt as the *one* who did not want to grow old, "like Mowgli."

Role Play and the Treatment of the Voice of Language

Ron Suskind has stressed the importance of the VCR as a technical device that makes it possible to find a new use for these dialogues, cutting them out of context and, by repetition, "eating them," transcribing them into new contexts. A number of other machines can also be used in this way, highlighting the multiple registers of the *letter*, which is another name for what functions as *one* in the process of speaking, writing, counting, constructing images, and so on. Each of us appropriates our faculties in a unique and heterogeneous way. Totally mute children can write a great deal, some of which is readable and some of which is completely illegible. Some children are situated not on the side of speech or writing but on the side of singing, while others can only count. A child may say, "I have forgotten everything; I just know that I know how to count." Different digital objects allow for the articulation of different registers of the letter. Keyboards make it possible to overcome difficulties with the fine motor skills that require a particularly efficient relation to the body and its image, from which not all subjects benefit. The role of computers in reconnecting the autistic subject to the Other is well known, from the procedure of *facilitated communication*, invented by Rosemary Crossley[19] and used, most notably, by Birger Sellin,[20] to the procedure of *assisted communication*, used by Jean-Claude Maleval and others.[21]

Treatments based upon the instance of the letter, understood in the widest possible sense, can be used to create a bond with the subject.

The mother of another autistic child recently underlined the creative relation her child has with the voice recognition software used in Apple's Siri:

> Gus has autism, and Siri, Apple's "intelligent personal assistant" on the iPhone, is currently his BFF. Obsessed with weather formations, Gus had spent the hour parsing the difference between isolated and scattered thunderstorms—an hour in which, thank God, I didn't have to discuss them. After a while I heard this:
>
> > Gus: "You're a really nice computer."
> > Siri: "It's nice to be appreciated." [. . .]
> > That Siri. She doesn't let my communications-impaired son get away with anything. Indeed, many of us wanted an imaginary friend, and now we have one. Only she's not entirely imaginary. [. . .]
>
> For most of us, Siri is merely a momentary diversion. But for some, it's more. My son's practice conversation with Siri is translating into more facility with actual humans. [. . .]
>
> The developers of intelligent assistants recognize their uses to those with speech and communication problems—and some are thinking of new ways the assistants can help. According to the folks at SRI International, the research and development company where Siri began before Apple bought the technology, the next generation of virtual assistants will not just retrieve information—they will also be able to carry on more complex conversations about a person's area of interest. [. . .]
>
> Ron Suskind, whose new book, "Life, Animated," chronicles how his autistic son came out of his shell through engagement with Disney characters, is talking to SRI about having assistants for those with autism that can be programmed to speak in the voice of the character that reaches them—for his son, perhaps Aladdin; for mine, either Kermit or Lady Gaga.[22]

These testimonies, of course, do not speak for a pure abandon of the child to the machine. A creative use of the machine allows the body-presence of the parents or therapist to search for the breaking point at which the subject goes beyond the limit, "the point beyond," as Cornelia Suskind puts it. This is what Antonio di Ciaccia calls "soft forcing."[23] It is only through the process of body-mediation, between the child and the new use of language as a "voice," that this point can be produced.

Tom and a New Modulation of the Voice

Other children, encouraged to make new use of their passional objects, speak for the fecundity of this approach. I will now turn to what Tom has taught us about this. Tom discovered a use of cartoons, quite different from Owen's. He has been in a specialized school since he arrived at the age of seven. He cannot bear the class. When he first arrived he practically never communicated with the others; instead, he would play alone with sentence fragments from cartoons. These decontextualized phrases, without meaning, penetrated him. His parents were worried when they saw him hypnotized by the cartoon *Cars* and certain songs.

The point of departure for Tom's treatment was his use of dialogue from the cartoon. The earliest sessions were explosive; he opened boxes, threw objects to the ground, snatched my glasses, and turned the lights off and on. He chose a halogen light equipped with two lamps; he used one to look at his reflection and he made the other into a microphone. He became interested in a box of rubber bands, which he kneaded while singing, and asked me to sing along with him.

He made use of my glasses to invent a treatment for the invading gaze and he sang to defend himself from the howling voice. He tried to regulate the energy and excitation that seized him. He hit the radiator and his entire body was set in motion. He threw himself to the ground, hid under the table, and mimed "Mr. Totem" by picking up a box and slamming its lid down as if it was a screaming mouth. At the same time, he set up rituals that allowed him to bear the end of the workshop more easily. For example, he would say, "Thank you, thank you, good bye" to the objects he used during the session that remained too alive; he also said, "Thank you, thank you, Éric." I replied, "Thank you, thank you, Tom," and we would shake hands.

Then, from the falling, disappearing body, he would act out snippets of stories with a catastrophic allure. For example, he cried, "They're coming, go, hurry up, hurry up; mommy; my child; everyone get to the anthill!" Tom huffs and puffs; something is really at stake for him! "Quick, catch him, to the rescue help me!" I intervene, "Can I help you Tom?" "No," he says: "Yes, look, someone is stuck in the building; open the window to save Flash McQueen and the other cars. Don't worry my friend, you're out of danger."

Tom repeats these phrases, which he contorts again and again, until there is a decrease in the drive and they become more coherent and contextualized. Furthermore, he integrates signifying oppositions learnt in class, such as "right-left," "night-day," "hot-cold," and so on.

In the spring, we once again had a meeting about Tom and everyone was unanimous, he was advancing and prerequisites were being installed. A primary school teacher spoke about his work with computer learning software: He plays with the voices of the program, whose demands he is learning to tolerate. He greets the director each day and knows the first names of all of the team members and certain children. During the recreational period he sometimes hits a ball back and forth with another pupil.

The following year, Tom showed signs of learning to endure being in class. He participated in a singing workshop that culminated in a year-end concert, at which he seduced the audience with his performance. He began to question language, not only the language of cartoons and songs but also the language used at school. He can now include himself among the others and address his anxiety of being excluded. He can stand firm before an adult and say, "You're fired!" then return later and apologize. He does the same role reversal with a teacher that he did with me the first year, asking her not to sing but to count. Tom opened up to the other but it was not without eruptions of affect, including tears and rage. In the therapy, little by little, he dared to construct himself with Lego and build a garage and house for his rubber bands and car. I reach out more and more to welcome what is at risk of falling. This is where the body of the therapist is crucial to prevent the explosion of his body.

This year Tom followed the class program. However, along with others struggling to read, he participates in a music workshop, which his speech therapist and teacher set up in view of establishing a link between music, reading, and writing. They use a code of signs that correspond to a sound or gesture. Contrary to preestablished methods, they have constructed a tailor-made method with regard to the pupils for whom music is a support. For the moment, this reading method excludes any dimension of meaning, which is precisely what allows the pupils to actively participate.

The Use of Screen Characters to Pass from Two to Three Dimensions

In the incarnation of characters that initially present themselves in two dimensions upon screen, there is a crucial passage from the flat colors of two to three dimensions. One subject, Jules, a twelve-year-old boy who arrived while in partial residency at an institution, made this perceptible for us. The relation with screens and digital objects need not simply be a relation of love; it can also be a relation of love and hate, and Jules bears witness to this. He is a researcher. Using Google Earth and Google Maps, he visualizes the places he has lived as well as his current abode. "I love going into countries," he says. On the globe he passes from France to the Bahamas: "I was there when I was little." He zooms in on all that encompasses his position upon the screen: the fish, sun, submarine, and so on. During these investigations, Jules hails us and solicits our gaze: "How did they film this? What is a good image? How does one make sure there are no reflections?"

Jules investigates screens as well: liquid crystal displays, the size of screens, touch screens, the deleted images of screens, and so on. And then there is his research into 3D—3D printers, 3D television, 3D tablets, 3D films. "I love 3D because you can't see right to the end," he tells us. Jules is interested not only in 3D but also in everything that develops around the number three, from the Citroën C3 car to triangles. He is capable of saying things like "You, you have a triangle head." There are also "the triangular baby-bottles" that accompanied him until he was eight. "3D, it's his triangular bottle, his obsession of the moment," his father says.

All of these investigations on the computer invariably end with Jules punching the screen. "Boom, boom. When can I break the computer? Why are we not allowed to break it? Is it forbidden? Is it a little bit bad or really bad to do that?" We do not answer, inviting Jules to leave the room.

The television screens meet with the same fate. Jules loves to watch cartoons, but then he gives the screen the finger or attempts to shatter the glass of the television. One day Celine, Jules's therapist, discovered that he was very agitated and wanted to make the computer "explode." He asked whether this was a "little bit bad or really bad." Then, in the garden, he threw a wheelbarrow in order "to score a point." Finally, he asked Celine to take him to the bathroom: "I promise, I'm not going to clog it." Celine stays behind the door, ready to intervene. Jules shouts, "but you're watching me." Then, he opens the door and urinates upon Celine's legs. He laughs and punctuates, "that was a really bad thing to do."

The relationship between the screen and what punches a hole in it finds itself reversed in front of the hole in the toilet, which he cannot confront without trying to obstruct it. The fact that he turns away from the hole in order to urinate upon the therapist follows the same pattern. The passage from 2 to 3D includes the hole and its plug. This is also why he proposes building endless cardboard constructions to which he gives the "3D" qualification; it is a way to build a body.

For each creation, Jules takes a long time drawing up plans that he compiles in a notebook. He meticulously draws his models from different perspectives: the top, front, side, and so on. Generally speaking, drawing seems to calm Jules and manages to mortify what is overly lifelike in 3D. We were able to observe that when, in a state of great excitement, he stages monster trucks crushing smaller vehicles that come smashing off the walls, drawing roads and circuits manages to limit the outburst.

In order to achieve his inventions in 3D, Jules agrees to let us do it, giving us his instructions. He is more concerned with choosing colors and papers to adorn his creations. Recently, he has embarked upon designs that he calls "cow designs"; they have patterns made with marks typical to cows. It should be noted that cow's milk plays a lively role in his daily life. Jules's parents, noting that he was more agitated after meals, linked it to the consumption of milk products and, thereafter, removed them from his diet. Since then, Jules constantly opens the fridge at Le Courtil in order to grab the milk cartons and crush them.[24] "It's too powerful, it's too powerful," he shouts with jubilation. But when Jules adorns his creations with "cow designs" he is calm. The "Traces" workshop ends with a photo shoot of Jules and his achievements. He is photographed with a cardboard car: "a Citroën C3 3D tuning, future racing car that can fly." There is very little staging of the scene. He takes a break, looks at the result, and asks for a second shot. Then we have to photograph the car with the door open, and then closed, the different sides, the bottom of the box, and, to finish, from above. Is this a way to deal with 3D, by making 2D with the different photos, a little like he does with his plans? He broadens his vocabulary and the contexts of his language use. Instead of repeating his tests of "bad things" to do, he switches to a new question. "What does *privé* mean?" he asks, hesitating between its two meanings in French, "private" and "taken away," like when his mother punished him for having made a "bad mistake." The initial question, "Is it private? What does private mean?" is accompanied by a great commotion. Subsequently, Jules questions us: "Do you remember what private means?" When occupied with his creations, Jules can say, "private is personal" or "private is the contrary of public." As for us, Jules exclaims, "Anyway you, you don't know what private means!" He does not expect a response from us and continues with his creation.

Jules's latest creation is a bicolored helicopter. He sticks both sides of the helicopter onto each other and, with great concentration, tells us, "We'll call it a private 3D helicopter."[25] Thus, he has produced a personal meaning for this ambiguous word "private." He gives an answer to what the meaning of a word is by building a machine within his own world. This is of the same order as the uses of *Minecraft* in the building of worlds that give possible uses to new words. The logician J. L. Austin wrote a book with the title *How to Do Things with Words*, but this is the reverse; the subject does things to build the meaning of a new word.

Lost in Cognition

The way autistic subjects "learn," in an interplay between their body and other bodies, by way of their object, gives us an idea of what is lost in the cognitive paradigm and its hypothesis about the embodiment of objects in the brain. That is what I explore in *Lost in Cognition*,[26] but it can be developed further. Before doing so, however, I would like to consider the correlation between psychoanalysis and the cognitive paradigm during the cybernetics period. In Seminar II, Jacques Lacan offers a version of Freudian repetition based upon the pure repetition of signifiers and, in so doing, makes reference to the feedback loops of Norbert Wiener's cybernetics.[27] We should look carefully at what is represented at this moment in the history of psychoanalysis.

In 1950, a manuscript in Sigmund Freud's own hand was found that was previously thought lost.[28] It was purchased by Marie Bonaparte and edited by the ego psychology band, which then published it. Ernst Kris's interpretation of the passage from Freud the neurologist to Freud the psychoanalyst is simple and robust: *Freud had gone from a mechanical, neurological model to a psychological model.*[29] This interpretation was set to dominate until, in France, Lacan and, in the US, David Rapaport, an important psychoanalyst who worked at the Menninger Clinic, took issue with it.

Rapaport, an eminent member of New York's Jewish intelligentsia associated with Columbia University, gathered together a group of brilliant students to study Freud's neurological models. One of them, Daniel Kahneman, who went on to win the Nobel Prize in Economics in 2002, said that they studied it like the Talmud.[30] Indeed, there was a concerted effort to step outside the framework of the psychoanalysis of ego psychology by taking into consideration a reading of these systems for neurological inscription.

Kahneman and Eric Kandel, the winner of the Nobel Prize in Physiology or Medicine in 2000, each have their own way of telling this story. Kahneman tries to resolve the tension between, on the one hand, everything that is for cognition, pattern recognition, and instantaneity, and, on the other hand, the long-term processes. He says that there are two types of processes: On the one hand, there are instantaneous processes, that is, everything that happens in a *blink*, as Malcolm Gladwell's popular science book has it,[31] including love at first sight, thin-slicing, spontaneous pattern recognition, and rapid cognition processes; on the other hand, there are the slow rational processes. Next, he speaks about the cognitive bias this can generate. In other words, cognition is a fundamentally biased mechanism: We are not really acquainted with the world; we are constantly mistaken. Kandel, meanwhile, tries to resolve the problem of memory by complicating the problem of the Hebb synapse put forward in 1949 to account for the trace left by a stimulation of the nervous system, and he came up with a very different model.[32]

At this same time, in France, Lacan broke away from neurological inscription. Whereas Freud speaks of traces, Lacan proposes a new topology, a space different from the biological body in which to register the traces of jouissance. These traces are not inscribed in the body or the nervous system because they are signifiers. Lacan turns his attention to cybernetics because it allows him to build the Other, the locus of the Other. On the one hand, there was the environment the psychoanalysts of the time were breathing in, including Sartrism, phenomenology, humanism, and empathy; on the other hand, Lacan was striving to have them take in the air of formal logic that is constructed in the locus of the Other.

Cybernetics only held Lacan's interest for a short while, however, because he had no time for the scientistic ideology that frequently spurred on the initiators of the movement, such as Warren Sturgis McCulloch.[33] Lacan was much closer to Wiener. When, at the end of his life, Wiener took fright at the prevailing eagerness to scale down contingency and happenstance under the influence of strict processes, Lacan naturally shared this point of view. The locus of the Other was constructed with the immediate addition of a bar upon the capital A of the Other (*Autre*), that is, it was put together with a fundamental hole in this locus of the Other. Lacan never shared Claude Lévi-Strauss's enthusiasm for complete structures. Having asked, in the 1960s, "What is a science that includes psychoanalysis?"[34]—a subversive question—he concludes in 1973, in an interview on Radio France Culture, that psychoanalysis is not a science; it is what allows a subject traumatized by science to breathe a little easier.[35] The cybernetic Lacan never loses the thread of what is stifling in the scientistic slide towards the ideal of a computable universal.

The cognitive paradigm sends us back to the founding moment of a great utopia, the utopia of building machines and robots. Engineers at the Massachusetts Institute of Technology have just published a book entitled *The Second Machine Age*, in which they explain that we shall soon be producing machines that are far more sophisticated than human intelligence, leading them to list all of the professions that are set to vanish.[36] Seventy-five percent of doctors are likely to disappear, replaced by software programs that will perform diagnoses.

Then, on the West Coast, there is Google and Larry Page, who have founded a "Singularity University," whose director holds forth in rather undemonstrative fashion upon how we shall soon have perfectly singular machines that will think better than we do, and so on and so forth. In an interview back in early July, Sergey Brin said that we should "presume that someday we will be able to make machines that can reason, think, and do things better than we can," and Google will see to it.[37] Indeed, Google already offers a driverless car that reportedly drives better than any human.

Jaron Lanier, who has written a book entitled *Who Owns the Future?*,[38] calls this ideology into question, arguing, "[w]e're still pretending that we're inventing a brain when all we've come up with is a giant mash-up of real brains. We don't yet understand how brains work, so we can't build one."[39] In the field of psychopathology, the consequence is, as John Horgan of *Scientific American* puts it, we are in a situation akin to where genetics was before the discovery of the double helix.[40] The field lacks a unifying scientific principle, and so we are a long way from being able to tie the various biological clues to the different clinical levels open to observation. Three decades of the *Diagnostic and Statistical Manual of Mental Disorders* (DSM) have failed to introduce any meaningful discoveries, but the Research Domain Criteria (RDoC) scientific project, which is supposed to be taking up the baton, remains up in the air. It wants to be linked with the BRAIN Initiative (Brain Research through Advancing Innovative Neurotechnologies) launched by the Obama Administration, but it will not easily solve the problem, as the crisis in the Human Brain Project (HBP) in Europe shows. The conflict between mathematical models of the brain and the experimental neurosciences led to a shake up in the top management of the project: "A thunderclap was heard on February 20th when the board of directors voted to dissolve the executive committee of the HBP."[41] New questions and anxieties have arisen: "The HBP will only be a success if the neurosciences and new information and communication technologies establish balanced and synergetic collaborations. The implementation of scientific experiments in the neurosciences is necessary not only to produce new forms of knowledge but also to develop highly sophisticated tools with real scientific value."[42]

The RDoC project, though it is still a dream of the National Institute of Mental Health (NIMH), remains a project that no less subverts the traditional form of the cognitive-behavioral compromise. Certainly the project will seek to integrate the alteration of cognitive functions and their objectifiable circuits across the three essential domains of cognition, emotion, and behavior, but the RDoC has the goal of mapping the entirety of these aspects across the continuum of the field, bypassing the DSM's various labels and subgroups that endlessly subdivide, and likewise bypassing an approach based upon behavioral observation alone. The search for an "objectification" of cognitive functions in neuronal circuits that can be observed through imaging implies breaking off from an observation of human conduct that reduces it to mere lines of behavior. Behavior will be admitted into the new project only upon the condition that it corresponds to the functioning of an observable neural circuit, but we are still a long way from being able to "objectify" behaviors that draw upon the body as a whole, such as sitting in a chair, for instance. If we put someone under a positron camera and ask him or her simply to associate "to sit" with the word "chair," the number of zones that light up and are mobilized just to utter "I'm sitting in a chair" is immense. When it comes to more complicated conversations, the number is practically incalculable, for example, when the subject does not know which chair or when he or she is instructed not to sit in the chair that is being shown. These mechanisms introduce a sum of information that makes one marvel at just how it can be deployed in real-time conversation. One can only wonder as to the whereabouts of the integrating center that would allow for these zones that treat the information associated with "sitting in a chair" to be unified so as to perform the action, not to mention when a slip of the tongue, a play upon words, or a witticism is uttered when one is speaking. Furthermore, the Harvard-based Nobel laureate David Hubel has objected that "[t]his surprising tendency for attributes such as form, color, and movement to be handled by separate structures in the brain immediately raises the question of how all the information is finally assembled, say[,] for perceiving a bouncing red ball. It obviously must be assembled, [but where] and how, we have no idea."[43]

From our current standpoint, what we have learned about the brain's functioning suggests that, within the coming decade, we shall know more about how it works and perhaps in detail that we can scarcely imagine at present, but we can also say that a certain number of fundamental points bearing upon subjectivity will remain enigmatic. How will the cognitive-behavioral program be modified? We shall see, but we can be sure that a good many different patchwork solutions will be put forward to save it.

The end of an era always brings with it peculiar jolts and jerks. We are emerging from a period in which a predominant paradigm was established that only allowed for opposition upon the fringes. Now the entire field is shot through with fresh contradictions between scientific hardliners, public and private healthcare bureaucracies, upholders of various clinical traditions, and those appealing for a clinic of the subject. The cards are going to be reshuffled and the divergent interests of the different players are not about to converge in an overhauled unifying paradigm anytime soon. Something new will remain "lost in cognition."

We shall continue to assume responsibility for the ongoing commentary upon this loss, and in this commentary we shall not lose sight of the extent to which the cognitive paradigm seeks to silence the body, which is reduced to its behavioral dimension so as to exalt only the cognitive process, even if this process is qualified as an emotional one. Lacan proposed, by way of an *aggiornamento* of the Freudian unconscious, the "speaking body" or the *parlêtre*.[44]

The text printed here was originally delivered as a talk on March 27, 2015, at a symposium at the University at Buffalo (SUNY), organized by the Center for the Study of Psychoanalysis and Culture, entitled "Psychoanalysis and Neurocognitive Disability."

Notes

1. There are three major forms of legislation that protect disabled workers in France: the French Labor Law (Code du Travail); the 1987 Disability Employment Act (Loi numero 87-517 du 10 juillet 1987 en faveur de l'emploi des travailleurs handicaps); and the 2005 Disability Act (Loi numero 2005-102 du 11 février 2005 pour l'égalité des droits et des chances, la participation et la citoyenneté des personnes handicapées).—Eds.

2. Marianne Niosi, "Autisme: Au Québec, l'hégémonie de l'ABA de plus en plus contestée," *mediapart.fr*, January 6, 2015, https://www.mediapart.fr.

3. See Johann Wolfgang Von Goethe, *Elective Affinities*, trans. R. J. Hollingdale (New York: Penguin, 1978).

4. See Ron Suskind, *Life, Animated: A Story of Sidekicks, Heroes, and Autism* (New York: Kingswell, 2014).

5. Don Oldenburg, "'Life, Animated': How Disney Films Rescued Autistic Boy," *USAToday*, April 16, 2014, http://www.usatoday.com/.

6. Hanna Rosin, "A Pathway, Not a Prison," *Slate*, April 1, 2014, http://www.slate.com/.

7. Ibid.

8. Beth J. Harpaz, "A Little Movie Magic: How Disney Films Unlocked an Autistic Boy's Emotions," *Columbia Daily Tribune*, April 25, 2014, http://www.columbiatribune.com/.

9. Rosin, "A Pathway, Not a Prison."

10. Ibid.

11. Keith Stuart, "Minecraft's creator will always be a hero to me, he gave my autistic son a voice," *Guardian*, March 4, 2015, http://www.theguardian.com/.

12. Ibid.

13. Eddy Wang, "Suskind Sparks Autism Research," *Yale Daily News*, April 15, 2014, http://yaledailynews.com/.

14. Rosin, "A Pathway, Not a Prison."

15. Harpaz, "A Little Movie Magic: How Disney Films Unlocked an Autistic Boy's Emotions."

16. Ibid.

17. Judith Warner, "A Family's Hard Journey, With Disney as a Guide: 'Life, Animated,' by Ron Suskind," *New York Times*, May 21, 2014, http://www.nytimes.com/.

18. Ron Suskind, "Disney Movies Give Voice to an Autistic Child," *Radio Boston*, May 28, 2014, http://radioboston.wbur.org/.

19. See Rosemary Crossley, *Speechless: Facilitating Communication for People without Voices* (New York: Dutton, 1997).

20. See Birger Sellin, *I Don't Want to Be Inside Me Anymore: Messages from an Autistic Mind*, trans. Anthea Bell (New York: Basic, 1996).

21. See Jean-Claude Maleval, *L'autiste, son double et ses objets* (Rennes: Presses Universitaires de Rennes, 2009).

22. Judith Newman, "To Siri, With Love: How One Boy with Autism Became BFF with Apple's Siri," *New York Times*, October 17, 2014, http://www.nytimes.com/.

23. Antonio di Ciaccia, "La práctica entre varios en la Antenne 110 de Genval, Bélgica" (intervention at the seminar of March 23, 2002, Clinical Section of Paris, directed by Marie-Hélène Brousse and Pierre-Gilles Guéguen).

24. Le Courtil is an institution for psychotic and pathologically neurotic children and young adults founded in 1982 and located along the French border in Belgium, upon the edge of the northern metropolitan area of Lille-Roubaix-Tourcoing. —Eds.

25. Sophie Louis, "Tentatives pour se faire partenaire" (paper presented at l'Association de la Cause freudienne study day, Brussels, Belgium, February 28, 2015).

26. See Éric Laurent, *Lost in Cognition: Psychoanalysis and the Cognitive Sciences*, trans. A. R. Price (London: Karnac, 2014).

27. See, in particular, Jacques Lacan, "Psychoanalysis and Cybernetics, or On the Nature of Language," in *The Seminar of Jacques Lacan, Book II: The Ego in Freud's Theory and in the Technique of Psychoanalysis, 1954–1955*, ed. Jacques-Alain Miller, trans. Sylvana Tomaselli (New York: W. W. Norton, 1988), 294–308.

28. See Sigmund Freud, *The Origins of Psycho-Analysis: Letters to Wilhelm Fliess, Drafts and Notes (1887–1902)*, ed. Marie Bonaparte, Anna Freud, and Ernst Kris, trans. Eric Mosbacher and James Strachey (New York: Basic, 1954).

29. See Ernst Kris, "Introduction," in *The Origins of Psycho-Analysis: Letters to Wilhelm Fliess, Drafts and Notes (1887–1902)*, by Sigmund Freud, 1–47.

30. See Daniel Kahneman, "Daniel Kahneman—Biographical," *Nobelprize.org*, July 11, 2015, http://www.nobelprize.org/.

31. See Malcolm Gladwell, *Blink: The Power of Thinking Without Thinking* (New York: Little, Brown, 2005).

32. See Eric R. Kandel, *In Search of Memory: The Emergence of a New Science of Mind* (New York: W. W. Norton, 2006); and Donald O. Hebb, *The Organization of Behavior* (New York: Wiley, 1949).

33. See Warren S. McCulloch, *Embodiments of Mind* (Cambridge: MIT Press, 1988).

34. Lacan, "The Four Fundamental Concepts of Psychoanalysis: Report on the 1964 Seminar," *Hurly-Burly* 5 (2011): 18.

35. See Lacan, "Intervention by Jacques Lacan, December 1973," *RadioLacan*, December 1, 1973, http://www.radiolacan.com/en/topic/213/2.

36. See Erik Brynjolfsson and Andrew McAfee, *The Second Machine Age: Work, Progress, and Prosperity in a Time of Brilliant Technologies* (New York: W. W. Norton, 2014).

37. Sergey Brin, "Fireside Chat with Google Co-founders, Larry Page and Sergey Brin," *khosla ventures*, July 3, 2014, http://www.khoslaventures.com/.

38. See Jaron Lanier, *Who Owns the Future?* (New York: Simon and Schuster, 2013).

39. Maureen Dowd, "Silicon Valley Sharknado," *New York Times*, July 8, 2014, http://www.nytimes.com/.

40. John Horgan, "Psychiatry in Crisis! Mental Health Director Rejects Psychiatric 'Bible' and Replaces with Nothing," *Scientific American* (blog), May 4, 2013, http://blogs.scientificamerican.com/.

41. Florence Rosier, "Wolfgang Marquardt: 'Il faut des changements notables dans la gouvernance du Human Brain Project,'" *Le Monde*, March 10, 2015, http://www.lemonde.fr/.

42. Ibid.

43. David Hubel, *Eye, Brain, and Vision* (New York: Henry Holt, 1995), 220.

44. See Lacan, "Joyce le Symptôme," in *Autres écrits*, ed. Jacques-Alain Miller (Paris: Éditions du Seuil, 2001), 565.

CHAPTER 16

The Insistence of Jouissance

On Inheritance and Psychoanalysis

Joan Copjec with James A. Godley

JAMES A. GODLEY: You have been professor of modern culture and media at Brown University since 2013, and for twenty-two years before that you were director of the Center for the Study of Psychoanalysis and Culture at the University of Buffalo (SUNY), where, together with its graduate student editorial collective, you founded and published the widely renowned journal of critical theory *Umbr(a): A Journal of the Unconscious*. I mention your academic posts and activities because your experience must have taught you a great deal about what psychoanalysis is and means within the American academy. What does it mean to you to teach psychoanalysis? Why is it worth fighting for? Why is it important to participate in the American academy specifically as a Lacanian?

JOAN COPJEC: Although my graduate degrees are in English literature and cinema studies, I was invited to come to Buffalo mainly to teach psychoanalysis and take over the directorship of what was called at the time the Center for the Psychological Study of the Arts. The center—founded by Norman Holland and Murray Schwartz (in 1970, I believe)—was one of the extraordinary intellectual hot spots that turned Buffalo into an academic mecca. The center's faculty members were pioneers, the first in the United States to attempt to insinuate psychoanalysis into the university curriculum. For nearly two decades, they succeeded brilliantly.

By the time I arrived, however, times had changed. A more conservative climate had descended over the academy, and the faculty in the English department no longer knew why they were housing a center for psychology; much of the original center faculty had moved elsewhere, retired, or run out of steam, and in a few years Bill Warner and Claire Kahane, who had originally invited me to Buffalo, would also leave. What is more, the original center had focused upon the intersection between ego psychology and object relations theory. I quickly realized that, while I had inherited the directorship of a justly famous and important center, I was at odds with it on several key points. First of all, I was an ardent Lacanian and adverse to the center's name, which was easily and immediately changed; it became the Center for the Study of Psychoanalysis and Culture in 1991. The rest required much more thought and a good deal of work. Naturally, I felt I had a duty to maintain the former center's distinguished reputation, but there was no way I could do this by following the same path it had initially laid down. Some betrayal was necessary, and I feel sure that those who originally invited me to Buffalo counted upon that. It was at this point that I began asking myself the questions you are asking me.

Some Lacanian burrowing had taken place before my arrival in Buffalo to loosen the floorboards of the center. Joel Fineman—a close friend of mine and an incredibly smart Shakespearean scholar, who argued that Shakespeare's "perjured eye" detected and brought forth through his use of language the form of subjectivity Jacques Lacan would later theorize—was a graduate of Buffalo's English and Comparative Literature departments who worked with the faculty at the center. Stuart Schneiderman taught at Buffalo briefly, before departing abruptly to Paris in order to study with Lacan and become a Lacanian analyst. By the beginning of the 1990s, however, Joel had passed away, far too prematurely. Stuart had completely disavowed his association with Lacanian psychoanalysis and instead became a life coach. And Lacanian theory, once considered one of the most radical component threads of film theory (and many other discourses as well), had been shoved to the side by New Historicism and a by-now neoliberal academy. Psychoanalysis did not fit into this structure and it was not in its best interest to try to; its only chance of survival lay in its determination to press its position as forcefully as possible and work toward changing the way things were.

When a question was posed in the 1970s about how psychoanalysis might be put to political use, Jacqueline Rose responded that psychoanalysis, Sigmund Freud's invention, was already political.[1] Her shrewd response determined the way I have thought about psychoanalysis ever since—*psychoanalysis is not a regional discourse.* It is not a private language, nor is it reducible to the historical moment or place of its invention. It operates, and has from its beginning, in an international frame. The job of the center was therefore clear; it had to resist the privatization and localization of Freud's science.

The single most consequential decision I made was to found a journal, ensuring that the center's graduate students were equal partners in its production. Well, that is not quite right. I could not ensure such an arrangement on my own; you, the students, had to make yourselves equal partners. This is why I am never able to speak or think about the foundation of the center's journal, *Umbr(a)*, without mentioning the crucial, early intervention of Sam Gillespie and Sigi Jöttkandt, two students who now stand in for a long list of extraordinary graduates. The journal came into being via an inheritance—or transmission, as it is known in psychoanalysis. The volume you are editing is a substantial contribution to the theorization of inheritance; *Umbr(a)*—its foundation and extended, spectacular run—is an exemplary instance, a unique case study of it. Something apart from knowledge was imparted through the process of teaching, of imparting knowledge. Despite constant shifts in the composition of the editorial collective, as members entered and graduated from the program, something was transmitted and the journal retained a consistency. Even after graduating and taking teaching posts elsewhere, many former members of the collective have, as you may know, retained, in various forms, what they gained by working together on the journal. Many have continued working together, editing book series, special issues, and organizing conference events. It has been very gratifying to witness the aftereffect of *Umbr(a)*.

The journal became the means by which the center gained widespread visibility; more importantly, however, it became the means by which it made visible the expanded field of psychoanalysis's purchase. Issues were focused not only upon topics that were considered to be part of the proper terrain of its discourse but also upon topics not normally thought to be within its range: law, the incurable, technology, and Islam, to name a few. We published the first English-language contribution to the study of Alain Badiou's philosophy. When everyone seemed, still, to be focused only upon Lacan's theory of desire, we published a volume that extensively considered the concept of drive. We also offered early responses to the budding turn toward object-centered philosophy. In each of these endeavors, what the editorial team delighted in most, I think, was the fact that we could not fall back upon already known psychoanalytic truths but had to invent such truths. Rose was, of course, right when she spoke of what was *already* there in psychoanalysis, but the questions the discourse never had to face earlier, the new questions that crop up every day in analysis (from one analysand to the next), and from one historical moment to another, forced what was already there to appear for the first time. When Lacan says "I do not seek, I find,"[2] I take him to mean that he understands what is there already in psychoanalysis as what was placed there by Freud, in a present that has since past, as well as what had not yet come to pass and, thus, had to be brought forth.

JG: One might say that the mainspring of your work—from *Read My Desire: Lacan against the Historicists* and *Imagine There's No Woman: Ethics and Sublimation* to more recent essays, including "May '68, The Emotional Month" and "The Sexual Compact"[3]—is a devotion to the psychoanalytic concept of sexual difference, and, with respect to this concept, you have written extensively about the potential for rethinking ontology as the ontology of sex. The field in which you have situated this intervention is at the border between psychoanalysis, radical politics, feminism, film theory, and philosophy, but with psychoanalysis, we might say, in the leading role. Why is it so important to engage with these other disciplines in light of psychoanalysis, and, specifically, to view sex in light of ontology?

JC: Psychoanalysis is the method I use to think; it is a method akin to—yet different from—philosophy. Like Stanley Cavell (I mention him because one is pleasantly surprised to hear from an American ordinary language philosopher the articulation of a position more common among Lacanians), I tend to think of psychoanalysis as the "fulfillment" of philosophy and am particularly interested in the way Freud aligns his project with that of Immanuel Kant, whose thinking he seemed intent upon developing, pushing further, and going beyond.[4] From *Project for a Scientific Psychology* and "Negation," which I read as mini "critiques of judgment," to "A Note upon the 'Mystic Writing-Pad,'" which culminates in a reference to Kant's conception of time,[5] to the final words written shortly before his death—"[i]nstead of Kant's *a priori* determinations [. . . , the p]syche is extended[,] knows nothing about it"[6]—Freud was, I am convinced, drawn to Kant's way of thinking.

How to describe the difference, then, between psychoanalysis and philosophy? The usual answer—psychoanalysis is not, like philosophy, just a friend of wisdom; it is a *practice*, a *savoir faire*; it operates within a *clinic*—is not without value. But while the clinical practice of psychoanalysis is essential to it, its practice cannot be confined to the clinic. Too much of what goes on in the clinic does not stay there, and too much about which psychoanalysis has to teach is disdainful or indifferent to it and, thus, never thinks of knocking at its door. It is possible to have an aptitude for psychoanalytic thinking without having an aptitude for clinical practice. For these reasons, many would agree that psychoanalysis has a dual vocation—cultural as well as clinical.

In my view, the specificity of psychoanalysis should be located in the
privilege it accords to the relation between meaning and pleasure—which
brings us to your question about the focus upon sexual difference in my
work. It was as a feminist that I was first drawn to psychoanalysis, the
unique, defining contribution of which lies in its refusal to relegate sexuality
to either the biological or the cultural domain, the opposing pitfalls between
which feminism has otherwise been forced to oscillate. Sexual difference is
not a biological given, nor is it imposed, historically, as a contingent definition or meaning, as the "performative" theory of "gender"—which regards
language as a tool of domination—would have it. The problem is not only
that language is not a tool or organon (to use Aristotle's word)—if there is
no such thing as a metalanguage, then there is no place from which language
can be wielded—but also that the theory of performance fails to ask or think
about what language is imposed *upon*. It assumes, per definition, that language does not impose itself upon anything but rather produces the very
thing it utters. This position considers itself an advance with respect to biological essentialism. It says that sexual difference is not a natural difference.
At the end of the day, however, it comes surprisingly close to the Lockean
position, according to which the subject is a tabula rasa, a blank slate upon
which culture writes. But, again, if there is no metalanguage, then language
produces meaning as well as the excess it cannot contain as meaning. This
excess should be considered *positively* as something that is *subtracted* from
meaning, or—in the terms Lacan uses at the end of Seminar XI—as *minus
one* (-1) rather than *zero* (0).[7] The denaturalization of the subject leaves in its
wake not an infinitely pliable subject—a subject without *resist*—but a head-
less, recalcitrant subject of drive. Thus, language both produces and imposes
itself upon drive, which is completely different from nature and a blank slate,
the essentialist and performative alternatives. The stubbornness of sexuality
is not that of a biological fact but of the insistence of pleasure, despite all
attempts to get rid of it; and meaning does not impose sexual categories
upon subjects otherwise freely enjoying labile pleasures but renders pleasure
more labile and social. Sexual difference, at this point, becomes the name
for the fact that there are two different ways in which the relation between
meaning and pleasure fails to unite or place them upon a continuum. On the
contrary, the relation destabilizes both of them.

Ontology . . . Having been an editor for a number of years, I have contracted the habit of editing everything I read, including my own work, endlessly. Often, after writing about sexuality and ontology, I edit out *ontology*
in subsequent versions of my texts, remembering each time that Lacan (at
one point insisting that the status of the unconscious is *not* ontological but

ethical)[8] distanced himself from Martin Heidegger's obsession with ontology. As you know, Heidegger distinguished an ontic level of particular, determined beings from an ontological level of Being that is more "general" (though not an abstraction), the *fact* of being rather than the *what* or *quiddity* of being. In "Sex and the Euthanasia of Reason," I thought in terms of this distinction as I argued that sexual difference was not a difference like others, insofar as it is not a predicate of the subject, a secondary or particular attribute like, say, height, weight, color, class, attractiveness, and so on.[9] Years after I published that essay I came across Jacques Derrida's "*Geschlecht*: Sexual Difference, Ontological Difference," which made me feel a bit sheepish, since I had argued that deconstruction was incapable of, or disinterested in, conceiving the sort of primary difference sexuality gives rise to, and here Derrida was doing just that in Heidegger's name.[10] But Lacan is not Heidegger, and I have become more interested in the dissimilarities between them and, therefore, more reluctant to speak in terms of the ontological character of sexual difference. There remains in Heidegger's thinking a kind of finalism—I call it *biofinalism*—manifest most clearly in his notion of *being-toward-death*, which makes his theory incompatible with psychoanalysis's radical rejection of finalism. In Seminar XI, where he also insists upon the nonontological nature of the unconscious, Lacan uses the term *unrealized*.[11] It is on the level of nonbeing, the unrealized, that psychoanalysis situates sexuality, not—I would now argue—on the general and encompassing ontological level. For Lacan, the question is not *Why is there something rather than nothing?* but *How can nonbeing "be"?*

JG: Could you say more about your statement *psychoanalysis is not a regional discourse*? I am curious to know, in particular, how this statement is linked to your ongoing quarrel with Michel Foucault's thinking, especially in *The History of Sexuality*, where he not only critiques psychoanalysis but also proposes his notion of biopower, which has been taken up by a wide range of thinkers.

JC: You are right to note that my quarrel with Foucault's thinking has gone on for some time. I just recently gave a talk entitled "Foucault's No / Freud's *Verneinung*"—the newest chapter in the ongoing quarrel.[12] One of the speakers who preceded me talked a bit about the implications of an interesting legal category, *the unusually persistent complainant*, and I began, while listening to her, to see how querulous my own persistent return to Foucault's misguided attack upon psychoanalysis might seem to some. However, I gave that same talk several weeks earlier at a conference in Beirut—"Lacan contra

Foucault: Subjectivity, Universalism, Politics"—the very title of which *invited* complainants.[13] Now, most of the conference participants were on one side or the other, but I believe this conference demonstrated that the confrontation is both necessary and productive, that Lacanian theory can and must respond directly to Foucault's charges. Since that conference, I no longer feel as isolated as I did at the beginning, when so many who had previously supported psychoanalysis retreated in the face of Foucault's full out attack. To me, these retreats signaled their concession to the common assumption that psychoanalysis is indeed a minor, parochial discourse that mistook itself as universal and ignored history. *History contra psychoanalysis*—this was the blackmail many accepted, choosing history, of course, without offering any counterproposals from the side of psychoanalysis. The sudden shift away from psychoanalysis transpired as if Freud had not provided the building blocks necessary for a robust theory of history—inheritance, transmission, historicity—far superior to what the historicists were offering.

Ironically, while many fair-weather advocates of psychoanalysis were, in the face of historicist critiques, busy jumping ship, ceding ground, sacrificing a serious analysis of language for an analysis of power (as though they faced off against each other), and generally whittling Freud's discourse down to a therapeutic parlor game, Foucault was engaged in enlarging it. His aim was to escort psychoanalysis out of the closed rooms in which sex was (supposedly) spoken in whispers in order to argue that the discourse of sexuality was the megaphone of powerful institutions, indeed, of capitalism and biopower, whose emergence psychoanalysis (supposedly) facilitated. This was in direct opposition to Lacan's position, which he states most succinctly in *Television*: "Back to zero, then, for the issue of sex, since [. . .] that was [capitalism's] starting point: getting rid of sex."[14] Here one really does have to choose: Capitalism either depends upon sexuality (or relies upon *governing* it) or tries to get rid of sex altogether. The choice is not simple; one cannot just pick a side but must labor to lay out a theory not only of sexuality but also of capitalism. It seems to me that psychoanalysis has the upper hand in this case. For, not only does it have a complex theory of sexuality (over and against Foucault's vague pining for a different economy of bodies and pleasures), it—Freud's discourse and critique of psychical economy—also has been linked historically to Karl Marx's critique of capitalism and political economy. While Lacan was working to strengthen this link, proposing that it operates on the level of homology, rather than mere analogy, Foucault, in *The History of Sexuality*, sought—clumsily, in my opinion—to use the link against Freud.

The most frustrating aspect of Foucault's "critique" of psychoanalysis is that it fails to confront its target directly. Instead of reading any of its texts and attacking what they say, it prefers to attack hearsay, what psychoanalysis is said to have said. The obvious problem is that that *doxa* from which Foucault works is an amalgam of confused ideas. At one point, in *The History of Sexuality*, even he realizes that something must be said about this mishmash, so he makes a distinction between "the theory of the law as constitutive of desire" (Lacan's theory, obviously, though Foucault declines to say so) and "the thematics of repression" (recognizable only as a vague, Freudo-Marxist conflation of Freud, Herbert Marcuse, and Wilhelm Reich, although, again, no names are named).[15] The distinction flickers for only a moment before it is put out; Foucault quickly moves to discount the distinction. His argument is that even when psychoanalysis says "Yes," it is actually saying "No." The entire field of psychoanalysis, Freud and Lacan included, are tarred with the same Freudo-Marxist brush, the contention that power seeks to repress the "life force" of the drives, while Marxists advocate for its liberation.

The "Marxist turn" in Lacan's thought avoids the mistakes of earlier attempts to link Freud and Marx. This avoidance becomes especially visible in the way Lacan (1) tirelessly foregrounds the death drive (the most direct way to approach the death drive is to take Freud's infamous statement "the aim of all life is death"[16] as a statement of opposition to Xavier Bichat's vitalist definition of life as "the totality of those functions which resist death")[17] and (2) prefaces his remark about capitalism's goal of "getting rid of sex" by distinguishing between repression and suppression. The failure to observe this distinction is the error the Freudo-Marxists perpetrated.

It would be interesting to pursue the question of what the concept of biopower inherits from this error, but I am drawn in a different direction at the moment. I would like to examine the difference between Foucault's reactions to the revolution both of May '68, on the one hand, and the Iranian Revolution, on the other. May '68 is a part of what has been called the "sexual revolution," and the Iranian Revolution, while beginning as a revolt against Western intervention and the increasing impoverishment of the downtrodden, ended in a foregrounding of sexual issues. I would like to examine the relation between sexuality and an event and the differences separating Lacan from Foucault on this question. But my thoughts are incompletely formed at this point, so I will stop here.

JG: In "The Sexual Compact," you point out that Lacan thinks of jouissance as the inheritance of some common that can be put to use but not used up.[18] Are you suggesting that this is Lacan's way of thinking about potentiality? What is the role of sublimation here, and how does this line of investigation relate to your current interest in the concept of fatigue?

JC: Wow! You have managed to embed several questions into this one question. First, thank you for assuming that I am attempting to link these various concepts—jouissance, potentiality, sublimation, and fatigue. They may appear to be merely points upon a haphazard trajectory, but they really are conceptual markers of a critical path I have been forging for myself, or at least that is the way I am treating them. Enmeshed as I am in this project, I am not sure I have enough distance to give an overview. But I will try.

Theory has been awash for a number of years in contemplations of potentiality (Giorgio Agamben's signature concept) and virtuality (Gilles Deleuze's), both of which seem to spring up within the problematic of relation. To my mind, Lacan's twentieth seminar is the best place to go if one wants to enter into this problematic. The concept of relation—the sexual relation, specifically, but also the concept of relation in general, which seems inseparable from sexuality—is central to that seminar, and it is that concept to which my own term *sexual compact* refers. The concept of compactness (a mathematical situation wherein an immeasurable closeness exists between two points)—and, in particular, sexual compactness—is not only, I suggest, superior to the concept of a social contract for designating relations among subjects but also exposes the latter as an obfuscation of the deadlock of the sexual (non)relation. The two of the sexual relation are not two completely individuated ones that set aside their differences and live together in harmony. Sexual compactness is not arrived at by adding two ones together, nor does it result in harmony.

We can start to understand what Lacan is up to in Seminar XX by focusing upon his statement "one can refuse the predicate and say 'man is' [. . .] without saying what. The status of being is closely related to this lopping off of the predicate."[19] The expression "lopping off" is perfect if you keep in mind that *sex* is often said to be derived from the verb "to cut" or "sever." I mentioned earlier that sex is not *a* predicate of the subject; I would now say that sex is associated with the avoidance of *all* predicates when it comes to the nature of the subject. If you lop them all off, you get a denatured, deessentialized—or sexualized—subject (*not* a simple tabula rasa). Thinking back to what we said about Lacan's attempt to link Freud to Marx in a way not tried before, we can make a connection to "Estranged Labour," one of the essays collected in *Economic and Philosophic Manuscripts of 1844.*[20] In order to critique political economy, Marx and Friedrich Engels must scrutinize and reject the psychological subject it presupposes. Capitalism cannot be accounted for, they argue, by the supposition that man is avaricious and so on; it cannot be accounted for by any qualities or predicates attributed to the human species. The ascription of predicates to man derives from a logic of private property that turns these predicates into determinations of human essence and considers them the cause of human action. Marx and Engels lop off all predicates, thus depriving man of nature; man is not avaricious, lazy, hardworking, or corrupt—he simply *is*. Now no longer just an inert link between man and the properties attributable to him, "is" becomes a productive act, a *life-activity* or labor. What makes (the species) man "man" is man himself, in concert with other men. In other words, the being of man is a matter of constant modulation and revision; the being of man has the potential to be other than it is now or has been in the past.

Looking backward at "Estranged Labour," one can discern in it a certain Lacanian logic. Lopping off or barring the subject's properties empties it, but this emptying does not eventuate in absolute loss. What emerges, rather, is an odd sort of gain or bonus, a "surplus object," which is here designated labor-power or *potential*. Paolo Virno points out that Marx frequently reminded readers that labor-power does not exist as something real or present but as something that must always be thought of as capacity or potential.[21] The trick, of course, is to hold onto the negativity this implies. If one substantializes or transforms potential into another kind of property, privately owned by an individual, one causes it to cease being what it is, namely, nonbeing or a suspension of being. Marx conceives of labor-power as *social*, not only because it produces the social order but also because it estranges the laborer from her own being.

It is against this backdrop, the one Lacan himself painted in the seminars leading up to Seminar XX, that we begin to make sense of Lacan's generous definition and discussion of jouissance, which is given an entire page near the beginning of Seminar XX (*generous*, I mean, by Lacanian standards, since his oracular style is not wont to tarry with definitions).[22] Lacan tells us that jouissance is derived from the archaic term *usufruct*, which relates jouissance (enjoyment) to that which is useful. I cannot help hearing the oscillating differences between *use value* and *exchange value* as well as *with* and *by means of* (foregrounded in "Kant *avec* Sade")[23] humming in the background. How does *being in relation to others* or *being with* become transformed into something's being the means, instrument, or tool by which we obtain our goals? Lacan reaches for the term *usufruct* in an effort to shed connotations of utility (the ablative connotation of means or instrument) from enjoyment and restore the sense of "being in common" or "being with."

Here is what he says: "'Usufruct' means that you can enjoy your means, but not waste them. When you have the usufruct of an inheritance, you enjoy the inheritance as long as you don't use up too much of it."[24] This is the point I take up, as you note in your question. With this, I think one sees that

Lacan successfully holds onto the *negativity* of jouissance and potentiality (as I argue), which is necessary for safeguarding jouissance/potentiality as such. Like labor-power, jouissance cannot be substantialized; it is not something. In other words, it is not a commodity that can be bought and sold on the market, and yet, under capitalism, it is. Jouissance and labor-power are both signs of the subject's self-estrangement; the subject cannot ever coincide with herself because her potential to be other than she is insists, even if she does not avail herself of it. But while jouissance and labor-power separate or estrange the subject from herself, neither is separable or isolatable from the subject, for the estrangement produced by each is the very condition of subjectivity. This does not stop capitalism, however, from dreaming of doing just that, separating labor-power (and jouissance) from its host, the living subject. This is the dream that has given us financialization, or what Aristotle centuries ago foresaw and accurately described as the "birth [or breeding] of money from money."[25]

When Lacan counsels us not to surrender our jouissance to the Other, he warns against engaging in financialist adventures, against putting off enjoyment in the hopes of accumulating reserves of capital, which will never be redeemable in the form of greater enjoyment. What is in store for us, rather, is "fake" enjoyment. Aristotle also gives us a glimpse of this fake—or, as he says, "most unnatural"[26]—enjoyment when he completes his description of "the birth of money from money": "[T]he offspring [of this breeding] resembles the parent."[27] Money (or *coin*, as Aristotle calls it) returns to itself but without coinciding with itself, for it returns to itself *with interest*, as surplus beyond itself. (M' is M with a return on itself, with interest.) If this return nets only fake jouissance—and not jouissance as such—it is because the surplus is merely an *increase*; what it is *not* is that alterity or estrangement of the self produced by the surprise appearance of a different kind of surplus, object *a*. In Seminar XI, Lacan says of this surplus object that "[i]t is precisely what is subtracted from the living being [note the *negativity* in this definition; it is what is *lost*] by virtue of the fact that it is subject to the cycle of sexed reproduction."[28] To my mind, it would be a mistake to reduce this reference to "sexed reproduction" to the biological fact that two parents of different sexes are necessary for the "breeding" of children. In the context of the Marxist distinction between production and reproduction and Aristotle's characterization of *usury* (as opposed, we might want to say, to *usufruct*) as "money breeding money," *sexed reproduction* takes on the meaning of *reproduction out of alterity*. The question of inheritance comes down to a question about the kind of future we inherit.

One can say a lot more about this, but I do not want to forget your question about sublimation, which I will try to answer by returning to the notion of *the common*, which Lacan himself brings up when he mentions the "fine common law [. . .] of concubinage, which means [. . .] sleep[ing] together."[29] As Lacan points out, *usufruct* is a legal term. While law ordinarily deals with legal marriages—and, thus, specific, coded laws of inheritance that fit in well with capitalism, insofar as it ensures the accumulation of wealth beyond the individual life of the capitalist—it also minimally acknowledges "common law" marriages, though not the kind of extralegal alterity at stake in sexuality. If coded law does minimally acknowledge what would normally be thought to be outside its domain, this is no doubt because law is obliged to rely upon something beyond itself for its legitimacy—in the same way as, let us say, the pleasure principle has to rely upon another principle (the death drive) for its legitimacy. The law's avoidance of full acknowledgment of its extralegal condition—and, indeed, law's attempts to obfuscate its condition—results in distortions of the latter. Thus, the common or preindividual nature of jouissance (the impersonal nature of libido, to use Freudian terminology) is transformed through strategies of obfuscation into a positive something that can be "divide[d] up, distribute[d], or reattribute[d]" and is, as Lacan says, the very "essence of law."[30] This is the specifically utilitarian idea of law but obtains in various ways in other theories of law as well. Once again, a subtraction of negativity ends up destroying the "thing" itself. The preindividual or common that defines jouissance is not divided or distributed *to* and *among* individuals as shares (as if it were already a thing); rather, jouissance is disseminated *by* individuals in and as various social forms. The traditional understanding of sublimation, as the process of foregoing raw sexuality in favor of some socially acceptable activity, must be put aside once and for all. Sublimation is, rather, the process by which we transform our sense of alterity by articulating a new social form, or the process of dignifying alterity by bestowing it with social existence in the form of some invention of thought or action.

Though I could go on with this argument, I am going to jump now to your query about my current project. At first it seemed to me that my interest in fatigue was haphazard, a matter of pure chance. The Pembroke Center at Brown held a meeting to discuss plans for future seminars, to which I was invited, along with other faculty members. When I learned that the seminars were committed to examining the question of war, I initially did not think I had a suggestion for a specific topic and so was surprised to hear myself blurt out *battle fatigue*, before immediately abbreviating my response:

fatigue. Over the course of the last year, as I have been leading a seminar on this topic, I realized that my seemingly out-of-the-blue response really did spring from the work in which I had been engaged. The ostensible reason for this is that *battle fatigue* had seemed by World War II to have replaced *shell shock* as the preferred term for what Freud originally conceived of as *war neuroses*: traumatic effects of battle that appeared to have no direct physical cause. I wondered how this terminological shift might allow us to recast Freud's ideas in a slightly different light.

However, I had in fact already been making mental notes for a long time of the instances in which Lacan evokes the phenomenon of fatigue, the *desire*, as opposed to the *need*, for sleep. There is plenty of evidence, I began to think, that the definition of the body (as psychoanalysis conceives of it) might be boiled down to this—*the body is what desires sleep*. To return to the relation of labor-power and the living body, fatigue can be seen as the enemy of capitalism. It interferes with workers' productivity and is thus a problem to be eliminated. Can Freud's definition of dreams as functions of the desire to sleep, I began to wonder, be rethought as refractory to the logic of capital? *Arbeit macht frei* (work sets you free), the official motto of the Nazis, is also the unofficial motto of capitalism, and yet the promise that work—whether the work of war or capitalist workers—would pay out as freedom has never been fulfilled, and it is the betrayal of this promise that has led to postworkerist movements and theories.

As the seminar has progressed I have been surprised by how frequently the topic of fatigue pops up in theoretical considerations. These considerations proceed in two different directions. The first condemns fatigue, the wearing out of the body, as a problem created by capitalism, which wants to work us 24/7 but does not want to pay the price for all the wear and tear that that ceaseless work entails—and, of course, it does not have to pay this price because the useless and worn-out can simply be replaced. This approach views the finitude of the body chronologically: The body is what wears down and eventually dies. The second approach to fatigue views the finitude of the body in structural terms. The body is not, in this case, reduced to its infirmity or caducity but is viewed as the site of jouissance and thus associated with the subject's capacity to surpass or renew itself. Here, fatigue names an interval that opens in time, suspends time momentarily, thereby opening up the possibility of charting a different course. These moments of suspended time, of duration, are programmatically elided by capitalism, which does not much care to know anything about them.

I can go on at much greater length, but an interview is one of those things that must finally end and I would rather end on a less abstract note.

Throughout the seminar on fatigue I have used films to steer our discussions of theory toward concrete depictions of fatigue. I screened the films of one filmmaker in particular—Chantal Akerman—as exemplary reflections/representations of the power of fatigue. She, more than anyone else, was able to show how fatigue enters the body and staves off fragility.

Notes

1. See Jacqueline Rose, "Femininity and its Discontents," in *Sexuality in the Field of Vision* (New York: Verso, 2005), 83–103.

2. Jacques Lacan, *The Seminar of Jacques Lacan, Book XI: The Four Fundamental Concepts of Psychoanalysis*, ed. Jacques-Alain Miller, trans. Alan Sheridan (New York: W. W. Norton, 1998), 7.

3. See Joan Copjec, *Read My Desire: Lacan against the Historicists* (Cambridge: MIT Press, 1994); *Imagine There's No Woman: Ethics and Sublimation* (Cambridge: MIT Press, 2002); "May '68, the Emotional Month," in *Lacan: The Silent Partners*, ed. Slavoj Žižek (New York: Verso, 2006), 90–113; and "The Sexual Compact," *Angelaki: Journal of the Theoretical Humanities* 17, no. 2 (2012): 31–48.

4. See Stanley Cavell, "Freud and Philosophy: A Fragment," *Critical Inquiry* 13, no. 2 (1987): 388, 391.

5. See Sigmund Freud, "A Note upon the 'Mystic Writing-Pad,'" in *The Standard Edition of the Complete Psychological Works of Sigmund Freud* (hereafter *SE*), ed. and trans. James Strachey et al. (London: Hogarth Press, 1953–1974), 19:231.

6. Freud, "Findings, Ideas, Problems," in *SE* 23:300.

7. See Lacan, *The Seminar of Jacques Lacan, Book XI: The Four Fundamental Concepts of Psychoanalysis*, 252.

8. See ibid., 34.

9. See Copjec, "Sex and the Euthanasia of Reason," in *Read My Desire: Lacan against the Historicists*, 201–36.

10. See Jacques Derrida, "*Geschlecht* I: Sexual Difference, Ontological Difference," in *Psyche: Inventions of the Other*, ed. Peggy Kamuf and Elizabeth Rottenberg, trans. Ruben Bevezdivin and Elizabeth Rottenberg, vol. 2 (Stanford: Stanford University Press, 2008), 7–26.

11. See Lacan, *The Seminar of Jacques Lacan, Book XI: The Four Fundamental Concepts of Psychoanalysis*, 30.

12. Copjec, "Foucault's No / Freud's *Verneinung*" (lecture, Duke University, Durham, NC, February 26, 2016).

13. Copjec, "No: Foucault" (lecture, American University of Beirut, Beirut, Lebanon, December 2, 2015), https://www.youtube.com/watch?v=zhT6NhiwbLo.

See also "No: Foucault," in *After the "Speculative Turn": Realism, Philosophy, and Feminism*, ed. Katerina Kolozova and Eileen A. Joy (New York: Punctum, 2016), 71–93.

14. Lacan, *Television*, in *Television: A Challenge to the Psychoanalytic Establishment*, ed. Joan Copjec, trans. Denis Hollier, Rosalind Krauss, and Annette Michelson (New York: W. W. Norton, 1990), 30.

15. See, in particular, Michel Foucault, *The History of Sexuality: An Introduction*, trans. Robert Hurley, vol. 1 (New York: Pantheon, 1978), 82–83.

16. Freud, *Beyond the Pleasure Principle*, in *SE* 18:36.

17. Xavier Bichat, *Physiological Researches upon Life and Death*, trans. Tobias Watkins (Philadelphia: Smith and Maxwell, 1809), 1.

18. See Copjec, "The Sexual Compact," 34.

19. Lacan, *The Seminar of Jacques Lacan, Book XX: Encore, On Feminine Sexuality, the Limits of Love and Knowledge, 1972–1973*, ed. Jacques-Alain Miller, trans. Bruce Fink (New York: W. W. Norton, 1999), 11.

20. See Karl Marx, *Economic and Philosophic Manuscripts of 1844*, in *The Marx-Engels Reader*, 2nd ed., ed. Robert C. Tucker (New York: W. W. Norton, 1978), 70–81.

21. See Paolo Virno, *A Grammar of the Multitude: For an Analysis of Contemporary Forms of Life*, trans. Isabella Bertoletti, James Cascaito, and Andrea Casson (New York: Semiotext[e], 2004), 81–84.

22. See Lacan, *The Seminar of Jacques Lacan, Book XX: Encore, On Feminine Sexuality, the Limits of Love and Knowledge, 1972–1973*, 3.

23. See Lacan, "Kant with Sade," in *Écrits: The First Complete Edition in English*, trans. Bruce Fink (New York: W. W. Norton, 2006), 645–68.

24. Lacan, *The Seminar of Jacques Lacan, Book XX: Encore, On Feminine Sexuality, the Limits of Love and Knowledge, 1972–1973*, 3.

25. Aristotle, *The Politics*, in *"The Politics" and "The Constitution of Athens,"* ed. Stephen Everson, trans. Jonathan Barnes (New York: Cambridge University Press, 1996), 1258b6.

26. Ibid., 1258b8.

27. Ibid., 1258b7.

28. Lacan, *The Seminar of Jacques Lacan, Book XI: The Four Fundamental Concepts of Psychoanalysis*, 198.

29. Lacan, *The Seminar of Jacques Lacan, Book XX: Encore, On Feminine Sexuality, the Limits of Love and Knowledge, 1972–1973*, 2.

30. Ibid., 3.

About the Contributors

Lorenzo Chiesa is director of the Genoa School of Humanities in Italy. He is the author of *Subjectivity and Otherness: A Philosophical Reading of Lacan*; *The Not-Two: Logic and God in Lacan*; and *The Virtual Point of Freedom*. He is also a coeditor (with Alberto Toscano) of *The Italian Difference: Between Nihilism and Biopolitics*, and editor of *Italian Thought Today: Bio-economy, Human Nature, Christianity* and *Lacan and Philosophy: The New Generation*.

Justin Clemens is senior lecturer in the School of Culture and Communication at the University of Melbourne in Australia. His most recent books include *Psychoanalysis Is an Antiphilosophy* and (with A. J. Bartlett and Jon Roffe) *Lacan Deleuze Badiou*. He is also the editor of numerous book collections, including (with Russell Grigg) *Jacques Lacan and the Other Side of Psychoanalysis: Reflections on Seminar XVII*; (with Paul Ashton and A. J. Bartlett) *The Praxis of Alain Badiou*; and (with Ben Naparstek) *The Jacqueline Rose Reader*.

Rebecca Comay is professor of philosophy and comparative literature and director of the program in literary studies at the University of Toronto in Canada. She is the author of *Mourning Sickness: Hegel and the French Revolution*; coauthor (with Frank Ruda) of *The Dash: The Other Side of Absolute Knowing* (forthcoming); editor of *Lost in the Archives*; and coeditor (with John McCumber) of *Endings: Memory in Hegel and Heidegger*.

Joan Copjec is professor of modern culture and media at Brown University. She is the author of *Read My Desire: Lacan against the Historicists* and *Imagine There's No Woman: Ethics and Sublimation*. She is also the editor of numerous book collections, including (with Annette Michelson, Rosalind Krauss, and Douglas Crimp) *October: The First Decade, 1976–1986*; *Television: A Challenge to the Psychoanalytic Establishment*; and (with Sigi Jöttkandt) *Penumbr(a)*. She was formerly an editor of *October*, the executive editor of *Umbr(a): A Journal of the Unconscious*, and director of the

Center for the Study of Psychoanalysis and Culture at the University at Buffalo (SUNY).

Patricia Gherovici is a psychoanalyst, supervising analyst at Après-Coup
Psychoanalytic Association, New York, and cofounder and director of the
Philadelphia Lacan Group. She is the author of *The Puerto Rican Syndrome*;
*Please Select Your Gender: From the Invention of Hysteria to the Democratizing
of Transgenderism*; and *Transgender Psychoanalysis: A Lacanian Perspective
on Sexual Difference*. She is also a coeditor (with Manya Steinkoler) of *Lacan
on Madness: Madness, Yes You Can't* and *Lacan, Psychoanalysis, and Comedy*.

James A. Godley recently completed his PhD in English at the University at
Buffalo (SUNY). He currently teaches American literature in Seoul, South
Korea.

Joel Goldbach is an independent scholar living in Toronto, Canada. He
recently completed his PhD in English at the University at Buffalo (SUNY).

Adrian Johnston is a professor of philosophy at the University of New Mex-
ico at Albuquerque and a faculty member at the Emory Psychoanalytic Institute in Atlanta. He is the author of *Time Driven: Metapsychology and the
Splitting of the Drive*; *Žižek's Ontology: A Transcendental Materialist Theory
of Subjectivity*; *Badiou, Žižek, and Political Transformations: The Cadence of
Change*; *The Outcome of Contemporary French Philosophy*, volume 1 of *Prolegomena to Any Future Materialism*; *Adventures in Transcendental Materialism: Dialogues with Contemporary Thinkers*; and *Irrepressible Truth: On
Lacan's "The Freudian Thing."* He is also a coauthor (with Catherine Malabou) of *Self and Emotional Life: Philosophy, Psychoanalysis, and Neuroscience*.

Sigi Jöttkandt is a lecturer in the School of Arts and Media at the University
of New South Wales in Australia. She is a cofounder (with Dominiek Hoens)
of *S: Journal of the Jan van Eyck Circle for Lacanian Ideology Critique* and the
author of *Acting Beautifully: Henry James and the Ethical Aesthetic* and *First
Love: A Phenomenology of the One*. She is also a coeditor (with Dominiek
Hoens and Gert Buelens) of *The Catastrophic Imperative: Subjectivity, Time
and Memory in Contemporary Thought* and (with Joan Copjec) *Penumbr(a)*.

Lydia R. Kerr is an assistant professor of English and literature at Utah
Valley University. Her work has appeared in *Umbr(a): A Journal of the
Unconscious*; *theory@buffalo*; *Centennial Review*; *Correspondances, courrier*

de l'École freudienne du Québec; and on the University of Chicago Divinity School's *Religion and Culture Web Forum*. She is currently preparing an edited volume (with Nathan Gorelick) that revisits the intellectual relationship between Lacan and Heidegger.

A. Kiarina Kordela is professor of German studies and founding director of the critical theory program at Macalester College. In addition to numerous articles in academic journals, she is the author of *$urplus: Spinoza, Lacan*; *Being, Time, Bios: Capitalism and Ontology*; and *Epistemontology in Spinoza-Marx-Freud-Lacan: (Bio)Power of Structure* (forthcoming). She is also a coeditor (with Dimitris Vardoulakis) of *Freedom and Confinement in Modernity: Kafka's Cages* and *Spinoza's Authority: Resistance and Power.*

Éric Laurent is a psychologist and psychoanalyst; the former president of the World Association of Psychoanalysis and the École de la Cause Freudienne; and a teacher in the clinical section of the Department of Psychoanalysis at the University of Paris-VIII in France. His most recent book is *Lost in Cognition: Psychoanalysis and the Cognitive Sciences.*

Donald E. Pease is professor of English and comparative literature; the Ted and Helen Geisel Third Century Professor in the Humanities; and chair of the Master of Arts in Liberal Studies program at Dartmouth College. He is the author of *Visionary Compacts: American Renaissance Writing in Cultural Context*; *The New American Exceptionalism*; and *Theodore Seuss Geisel*. He is also the editor of several volumes, including (with Walter Benn Michaels) *The American Renaissance Reconsidered*; *National Identities and Post-Americanist Narratives*; and (with Robyn Wiegman) *The Futures of American Studies.*

Frank Ruda is an interim professor of philosophy of audiovisual media at the Bauhaus-University in Weimar, Germany. He is the author of *Hegel's Rabble: An Investigation into Hegel's Philosophy of Right*; *For Badiou: Idealism without Idealism*; *Abolishing Freedom: A Plea for the Contemporary Use of Fatalism*; and (with Rebecca Comay) *The Dash: The Other Side of Absolute Knowing* (forthcoming). He is also the editor of numerous book collections, including (with Mark Potocnik and Jan Völker) *Beyond Potentialities? Politics between the Possible and the Impossible*; (with Jan Völker) *Art and Contemporaneity*; and (with Agon Hamza) *Slavoj Žižek and Dialectical Materialism.*

Oxana Timofeeva is a senior research fellow at the Institute of Philosophy of the Russian Academy of Sciences in Moscow, Russia, and a member of the collective Chto Delat? In addition to many articles on animality, philosophy, psychoanalysis, and literature, she is the author of *History of Animals: An Essay on Negativity, Immanence and Freedom* and *A History of Animals in Philosophy* (forthcoming).

Samo Tomšič is a research assistant in the interdisciplinary cluster Image Knowledge Gestaltung at Humboldt University in Berlin, Germany. He is the author of *The Capitalist Unconscious: Marx and Lacan* and coeditor (with Andreja Zevnik) of *Jacques Lacan: Between Psychoanalysis and Politics* and (with Michael Friedman) *Psychoanalysis: Topological Perspectives.*

Philippe Van Haute is a psychoanalyst; professor of philosophical anthropology at Radboud University in Nijmegen, Netherlands; and extra-ordinary professor of philosophy at the University of Pretoria in South Africa. He is the author of *Against Adaptation: Lacan's "Subversion" of the Subject*; coauthor (with Tomas Geyskens) of *Confusion of Tongues: The Primacy of Sexuality in Freud, Ferenczi, and Laplanche*; *From Death Instinct to Attachment Theory: The Primacy of the Child in Freud, Klein, and Hermann*; and *A Non-Oedipal Psychoanalysis? A Clinical Anthropology of Hysteria in the Works of Freud and Lacan*; and coeditor (with Herman Westerink) of *Deconstructing Normativity? Re-reading Freud's 1905 Three Essays.*

Daniel Wilson lives in Montreal, Canada, where he studies and writes about psychoanalysis. He recently completed his PhD at Cornell University. His dissertation addresses the relationship between Freud's invention of psychoanalysis and the nineteenth-century science of energetics. He has published several articles on the intersection between psychoanalysis and the history and philosophy of science.

Index

Abraham, Karl, 255, 291–92
addiction, 68, 147–49, 158–59n31, 159n34, 307
Adorno, Theodor W., 105n13, 163, 290
affect (*Affekt*), 36–37, 62–63, 65, 144, 146, 153, 176, 186, 262, 283, 322; unconscious, 62–63, 65. *See also* anxiety; emotion
affinity therapy, 18, 314–16
Agamben, Giorgio, 178, 340. *See also* potentiality
American literature, 196–98; canon of, 14, 196–97, 200–201, 210n5; Matthiessen's Salzburg Seminar in, 197, 202; race and, 236 (*see also Mumbo Jumbo*; Reed, Ishmael)
anamorphosis, 222–23, 226–27
anatomy, 32–33, 38, 57, 175, 291, 295–96, 299, 305
animal multiplicity, 182–84, 187, 189, 191
animal negativity, 14, 192
animality, 76, 177–78; mammalian, 69
animals, 45, 47, 55n14, 61, 66, 68–69, 76, 97, 171, 183–84, 258; counting and, 179–80; domestic, 182; herd, 188–92; humans and, 177–79, 188; Lamarckian, 264–65; language and, 177–78; pack and, 186–87; unconscious/as the unconscious, 14, 176, 178, 180, 185, 192. *See also* beasts
animism, 48–49, 51
Ansermet, François, 60, 66
anthropocentrism, 47, 53n26
anthropology, 86–92, 105n13, 137; clinical, 287n5; emancipatory, 86; Hegel's, 90; philosophical, 85–86, 88–89
anxiety, 12, 63, 139–40, 150, 153, 156n9, 237, 261–63, 266, 322; castration, 122; dreams, 31

The Archaeology of Mind (Panksepp and Biven), 58–60, 62–72
Arendt, Hannah, 13, 164, 166–67
Aristotelianism, 23–24, 26, 28, 39, 40n2, 48, 85–86, 89; anti-, 26, 276
Aristotle, 10, 26, 133n86, 336, 342
attachment, 266; objects and, 295; Oedipal, 277; theory of, 289n30, 296
autism, 17–18, 313–15, 317–18, 320

Badiou, Alain, 219, 230n18, 334
beasts, 14, 176–81, 183–86, 188, 194n23. *See also* animality; animal negativity; animals
becoming, 28, 30, 41n12, 186, 198; becoming-wolf, 182, 186; of nature, 107n31
being, 11, 31, 41n12, 61, 95, 97, 109–110, 113, 118–27, 132n70, 152, 178–79, 192, 216, 223, 298, 307–308, 337, 340–41; bodily, 208; as herd, 179; hole in, 263; manners of, 14; "natural," 149; organized, 259; sexed, 295–96, 298; sexual, 300; social, 189; speaking, 12, 16, 39
being-toward-death, 339
Benjamin, Walter, 13, 146, 163–64, 167–72, 220–21, 230n30, 232n58; *The Arcades Project*, 13, 172. *See also* Scholem, Gershom
Bercovitch, Sacvan, 210n2, 211n8
Bergson, Henri, 223, 231n36
Berridge, Victoria, 147, 161n44
biology, 9, 31, 38, 44, 46, 48–49, 51, 55n41, 57, 70, 113, 116, 143, 266; evolutionary, 46, 77, 257; Freudian, 9, 49; Lamarckian, 257, 264; molecular, 48; nineteenth century, 258; sex and, 45 (*see also* sexuality: biological)
biopolitics, 12, 111–13, 122–24, 127